Introduction to Law

Jaap Hage
Antonia Waltermann
Bram Akkermans
Editors

Introduction to Law

Second Edition

Editors
Jaap Hage
Foundations and Methods of Law
Maastricht University Faculty of Law
Maastricht, The Netherlands

Antonia Waltermann
Maastricht University
Maastricht, The Netherlands

Bram Akkermans
Private Law
Maastricht University Faculty of Law
Maastricht, The Netherlands

ISBN 978-3-319-57251-2   ISBN 978-3-319-57252-9   (eBook)
DOI 10.1007/978-3-319-57252-9

Library of Congress Control Number: 2017949293

Printed on acid-free paper

This Springer imprint is published by Springer Nature
The registered company is Springer International Publishing AG
The registered company address is: Gewerbestrasse 11, 6330 Cham, Switzerland

Preface

The *Introduction to Law* that you are now holding in your hands is special in the sense that it introduces students to law in general and not to the law of one specific jurisdiction. It has been written with two goals in mind. First, this book is meant to be used in the course Introduction to Law of the Maastricht European Law School. This course aims to provide law students with the global knowledge of the basic legal concepts, elementary philosophy of law, and main fields of law. Since the European Law School does not exclusively focus on the law of one particular European jurisdiction, there is a need for an introductory course that also abstracts from the law of specific jurisdictions.

Second, and perhaps more importantly, this book reflects a special way of looking at legal education. We believe that it is of crucial importance for lawyers to be aware of the different ways in which societal problems can be solved and to be able to argue about the advantages and disadvantages of different legal solutions. Being a lawyer involves, on this view, being able to reason like a lawyer, even more than having detailed knowledge of particular sets of rules. The present *Introduction to Law* reflects this view by paying explicit attention to the functions of rules and to ways of reasoning about the qualities of different legal solutions. Where «positive» law is discussed, the emphasis is on the legal questions that must be addressed by a field of law and on the different kinds of solutions that have been adopted by—for instance—the common law and the civil law tradition. The law of specific jurisdictions is mainly discussed by way of illustration of a possible answer to, for instance, the question when the existence of a valid contract is assumed.

This is the second edition of the book. The list of persons who deserve gratitude for their contributions to the present and earlier editions has become too long to mention in full. Therefore we will confine ourselves to those whose role has been particularly important for this second edition. The chapter on tort law is based on an original text written by Gerrit van Maanen, and its present version has benefited from extensive comments by Cees van Dam. Sjoerd Claessens improved the chapter on the law of Europe. Daniel Hannappel has taken care of the format of the text, and Rebecca Kumi has improved the quality of the English. Last but not least, thanks go to all the students and tutors who used this book in our Maastricht Introduction to Law course and reported on their findings.

The editors of *Introduction to Law* are interested in your opinion of this book. We therefore invite you to send comments, suggestions, and questions to jaap.hage@maastrichtuniversity.nl.

Jaap Hage
Antonia Waltermann
Bram Akkermans
Maastricht, The Netherlands
February 2017

Contents

Contributors

Bram Akkermans
Maastricht European Private Law
Institute (M-EPLI),
Maastricht University
Maastricht, The Netherlands
b.akkermans@maastrichtuniversity.nl

Gustavo Arosemena
Maastricht University
Maastricht, The Netherlands
gustavo.arosemena@maastrichtuniversity.nl

Chris Backes
Utrecht University
Utrecht, The Netherlands
c.w.backes@uu.nl

Mariolina Eliantonio
Maastricht University
Maastricht, The Netherlands
m.eliantonio@maastrichtuniversity.nl

Fokke Fernhout
Maastricht University
Maastricht, The Netherlands
f.fernhout@maastrichtuniversity.nl

Jaap Hage
Maastricht University
Maastricht, The Netherlands
jaap.hage@maastrichtuniversity.nl

Aalt Willem Heringa
Maastricht Montesquieu Institute
Maastricht University
Maastricht, The Netherlands
aw.heringa@maastrichtuniversity.nl

Menno T. Kamminga
Maastricht Centre for Human Rights
Maastricht University
Maastricht, The Netherlands
m.kamminga@maastrichtuniversity.nl

Johannes Keiler
Maastricht University
Maastricht, The Netherlands
johannes.keiler@maastrichtuniversity.nl

Michele Panzavolta
Katholieke Universiteit Leuven
Leuven, Belgium
michele.panzavolta@kuleuven.be

David Roef
Maastricht University
Maastricht, The Netherlands
david.roef@maastrichtuniversity.nl

Marcel Schaper
Maastricht University
Maastricht, The Netherlands
mgh.schaper@maastrichtuniversity.nl

Jan Smits
Maastricht European Private Law
Institute (M-EPLI)
Maastricht University
Maastricht, The Netherlands
jan.smits@maastrichtuniversity.nl

Remco van Rhee
Maastricht European Private Law
Institute (M-EPLI)
Maastricht University
Maastricht, The Netherlands
remco.vanrhee@maastrichtuniversity.nl

Sources of Law

Jaap Hage

© Springer International Publishing Switzerland 2017
J. Hage et al. (eds.), *Introduction to Law*, DOI 10.1007/978-3-319-57252-9_1

1   What Is Law?

The main question that any introduction to law must answer deals with the nature of law. Although the need for the characterization of the nature of law is obvious, it is a need that is not easily satisfied. The law is multifaceted, and arguably has been in flux over the centuries. In this current age of globalization and Europeanization, it is changing at such a high speed that it is impossible to give a short definition of law from the outset. What is possible, however, is to mention a few characteristics of law. The majority of legal phenomena share most of these characteristics, but not all legal phenomena share all of them.

Rules

A substantial part of law exists in the form of rules. These rules do not only specify how people should behave («Do not steal», «Everybody with an income must pay income tax»), but they also contain definitions of terms, create competencies, and much more.

An example of a rule that gives a definition of a term can be found in Article 1 of the International Convention on the Elimination of All Forms of Racial Discrimination, which defines racial discrimination as

«… any distinction, exclusion, restriction or preference based on race, color, descent, or national or ethnic origin which has the purpose or effect of nullifying or impairing the recognition, enjoyment or exercise, on an equal footing, of human rights and fundamental freedoms in the political, economic, social, cultural or any other field of public life».

Article 37, Section 1 of the International Covenant on Civil and Political Rights provides an example of a rule that creates a competency for the Secretary-General of the United Nations. It states, in connection with the Human Rights Committee:

«The Secretary-General of the United Nations shall convene the initial meeting of the Committee at the Headquarters of the United Nations».

Society is governed not only by legal rules but also by other types of rules. In the next section, we will have a closer look at the law's most important relative – morality and moral rules – but there are also other types of rules, such as the rules that belong to:

- A religion (e.g., the Ten Commandments)
- Etiquette (e.g., «Eat with a knife and fork»)
- Special organizations such as student associations (e.g., «Every member must perform bar service twice a month»)

Legal rules are normally enforced by collective means and in particular by organs of the State, while other rules typically are not. Moreover, legal rules have very specific sanctions, such as incarceration, fines, compensation of damage, etc., while the sanctions of non-legal rules are less specific. For instance, someone who has committed a crime and broken a legal rule is liable to be punished by State organs such as the police and the prosecution service. However, from a moral point of view it is wrong to lie. While liars may be liable to informal and private sanctions such as reproach and avoidance, they will seldom be sanctioned by collective means.

Collective enforcement

At present, most laws are explicitly created by means of legislation or judicial decisions. These laws are called «positive law». The word «positive» in this connection is derived from the Latin *positus*, which literally means «laid down». The idea that law is explicitly created seems so obvious that the expression «positive law» has almost become synonymous with «the law that is valid here and now». However, the increasing importance of non-State rules is a reason to question this obviousness.

Positive law

It is often easy to establish the contents of positive law. The rules only need to be looked up in legislation or in judicial decisions. This may take some time, but in the end, it is often possible to establish the contents of the law beyond a reasonable doubt: positive law offers *legal certainty*. Therefore, it is usually unnecessary to invoke an authority such as a judge to settle a legal dispute. The parties can predict what the judge's decision would be, and in that way save both them and society at large, time and money.

Legal certainty

If the issue at stake is not what the positive law is, but rather what is «really» right, it may be much harder to reach an agreement. People often disagree about what is right or wrong. This predicament creates less favorable conditions for a smooth functioning society than the certainty of positive law. Often it is better to have no conflicts or fast solutions for conflicts, than to have a laboriously reached «right» solution. Therefore, law often prefers the certainty of a clear result over the uncertainty of the «best» solution for a problem.

Positive law also offers legal certainty in a different manner, namely by providing collective support for the enforcement of legal duties. If people are left to their own devices when it comes to enforcing their rights, this decreases the certainty that the rights will be respected.

A third aspect of legal certainty is that similar cases are treated in a similar fashion or – in other words – that the law will be applied consistently. For instance, if one citizen is granted a building permit, legal certainty requires that another citizen in exactly the same position should also be granted a building permit.

So legal certainty has at least three aspects:
1. Certainty about the content of the law
2. Certainty that the law will be enforced
3. Certainty that the law will be applied consistently

2   Roman Law

Our present-day law did not fall out of the blue sky; it is rather the outcome of a historical development in which the sources of law play an important role. As the easiest way to obtain an understanding of legal sources is through history, we will sketch the development of the law in Europe through time. In this examination, Roman law and common law play a central role.

Historical descriptions of the development of law in Europe often start with the impressive legal system built by the Romans in the period ranging from the eighth century BCE (Before Common Era) until the sixth century CE (Common Era). Impressive as the Roman system may have become over the course of these centuries, it started out in a simple form: tribal customary law.

2.1   Tribal Customary Law

Nowadays, we are very much accustomed to the idea of law as being the law of a particular country, such as German law or English law. More recently, we have seen the emergence of European law existing concurrently with national laws in the countries that make up the European Union. Moreover, for a number of centuries, a body of law has existed that governs the relations between States. This body is called «public international law».

However, the law of the Romans was not the law of a country or a State, but the law of a *people*, namely the Roman people. Since they were comprised of a tribal group whose members were connected mostly by family ties, the early law of the Romans was *tribal law*.

It is also possible to have law that is not connected to a particular territory or a particular people, but to a particular religion. Examples are Talmudic law, attached to the Jewish religion, and Shari'a law, attached to the Islam.

As a people grows larger, the main ties between its members can no longer be family ties, or at least not close family ties. The binding factor will then be a shared culture, for instance based on a common religion or language. We call such a people with a shared culture a «nation».

As are most tribal laws, early Roman law was customary   Customary law
law. Customary law consists of guidelines for behavior that have grown spontaneously in a society, such as a tribe, in the form of mutual expectations. After some time, these expectations are accepted as binding.

An example would be that the head of the tribe gets the first pick when an animal is caught in a hunt. For the first few times, this may be merely a kind gesture by the hunters towards the tribal leader. However, if it is repeated over a period of time, members of the tribe will count on its reoccurrence and there will be reproaches if the chief does not get the first pick. In the end, these reproaches may become so serious that the hunters will be punished if they do not offer the chief the first pick.

These guidelines are transmitted from generation to generation and are considered to be «natural» and rational. As such, their origin is frequently attributed to a historical, often divine, legislator.

An example would be the Ten Commandments and other rules that were, according to the Torah, given to the Jewish people by God on Mount Sinai, through the intermediary of Moses.

This ascription to a historical legislator explains another characteristic of customary law, namely that it is taken to be immutable. The law was such since time immemorial and will never change. However, as customary law starts as unwritten law, there may be gradual changes that go unnoticed because there are no texts that facilitate the comparison of recent law with that of older generations. As a consequence, customary law may change slowly over the course of time, adapting itself to circumstances, while its image of being natural and immutable may remain intact.

Although customary law is often retrospectively ascribed to a legislator, it is typically *not* the result of legislation. It consists of rules that are actually used in a society to govern the relations between the members of this society and are usually not easily distinguishable from religious and moral precepts. It is only at a later stage of the development of a legal system that the distinction between legal, moral, and religious precepts can be made.

Arguably, such a sharp distinction presupposes a separation between church and State, a separation that has gradually grown in the Western world since the late Middle Ages. It should be noted that this separation has not been accepted in a number of non-Western countries, particularly those that aim to follow some form of Islamic law.

2.2   Codification

Customary law starts as unwritten law, but this does not preclude it being written down at some stage. Part of Roman law, for instance, was written down in 451 BCE on what is now called the «Twelve Tables». The reason for this was that if there was any doubt, customary law could be interpreted by the *pontiffs*, officials who came from the cast of *patricians*, the societal upper class. The *plebeians*, the lower social class, objected to this practice of interpretation, because they feared that the pontiffs might use their power to interpret the law to the advantage of the patricians. If customary law were written down and published, its contents could be inspected by anyone who could read. This is another example of why the certainty of law is important: it makes it more difficult for rules that govern society to be manipulated to the advantage of a few.

If customary law is written down, the law is then described as having been *codified*. All codified laws are written law, and in this sense resemble law that was created by means of legislation. Still, there is a difference: law that was codified already existed before the codification, while law that was created through legislation did not exist before it was written down.

The terminology concerning codification is not always consistent, however. Sometimes the expression «codified law» is used in general for law contained in legislation.

2.3 Praetor and Iudex

If two parties have a dispute about a particular case, the legal solution will depend on two factors: the facts of the case and the contents of the law. In Roman law, these two factors were linked with two roles in the legal procedure, namely the role of the *praetor* and the role of the *iudex* (judge).

If one party wanted to sue another, he had to first approach a *praetor* and explain his case. If the *praetor* was of the opinion that the case might be successful, he would formulate a kind of legal instruction (the *formula*) for the *iudex*, in which this judge would be told to grant the suing party a legal remedy if he believed that the factual conditions had been fulfilled. It was then up to the judge to determine what the facts of the case actually were and whether these facts, in light of the formula provided by the *praetor*, justified the remedy. This division of roles made the *praetor* responsible for establishing the precise content of the law and the *iudex* responsible for the determination of the case facts. As the role of the *iudex* did not require any special legal knowledge, it was fulfilled by laymen.

In modern times, we find a role similar to that of the *iudex* in juries, consisting of laymen who must decide about the facts of the case. In criminal cases, the finding of the juries will be «guilty» or «not guilty». If a jury fulfills the function of the iudex, the function of the judge will resemble that of the *praetor*.

Because the *praetor* had the task of interpreting the law, he had a considerable influence on the content of the law. However, the function of the praetor was first and foremost a political one, a stepping-stone to becoming a *consul*. The praetor was therefore not necessarily a trained lawyer, and perhaps to remedy this deficiency, was advised by *jurists*, who also advised the process parties. As a consequence, jurists had, through their advice, a great degree of influence on the development of Roman law.

Jurists

2.4 The Corpus Iuris Civilis

In the year 395 BCE, the Roman Empire, which had come to encompass large parts of Europe, North Africa, and parts of the Middle East, was split into Western and Eastern halves. Not long thereafter, the Western Empire succumbed to an invasion by the Germanic tribes, precipitating the fall and plunder of Rome in 455 CE.

The Eastern Empire survived until the fall of its capital Constantinople (now Istanbul), in a war against the Turkish Ottoman Empire in 1453. However, long before that, the Eastern Empire reached a cultural summit with the *Corpus Iuris Civilis*. This *Corpus* was an attempt to codify the existing Roman law and was published in several parts on the order of Emperor Justinianus from 529 to 534. The first part, *the Codex,* contained imperial legislation spanning several centuries. The second part consisted of the *Digest,* a collection of excerpts from writings of jurists from the period of about 100 BCE until 300 CE. The third part, the *Institutions,* was a student textbook.

3   Common Law

After the fall of the Western Roman Empire, the law of Western Europe to a large extent returned to customary tribal law, namely to the law of the Germanic tribes that had taken possession of the area. In the High Middle Ages (the eleventh century until the fifteenth century), several developments took place that had an enduring influence on the evolution of law in Europe. One of them was the rediscovery of Roman law, starting from the eleventh century. This rediscovery and subsequent «reception» of Roman law turned out to be very influential on the development of private law on the European continent. In England however, Roman law had much less influence, due to another important development, specifically the rise of common law.

3.1   Royal Justices

The development of common law as a separate legal system dates back to 1066 when the Norman King William I (the Conqueror) invaded and conquered England. This initiated a movement towards the unification of the English legal system, which until then mostly consisted of local customary law.

The unification was brought about by means of a system of royal representatives who traveled through the country to administer the law. The task of these royal justices was to apply everywhere the same law, the law which would eventually become the *Common Law of England.* The emergence of central courts of justice in the thirteenth century further contributed to the promulgation of common law as they facilitated uniform application of the law all over the country. For law to be uniform, it is not only essential that the rules are the same everywhere, but also that these rules are applied in the same way. The law consists as much of its rules, as it does in the way these rules are applied.

The existence of a uniform legal system in England is one of the reasons why the rediscovery of Roman law, while having tremendous influence on the development of continental European law, left English law largely unaffected. As a consequence, the English legal system and the legal systems of the continent developed more or less independently of one another. One of the most conspicuous differences resulting from this separate development is that continental legal reasoning focuses on the creation and the application of mostly statutory rules, while the emphasis in the common law tradition has been on reasoning by way of analogy to previous cases. This is a consequence of the doctrine of *stare decisis*, to which we will now turn.

3.2   **Precedent**

Customary rules come into being if they are actually used by judges and other legal decision makers, among others. An example would be the following: A peasant sells a cow to another peasant. The cow turns out to be sick and dies within a few weeks. The second peasant wants his money back. The seller refuses to return the money and says that the buyer should have paid more attention to his purchase. If he had done so, he might have known that the cow was sick. The case comes before a judge, who agrees with the seller: the buyer should have been more attentive, since the illness of the cow would have been detected had there been a more careful inspection of the animal. In future cases, there is no longer a need to go to a judge about the sale of an unhealthy animal, if the animal's bad condition might have been discovered through careful inspection. In such cases, no money will be returned from the seller to the buyer. The decision of the judge will function as a *precedent* for future cases. Moreover, after some time, the rule that previously discoverable illnesses in cows does not constitute a reason to request the return of the sale price will be considered customary law.

Judicial decisions can and often will function as precedents. There are two ways to interpret this. The first interpretation is that the decision of the judge is *evidence* of the law already existing before the judge gave his decision. If the rule already existed, it is clear that the same rule should be applied in future cases and by other judges. A second interpretation is that the judge, in giving his decision, created a new rule that did not yet exist, but will exist from that moment onwards. It is also understandable that in this interpretation, other judges will have to apply the rule in future cases. It is this second interpretation, namely that courts' decisions *create* the law rather than merely state it, that has become prevalent in the twentieth century.

In earlier centuries, the view that judicial decisions were merely evidence of pre-existing law was the fashionable one. Blackstone, a famous English lawyer from the eighteenth century, wrote that: «[...] the decisions of courts of justice are the *evidence* of what is common law». (Emphasis added.)

Stare decisis

The second interpretation is confirmed in the doctrine of *stare decisis* (Latin for «stand by your decisions»). According to this doctrine, if a court has decided a case in a particular way, then the same court and the courts that are inferior to it, must give the same decision in similar future cases.

In 1966 the highest English court, the House of Lords (since 2009: the Supreme Court, and to be distinguished from the political «House of Lords»), announced that it would not consider itself bound by its own previous decisions anymore. By this announcement, it created for itself an exception to the *stare decisis* rule.

Case-based reasoning

The custom to decide cases by analogy to previous cases combined with the doctrine of *stare decisis* means that common law has developed on the basis of precedents and case law. English legal reasoning has therefore become a form of case-based reasoning, comparing and contrasting new cases with old cases that have already been decided. Although legislation also plays a role in English law, the emphasis has traditionally been on common law, which consists of a large body of cases. It may be argued, however, that this focus on cases instead of legislation has lost importance with the United Kingdom's membership in the European Union, as the laws of the European Member States are converging.

Common Law tradition

The English legal tradition has been exported to the members of the British Commonwealth. Consequently, it is not only England using common law, but also Ireland, Wales, most States in the USA, Canada, Australia, and many of Britain's former colonies. While the common laws of these countries have their basis in old precedents stemming from the time the British Empire, they have grown apart since becoming independent. Nevertheless, precedents set in one common law country may often still play a role in another common law country. In this way, common law is a major legal tradition, standing side by side with the civil law tradition of continental Europe.

3.3   Equity

This picture of the common law tradition would be one-sided if it did not pay some attention to the phenomenon of *equity*. Just like case law and legislation, equity forms part of the law in common law countries. Following the tradition of common law, equity is also a kind of judge-made law. However, there are some important differences.

Equity originated in the fourteenth century in England, when those who were unhappy about the outcome of common law procedures petitioned the King to intervene on their behalf. If the outcome of the common law for a particular case was found to be very inequitable, the King, or rather his secretariat, the Chancery, might ask the common law courts to reconsider the case. In time, the Chancery began to deal with such cases itself, and petitions came to be directed immediately to the Chancellor (the King's secretary) rather than to the King. A subsequent Court of Chancery eventually developed over centuries, creating a separate branch of law: equity.

Equity consists of a body of rules and principles that were developed to mitigate the harsh results that may, in some cases, arise from the application of common law. As the term "equity" suggests, this part of the law is particularly focused on obtaining fair results.   Fairness

Originally, equity may have been merely a correction to common law. However, in the course of time, some branches of law were only developed in equity, the law of trusts being the most prominent example.

The following example illustrates how equity differs from the common law. Angela is an unmarried woman of means who has a 2-year-old son Michael. Angela wants to give £50.000 to Michael, in the unexpected case that she might die. However, Michael is too young to deal with this sum of money. Therefore, Angela trusts the money to her friend Jane, who will act as a safe keeper for Michaels' money. Under the regime of the common law, Jane would be the sole owner of the money and it would depend on her benevolence whether she keeps the money for Michael. Michael would have no legal remedy if Jane abused her position. That is unfair, since the money was meant for Michael, and Jane was entrusted with it for Michael. In equity, it is possible to provide Michael with a more robust legal position. Jane will be the legal owner of the money (in common law), but acts as a «trustee». Michael will be the «beneficiary owner» (owner in equity) of the same money, and has a legal remedy against Jane if she does not keep the money for him.

Although nowadays it may be correct to state that equity is part of the common law tradition, originally equity was meant as an exception to the law. This difference is still reflected in English terminology, where the distinction is made between what holds *at law* (the common law) and *in equity*.

The historic roots of equity, namely that equity was applied by the Court of Chancery as a correction to «ordinary» common law courts, explains that equity was originally applied by separate courts. Reforms in the court structure of England in the nineteenth and twentieth centuries have meant that a single court can now apply both common law and the principles of equity to resolve disputes.

It is a matter of on-going debate whether this fusion of courts has also led to the fusion of common law and equity, or that – as metaphor would have it – «the two streams of jurisdiction, though they run in the same channel, run side by side and do not mix their waters».

4   Ius Commune

For most of the Middle Ages (roughly the fifth to fifteenth centuries), Western Europe was divided into a variety of smaller and larger territories, inhabited by different peoples. These territories had their own local customary law, and as a consequence the law in Europe was diverse. As far as legal science was concerned, this situation gradually changed after the rediscovery in Northern Italy of the *Digest*, around 1100. The *Digest* became an object of study at the newly founded University of Bologna.

Canon law

Alongside the *Digest* becoming the renewed object of scientific study, so did the law of the Roman Catholic Church, Canon law. Canon law dealt with the internal organization of the church, but also with civil affairs such as marriage, contracts, and wills.

There were a lot of diverse texts which discussed this Canon law and they were not always consistent. In 1140, the *Decretum Gratiani* was compiled: a collection of existing texts that were relevant for Canon law. This document was an attempt to make these diverse texts consistent.

Roman law and Canon law were usually studied together. This is still reflected in the titles «Bachelor of Laws» and «Master of Laws» (plural). In the abbreviation «LLM», which stands for «Master of Laws» the two L's represent these two branches of law.

The law schools in an increasing number of universities (such as Bologna and Orléans) became quite popular and attracted students from all over Europe. When the students returned home, they took knowledge of Roman and Canon laws with them. In this way, the same body of legal knowledge was spread over Europe.

Reception of Roman law

At first, the practical relevance of this European «common law», which is known under the Latin name *ius commune*, was not very substantial because local customary law was still the standard. Gradually however, local customary law was found to be inadequate, either because of its less sophisticated contents, or because it was difficult to access given its unwritten character, and the *ius commune* became more influential. This process, in which Roman law in a sense «conquered» legal science in Europe from the twelfth to the seventeenth century, has become known as the «Reception» of Roman law.

One of the reasons why Roman law gained acceptance is that it was considered to be rational; well-informed people would readily see that it contained good, if not the best possible, rules. Roman law was seen as *ratio scripta*, «reason written down».

Natural law

Being rational has always been one of the modes of existence of the law: rules were considered to be legal rules because they were rational. We can find evidence of this in the definition of law given to us in the thirteenth century by the Christian theologian and philosopher Thomas Aquinas.

According to his definition, the law is «a *rational* ordering of things which concern the common good, promulgated by whoever is charged with the care of the community». This definition was, by the way, not intended as a characterization of Roman law.

During the seventeenth and eighteenth centuries, there was a strong movement among learned legal writers emphasizing the rational nature of the law, and many authors attempted to establish the contents of law purely by means of reasoning. Law that was established by means of reason was usually discussed under the heading of «natural law».

Hugo Grotius (1583–1645) developed in his book *De iure belli ac pacis* (On the Law of War and Peace) the outlines of international law and private law on a rational basis.

Samuel von Pufendorf (1632–1694) in his book *De officio hominis et civis juxta legem naturalem libri duo* (On The Duty of Man and Citizen According to the Natural Law) developed large parts of private law, also on the basis of reasoning alone.

Christian Wolff (1679–1754) undertook a similar enterprise in his *Jus naturae methodo scientifica pertractatum* (Natural Law Dealt With by the Method of Science).

5   National States and Codification

Peace of Westphalia

England was already, to a large extent, united by the eleventh century. On the European continent however, the unification, in which small territorial units combined into bigger ones, was a longer process. Although the unification of Italy and of Germany took place only during the nineteenth century, it is often assumed that the process of State formation on the continent reached a provisional end point in 1648, when a number of wars were ended with the peace treaties of Westphalia. In this series of treaties, Europe was divided into individual Nation-States (each corresponding to a nation), which were assumed to be sovereign, meaning that each State would have exclusive power over its own territory.

National law

One of the consequences of this development was that law was to become primarily national law. Originally, the law was the law of a people or tribe rather than that of a territory. Later, when the different peoples who had flooded Europe in the period of mass migrations (fourth to sixth centuries CE) had settled down and began to mix, the law became local law and attached to territories of varying sizes. Only when the national States had formed could the law become the law of a Nation State.

Westphalian duo

Alongside this national law, there was law that dealt with mutual relations between the national States. This law is called *International Public Law*. National State law and international public law were taken to exhaust the forms that the law could take. These two became known as the «Westphalian duo». See ◘ Fig. 1.1.

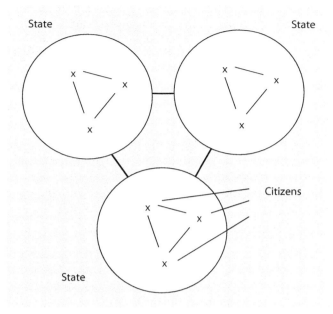

State

State

Citizens

State

● **Fig. 1.1**   The Westphalian duo

5.1   **Codification**

With the arrival of national States, law could become national law, but it still took several centuries before this process of nationalization was finished. A major step was taken with the French Revolution (1789–1799), in which the line of French kings was replaced, first by revolutionary agents and later by an emperor, Napoleon Bonaparte. It was Napoleon's reign that led to the codification of French law.

Shortly after the French Revolution, French law was codified in the form of a number of «Codes». They included the *Code civil* (private law), the *Code de commerce* (commerce law), the *Code de procédure civile* (law of civil procedure), the *Code pénal* (substantive criminal law), and the *Code d'instruction criminelle* (procedural criminal law). This codification, like others, served several purposes:

- It brought about legal unity in France, where the law, at least in part, had differed from region to region.
- It created legal certainty as the law was written down and could, at least in theory, be inspected by anyone.
- It emphasized the legal power of the central lawmaking agencies as opposed to the local judges.

— It guaranteed the influence of the people on the contents of the law because democratic organs have influence on the legislative process. (This last purpose only became relevant later, when democracy became more important).

Partly under the influence of the Napoleonic conquest of large parts of Europe, codifications were introduced at the beginning of the nineteenth century in several European countries, including Belgium and the Netherlands.

Historical School

Germany notably lagged behind because a strong resistance movement rose against codification. This is remarkable since some codifications in Germanic countries such as Bavaria and Prussia actually preceded French codification. However, on the whole, codification for the full German empire was (temporarily) postponed.

Under the leadership of Von Savigny (1779–1861), a famous law professor in Berlin, it was argued that the law of a nation reflected the «spirit» of that nation (the *Volksgeist*). Codification would fossilize the law, meaning that the crucial connection between the law and the spirit of the people would be lost. Respectively, codification should be preceded by historical research on the origins of law and the reasoning behind the law. The perspective of this movement, of which Von Savigny was one of the most important representatives, gave the «Historical School» its name.

In practice, this alleged relationship between the spirit of the people and the development of law was maintained by legal scholars. They wrote comments on the *Digest* and, in doing so, gradually adapted the law to the needs of society. The development of law in Germany was as a consequence driven by legal scholars. By the end of the nineteenth century, the resistance against codification lost its battle. In 1900, a codified German civil code, the *Bürgerliches Gesetzbuch*, entered into force.

5.2   Legal Families

Common law family

Developments in the law of Europe during the second millennium divided the national legal systems in Europe into two «legal families». The common law family, which includes England, Wales, and Ireland, were not as influenced by the reception of Roman law as were their counterparts on the continent. This is because common law development of was driven by the judiciary, as judges made new law through their decisions. It must be said that more recently, legislation has become an important source of the law in common law countries as well.

Scottish law was influenced by both the common law and the civil law tradition. It is a «mixed legal system».

The great counterpart of the common law family in Europe is the civil law family. The law of most countries on the European continent has been greatly influenced by the combination of Roman and Canon laws. However, it is also possible to detect a further subdivision within this civil law tradition. On the one hand, there are countries that have been strongly influenced by the French codification movement. This movement emphasized the role of parliament and democratic input in making the codification. The creation of law is, from this viewpoint, firstly a political process. Countries that belong to this *French family* include France, Belgium, Spain, and Portugal. On the other hand, there are countries that belong to the *German family*, in which the development of law was driven by legal scholars. Countries that belong to this tradition include Germany, Austria, and Switzerland.

Civil law family

The Nordic countries do not fall neatly in this twofold division, and many European countries, including Italy, the Netherlands, and Poland, have been influenced by both the French and the German tradition.

5.3 **Transnational Law**

The period of codification initiated a development towards the use of more and more positive law, although until the twentieth century, codifications still largely reflected preexisting law. However, during the twentieth century, and especially after World War II, legislation was increasingly used to create new law. This development took place both on the European continent and in Great Britain. In particular, it was the large increase in administrative law, which regulates relations between a government and its citizens, that caused a growth in the overall amount of law. This law was mostly positive, State-made, national law.

However, after World War II, there were also several developments that challenged the *Westphalian duo*. This led to the claim that national State law and public international law exhaust the kinds of law, to appear obsolete. These developments included the rise of human rights, the creation and development of the European Union, and the revival of the *Lex Mercatoria*.

Human rights

Traditionally, human rights were conceived as rights of individuals against their governments. They were part of the national law of States and were safeguarded in national constitutions. The scope of these human rights was determined by national judges, who decided in concrete cases whether a State had violated a human right.

After World War II, human rights came to be protected under treaties. Some of the most important ones have been created under the aegis of the United Nations.

Examples of treaties with a global scope are the International Covenant on Civil and Political Rights and the International Covenant on Economic, Social and Cultural Rights (both 1966). The Universal Declaration of Human Rights, which was adopted by the General Assembly of the United Nations in 1948, is very important. It is not a treaty properly speaking, as it was not created by an agreement between States. In Europe, the European Convention on Human Rights (1953) has also been an influential source of human rights.

When human rights were proclaimed and protected by international treaties, they were no longer the exclusive domain of national law. Although States can theoretically withdraw from treaties, in practice this is often not a viable option. States that have committed themselves to the protection of human rights have undertaken commitments towards their citizens, commitments which are, to a large extent, outside of their control. This phenomenon is enforced even if the application and interpretation of the treaties are assigned to judicial bodies that are beyond the power of national States.

An example of such a body is the *European Court of Human Rights*, which can deliver rulings that interpret the application of the European Convention on Human Rights, and is binding on States.

As such, while States can still determine to which human rights they bind themselves by means of treaties, it is independent courts that determined the scope. In this way, States have lost control over part of the law that is binding on their territories and which also binds them.

European Union law

In the treaties that created the European Union (EU), the institutions of the European Union have been given powers to make new and independent European legal rules. In two famous decisions – *Van Gend & Loos* (CJEU Case C-26/62) and *Costa/ENEL* (CJEU Case C-6/64) – the Court of Justice of the European Union decided that these European legal rules belong to a separate and autonomous legal system.

The rules that stem from the EU do not only bind the Member States but also their legal subjects. Moreover, these European legal rules have precedence over the States' domestic legal rules. As a consequence, the Member States of the EU and their legal subjects are bound by a legal system that is neither the system of a Nation State nor a system that regulates the mutual relations between Nation-States. In other words, the existence of EU law does not fit in the Westphalian picture that takes national States as its starting point.

The *Lex Mercatoria* is a set of rules created by merchants to regulate their mutual commerce. In principle, commercial relations are already governed by the rules of private law, the law that deals with mutual relations between private actors. However, the existing rules of private law were not always suitable for the particular needs of trade relations. Therefore as early as in the Middle Ages, a separate and independent body of rules emerged. For the same reason, separate courts originated, which had more expertise in commercial matters and which operated more swiftly.

Lex Mercatoria

Today, there still exists a body of rules that govern international commercial relations. This body consists of treaties such as the *Vienna Convention on the International Sale of Goods* (1980), and conventions that are not officially binding, but nevertheless exercise influence on the behavior of commercial partners (soft law). A typical example is the *Unidroit Principles of International Commercial Contracts*.

Because much of the *Lex Mercatoria* operates outside the traditional framework of national States and their relations towards each other and towards their legal subjects, it also provides counterevidence to the exhaustive nature of the Westphalian duo.

What is illustrated by the emergence of human rights, European Union law, and the revival of *Lex Mercatoria* is that there are many important legal phenomena that do not fit into the description of law created by the Treaties of Westphalia. These types of law have been categorized under the name of *transnational law*. Transnational law might be characterized as law that is neither made nor enforced by national States. This is a negative characterization: but simply put, transnational law is law that does not belong to the Westphalian duo. The increasing importance of this branch of law marks an important development in the long history of the law, which gives rise to new questions about the nature of the law.

Transnational law

6   Conclusion

In this chapter, we have seen how the law has taken different shapes over the course of time. Originally all law was customary law, but the oldest legislation that is presently known appeared around 2100 BCE (the *Codex Urnammu*), from the area that is now known as Iraq. The oldest legislation from the Roman tradition consists of the Twelve Tables. After the French Revolution, much of the existing law on the European continent was also codified, using the five aforementioned French Codes as examples.

Although it is likely that decisions made by judges had been a source of law long before the era of codification, case law as an official source of law in the common law tradition started with the conquest of England by William the Conqueror in the eleventh century. On the European continent, precedents also play an important role; however, they are seen as not officially binding.

Treaties and conventions are kinds of contracts between States. In theory, contracts only create obligations between States. Recently, however, some treaties such as ones pertaining to human rights or the treaties of the European Union, also assign rights to individuals as legal subjects. These legal subjects can in turn invoke their rights in court. As a consequence, the function of these treaties has started to resemble that of legislation.

The Peace of Westphalia (1648) established a kind of State system in Europe, and with it the idea that this system includes two kinds of law (the Westphalian duo). The first, National Law, concerns the citizens of a State, their mutual relations, and their relation to their own State. The other, International Public Law deals with the mutual relations between States. These two kinds of law were considered mutually exclusive and together exhaustive of all law. This idea of only two kinds of law was already incorrect for the time preceding the Westphalian Peace Treaties, and has become more incorrect over the last few decades with the rise of transnational law.

Recommended Literature

Merryman JH (2007) The civil law tradition, 3rd revised edn. Stanford University Press, Redwood City

Stein P (1999) Roman law in European History. Cambridge University Press, Cambridge

Legal Reasoning

Jaap Hage

© Springer International Publishing Switzerland 2017
J. Hage et al. (eds.), *Introduction to Law*, DOI 10.1007/978-3-319-57252-9_2

The sources of law have two different functions. They indicate what the various shapes are that law can take: customary law, precedent-based law, law based on legislation and treaties, and law based on legal doctrine and reason. We have seen examples of all these shapes in the chapter on the sources of law. Sources of law also play an important role in legal reasoning; they are used to substantiate the assertion that a particular rule is a legal rule and therefore can be used to support claims in law. Conversely, if a rule cannot be traced to a source, it can be concluded that the rule in question is not a legal rule and therefore cannot be used to support claims in law. In this chapter we will focus on the role that the sources of law play in legal reasoning.

1   The Legal Syllogism

With some simplification, the most important form of legal reasoning can be represented as a logical syllogism. A syllogism is an argument with two premises (starting points) and a single conclusion. The first premise contains the formulation of a legal rule in the format: IF condition THEN legal consequence. The second premise is the description of the facts of a case that satisfy the conditions of the rule. The conclusion describes the legal consequence that results from the application of the rule to the facts of the case.

Let us consider an example inspired by Dutch tort law. Tort law deals with the compensation of damage that a person has suffered as the result of a wrongful act by another person. The facts of the case are as follows: Pierre, 18 years old, visits the house of his neighbors. He is distracted by the daughter of the house, does not look where he is walking, stumbles over the carpet, and falls against an antique Chinese vase, which breaks as a consequence. The value of the vase was €3.000. Must Pierre (or his insurance) pay his neighbor €3.000?

The relevant rule, rendered in IF ... THEN- format, reads as follows:

» IF somebody acted wrongfully toward another person,
   and if he thereby caused damage to this other person,
   THEN he must compensate this damage.

The factual premise that can be reconstructed from the case description reads:

» Pierre acted wrongfully toward his neighbors and thereby
   he caused damage to his neighbors.

The conclusion that logically follows from these two premises is:

» Pierre must compensate the damage to his neighbors.

2   Classification

Although this argument refers to Pierre and his neighbors, it is formulated rather abstractly. It does not mention the daughter by whom Pierre was distracted, the role of the carpet, Pierre's stumbling, nor the vase. Perhaps some of these facts are not relevant to the question of whether Pierre must pay €3.000. Some other facts, however, will be relevant. These auxiliary facts are not mentioned because the description of the facts in the second premise of the syllogism must match the conditions of the rule that was formulated in the first premise.

While the description of the facts must be based on a real and concrete case, the given rule is in the abstract. It follows that the description of the case facts in the second premise must also be in the abstract. As such, a «translation» needs to be made from the concrete case description to the abstract case description that matches the rule conditions. This «translation» is called a *classification* of the facts. The facts that Pierre was distracted, stumbled over the carpet, and fell against the vase are taken together and classified as the fact that Pierre acted negligently. The fact that the vase broke as a consequence is classified as the fact that Pierre's act caused damage. Finally, the fact that the vase represented a value of €3.000 is classified as the fact that the damage amounts to €3.000.

Classification of case facts is often also based on the application of legal rules. Therefore, a classificatory argument can usually be cast in the shape of a legal syllogism. For instance,

» IF somebody acted negligently toward another person, THEN the former acted wrongfully against the latter.

» Pierre acted negligently toward his neighbors.

Pierre acted wrongfully toward his neighbors.

This classificatory argument still has an abstract factual premise. Therefore, we need yet another classificatory argument to justify the intermediate conclusion that Pierre acted negligently toward his neighbors:

>> IF somebody paid insufficient attention and thereby caused damage to another, THEN the former acted negligently toward the other.

>> Pierre paid insufficient attention and thereby caused damage to his neighbors.

Pierre acted negligently toward his neighbors.

3   Justification of the Rule: Official Legal Sources

Both the main argument, leading to the conclusion that Pierre must compensate the damage to his neighbors, and the classificatory arguments, leading to the intermediate conclusions that Pierre acted negligently and unlawfully toward his neighbors, are based on rules. In fact, most legal arguments are based on rules. Often, the rules used in legal arguments are uncontroversial. This is the case for many classificatory rules that express the normal meanings of words. For instance, if a legal reasoner classifies that a car is a vehicle, the rule that cars count as vehicles will normally be accepted without additional argument.

Other rules, however, are potentially more controversial. Take, for instance, the rule that if someone acted wrongfully toward another, and if he thereby caused damage to that person, he must compensate this damage. The person who must compensate the damage may demand that the use of the rule be justified. Why must he pay damages, if he did not intend to damage anybody? Here is where the sources of law come into play, because the use of a rule in a legal argument is typically justified by pointing out that the rule can be found in an official source of law.

For instance, the use of the rule «If somebody acted wrongfully towards somebody else and if he thereby caused damage to this other person, he must compensate this damage» can be justified by referring to the rule formulated in Article 6:162 Section 1 of the Dutch civil code (*Burgerlijk Wetboek*). If pressed even further, the person using the rule can also point out that the Dutch civil code is valid legislation, and that legislation is an official source of Dutch law.

The official sources of a modern legal system are typically leg- Official Sources
islation, including treaties, and – in the case of the common
law – precedents. Notice that these official sources are a more
limited category of legal sources than the sources discussed in
the previous chapter. Taken together, legal sources are indicative of the different shapes law can take. They are identified by
looking at different legal systems at different times. Not all of
these sources, however, can be used as reasons why a particular rule is a valid legal rule here and now; only «official»
sources can. What counts as «official source» varies from one
legal system to another and from one time to another. For
example, before 1066 (the Battle of Hastings), case law was not
an official source of English law. Presently, case law is an official source of English law, but not of continental Europe.

The justification of a legal rule by means of an official legal
source can be presented as a syllogism:

» IF a rule can be found in an official legal source, THEN this
rule holds (is valid).

» The rule «If somebody acted wrongfully towards another,
and if he thereby caused damage to this other person, he
must compensate this damage» can be found in an
official legal source.

IF somebody acted wrongfully toward another, and if he
thereby caused damage to this other person, THEN he
must compensate this damage.

In the common law tradition, judges are not bound by every *Ratio decidendi*
element of an earlier court decision, but only by its *ratio deci-*
dendi. Rather than all possible factors, this *ratio decidendi*
consists only of the decisive grounds that led the court take
the decision.

Apart from these decisive reasons, the court may have mentioned other
reasons that are relevant but did not determine the court's decision.
These other reasons are called *obiter dicta* (things that were also said),
and courts are not bound by these *obiter dicta*.

This *ratio decidendi*, together with the outcome of the case, is
comparable to respectively the conditions and the conclusion
of a rule. Where case law is an official source of law, the fact
that a court has decided a precedent in a particular way can be
used as a reason why this rule is valid law and can support new
legal decisions.

A simplified version of the *Donoghue v Stevenson 1932* case can illustrate this. Miss Donoghue visited a bar and drank from a bottle of ginger beer. It turned out that the bottle contained a partly decomposed snail. She fell ill and demanded damages from the manufacturer of beer. The court awarded the damages, because it argued that the manufacturer owed a duty of care to the woman and had violated this duty. The reason why the manufacturer owed the woman a duty of care (the *ratio decidendi* for this case) was that the women was considered a «neighbor» of the manufacturer. Such a «neighbor» is a person who is so closely and directly affected by the manufacturer's acts that the manufacturer ought reasonably to have had her in contemplation when directing its mind to the production and distribution of its products.

The fact that the court awarded Miss Donoghue damages can be adduced as a reason why this *ratio decidendi* is a valid English law and can be used in subsequent arguments before English courts.

The Sources Thesis   Legal positivism can briefly be described as the view that all law is positive law, that is: law that was created by being laid down. According to a particular view of legal positivism, there is an official source for every legal rule. If a rule stems from an official source, it is a legal rule. Conversely, if there is no source for it, a rule cannot be a legal rule. This thesis, that those and only those rules which can be traced to an official legal sources are legal rules, is called the «sources thesis».

This sources thesis was defended by the twentieth century English legal positivist Joseph Raz. Raz defended the thesis by pointing out that the existence of an official easily recognizable source for every legal rule contributes greatly to certainty about what the law is.

4   Interpretation

The texts by which legal rules are created are sometimes ambiguous. Take, for example, Article 6:162 Section 1 *Burgerlijk Wetboek*:

He who commits a wrongful act against another, which can be attributed to him, is obliged to compensate the damage suffered by that other as a consequence thereof.

It is not easy to translate this section of the *Burgerlijk Wetboek* into the structured rule «IF somebody acted wrongfully towards another, and if he thereby caused damage to this other person, THEN he must compensate this damage». The step from the text of an official legal source to the formulation of a rule with a clear structure is not always an easy one. Lawyers call this step «interpretation».

The term «interpretation» is used for a variety of related phenomena. They include the process of making the step from a source text to a rule formulation, the classification of case facts to allow their description fit the conditions of a rule, and the establishment of the legal consequences of juridical acts such as a contract, last will, or permit.

Lawyers use a number of techniques to deal with interpretation, which are called the «canons of interpretation». These canons are used in all three mentioned contexts: the determination of the rule formulation, the classification of facts, and the determination of the consequences of juridical acts.

Canons of Interpretation

Interpretation is sometimes also necessary to decide about the proper scope of application of a rule. For instance, does a rule that forbids the presence of dogs in a butcher shop also apply to guide dogs? If an issue arises about a guide dog in a butcher shop, it is necessary to take a decision about whether guide dogs are dogs for the purpose of the regulation. Further, this decision should be motivated.

One method of interpreting a rule requires that the interpretation matches the literal meaning of the words in the rule. Guide dogs are dogs, are they not? Therefore, a rule about dogs in general also applies to guide dogs. The canon of interpretation that states that rules should be interpreted literally is called the «literal rule», and the resulting interpretation is called a «grammatical» or «literal interpretation».

The Literal Rule or Grammatical Interpretation

Often rules are created to solve problems. The legislator intended to achieve particular results, and the rule is thus a means to obtain those results. If a legal decision maker gives the rule an interpretation that suits the original intention of the legislator, she is said to apply the mischief rule.

The Mischief Rule or Legislative Intent

Suppose that the legislator created the prohibition of dogs in butcher shops in order to prevent unhygienic situations in food stores. He considered the case of guide dogs but nevertheless decided not to make an exception, because hygiene was considered more important. If a legal decision maker wants to follow legislative intent, she must interpret the rule to make it also apply to guide dogs.

When an interpreter looks at the purpose of a rule, she may revert to the intention of the legislator who formulated the rule. This is the application of the mischief rule. However, she may also try to determine the purpose of the rule herself. When we speak of purposive or teleological interpretation, the decision maker applies the so-called golden rule.

The Golden Rule: Purposive or Teleological Interpretation

Assume again that the legislator created the prohibition of dogs in butcher shops in order to prevent unhygienic situations in food stores. If a legal decision maker recognizes this interest but finds the interest of visually handicapped persons more important, she might interpret the rule teleologically to make guide dogs fall outside the rule's scope.

Interpreting Precedents

Not only legislation and treaties require interpretation; the same holds for precedents. Above we discussed a simplified version of the *Donoghue v Stevenson* case and formulated – tentatively – a *ratio decidendi* for this case. Courts typically do not specify the *rationes decidendi* for their decisions themselves. Later courts or legal practitioners and scientists must interpret the precedents in order to extract the *ratio decidendi* from them. Canons of interpretation, however, as they have been developed for statutory interpretation, seem to be lacking for the extraction of *rationes decidendi* of precedents.

5   Reasoning with Rules and Cases

Applicability

Even after the precise conditions and conclusion of a rule or the *ratio decidendi* of a precedent have been established, and the facts of a case have been classified as being covered or not by this rule or ratio, the possibilities of a legal reasoner are not exhausted. A rule is *applicable* to a case only if the facts of the case after classification satisfy the conditions of the rule. The normal situation is that an applicable rule attaches its consequences to the case. For example, Pierre has to pay €3000 to his neighbors to compensate the damage of the broken vase. If a rule is not applicable, it does not attach its consequences to the case.

Analogy

Sometimes it happens that a rule is, strictly speaking, not applicable to a case. Yet, the new case may have so many similarities to older cases to which the rule was applicable, that it seems desirable to apply the rule by analogy. Assume, for example, that a civil code contains the rule that the owner of a piece of land is not allowed to have trees less than two meters from the border with his neighbor's land. In a particular case, it is not the owner of a piece of land who has a tree less than two meters from the border, but a lessee. The lessee is not the owner, so strictly speaking the rule is not applicable to his tree. However, given the similarity of the cases, and given the purpose of the rule, there is reason to apply this rule to lessees with wrongly planted trees. Because the rule was not strictly applicable, we then say that the rule was applied by analogy.

Application of rules by analogy is a somewhat hazardous enterprise, because a court that does this deviates from a decision of the legislator who created the rule. In criminal law and in tax law, rule application by analogy is therefore regarded with great suspicion.

It is possible to extract *rationes decidendi* from precedents, which can then be applied to new cases in the same way as rules based on legislation. However, it is also possible to use precedents in a different way, namely, for reasoning by analogy. A new case is seldom completely identical to a precedent. There will be similarities but also differences. An old case should function as a precedent for a new case when it is the most «on point» case of all potential precedents. The number and relevance of both the similarities and differences play a role in determining which case is most «on point» and should support the decision in the new case. The reasoning for which a potential precedent is most «on point» is similar to the reasoning that is required for determining whether a non-applicable rule should be applied by analogy.

Case-Based Reasoning

The binding nature of precedent only applies to cases that are *similar* to the already decided case. Here, «similar» means identical in *all* relevant aspects. This creates leeway for the development of law because a court that must decide on a new case has to determine whether the new case is really similar to the alleged precedent. By pointing out relevant differences (distinguishing), the court can argue that the cases are not similar and that it is therefore not bound by a particular precedent.

Distinguishing

Suppose that in an old case someone sold a sick cow. The buyer wanted to undo the sale because the cow was ill, but the court refused to do so because the buyer could have, or should have, seen that the cow was sick. This is a precedent for future cases, but for which ones precisely? Suppose that in a later case the seller explicitly stated to the buyer that the animal was healthy. Would that make a difference to the buyer who bought the cow and now wants his money back? If the court decides to distinguish this case from the prior case, the law will be changed, and this decision will also function as a precedent for future cases.

It is possible that a court treats cases as similar when their similarity is not obvious. If a judge applies the rule that there will be no money back for unhealthy animals if their illness was detectable to a case involving defective products bought in a shop, the rule will be broadened considerably. This broadened rule will also come to function as a precedent.

Broadening

6   Principles to Deal with Rule Conflicts

There is no guarantee that all legislation brought about by one body will be consistent. However, if there are several bodies that produce legislation, such as national laws and laws of provinces, it is almost guaranteed that there will be some conflict of rules. To deal with such conflicts, several principles have been developed over the course of time. Here we will focus on three of them.

Lex Superior

Sometimes rules stand in order based on a hierarchy between legislative bodies. This is usually the case if in a particular State legislators operate on different levels. Here, the rules of the «central» legislator are considered to be superior to the rules of the local legislators. The *Lex Superior* principle then holds that in case of conflict, the superior rule overrides the inferior rule. Thus, Lex Superior holds that national laws will prevail over laws of the province and that laws of the province prevail over municipal laws. Another example would be the supremacy of EU law over the national laws of the EU member states.

Lex Specialis

It is very difficult for a legislator to foresee all possible situations to which a rule may apply. As a consequence, a rule may be either *over-inclusive* or *under-inclusive*. A rule is *over-inclusive* if it applies to cases in which it was not meant to apply. An example would be a prohibition of dogs in a butcher shop, which is not meant to apply to guide dogs for the blind. A rule is *under-inclusive* if it does not apply to the cases to which it was meant to apply. An example would be a rule against dogs in a butcher shop, which should also apply to the monkey that Mrs. Jackson likes to take for a walk.

Both problems can be dealt with by means of a rule that deals with the specific situation. This specific rule will be in conflict with the more general rule, to which it is meant as an exception. This conflict is dealt with by means of the *Lex Specialis* principle. This principle holds that the more specific rule prevails over the more general rule.

The position of guide dogs might be dealt with by a rule that blind people are allowed to bring their guide dogs to all public places. This rule would be more specific than a general prohibition in butcher shops and would therefore prevail according to the *Lex Specialis* principle. Notice that it is not always easy to see which of two conflicting rules is the more specific one.

Lex Posterior

Most often, when a new rule is created that is in conflict with a preexisting rule, the old rule is simultaneously and explicitly repealed. However, in cases where this has not happened, the *Lex Posterior* principle may be useful. It states that the newer rule prevails over the older one.

7   The Lawyer's Toolbox

We have seen that a legal decision maker, who must justify her choice for a particular outcome for a case, has a choice of several different techniques. Some of these techniques are relatively formalist: the decision maker refers to the decision of someone else, a legislator, or a court and avoids giving a value judgment herself. Other techniques are more substantive: the decision maker engages in reasoning about what would be a good rule. She makes her own value judgment and bases her interpretation of the rule, the classification of the facts, and the way the rule is used in a legal argument, on this value judgment. In all cases, however, the decision maker must choose a technique. The different legal sources, the reasoning techniques, and the canons of interpretation can be compared to a set of decision-making tools in a lawyer's toolbox. Depending on the needs of the case, a legal decision maker picks a tool that helps her reach a desirable result.

Recommended Literature

Schauer F (1991) Playing by the rules. Clarendon, Oxford

Raz J (2009) Legal positivism and the sources of law. In: Raz J (ed) The authority of law. Essays on law and morality, 2nd edn. Clarendon, Oxford, pp 37–52

Basic Concepts of Law

Jaap Hage

© Springer International Publishing Switzerland 2017
J. Hage et al. (eds.), *Introduction to Law*, DOI 10.1007/978-3-319-57252-9_3

This chapter deals with a number of basic concepts that play a role in law and legal science. ▶ Section 1 addresses the different fields of law, such as tort law and administrative law. Legal subjects such as natural and legal persons are the topic of ▶ Sect. 2. ▶ Section 3 deals with the operation of rules and discusses operative facts and legal consequences. Juridical acts, by means of which legal agents can intentionally change the legal positions of themselves and others, are the topic of ▶ Sect. 4. ▶ Section 5 addresses the relations between duties, prohibitions, and permissions, while ▶ Sect. 6 goes into some detail concerning competences and immunities. ▶ Sections 7, 8, 9, and 10, finally, discuss different kinds of rights.

1   Fields of law

Law is not a homogeneous body of rules; it consists of many «fields of law» that sometimes exhibit large differences. Most of what has to be said about law is therefore included in the chapters that deal with the different legal fields, such as property law, constitutional law, international law, and criminal law. This section deals with the fields of law in a more general way. It focuses upon two major divisions within law, namely, the divisions between public and private law and between substantive and procedural law.

1.1   Public Law and Private Law

The first major division is between public and private law. In this division, the role of the government is central. Simply stated:

- Public law is that part of the law in which the government as such plays a role.
- Private law is that part of the law in which the government as such does not play a role.

The above characterizations refer to the government «as such» because the government can at times act as a private party. An example is that the police force owns a number of police cars. This is not different from ownership by a private person.

Private Law

Private law deals with the mutual relations between citizens. *Property law* and *contract law* are major branches of private law, which regulate things such as sales, ownership, and mortgages. A third branch of private law is *tort law*, which deals with the compensation for damage that occurs when there is no contract. Other branches of private law include the *family law* (marriage, adoption, right to a name) and the *law of commerce*, which regulates, among other things, the transport of goods. A special branch is *private international law*, which determines which laws are applicable if a case falls under more than one jurisdiction. For instance, it determines which family law governs the divorce of persons with different nationalities.

Public law is characterized by the fact that the government, as such, plays a central role. There are four main branches of public law. The best known of these may be *criminal law*. This is a branch of public law because the tracing, prosecution, and punishment of criminals are handled by, or on behalf of, the government.

Public Law

A second important branch of public law organizes the State and the government. This branch is called *constitutional law* and deals with topics such as the division of government powers (Trias Politica), the functioning of democracy, the creation of legislation, and the relationship between central and local government agents. Traditionally, it also deals with human rights, but that field now also falls under public international law.

The third branch, *administrative law*, covers the most expansive part of public law and deals with the many interactions between government agents and civilians or private organizations. Administrative law has many branches of its own, including social security law, environmental law, and tax law.

Public international law regulates relations between States and international organizations and is also a branch of public law.

European Union law illustrates that the division between private and public law is not always clear-cut. On the one hand, there are treaties between the member States of the European Union (EU) in which the main institutions of the EU are regulated. These rules very much resemble the constitutional law of the individual member States and would therefore be a kind of public law. As this law is created in the form of treaties between States, it is a kind of public international law. On the other hand, the institutions of the EU also make law themselves. This law deals with the organization of the EU, in a manner similar to constitutional law. However, it also deals with the relationship between citizens and companies within the EU. There are, for instance, EU rules about fair competition, and many of these rules focus on citizens and companies. Arguably, these rules belong to private law.

European Union Law

1.2   Substantive and Procedural Law

A second twofold division of law, which is perpendicular to the division between public and private law, is the division between substantive and procedural law. *Substantive law* consists of rules that give people rights and determine what people should do.

Not everyone always complies with all duty-imposing rules nor are all the rights of legal subjects always respected. Therefore, if law is to function well, it has to provide the means through which compliance with duties and respect for rights can be enforced. These means are given by *procedural law*. This field of law provides the rules for court procedures and for the organization of the judiciary. It also includes rules that specify how judicial orders can be enforced.

There are branches of procedural law for each of the major branches of substantive law. This means that there exist rules for *civil procedure*, which deal with the enforcement of private law. There are also rules for *criminal procedure*, which specify how criminal suspects can be traced, prosecuted, and—after conviction— punished. Further, there are rules of *administrative* procedure, indicating, for example, how environmental law or tax law can be enforced. The European Union has its own procedural rules, which govern, among others, the operation of the Court of Justice of the European Union.

1.3   «Functional» Fields of Law

European Union law is not the only field of law that does not sit well within the established divisions between public and private law and between substantive and procedural law. In fact, there are many fields of law that have traits of both private and public law and/or both substantive and procedural law. Those fields of law are sometimes called «functional» fields of law because they are characterized by the function they fulfill rather than by belonging to one of the main areas of law. The function then consists mainly of the topic that is regulated by the field, such as the European Union (EU law), the environment (environmental law), or information and communication technology (ICT law).

The relationship between the main areas of law and the functional fields can be depicted as in ◘ Fig. 3.1.

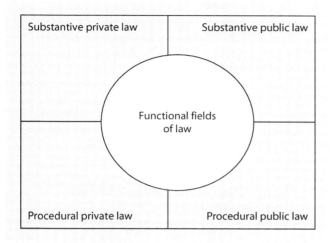

□ **Fig. 3.1**   Functional fields of law

2   Legal Subjects

Legal rules impose duties upon and attribute competences and rights to legal subjects. These legal subjects are typically human beings, but in theory law can give the status of a legal subject to anyone or anything it wants. For example, a foundation, a company with limited liability, a State, or a municipality, can—and in many countries do—be counted as legal subjects. Under the law, human beings are called «natural persons» (*personnes physiques, natürliche Personen*), while organizations that have received the status of legal subjects are called «legal persons» (*personnes morales, juristische Personen*).

The consequences of being a legal subject vary from one field of law to another. In criminal law, being a legal subject means to be addressed by rules of criminal law and to become punishable in case of violation. Natural persons are legal subjects in this sense, but it is not evident that legal persons are also addressed by criminal law rules. For instance, it is not immediately clear that one can speak about an «intention to act» in case of a municipality, even though an intention is an essential condition for many crimes.

Furthermore, natural persons are protected by the human rights that are assigned to them. They have a right to privacy, freedom of expression, freedom of religion, and a right to physical integrity. Not all of these rights make sense when applied to legal persons. It is conceivable, for instance, that a legal person such as a newspaper company exercises its freedom of expression. Conversely, it is not immediately clear what the protection of physical integrity would mean in the case of legal persons.

In private law, legal subjects have rights, such as property or a claim to be paid money, and legal subjects can perform juridical acts. These consequences pertain to both natural and legal persons. For example, both a natural person and a foundation can own property and are able to contract.

3   Rules, Operative Facts, and Legal Consequences

Structure of Rules

A common understanding of law is that it consists of rules that prescribe behavior. However, there are also rules that give definitions, create rights and competences, define procedures, and fulfill still other functions. Although there are many different kinds of legal rules, most of them can be analyzed as having a conditional structure. They have a condition part, which states when the rule is applicable, and a conclusion part, which indicates what the consequences are when the rule is applied. This structure of rules is not always obvious from the literal wording of the rule. Take, for instance, Book 1, ▶ Sect. 7.1 of the German Civil Code, which reads (if translated into English):

A person who settles permanently in a place establishes his residence in that place.

With some good will, the following conditional structure can be discovered in this statutory provision:

» If P settles permanently in a place
Then P has established his residence in that place

where «P» stands for an arbitrary person.

Operative Facts and Legal Consequences

A legal rule is applicable to a case if the facts of the case satisfy the conditions of the rule. The facts of a case that match the conditions are called *operative facts*. A fact can only be an operative fact if a rule attaches *legal consequences* to it. For instance, if Claus Ziegler settled himself permanently in Bonn, this is an operative fact because the rule in ▶ Sect. 7.1 of the German Civil Code attaches to this fact the legal consequence that Claus Ziegler has established his residence in Bonn.

Other examples of operative facts are:

- Someone passes away. This has the legal consequence that the property of the deceased person is inherited by his heirs.
- Someone is the owner of a book. This has the legal consequence that this person will be competent to alienate the book (alienation is moving ownership to somebody else).
- A legislator creates a statute. This has the legal consequence that new rules come into existence.
- A court sentences a criminal suspect. This has the legal consequence that it becomes allowed to incarcerate this person.

4   Juridical Acts

Law is dynamic, both in the sense that the rules change over the course of time and in the sense that the legal positions of individual persons are subject to modifications. An example of the latter is that Jeanine Dabin was the owner of a Lamborghini sports car, and then because she sold it, she was no longer the owner. Some of these changes occur spontaneously; when a baby is born, it immediately has the right to privacy, or when a building collapses, the possessor of the building becomes liable for damages. However, not all operative facts just happen; some of them were brought about intentionally. If Jeanine Dabin sold her car, she intentionally brought about her loss of ownership of the car.

It is attractive if legal subjects, whether they be private citizens, organizations, or government agents, are able to change legal positions and legal rules as they deem fit. This adds to the autonomy of these agents. Of course, not everyone should be able to bring about any change he likes. Private persons should, for example, not be able to appropriate what belongs to others nor should they be able to marry two other persons who do not want to be married. A municipal legislator should not be able to create rules that apply to everyone in the world, and the EU should not be able to prohibit European citizens from expressing their opinions. However, within certain limits, legal subjects should have the power to intentionally change legal positions or even legal rules. This power is given to them through the possibility to perform juridical acts. Examples of juridical acts are contracts, last wills, legislative acts, judicial decisions, and administrative dispositions.

3

Intention

The phenomenon of juridical acts exists in most, if not all, legal systems of the world. The concept of a juridical act, however, has mainly become popular in the legal systems that belong to the civil law tradition. In common law countries, one rather speaks of the exercise of a legal power. A consequence of this difference between legal cultures is that the English term «juridical act» has not reached the level of general usage.

Legal subjects perform juridical acts with the intention to bring about legal consequences. The very idea of a juridical act is that its performance leads precisely to these intended consequences. If one wants to know what the legal consequences of a juridical act are, the first place to look is at the intention of the agent.

For example, legislation is a juridical act. If a State agent legislates, the typical legal consequence is either that a new law is created in line with what the agent had intended or that rules the agent intended to repeal are repealed. If two parties enter into a contract—another juridical act—the legal consequences are in the first place those which the parties wanted to bring about.

Definition

A *juridical act* is an act performed with the intention to bring about legal consequences, specifically one where the law connects legal consequences to the act for the reason that they were intended. If Daniel contracts with Rebecca that he will paint her house, he does so with the intention to undertake a legal obligation. Because of this intention, Daniel is bound by the contract. However, if Johnnie commits a murder, it does not matter whether he had the intention to bring about the legal consequence that he is criminally liable, because the law attaches the legal consequence independently of his intention. This shows that murdering someone is not a juridical act, even though it has legal consequences.

Alternative expressions for «juridical act» in English are «legal act» and «legal transaction.» More common is the German term «Rechtsgeschäft» or the French term «acte juridique.» In Germany, the notion of a juridical act is confined to private law. This means that legislation, judicial decisions and administrative dispositions, which belong to public law, would not count as juridical acts in Germany.

Factual Acts

Sometimes it is useful to dispose of terminology to refer to acts that are not juridical acts. For instance, a municipality can pursue its parking policies both by creating prohibitions (which is a juridical act) and by making it physically impossible to park in certain places. We will use the expression «factual acts» to refer to acts, usually performed by the administration, that are not aimed at creating legal consequences.

Sometimes the performance of a juridical act requires that formalities are respected. Only if these formalities are taken into account will the act in question, for instance, signing a document in the presence of two witnesses, count as making a last will. This is also very clear in the case of legislation: a legislator must follow precisely specified steps in order to create a valid law. Other juridical acts have no formal requirements. Most contracts fall under this category; they come into existence merely through the exchange and the intention to create legal consequences. **Formalities**

We have already seen that not everyone can bring about a legal consequence by means of a juridical act. To begin with, juridical acts such as legislation that belong to the sphere of public law cannot be performed by ordinary citizens. Moreover, private persons cannot impose obligations on persons other than themselves. In general, there is a limitation on the kinds of juridical acts that can be performed by particular agents and on the kinds of legal consequences that can be brought about by means of juridical acts. This limitation is evidenced by the fact that one can only bring about particular legal consequences by means of a juridical act if one has the competence to do so. **Competence**

Sometimes the act has legal consequences, despite the incompetence of the agent, because the act has created justified expectations that the laws want to honor. For instance, if a public servant has granted a building permit without having the relevant competence, legal certainty may nevertheless require that the permit remain valid, at least until it has been avoided.

The competence to create legal consequences by means of juridical acts is typically attached to a legal status by a legal rule. For instance, if an organization is the parliament of a country (a legal status), a legal rule may attach to this status the fact that this body has the competence to legislate. If somebody owns a house (another legal status), a legal rule attaches to this right of ownership the competence to sell the house to somebody else. Another rule attaches a competence to the bank which has a mortgage on the house, in case the owner does not repay his debt to the bank. If someone is the mayor of a city, a legal rule attaches to this fact the competence to make emergency regulations for her city.

If a person or an organization attempts to perform a juridical act for which they lack the relevant competence, the act in question will normally not have the intended legal consequences. The act is then said to be *null and void*. **Nullity, Validity, and Avoidance**

If the intention of an agent to create a particular legal consequence was brought about in the wrong way, for instance, because the agent was cheated, the juridical act is typically still *valid*, meaning that it retains its legal consequences. However, the law often gives such an agent the competence to *avoid* the juridical act. If a juridical act is avoided, its legal consequences are taken away retrospectively. This means that the law treats the juridical act as if it never had been valid and never had any legal consequences. Sometimes the agent can avoid his juridical act himself, but it is also possible that a judicial decision is required for the avoidance. After avoidance, a juridical act is null and void.

Grounds for Avoidance

There are several possible reasons why a juridical act is avoidable. One of them is that the intention of the agent was brought about in a wrong way. An example would be that a crook puts a false signature under a painting and succeeds in selling the painting for far more than its actual value. The intention to buy this painting was therefore brought about in a wrong way.

Another reason would be that a public officer has made a legal mistake in refusing a license. The applicant for the license may ask a court to avoid this refusal.

Yet another example of why a juridical act may be avoidable is that its content is in some way undesirable. If a municipality makes a bylaw that violates one of the human rights enshrined in the constitution or a human rights treaty, this bylaw is avoidable. That would, for instance, be the case if the municipality prohibited the exercise of a particular religion.

In private law, undesirable content often leads to nullity, rather than avoidability, of a contract. If a hired killer contracts to murder an enemy of his contract partner, the contract will be null and void, both because the contract conflicts with existing law and because it is immoral. This difference between public and private law can be explained by the demands of legal certainty. In public law, administrative and legislative acts that are «wrong» are nevertheless often considered to be valid, because legal certainty demands this. However, in private law the demands of legal certainty are often less strict, which makes the sanction of nullity possible.

5   Duties, Prohibitions, and Permissions

Two of the most important notions in law are those of «duty» and «right». It is sometimes thought that the two are closely related in the sense that the duty of one person corresponds to the right of another and vice versa. As we will see, this is often not the case.

3

5.1   Duties and Prohibitions

If somebody has a duty to do something, this means that he is obligated to do it. Every duty has two elements:
1. The agent who has the duty
2. The kind of action which the agent is obligated to perform

Duties are meant to guide persons in their behavior. This means that duties are always addressed to one or more specific agents. We use the general term «agent» because not only natural persons but also groups and organizations can have duties.

Addressees

For instance, John Doe has the duty to stop when the traffic light is red; John and Jean Doe have the duty to clean away the snow from the pavement in front of their house; the Apple Company has a duty to treat its employees in a decent way.

Duties are typically imposed on agents by a rule that attaches the duty to a particular status of the agent. For instance, only car drivers have the duty to turn on their car lights when it gets dark. The rule mentions car drivers in general, while the duty pertains to individual agents who happen to drive cars. Another example would be the rule that natural and legal persons with taxable incomes have the duty to make a yearly tax declaration. This rule imposes a duty on Alphabet (the company that owns Google) to make a yearly tax declaration. Some rules impose duties on everybody. An example is the rule not to torture. Rules that impose duties are also called «mandatory rules».

Duty-Imposing Rules

Every duty has a *content*, which indicates what the addressee of the duty is obligated to do. The action that a duty prescribes can either be doing something or abstaining from doing something. An example of a duty to do something is the duty to pay one's income tax. An example of a duty to abstain from doing something is the duty not to commit theft. A *prohibition* is nothing other than a duty to refrain from doing something. The duty not to commit theft is therefore the prohibition of theft.

Content of Duty

5.2   Permissions

If an agent is permitted (allowed) to perform some kind of action, this means that the agent is not forbidden to perform that kind of action. For instance, if Maria is allowed to walk on the lawn, this means that Maria is not prohibited from walking on the lawn or that Maria does not have the duty not to walk on the lawn.

It is generally assumed that everybody is allowed to do anything that has not been explicitly forbidden. This means that if there is no rule that forbids the agent to do something, and if nobody forbade the agent to do it, the agent is allowed to do it. Permission is thus usually the mere absence of a prohibition; no permissive rule or explicit permission is required. For instance, if there is no applicable rule forbidding Maria to walk on the lawn, and no competent person forbade her to do so, Maria has permission to walk on the lawn.

Nevertheless, law has a function for permissive rules and explicit permissions. This function is to make an exception to what is generally forbidden. Police officers, for instance, are usually permitted to perform a body search on suspects of serious crimes. This permission is not merely the absence of a prohibition. In fact there *is* a prohibition against such an action: it is generally forbidden to search persons in this way. However, next to this general prohibition, there is an exception for the police. Police officers are permitted to do what no one else may do, namely, to search, interrogate, and apprehend suspects of serious crimes. While this permission applies only to police officers, it applies to police officers in general and is therefore based on a permissive rule.

Permissions are also often the result of a juridical act by which a permission is granted. If the lawn belongs to Dietmar, nobody else is permitted to walk on it, unless Dietmar gives permission. Giving permission is a juridical act through which an exception is created on a general prohibition. If Dietmar authorizes Maria to walk on the lawn, Maria has permission/is allowed to do so. This permission only applies to Maria; it is therefore not based on a permissive rule but on the explicit permission given by Dietmar.

Permission and Competence

Two concepts that are easily confused are those of permission and competence. Nevertheless, there are clear differences between the two. Competence is a precondition for the intentional creation of a legal consequence *by means of a juridical act*. If one tries to perform a juridical act for which one lacks the required competence, one will normally not succeed in bringing about any legal consequence. However, an attempt to do so is not necessarily illegal.

For instance, if an ordinary citizen tries to create a statute, this is not necessarily illegal, but an attempt to do so will not result in the intended consequence (the legislation will be considered non-existent or void) because ordinary citizens lack the required competence.

Permission has to do with what one is allowed to do. Any kind of action, whether juridical or ordinary, may be the object of permission. If an act is done without having the necessary permission to do so, this amounts to a norm violation or perhaps an unlawful act.

The difference between competence and permission becomes especially clear when it is approached from the perspective of a legislator who wants to prevent certain kinds of behavior. If the behavior in question is a juridical act, for instance, selling drugs, his task is quite easy. The only thing the legislator has to do is to make sure that no one has the competence to sell drugs. That can easily be done by means of legislation. Without competence, it is impossible to buy or sell, and as such the trade of drugs can be removed from the world by means of simple legislation.

Legally speaking, the argument above is correct: without competence it is not possible to buy or to sell, since sales contracts are juridical acts. However, it is still possible to give somebody drugs and to take money in exchange, because those are both purely factual acts. What is made impossible by legislation is the creation of an obligation to deliver the drugs and an obligation to pay money for them.

If the legislator wants to prevent something that is not a juridical act, the task is more difficult. Often the best that can be done is to prohibit the undesired behavior and use the threat of sanctions in case the prohibition is violated. This may work, but there is no guarantee. For example, a prohibition against speeding on the road is easily violated.

As an alternative, the administration can make some kinds of behavior physically impossible, for instance by making a road so rough that it is impossible to drive faster than 30 miles an hour.

6   Competences and Immunities

An agent exercises a competence by performing the juridical act for which this competence is required. Parliament exercises its competence to make legal rules by legislating; the owner of a book exercises his competence to alienate the book by selling it. Sometimes the performance of a juridical act has as an immediate legal consequence, changing the legal position of the agent or of someone else related to the act. For example, if two parties enter into a contract, they not only change their own legal positions by undertaking obligations but those of their counterparts as well, by giving them rights.

The possibility that an agent changes the legal position of someone else seems problematic, especially if the change involves the imposition of a burden and if the agent is not a public authority. If Jan and Catalina are private persons, Jan should not be able to alienate Catalina's book, and Catalina should not be able to impose duties on Jan. Jan and Catalina are not able to do so because the acts in question are juridical acts, and Jan and Catalina lack the required competences.

The flip side of an agent lacking the competence to modify someone else's legal position is that this other person is *immune* to having his or her legal position modified by the agent. Catalina is immune to Jan alienating her book, while Jan is immune to Catalina imposing duties on him.

In private law, legal subjects are generally immune to having their legal positions modified by other legal subjects. However, they have the required competence for, and are therefore not immune to, the modification of their own legal positions. In public law, this is different: public officers often do have the competence to modify the legal positions of private citizens. A tax inspector can impose a duty to pay income tax on a citizen, a parking officer can fine the driver of a wrongly parked car, a public servant can grant a building permit, and a court can sentence a defendant to pay damages. Citizens are generally not immune to having their legal positions modified by public officers.

7   Rights as Pincushions

There are many different kinds of rights which differ considerably from each other. If one seeks a common denominator for the different kinds of rights, there are two characteristics that most (but not all) rights share. One is that rights represent interests that are protected by law. The other characteristic is that rights are like pincushions. They are points in legal space where other legal positions are grouped together, analogous to how a pincushion group pins together. These «other legal positions» include permissions, duties, prohibitions, powers, and immunities, in different combinations and with different contents for different rights (◻ Fig. 3.2).

The different kinds of rights can, with some good will, be grouped under three headings, that is, rights against a person (*rights in personam* or claims), rights on an «object» (*rights in*

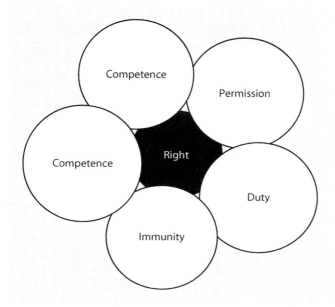

◘ Fig. 3.2 Rights as pincushions

rem or *property rights*), and human or fundamental rights.
► Section 8 discusses claims and their counterparts and obligations. ► Section 9 will deal with property rights, and ► Sect. 10 covers a few fundamental rights.

8   Claims and Obligations

Personal rights, which are also called «claims» or «relative rights», mainly belong to the field of private law and are the counterparts of obligations in a narrow sense. Legal obligations are the results of events to which private law attaches an obligation as its legal consequence. Typical examples of such events are contracts and the unlawful actions that are grouped together under the denominator «torts». Take, for instance, a sales contract. When two parties enter into a sales contract, the seller has the obligation to deliver what he has sold, and the buyer has a corresponding right to its delivery. This right is only directed to the seller and is therefore a personal right or a claim. The word «obligation» is used both to describe the obligation that is the counterpart of the claim («obligation» in the narrow sense) and to describe the combination of the obligation in the narrow sense and the claim that resulted

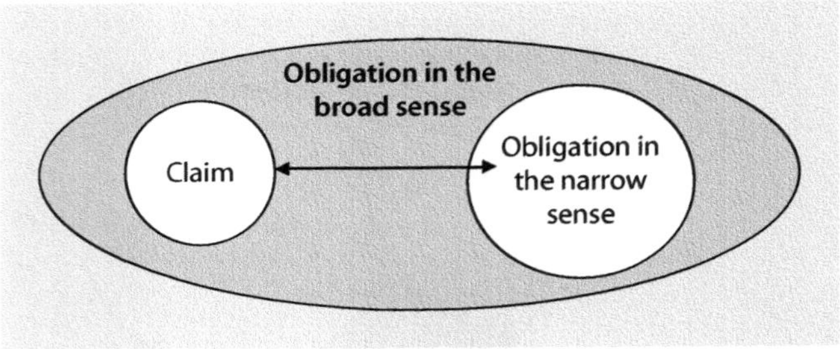

◘ Fig. 3.3   Obligations in the wide and narrow sense

from the contract or the tort («obligation» in the broad sense). From now on, we will use the word «obligation» to refer to obligations in the narrow sense only (◘ Fig. 3.3).

Obligations and Duties   Obligations and duties are quite similar. In fact, in English legal literature, the words are used interchangeably. In the civil law tradition, however, for every obligation there is a creditor, while in the case of duties there is not. Therefore, the word «obligation» refers to what a person, the debtor, is obligated to do in favor of another person, the creditor. For example, if Antonia borrows €5.000 from William, she has an obligation *toward William* to repay the money. If Gerald approaches a red traffic light, he has the duty to stop, but this is not a duty toward someone in particular. This difference in directedness—obligations being directed to someone while duties are not—is reflected in the counterpart of an obligation, the claim, or personal right. If Antonia has an obligation toward William, William has a claim against Antonia. There are no claims corresponding to duties.

However, if somebody violates a duty, and damage results, the law may attach an obligation to compensate the damage to this violation. This obligation has a corresponding claim.

What a Claim Involves   A claim is more than merely the flip side of an obligation. Like other rights, it is best seen as a point in legal space where several legal positions are joined together, attached to the claim.

One of these positions is the competence to transfer a claim. If William transfers his claim against Antonia to Mark, Mark will be the new claim holder. This means that the content of Antonia's obligation has changed: after the transfer, she is obligated to pay €5.000 to Mark and not to William. Moreover, if William transfers his claim to Mark, all the competences that are attached to the claim also move from William to Mark.

Another possible legal position attached to a claim is the competence to enforce that claim. If Antonia does not repay the €5.000 to William, William can start a court procedure which may end with a bailiff enforcing the claim against Antonia.

Finally a claim holder has the competence to waive his right. If William informs Antonia in the proper way that she no longer has to repay the money, this will end both Antonia's obligation and William's claim.

As we can see, a claim held by a creditor does not only involve an obligation on the side of the debtor but also a number of competences for the claim holder. Neither the obligation nor the competences are identical to the claim, but having a claim involves the presence of the obligation and the competences. If a claim is transferred, the content of the corresponding obligation is adapted, and the associated competences move with the claim to the new holder.

9   Property Rights

Where claims correspond to obligations and are therefore rights that correspond with doing or not doing something, property rights are the relations between the right holder and the object of the right (the property). The most familiar example of such a right regarding an object is the right of ownership, which the owner has with regard to the owned object. Other examples of property rights are copyright and mortgage.

The term «property right» is somewhat misleading, because it suggests that there is always property in the sense of ownership. Perhaps the expression of a «right regarding an object» describes more precisely the definition of property rights. However, since the name «property right» is well established, we will use it here too.

What distinguishes property rights from claims is that the latter can only be invoked against the specific person who is bound by the corresponding obligation, while the former can potentially be invoked against everyone. In Latin, the property right is therefore a right *erga omnes*. The owner of a car, for instance, can in principle invoke his ownership against everyone who happens to have the car in his possession.

The French speak of this as a «droit de suite»; a right to follow the object of the right wherever this object may find itself.

A property right on a physical object normally involves a general prohibition against everyone except the right holder to use, damage, or destroy the object of the right. The property right then typically involves a permission for the right holder to use, damage, or destroy this object.

For example, if Johannes owns a car, no one is allowed to use the car, except for Johannes.

The holder of a property right typically has the competence to transfer his property right to somebody else. Moreover, he also has the competence to give other persons permission to do things with the property which would normally count as infringements of the right.

Johannes is competent to transfer the ownership of his car to Dorothée. Moreover, he can give André permission to use his car.

10   Fundamental Rights

Fundamental rights, such as the freedom of religion, freedom of expression, freedom of association, the right to bodily integrity, but also the right to privacy, the right to health care, the right to schooling, and the right to employment, are traditionally seen as the rights which human beings hold against their governments. These rights are also known as «human rights», and as they are seen as rights against governments, they can often be found in constitutions. This heading should not bother us here; the issue that needs to be discussed at this point is what these fundamental rights involve. Thus, the main message is that although the common denominator of «fundamental rights» may suggest the contrary, there is little that all the respective fundamental rights actually have in common. To show that this is the case, we will take a closer look at three of these rights.

The Right to Bodily Integrity

Let us start from the assumption that fundamental rights are first and foremost rights against the government, which bears a duty corresponding to the right. In this respect, they are like relative rights, which are also rights against a specific legal subject. However, unlike relative rights, the right to bodily integrity does not belong to an obligation in the broad sense, and the right does not originate from a specific event as relative rights do.

The holder of the right to bodily integrity has the competence to enforce this right through a judicial procedure. Moreover, he has the competence to waive his right by giving permission to affect his body, for instance, for a medical operation. However, such a waiver does not end the right to bodily integrity as it would for a personal right. A permission for a single operation does not mean that from that moment on, the government has permission to affect the body of the right holder.

The right holder does not have the competence to transfer his right of bodily integrity to someone else. It is not even clear what such a transfer would mean. Moreover, he is immune to someone else taking his right away.

The freedom of expression involves not only a prohibition for the State to withhold legal subjects from expressing themselves but also an immunity. However, it is not a permission. The holder of this right is permitted to express his or her opinions, but since there is no general prohibition to do so, the right does not add anything to the permission that consists in the absence of a prohibition. The very point of the freedom of expression is that the government lacks the competence to prohibit the expression of opinions. Because the government lacks this competence, the right holder enjoys an immunity against having her permission to express herself taken away by the government, for instance, through legislation that curbs free expression.

Freedom of Expression

The right holder also has the competence to enforce her freedom of expression through a judicial procedure against the government. For instance, the right empowers courts not to apply legislation that would infringe upon the freedom of expression.

The right holder does not have the competence to waive her right against the government; however, she can waive her right to the extent that it is also a right against private legal subjects. For instance, a labor contract may include the clause that the employee is not permitted to talk about secret company information. Such a clause would not be null and void because it violates the freedom of expression.

The right to health care is partnered with the duty of the State to provide adequate health care. However, the right does not involve the competence of a private person to enforce this State duty. This is perhaps because it is not sufficiently specified what the duty of the State actually involves in fulfilling this right. In this respect, the right to health care differs from the right to bodily integrity.

The Right to Health Care

It is unlikely that the holder of a right to health care can transfer his right to somebody else or is competent to waive his right. Moreover, he is immune against having his right taken away through actions of the State.

Conclusion   The rights to bodily integrity, free expression, and health care turn out to involve rather different combinations of duties, permissions, competences, and immunities. This goes to show that there is no common measure for what a fundamental right is. Moreover, personal rights and property rights do not only differ from each other but also from all kinds of other fundamental rights. The only thing that rights seem to have in common is that they protect an interest of the right holder and that they function as points in legal space in which duties, obligations, permissions, competences, and immunities are tied together in various combinations.

Recommended Literature

Hohfeld WL (1920) Fundamental legal conceptions as applied in judicial reasoning, and other legal essays. Yale University Press, New Haven

The Law of Contract

Jan Smits

© Springer International Publishing Switzerland 2017
J. Hage et al. (eds.), *Introduction to Law*, DOI 10.1007/978-3-319-57252-9_4

1   Introduction

Modern society is unthinkable without the possibility to conclude binding contracts. Contracts not only allow businesses
to trade goods and offer services, contracts are also used by
citizens to pursue the things they are after, even if they do not
always realize it. Thus, people conclude contracts when they
buy products in a supermarket, rent an apartment, take out
insurance, open a bank account, download software, take up a
new job, are treated by their doctor, go to the hairdresser, or
order tickets over the Internet to go to a Lady Gaga concert.
The set of rules and principles that governs these transactions
is the law of contract. It governs not only so-called consumer
contracts like those just mentioned but also commercial contracts. One only needs to visit a random news site to find
examples of the latter. They range from contracts for the sale
of goods to franchising and distribution contracts and also
include agreements to create a joint venture, take over a company, build an airport, or invest in a foreign country.

Contract law is such an integral part of present society that it is almost
impossible to imagine society without it. However, societies without
contracts are conceivable in situations where the State or the community takes care of everything, including the provision of the necessities of
life (such as, in today's world, food, housing, and health care). In such a
society, the need to contract with other people is absent. It is not only
Communism that provides—at least in theory—an example of such a
society. A better example is the type of community that existed in pre-
historic times before there was any division of labor: small groups of
nomadic people who shared what they found by hunting, fishing, and
gathering had nothing to contract about among themselves or with
other groups.

Exchange

The core of a typical contract is exchange: one party gives
something to another party and receives something in return.
This exchange is prompted by the belief of both parties that
they benefit from it: the buyer offers to buy goods because she
values these more than the money she holds in her pocket,
whereas the seller would rather have the money than the
goods. Yet while this economic rationale underlies most contracts, it is not true for all contracts. In particular, in the case
of *gratuitous contracts*, such as a promise to make a gift, the
law can make the promise enforceable even if only one party
will benefit from it.

Questions

This chapter presents the main questions that contract law
seeks to answer. These questions are structured in accordance
with the chronology of the contract. The first question asks
when exactly is there a binding contract: can any promise to

do or to give something (or to abstain from something) be enforced in the courts? Once we have decided that a contract has been validly concluded and is enforceable, another question emerges: what exactly should the parties do as a result of this contract? This question may seem superfluous when parties have agreed upon all their mutual obligations under the contract, but the reality is different: in many cases, disputes arise about what parties are actually bound to do. Contract law provides the tools to establish the exact contents of the agreement. If it is clear that the contract is binding and we know about its contents, yet another question can arise: what rights does a party have if the other party does not perform? Can a contracting party always claim performance of the contract? Can it bring a claim for damages? Or is it even possible for it to claim termination of the contract, meaning that the frustrated party no longer has to perform itself? These three questions on formation, contents, and remedies are discussed in ▶ Sects. 3, 4, and 5. They are preceded by ▶ Sect. 2, which is devoted to an overview of the sources of contract law, and followed by ▶ Sect. 6, which offers a brief outlook on the topic.

2 Sources of Contract Law

Contract law in the sense mentioned above (as a set of rules and principles that governs transactions among parties, thereby setting the rights and obligations of these parties) is made up of a large number of different rules. In this section, a distinction is made on the basis of the origins of these rules. Such a categorization on the basis of *sources* allows us to distinguish between three types of rules relevant to contract law: rules that are made by the contracting parties themselves; rules that emerge from the official national, European, and supranational sources; and finally, informal rules that are made by others (including non-State organizations and academics).

2.1 Rules Made by the Contracting Parties

Compared to many of the other fields of law discussed in this book, contract law is special in at least one important respect: the question of what the law is (in the sense of the enforceable rights and obligations of the parties) can, to a large extent, be decided by the parties themselves. This is because one of the

Freedom of Contract

most important principles in this field is freedom of contract: not only are parties free to decide whether they want to contract at all and with whom, but they can also determine the contents of their contract. This means that no one is obliged to enter into a contract, but if one *does*, one is bound by it in the same way as if the rules had been made by the legislature. The French Civil Code of 1804—drafted in the heyday of the autonomy of the individual citizen—encapsulates this succinctly in its famous Art. 1103: «Agreements lawfully entered into take the place of the law for those who have made them».

General Conditions

Contractual rules need not be made for one contract only. In practice, parties often make use of standardized sets of rules that are suited to their own interests. The so-called general conditions are one very popular type of such standardized rules. Almost all professional parties (including supermarkets and retailers) use such conditions for the contracts they conclude with consumers or other professional parties. The advantages of this are clear: it saves a party from having to draft contract conditions for every new contract it wants to conclude. This makes the use of general conditions indispensable in a world as dominated by efficiency as ours.

2.2 Official National, European, and Supranational Rules

Default and Mandatory Rules

It is clear that, in most cases, a party agreement alone cannot set all rights and obligations under the contract. Often, parties only discuss those elements of the contract that they consider essential (such as the price and the time of delivery), but not many other aspects (such as the place of delivery or what will happen if the other party does not perform the contract). In so far as such matters are not covered by general conditions, the law should provide so-called default (or «facilitative») rules that are automatically applicable if the parties have not made any other arrangements. It may also happen that parties would like to contract in a way that is considered contrary to law or morality (such as hiring someone to steal a painting or—to give a more disputed example—paying someone to give birth to a baby). In that case, the law must intervene with so-called mandatory rules that declare such a contract void or at least avoidable by one of the parties. These facilitative and mandatory laws flow from «official» national, European, and supranational sources.

National Rules

At the national level, the official contract law is primarily produced by the legislature and the courts. Despite many differences in detail, contract law is arguably the field of law in which we find the most commonalities among the world's jurisdictions.

In civil law countries, general rules on contract law can be found in civil codes. The French Code Civil places contract law in its Third Book on ways to acquire ownership, whereas the German Bürgerliches Gesetzbuch has general provisions on juridical acts (Rechtsgeschäfte) in Book 1 and specific rules on contracts in Book 2. This does not mean that case law is not important: the older the civil code, the more important it is to take cognizance of the decisions of the highest national courts in order to understand contract law properly. Together with the code, many countries often have more specific statutes in which contract law can be found (France, e.g., has a separate Consumer Code), and we should also note that national civil codes have frequently undergone major changes over the years (such as the German law of obligations that was fundamentally revised in 2002 and the French law of contract that underwent a major reform in 2016).

In the common law, the starting point is rather the opposite: contract law is to a large extent laid down in cases decided by courts. Statutes however (including the important Sale of Goods Act 1979 in England) have come to play an increasingly important role in the last century. Most of these rules created by national legislatures and courts are facilitative, and it is clear why the State should provide them: in most cases, it is impossible for the parties to imagine all the contingencies that may occur during the lifecycle of their contract, and, for those they can foresee, the parties may not want to invest the time and money to formulate minute contractual rules for them.

Contract law also flows from European sources. In the last two decades, the European legislature has promulgated almost 20 directives with relevance to contract law, which the Member States have had to implement in their national legislation. However, unlike national contract law, the European legislature can only create law in so far as it has a competence to do so provided by one of the European treaties. For contract law, the source of this competence is usually found in Art. 114 of the Treaty on the Functioning of the European Union, which allows the European legislature to adopt measures harmonizing national provisions «which have as their object the establishment and functioning of the internal market». The result is a rather fragmented European contract law: directives only deal with specific contracts (e.g., package travel, doorstep sales, and consumer sales) and only with certain aspects of these contracts (e.g., information duties vis-à-vis the consumer and the possibility to withdraw from the contract). **European Rules**

A third source of official contract law consists of supranational rules. The most important international convention in this field (and arguably in private law as a whole) is the 1980 **Supranational Rules**

United Nations *Convention on Contracts for the International Sale of Goods* (CISG). The CISG has been ratified in 85 countries and contains rules that apply to commercial cross border transactions. If the contracting parties reside in a country that has ratified the CISG, these rules are applicable to the contract unless the parties have explicitly excluded this.

As Germany and the Netherlands are both a party to the CISG, a contract between a German and a Dutch businessperson is therefore governed by the rules of the convention on, e.g., formation of contract and remedies.

2.3   Informal Rules

Soft Law

As is the case in many other areas of law, contract law is increasingly influenced by rules that are not officially binding but have the status of soft law. This soft law can take the form of model rules, which are intended to influence the setting of norms or the deciding of cases by the formal institutions (including European and national legislatures and courts), or can be a source of inspiration for parties drafting a contract. In addition to these two functions, soft law rules have come to play an important role in legal research and in teaching the law.

The best-known soft law rules in the field of contracts are the Unidroit Principles of International Commercial Contracts (UP) of 1994, the Principles of European Contract Law (PECL) of 1995, and the Draft Common Frame of Reference of European Private Law (DCFR) of 2009. All three sets can be seen as «restatements» of the law: they aim to identify commonalities among the jurisdictions they seek to cover and to put these down in succinct common «principles». In so far as commonalities were difficult to find, the drafters made a choice for what they considered to be the «best» rule. Although these sets of rules are not formally binding, they are often seen as a blueprint for a future legislative instrument in the form of, e.g., a European Code of Contracts. In the remainder of this chapter, reference is made in particular to the PECL.

3   Formation of a Binding Contract

As long as economic activity consists only of exchanging goods on the spot (as was the case in early societies), there is no real need to answer the question as to when a contract is binding. This is different if a party *promises* to do or to give something in the future. The law should then provide an answer to the question whether this promise is enforceable or not (meaning that the promisee can go to court and force the promisor to, e.g., deliver the good or pay the price). This section considers when there is a basis for such an enforceable promise: ▶ Sect. 3.1 looks in general into the requirements that the law applies in order to determine whether a promise is binding, while the subsequent sections consider how the contracting process usually takes place (▶ 3.2), whether any formalities need to be fulfilled and how the weaker party is protected (▶ 3.3). The final Section pays attention to what happens if a party breaks off contractual negotiations (▶ 3.4).

3.1 From a Promise to a Binding Contract

No legal system allows all promises to be enforceable. If I promise my fiancée to take her to dinner tomorrow evening, no sensible person would claim that she could go to court and force me to feed her. Of the vast majority of promises that we make in our life, we can say at best that it would be *morally* wrong not to keep them. Breaking a promise may have many negative consequences for the friends we keep, for the people we love, and for the reputation we have—but none of this is the law's business. A contrary view would make society unlivable and would flood the courts with futile cases. This makes it important to ask what the criterion is for the *legal* enforceability of promises.

All modern jurisdictions accept that the main criterion for the enforceability of a promise is the intention of the parties to enter into a legal relationship. The PECL puts this succinctly in Art. 2:101 s.1 in stating that a contract is concluded «if the parties intend to be legally bound» and «reach a sufficient agreement». This principle is the end result of a long historical process.

Intention to Be Legally Bound

It is not self-evident that parties can bind themselves by merely expressing their intention to be legally bound. In fact this principle was not accepted on the European continent until the seventeenth century. In Roman times, only specific types of contracts were seen as enforceable, for example, because they were in a certain form, or consisted of the actual handing over of the good. Roman law also recognized purely «consensual» contracts but only in a limited number of cases (including sale of goods and mandate). It was only with the development of the economy and with the growing influence of natural law in the seventeenth century that the general principle of all contracts being enforceable on the basis of consent (pacta sunt servanda) came to be recognized.

English law underwent a similar development; it sought to base the enforcement of promises on a particular doctrine called consideration. The English courts found such consideration to be present if a promise met all the requirements for its enforceability. The requirement still exists today, but as modern English law also adheres to the view that a contract requires the intention to be legally bound, the separate consideration doctrine has become much less important—its main role today lies in making gratuitous promises unenforceable (see below).

It is important to realize that the question of whether there is an intention to be legally bound is a *legal* question: the law decides when such an intention exists. It is usually not a problem to «find» this intention in cases where the respective promises of the parties are more or less of the same value or if the parties are sophisticated businesspeople who can take care of their own interests. However, the law is much more reluctant to enforce purely gratuitous promises or promises among family members or friends, as it finds it much less likely that someone would wish to be legally bound in these situations. The law, suspicious as it is of altruism, presumes that a party will only bind itself *legally* if it is to gain from the transaction.

Gratuitous Promises   A purely gratuitous promise, such as the promise to make a gift, is usually viewed with so much suspicion that most civil law jurisdictions require this promise to be put in a *notarial deed*. This forces the donor to think through his act of benevolence and allows an independent notary (in most countries, a trained lawyer) to warn the donor of the consequences of his act.

Consideration   Under English law, a gratuitous promise is equally unenforceable but for the reason that it does not have consideration. Consideration requires that there is a quid pro quo: a promise must be given for a (promise of) counter-performance by the other party. It is clear that a gratuitous promise lacks such consideration. In the absence of a notary as in the continental model, English law therefore requires the donative promise to be put in a *deed*. This written and signed document that is attested by witnesses may not offer the same security as a notarial deed on the continent, but it does make the donor reflect upon his plan to perform an act of altruism and forces him to put his promise in precise writing.

Unequal Obligations   A promise need not be purely gratuitous for it to raise suspicions about the earnestness of the intention. I can sell my car worth €20,000 for €10, or my neighbor can allow me to live in her house on the sole condition that I regularly water her plants. These contracts do not require any particular form, but whether or not they are enforceable depends on how likely it is that the court will find an intention to be legally bound on the part of the promisor. Decisive is whether the promisee could reasonably expect from the words and the conduct of the promisor that the latter intended to be bound. This is dependent on what the reasons for making the promise were and what the consequences would be for the promisee if the promise were to be held unenforceable. Thus, in the examples above, if the buyer of my car already sold her own car in reasonable reliance on my promise or if I immediately gave notice to my landlord after hearing my neighbor's generous offer, thereby leaving me without a home if she reneges on her promise, there are strong arguments to show that there was a binding contract.

Another category of cases concerns promises in the domestic or social sphere. If a father promises his daughter to pay for her driving lessons if she does not smoke until she is 18 years old, no sensible lawyer would advise her to take her father to court if he does not keep his promise. But what about my colleague's promise to pick me up every workday around 07.00 and «carpool» me to Maastricht? This promise already lies in the economic sphere, and it would depend on the exact circumstances of the case to what extent I could claim, at the very least, compensation for the time it takes me to find an alternative way of getting to Maastricht.

Promises in the Domestic or Social Sphere

3.2 Offer and Acceptance

We saw in the previous section that the consent of the parties is a necessary requirement for a binding contract. Lawyers tend to split this consent into two different elements: an *offer* by the offeror and the *acceptance* of this offer by the offeree. Art. 2:201 s. 1 PECL is a good reflection of the world's legal systems on this point:

> A proposal amounts to an offer if:
> 1. It is intended to result in a contract if the other party accepts it.
> 2. It contains sufficiently definite terms to form a contract.

Lawyers usually ask three different questions regarding offer and acceptance:
1. When can a proposal be qualified as an offer?
2. Can the offeror go back on its offer before acceptance by the offeree (*revocation*)?
3. At what moment in time does the acceptance of the offer lead to a binding contract?

Offer

The importance of the first question is immediately clear: if a proposal can be qualified as an offer, it means that a binding contract comes into being upon the mere acceptance of the offer by the offeree. This is exactly the reason why an offer can only exist if it reflects the intention to be legally bound and is sufficiently clear about the contents of the resulting contract.

If Gary sends an email to Caroline in which he offers his car for sale, it needs to define at least the price and the main characteristics of the car (such as the type, the year in which it was built, the State it is in, etc.) before it can be seen as an offer that is definite enough—unless Caroline knows exactly what car and price Gary is referring to because of the previous contact between them. If the offer is not definite enough («for sale: an interesting book»), it would at best be an invitation to enter into negotiations about a contract.

Not all jurisdictions make the distinction between offers and mere invitations to enter into negotiations in the same way.

An advertisement in a newspaper in which goods are offered for sale would usually not be seen as a binding offer under English or Polish law, but it would be under French law. The display of goods in a shop is seen as an offer in French and Swiss law but as a mere invitation to treat in English law.

Much more important than what the law in a specific jurisdiction says, however, is the need to recognize the policy reasons behind it. To consider an advertisement or display of goods in a shop as an offer means that the seller cannot go back on her intention. This is clearly in the interest of the prospective buyer, who may have been tempted to respond to the advertisement or enter the seller's shop, because of the attractiveness of the product being offered. He should not be confronted with a seller who can withdraw her proposal at will. It would, on the other hand, be unfair on the seller if she were forced to sell the product to anyone and everyone that is interested, even if the product is out of stock.

It seems that Art. 2:201 s. 3 PECL fares a middle way between these two interests by stipulating that a proposal to supply goods or services at stated prices made by a professional supplier in a public advertisement or catalogue, or by a display of goods, is presumed to be an offer to sell or supply at that price until the stock of goods, or the supplier's capacity to provide the service, is exhausted.

Revocation

Once it is established that the proposal amounts to an offer, a second question can arise: can the offeror revoke their offer before acceptance by the offeree? If Catalina offers her iPhone to William, it would be in her interest to be able to change her mind at any time and sell it to a higher bidder instead. It would, on the other hand, create hardship for William if he did not have at least some time to think about Catalina's offer and perhaps try to borrow money from a relative or a friend to buy the gadget. It is by balancing these two interests that each jurisdiction adopts its own solution.

The German (§ 145 BGB), French (art. 1116 CC), and Dutch (Art. 6:219 BW) Civil Codes protect the offeree by making an offer irrevocable for the period that is fixed in the offer (or for a reasonable period if no such period is fixed) unless the offer states explicitly that it is freely revocable. This civil law position seems to have been codified as the European model rule in Art. 2:202 PECL.

English law adopts the other extreme by allowing an offer to be revoked at all times. As harsh as this latter position may seem, it is consistent with the English doctrine of consideration that one cannot be bound if the other party has not done or promised something in return (see above, ► Sect. 3.2).

Acceptance

The third and final question asks when the acceptance of an offer leads to a binding contract. This is a very relevant question in commercial practice: parties need to know at what moment they are bound to a contract because all kinds of rights and obligations may follow from this. Art. 2:205 s. 1 PECL aptly reflects the rule that many jurisdictions accept: «If an acceptance has been dispatched by the offeree the contract is concluded when the acceptance reaches the offeror». This rule also applies to electronic communication, in which case the acceptance is supposed to have reached the offeror if the message has entered into an electronic mailbox.

A well-known exception to the widely accepted rule of Art. 2:205 s.1 PECL can be found in English law: in case the acceptance is sent by (regular) mail, the contract is concluded when the acceptance is dispatched by post. It is clear that this rule benefits the offeree, who can no longer be confronted with the revocation of an offer once he has put his acceptance in the mailbox. However, the importance of this «mailbox rule» is rather limited in practice: most communication in today's world takes place through email, fax, or telephone, significantly limiting the time between the sending and the arrival of the message. To such instantaneous communication, the mailbox rule does not apply (as the English Court of Appeal made clear in 1955 in Entores v. Miles Far East Corp).

3.3   Formalities and Protection
of the Weaker Party

If the consent of the parties is sufficient for the contract to be binding—as we just saw—this implies that no other formalities are needed. A fundamental principle of contract law is therefore not only that contracts are binding but also that they can come about in any form. It may be that it is often difficult to prove the exact content of a contract if it was concluded orally, but there is no doubt that such a contract is valid as a matter of law. And yet, there are cases in which this is different. In ▶ Sect. 3.1, it was seen that gifts often require a (notarial) deed in order to make the giving party aware of the risks and (in civil law) to allow a legal expert to give advice.

Consumer Protection   However, in most cases in which formalities exist, it is to protect a party who is presumed to be weaker vis-à-vis the other party. In particular, in European legislation, we find many rules that aim to protect the «weak» consumer against the professional seller or provider of services. The formalities do not only consist of the need to put the contract in writing (as in the case of consumer credit) but must also include the need to comply with information duties: the professional party needs to provide consumers with all kinds of information on the product and often on their right to withdraw from the contract (as in doorstep selling and distance sales).

Withdrawal Rights   Withdrawal rights allow the cancellation of a contract without giving any reason: consumers only need to return the good or send the seller a notice of cancellation within the «cooling off-period» (usually 14 days). This is an important deviation from traditional contract law, in which the binding force of contracts cannot in principle be set aside.

Withdrawal rights can, for example, be found in Directive 2011/83 on consumer rights (Art. 9), Directive 2008/122 on timeshare (Art. 6) and Directive 2008/48 on consumer credit (Art. 14). These statutory rights must be distinguished from the policy of many shops allowing the consumer the possibility to «bring back» the purchased product within a certain period: no shop is legally obliged to offer this service to the consumer. But once a seller has given the consumer this extra right to return goods, it must keep its promise and take the product back.

Incapacity   Another device to protect weaker parties is the institution of legal incapacity. The law considers certain persons to be incapable of entering into a valid legal transaction *at all*. In particular, two categories of people are put under this special protective regime: young children and the mentally ill. The law has to balance the interests of these weaker parties against those with whom they deal with. In particular, in the case of mentally ill persons, it is not always apparent to the outside world that a party is not capable of making a rational decision.

If Jack, on his weekly trip to the town close to the mental institution he lives in, buys a new car, it may not be clear to the local Mercedes dealer that he is dealing with a patient suffering from a psychiatric disorder. If, on the other hand, a 15-year-old buys a copy of Richard Dawkins' book *The God Delusion* to enlighten herself, it should not be possible to invalidate this transaction, which is clearly in the interest of the incapacitated person.

In balancing the conflicting interests of the incapacitated and the parties with whom they deal, any legal system takes as a starting point that contracts entered into by minors (in most countries, persons under 18 years of age) and by persons formally incapacitated by a court decision can be invalidated by their legal representatives (in the case of minors, usually their parents). This does not grossly violate the interests of the other party: in case of doubt, it can always ask for the ID card of the minor or check the national register of incapacitated persons.

Many jurisdictions also accept that the contract is valid anyway if it is to the benefit of the incapacitated person. This may be because someone contracts for necessities (like food or medicine) or because a minor is contracting for something that is seen as «normal» for someone of his age. A 10-year-old can validly buy candy, but the seller of a scooter would have a hard time convincing the court that the parents of this child cannot invalidate the transaction. Rather important in practice is the fact that the parents may also *agree* with the minor's transaction, in which case the contract cannot be invalidated either.

Next to these more formal devices to protect a weaker party (usually allowing the weaker party to invalidate the contract), courts can make use of more subtle instruments to remedy information asymmetries among the parties or simply not allow a party to invoke a contractual clause for reasons of procedural or substantive injustice (see ▶ Sect. 4.2).

3.4   **Pre-contractual Liability**

The principle of the binding force of contract suggests that a party is *only* bound toward the other party once the contract is concluded. This suggestion is wrong. Even during negotiations, a party might justifiably rely on the conclusion of the contract and be subsequently disappointed in this reliance because the other party breaks off the negotiations. In these situations, some jurisdictions allow this party to ask for compensation of the costs that have been incurred.

In particular civil law courts are prone to argue that such a pre-contractual liability can be based on the general principle of fairness and reasonableness (cf. Art. 6:2 Dutch Civil Code), on a specific liability for fault in contracting (cf. the German culpa in contrahendo, codified in § 311 II BGB), or simply on delict in general (cf. Art. 1112 French Civil Code). The underlying idea of such a liability is that negotiating parties have to take into account each other's interests because they would form, as it was once put by the French author Demogue, «un sorte de microcosme: [...] une petite société où chacun doit travailler pour un but commun qui est. la somme des buts individuels poursuivis par chacun (...)» («A kind of microcosm: [...] a small society where everyone must work for a common goal which is, in fact, the sum of the individual goals pursued by each person»). If Jaap from Maastricht enters into lengthy negotiations with Mark from Chicago and Jaap decides to travel repeatedly to the Chicago O'Hare Airport Hilton to discuss the deal, while Mark already knows he will sell to somebody else, this is not the type of conduct that most jurisdictions encourage. If Jaap can prove Mark's dishonest behavior, he would be able to claim back his travel costs from Mark.

In a more liberal—and perhaps economically more viable—legal system, the point of no return in contracting does not come to pass until the contract is actually formed. This is the position of English law. In the famous case of Walford v. Miles (1992), the House of Lords held per Lord Ackner that «(...) the concept of a duty to carry on negotiations in good faith is inherently repugnant to the adversarial position of the parties when involved in negotiations. Each party to the negotiations is entitled to pursue his (or her) own interest (...). A duty to negotiate in good faith is as unworkable in practice as it is inherently inconsistent with the position of the negotiating parties. (...)».

4   The Contents of the Contract

Once the contract is validly concluded, the second stage of its life begins: the parties have to perform in conformity with what they promised. Fortunately, this does not pose a problem in the great majority of cases; the parties doing what they should do will automatically lead to the extinction of their respective obligations. However, the law also needs to provide rules for those cases in which problems do arise. It can be that the parties are in disagreement about what they actually agreed upon (► Sect. 4.1) or that a party refuses to perform because of manifest «unfairness» in one or more of the contract terms (► Sect. 4.2). A third problem arises when the contents of the contract are considered as illegal or immoral by the State (► Sect. 4.3).

4.1   **Interpretation**

The law shares with literature and theology the characteristic that it is an interpretative discipline: legislative statutes, governmental decisions, treaties, and written contracts may be unclear and therefore have to be interpreted. In contract law, this interpretation often takes place implicitly, even without the parties realizing it. However, it may also happen that parties differ explicitly about what they actually agreed upon. If Newcom Ltd. agrees that its customer Agri Gmbh is allowed to «give back» the machine it purchased within 3 months after delivery, it could well be that Newcom intended Agri to be allowed to terminate the contract only in the event of a defect with the machine, while Agri understood the term as allowing it to simply end the contract at its own will. This raises the question of how the contract should be interpreted.

Interpretation of contracts can take place starting from two fundamentally different positions. One view is to give preference to the intention of the promisor: since the words she used are only the expression of her intention, it is the intention that should prevail. The opposite view is to give priority to the declaration and therefore to the external expression of the intention, this being the only thing that is apparent to the other party.

The tension between giving priority to the party's (subjective) intention and to its (objective) declaration is clearly visible in the great codifications of private law. Art. 1188 of the French Civil Code requires the court to find the «common intention of the parties», but it also considers that where the intention cannot be discerned, «the contract is to be interpreted in the sense which a reasonable person placed in the same situation would give to it». §133 BGB states as the aim of interpretation «to discern the real intention» but continues in §157 BGB with the rule that interpretation should take place «in accordance with fairness and reasonableness as understood in good commercial practice».

All European jurisdictions adopt a compromise between attaching importance to intention and declaration. As a general principle, interpretation is aimed at ascertaining the meaning that the text would convey to a reasonable person having the same knowledge that would have been available to the parties at the time of the contract. The contract is thus interpreted in the way in which a reasonable person would understand it.

Reasonable Person

Civil law and common law reach this result from two different perspectives. In civil law countries, the subjective intention of the parties is the starting point: in case of a dispute the meaning that a reasonable man in the position of the party would give to this intention is decisive. In English law, it is rather the objective meaning of the words of the contract that is given preference, although this is also mitigated by what is reasonable. This is reflected in Art. 5:101 PECL:

1. A contract is to be interpreted according to the common intention of the parties even if this differs from the literal meaning of the words.
2. If it is established that one party intended the contract to have a particular meaning, and at the time of the conclusion of the contract the other party could not have been unaware of the first party's intention, the contract is to be interpreted in the way intended by the first party.
3. If an intention cannot be established according to (1) or (2), the contract is to be interpreted according to the meaning that reasonable persons of the same kind as the parties would give to it in the same circumstances.

4.2 Unfairness of Contract Terms

Fairness and Reasonableness

An eternal question of contract law is whether only «fair» contracts should be enforced. Until well into the nineteenth century, an important strand of thought was that without some equivalence among the performance and counter-performance, a contract of sale would not be valid. Indeed, this prohibition of *laesio enormis* can still be found in various European codifications, including Art. 934 of the Austrian Allgemeines Bürgerliches Gesetzbuch (ABGB) of 1812, allowing a party to invalidate a sale for less than half of the value if it did not explicitly agree with it at the time of conclusion of the contract. This means that if a party did not know the true value of the good, it is allowed to ask for the good back.

Procedural Unfairness

Contract law is impregnated with devices that aim to avoid so-called procedural unfairness. Such unfairness exists if a party is not able to form its will in a manner that is sufficiently free. If Amy holds Clint at gunpoint while telling him to sign a document, every jurisdiction would allow Clint to invalidate the contract for threat (cf. Art. 4:108 PECL). And if a 4-year-old were to buy a Roman artifact from the online store of an Amsterdam antique dealer, his parents could invalidate the contract for incapacity (see ► Sect. 3.3).

Threat and Incapacity

Threat and incapacity lead to an avoidable contract because the law presumes that the will of a party could not be formed in the right way. Other applications of such procedural fairness are *fraud* and *mistake*. In the case of the latter, a party contracts under an incorrect assumption: it can be under the impression that it buys a secondhand car in excellent shape, although it is in reality a death trap. While it is clear that this affects the proper formation of the party's intention to buy, it is less clear what this should lead to. The law has to find a balance between the duty of the buyer to investigate for himself what shape the car is in and the duty of the seller to inform the prospective buyer about possible defects. Each jurisdiction balances these interests in a different way.

It was already noted (in ▶ Sect. 2) that many professional parties make use of general conditions. This poses a problem for the fairness of consumer contracts in particular. In practice, consumers that are confronted with these standard contracts cannot influence their contents (assuming they are able to understand them at all) and have to decide either to accept the general conditions or not to enter into the contract at all. Here, too, it is possible for the law to intervene on the basis of deficiencies in the formation of the contract, holding that—as Lord Bingham stated in the English decision of *Director General of Fair Trading v. First National Bank* (2001) in a case about consumer credit—the contract terms «should be expressed fully, clearly and legibly, containing no concealed pitfalls or traps. (…) Fair dealing requires that a supplier should not (…) take advantage of the consumer's necessity, indigence, lack of experience, unfamiliarity with the subject matter of the contract, weak bargaining position (…)».

General Conditions

However, practice shows that safeguarding procedural fairness may not be enough, particularly in the case of standard form contracts. Preceded by statutes in many individual Member States, the European legislature therefore issued Directive 93/13 on unfair terms in consumer contracts, allowing courts to hold a standard clause in a contract invalid «if, contrary to the requirement of good faith, it causes a significant imbalance in the parties' rights and obligations under the contract». This test of *substantive* fairness invites the court to consider the actual contents of the contract, even if its formation did meet the necessary standard.

While testing the substantive fairness of general conditions is now daily practice in the national courts of the European Union, this is different for the part of the agreement that the parties explicitly discussed. If Rafael is unequivocally clear about his intention to sell his Ferrari to Roger for only a tenth of its actual value but subsequently realizes that he has entered into a disadvantageous agreement, he cannot go back on his promise arguing that this contract is manifestly unjust.

The notion of good faith (fairness and reasonableness) referred to in Directive 93/13 is well known in civil law countries, to such an extent that it is often seen as a principle that permeates the entire law of contract or is even, as was once remarked, the «queen of rules». The English judge Lord Bingham excels in describing the principle:

«In many civil law systems, and perhaps in most legal systems outside the common law world, the law of obligations recognizes and enforces an overriding principle that in making and carrying out contracts parties should act in good faith. This does not simply mean that they should not deceive each other, a principle which any legal system must recognize; its effect is perhaps most aptly conveyed by such metaphorical colloquialisms as «playing fair», «coming clean» or «putting one's cards face upwards on the table». It is in essence a principle of fair and open dealing (…)».

This fair and open dealing implies that parties have to take into account each other's legitimate interests, not only in interpreting the contract (which should take place in a reasonable way: see ▶ Sect. 4.1) but also in supplementing the party agreement with duties to give information to, and cooperate with, the other party. In countries like Germany (§ 242 BGB) and the Netherlands (Art. 6:248 s. 2 BW), the principle is even used to limit the exercise of contractual rights, namely, where it would be grossly unfair to invoke a contractual provision.

4.3   Prohibited Contracts

Despite the prevalence of the principle of freedom of contract, parties are not free to enter into any contract whatever its contents. Every legal system places limits on the freedom of contracting parties by declaring contracts void if they are contrary to law, public order, or morality. If Marjolein were to sell nuclear arms to a terrorist group or if Jens were to agree to act as a hired assassin in return for a sum of money wired to his Swiss bank account, not many would doubt that these contracts interfere with the public interest and should not be enforced. The same is true for agreements among companies to divide the market among themselves and to refrain from competition.

Other cases, however, give rise to more doubt. One problematic category of cases is where it is not necessarily apparent to the other party that the contract is concluded to engage in an illegal activity.

If I were to buy a knife in a nearby supermarket with the aim of killing my neighbor, it is not likely that I will tell the seller about this motive. But if the other party should reasonably know about my intentions, one can argue that this contract should be void as well.

Another type of case is where sensible persons would doubt the extent to which the contract violates public order or morality. This is, in particular, problematic if one would like to base one's decision on a notion of shared European values, as Art. 15:101 PECL suggests. This provision states «A contract is of no effect to the extent that it is contrary to principles recognized as fundamental in the laws of the Member States of the European Union».

If Xaviera borrows money to set up a brothel, it is not likely that all European countries share one view on the validity of this contract.

But even within one country, views can differ on what should be recognized as fundamental.

Does it violate human dignity if Manuel, who is 25 years old and 114 cm tall, is employed in a discotheque by allowing himself to be thrown short distances onto an airbed by clients (so-called dwarf-tossing)? This is a question of balancing the personal freedom of Manuel to work in the way he chooses with the responsibility of the State to guard people against themselves. The court may have a difficult job in deciding what national public morality has to say in this respect.

5   Remedies of the Parties

If the contract is validly concluded (► Sect. 3) and if it is clear what the (valid) contents of the contract are (► Sect. 4), a third question arises: what if the other party does not perform the contract? This *nonperformance* could be because the other party did not perform at all, performed too late (delay), or performed in the wrong way (defective performance). Every jurisdiction has an elaborate set of rules on the remedies that a party can claim in the event of such a breach of contract. These include the action for performance (► Sect. 5.1), for damages (► Sect. 5.2), and for termination of the contract (► Sect. 5.3).

5.1   Performance

Civil Law Approach

It seems to follow from the principle of the binding force of contract that if a party does not perform, it can be forced to do so by a court of law. This is indeed the position of all civil law jurisdictions. In countries like Germany, France, and Poland, the claim for performance is seen as the natural remedy that follows automatically from the fact that a valid contract exists. And if a party does not abide by the court decision to perform, it can be forced to do so by an official (*Gerichtsvollzieher*, *huissier*, *deurwaarder*, or *bailiff*) who would take the goods or the money from the defaulting party and give it to the creditor.

However, this main rule cannot always be applied. If the computer that Sarah sold to Lena is stolen from Sarah before delivery is due, it does not make much sense for Lena to claim performance. Such a case of *objective impossibility* also exists if performance is only useful if it takes place before a fixed date. If Christa is to marry on 8 August, it would be futile to claim performance from the manufacturer of the wedding dress on any later date.

In addition to these cases of objective impossibility, it can happen that performance is still possible but would cause the debtor unreasonable effort or expense. No reasonable person would require the seller of a ring who accidentally dropped it in the River Meuse to dig it up, even though this would technically be possible at the expense of a large sum of money.

A final situation in which a claim cannot be brought is where performance requires specific personal qualities of the debtor, or as Art. 9:102 PECL states: «the performance consists in the provision of services or work of a personal character or depends on a personal relationship». A music company cannot force Coldplay to make a record to the best of its artistic ability, and the organizers of the Zurich Grand Prix cannot make an athlete run. This does not mean that contracts with artists or sportspeople do not contain provisions to this effect, but they only allow the other party to bring a claim for damages or termination in case of breach of the contract.

It is clear why a court in these cases would not allow a claim for performance: not only would this turn the debtor into some sort of slave, but it is also difficult to believe that an unwilling debtor will in fact perform to the best of its abilities when being forced to do so.

Common Law Approach

Although the general availability of the claim for performance seems logical in view of the aim of the contract (to hold a party to its promise), common law adopts a different standpoint. Under English law, the normal action is for *damages*, so-called specific performance being the exception. There is a lot to say about the exact reasons for this radically different position, but in essence it finds its origins in an alternative view of the contract itself. This view is perhaps best expressed by the famous American judge and jurist Oliver Wendell Holmes, who wrote in 1881 that «… the only universal consequence of a legally binding promise is that the law makes the promisor pay damages if the promised act does not come to pass. In every case it leaves him free (…) to break his contract if he chooses». This is a view of contract, not as a *moral* conception but as an *economic* device: people conclude contracts to increase their welfare, and if the debtor prefers to bring the other party in the financial position in which it would have been had the contract been properly performed, this is just as good.

However, English law does recognize that this so-called specific performance should be available in certain situations. This is why, in equity, it has long been recognized that if damages are «inadequate», the court can grant a claim for performance. In particular, in the case of contracts concerning specific goods (such as land, works of art, or other objects having unique qualities), the court allows the creditor to force the other party to perform *in specie*.

The difference between civil law and common law is best visible in the case of sale of so-called generic goods. These are goods that are readily available on the market, including bulk products such as (to name but a few) potatoes, bananas, water, oil, steel, and plastics. In German, Italian, or Dutch law, it is beyond doubt that the buyer of such goods can claim delivery from the seller. In English law, however, the buyer has to satisfy itself with a claim for damages as these goods are not unique and can easily be found elsewhere. Art. 9:102 PECL also adheres to this view (cf. Art. III.3:302 DCFR).

Generic Goods

This age-old difference between civil law and common law in the field of performance has considerably diminished as a result of European Directive 1999/44 on consumer sales. If a professional seller delivers goods to a consumer that are not in conformity with the contract, the consumer can require the seller to have the goods brought into conformity by repair or replacement.

5.2   Damages for Nonperformance

If performance of the contract does not take place at all, or is too late or defective, the creditor may have the possibility to claim damages for nonperformance of the contract. This is in line with the principle that an aggrieved party should be brought as much as possible in the position in which it would have been if the contract had been properly performed.

Common Law Approach

There are two ways to reason about the availability of this claim. The first is to hold the nonperforming party liable simply because it did not perform. In this view, it does not matter whether the party was at fault or not: the mere fact of nonperformance gives rise to liability in damages. This is the position of common law, well captured in the English case of *Nicolene Ltd. v. Simmonds* (1952): «It does not matter whether the failure to fulfill the contract by the seller is because he is indifferent or willfully negligent or just unfortunate. It does not matter what the reason is. What matters is the fact of performance. Has he performed or not?» Even if the IT company could not help it that the network was down for more than a day, it still needs to compensate its customers.

Civil Law Approach

The other way of reasoning is to allow a claim for damages only if the party in breach was at fault or can at least be held responsible for the nonperformance. This is the position of civil law jurisdictions. Thus, Art. 1231-1 of the French Civil Code states that no damages are due when the person who is to perform was prevented from doing so by *force majeure*. This means, in most cases, that a party is freed from any liability if it can prove that it used its best efforts in performing the contract.

Despite these different mentalities of common law and civil law, both legal traditions come close in the practical results that they reach. If the Rolling Stones hired Wembley stadium for a series of three concerts and the stadium were set on fire by Manchester United supporters before the first concert took place, the rock group could not claim any damages because an English court would construe a so-called implied condition, according to which the parties are excused in case performance becomes impossible through no fault of their own (cf. *Taylor v. Caldwell*, 1863). Many civil law jurisdictions make use of a similar fiction but then to hold the debtor *liable* even though there was no fault on its part. They can do this by implying that the seller has given a *guarantee* that the goods it sold are fit for its purpose.

5.3   Termination for Nonperformance

If a party claims damages instead of performance, it still has to perform its own obligations. However, this may not be what a party wants. It can happen that a party loses all confidence in its counterpart and simply wants to end the contract, meaning that it is no longer bound to it, and if it already performed, to give back the good or ask for the money back. The action for termination allows this, but it is clear that this action cannot be used lightheartedly in view of the interest of the nonperforming party in upholding the contract. If the bell is missing on the bike that Bart buys from Herman, this does not usually justify termination because the breach is not serious enough (although it would be possible for Bart to claim performance of the contract or damages). This is why legal systems only allow termination in respect of breaches that are sufficiently serious. The test for this is different in each jurisdiction. While English law holds that the breached contract term must be «essential», German law only allows termination in case of nonperformance of a *Hauptpflicht* (main obligation) or after a so-called grace period was given to the debtor within which it could still perform but did not. The CISG and PECL require a so-called fundamental nonperformance.

Art. 8:103 PECL gives the following definition of fundamental nonperformance:

A non-performance of an obligation is fundamental to the contract if: strict compliance with the obligation is of the essence of the contract; or the non-performance substantially deprives the aggrieved party of what it was entitled to expect under the contract, unless the other party did not foresee and could not reasonably have foreseen that result; or the non-performance is intentional and gives the aggrieved party reason to believe that it cannot rely on the other party's future performance.

6   Outlook

It was seen in the above that the three main questions in contract law receive different answers depending on the jurisdiction one looks at. One cannot say that one solution is necessarily better than the other. What is important, however, is to recognize that the different outcomes are usually based on underlying assumptions about the aim of contract law. At the risk of generalizing too broadly, one can say that English contract law seems more geared toward the interests of like-minded commercial parties, while civil law jurisdictions tend to attach high value to remedying an unequal position among the contracting parties. Both legal traditions thus offer alternative views of how to shape contract law.

Contract law cannot be separated from other fields of private law. In the civil law tradition, it is intrinsically linked to the fields of tort law and property law. Both contract law and tort law can give rise to so-called obligations, a legal term indicating an (usually) enforceable duty of one person vis-à-vis another person or several other persons. While in case of a contract an obligation arises voluntarily because a party intends to be legally bound, in case of a tort the obligation is imposed upon a person independent of its intention, usually because the law wants to attach consequences to wrongful behavior. This distinction between voluntary and nonvoluntary obligations is as old as the civil law tradition itself: it was already set out as the *summa divisio* in a textbook for law students written by the Roman jurist Gaius in the year 160.

Property law deals, inter alia, with the consequences the performance of obligations may have for proprietary rights. The transfer of property or the creation of a real right (such as a mortgage; elsewhere in this book the term «lesser property rights» is used) is invariably accompanied by a contract in which the parties agree to transfer a good or create the mortgage. As a result, the sale of goods is said to have both contractual and proprietary aspects. It is contractual in that it obliges the parties to perform an obligation, i.e., for the buyer to pay a price and for the seller to deliver the good. The sale also has a proprietary aspect because it will lead to the transfer of property of the good, either because the property passes with the contract itself (as in France and Belgium) or because the seller's obligation to deliver the good is performed, leading to the actual delivery of the good (as in the Netherlands).

On a final note, it is important to emphasize that a particular characteristic of contract law is that it can often be subject to the choice of the parties: thus, commercial parties located in different countries can choose the national contract law of their liking to govern a contract, even if this is the law of a third country. This turns the availability of different approaches toward contract law into an enormous asset for the European Union: it allows parties to *opt in* to another legal system. This has not gone unnoticed by the European Commission and Parliament, which have pursued the idea of adding a 29th European system of contract law to the existing

28 national jurisdictions. Such an optional instrument would add to the choices that parties already have today and would also have the advantage that it could be made available in all official languages of the European Union. So far this plan has not materialized.

Recommended Literature

Beale H et al (eds) (2010) Cases, materials and text on contract law, ius commune casebooks for the common law of Europe, 2nd edn. Hart, Oxford

Kötz H (1997) European contract law, vol 1 (trans: Weir T). Oxford University Press, Oxford

McKendrick E (2015) Contract law, 11th edn. Palgrave Macmillan, Basingstoke

Smits J (2017) Contract law: a comparative introduction, 2nd edn. Edward Elgar, Cheltenham

Zimmermann R (1996) The law of obligations: roman foundations of the civilian tradition. Oxford University Press, Oxford

Property Law

Bram Akkermans

© Springer International Publishing Switzerland 2017
J. Hage et al. (eds.), *Introduction to Law*, DOI 10.1007/978-3-319-57252-9_5

1   Property Rights and Property Law

Rights play an important role in private law. The owner of a car that has been damaged unlawfully by someone else has a right against the tort-feasor to be compensated. The seller of a car has the right against the buyer of the car to be paid the price for which the car was sold. And, finally, the owner of a car has a right to the car itself. This last right differs from the former two. It is not a right against a particular person such as the tort-feasor or the contract partner; it is a right on a tangible object, namely, the car.

1.1   Property Rights

Absolute and Relative Rights

Rights against a particular person are called *personal rights* or *relative rights*. Rights that are not against a particular person are called *absolute rights*. These absolute rights always pertain to «something», and this «something» is called the *object* of the right. The objects of rights may be *tangible*, such as land, buildings, cars, and books. They may also be *intangible*, such as trademarks, intellectual property (including copyrights and patents), shares, and claims. Absolute rights in private law are called *property rights*, and *property law* is the branch of private law that governs these property rights. See ◘ Fig. 5.1.

Effects *erga omnes*

Strictly speaking, property rights are not directed at any particular person, but because they pertain to an object, they have effect *erga omnes*. The expression *erga omnes* is Latin and refers to an effect against «everyone». Property rights are therefore rights with effect against everyone. This effect is a defining characteristic of property rights and means that

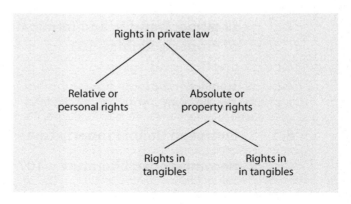

◘ **Fig. 5.1**   Rights in private law

property law, the law that governs property rights, differs from, for instance, the law of contract, which deals with legal relations between the contract parties only:

If Peter is the owner of a car, nobody else in the world is entitled to use this car without Peter's consent. If Jane has contracted with Sam that Sam will clean Jane's house for money, only Sam is under an obligation to clean Jane's house, and only Jane is under an obligation to pay Sam this money.

An immediate consequence of the fact that property rights have effects against everyone is a phenomenon that is best known under its French name *droit de suite* (literally, «right to follow»). If the object of a right falls into the hands of a person who does not hold the right, the right holder can exercise his right against that person:

Droit de suite

For instance, Elisa has the property right of usufruct on a house which belongs to her former husband James. This right involves that Elisa is entitled to use the house as long as she lives. Suppose that James sells the house to Joan, who becomes the new owner of the house. Because Elisa's right pertains to the house, and is not a right specifically against James, Elisa is still entitled to use the house. Joan must respect the usufruct which Elisa has on the house. And if Joan were to sell the house again, the new owner must also respect the usufruct. The right which Elisa has on the house so to speak 'follows' the house, regardless of whoever is the owner.

1.2 **Central Questions**

This chapter deals with a number of central questions of property law. The first question, addressed in ▶ Sect. 2, is why there should be property rights and property law at all.

The second question is what the main types of property rights are in the common law and in the civil law traditions. This question will be answered in ▶ Sects. 3, 4, and 5.

Although there are different property rights, they have a number of characteristics in common. In ▶ Sect. 6, the question what these common elements are will be answered by discussing seven principles and rules of property law.

The fourth question concerns the dynamics of property rights. How are these rights created, how are they transferred from one holder to another, and how are they terminated? This is the topic of ▶ Sect. 7.

A final question, to be answered in ▶ Sect. 8, is how property law will develop, in particular in light of further integration within the European Union.

2   Why Property Rights?

We are all accustomed to the idea that it is possible to have exclusive rights on objects. There seems to be nothing strange about the fact that someone who owns a book can prevent everyone else from reading it. And still, if one comes to think of it, it is less obvious than it seems at first sight. Why should there be property rights at all? Would it not be better if everyone were allowed to use everything? There is a theoretical (freedom of ownership) and an economic perspective (tragedy of the commons) to answering these questions.

Freedom of Ownership

Property rights actually facilitate the free circulation of goods by enabling these goods to change owners. A free market economy functions on the basis of what is known as the freedom of ownership. In such a system, every individual is free to acquire and dispose of their own property. The right of ownership and other property rights are the means by which individuals hold entitlement to their objects. Property law firmly establishes the presumption that all objects and things are freely transferable unless explicitly prohibited:

To illustrate this: After the fall of the Berlin wall and the removal of the Iron Curtain at the end of the 1980s and the beginning of the 1990s, former socialist countries had to change their system of property law from shared or communal ownership to a free market economy based on freedom of ownership. This change did not only concern movable things, but also land, which previously also had been held by a community of people. Transition to a free ownership regime was not always without problems, especially not since most people were accustomed to sharing objects, in particular land. It is sometimes held that the incentive to individually own needed to grow first.

Tragedy of the Commons

Economic theory also gives us a good indication as to why there are property rights and therefore also why there is property law. A good illustration of why it is good to allow ownership of material objects, as a primary property right, is offered by the idea of the «tragedy of the commons»:

The tragedy of the commons concerns an observation of what can go wrong with herders sharing a common parcel of land, on which they are each entitled to let their sheep graze. It is in each herder's interest to put as many sheep as possible onto the land, even if the quality of the commons is thereby temporarily or permanently damaged as a result of overgrazing. The herder receives all of the benefits from the sheep he puts onto the land, while the damage to the commons is shared by the entire group. If all herders make this individually rational economic decision, the commons will be depleted, or even destroyed, to the detriment of all.

It is therefore in the interest of all if fewer sheep are put onto the land, and if the land is assigned to those herders who profit most from it. This can be accomplished by making one person or group of persons the owner of the land. The owner of the land is by definition the person who may decide what will happen to the land. If other persons want to use the land, they need permission from the owner.

The herders can then gain rights from the owner, such as a lease of the entitlement, to put their sheep onto the land (a grazing right). Those herders who profit the most from the land will be able and willing to pay the highest price for the grazing right, which means that the rights will end up with those who profit the most from them. The owner will receive the money, but since the owner may be a collective, such as the municipality, or a whole set of herders, this does not have to be detrimental.

Recent examples of the same problematic are overfishing and pollution of the environment. The creation of fishing rights and pollution rights and of a market to trade them may have similar advantages to the introduction of private ownership of land.

3   Property Rights in Civil Law and Common Law

There are different kinds of property rights, both on tangibles, e.g., ownership, title to land and to chattels, mortgage, servitudes, and on intangibles, e.g., what are called «intellectual property rights» such as copyright, patents, and trademarks.

In this chapter, intellectual property rights will not be discussed, but even so, it is possible to distinguish many different property rights.

Which specific rights exist differs from one legal system to another, and for that reason it makes little sense to provide a list of «all» property rights. However, it is possible to divide property rights into subcategories:

- Primary property rights, as, for example, the right of ownership
- Secondary property rights to use
- Secondary property security rights
- Secondary rights to acquire a property right

Primary property rights are discussed in ▶ Sect. 4; secondary property rights are the topic of ▶ Sect. 5.

In property law, there is a major divide between continental European systems, the civil law systems, and the law of England and Wales, the common law. Civil law systems are dealt with in ▶ Sect. 3.1, while common law property law will be dealt with in ▶ Sects. 3.2 and 3.3.

3.1   Civil Law Property

Ownership, Possession, and Detentorship

In the civil law tradition, a distinction is made between ownership, possession, and detentorship of a good.

Ownership

Ownership is a property right that a person has in respect to some object. This is an immaterial relation between the person and the object, without the need for any physical equivalent. For instance, Jean can own a book even if she lent the book to Louise or if the book was stolen from her.

Possession

Possession is not the same as ownership; it is a factual relation between a person and an object. A person who possesses an object exercises factual control over this object. Usually, ownership and possession coincide so that the owner is also the possessor of a thing. Even though it is a factual state, property law attaches importance to possession, usually allowing someone who was dispossessed to recover possession:

An example would be the person who has bought a good and has received it from the seller. Normally he has also become the owner – possession and ownership usually go together – but this does not have to be so. If the seller was not the owner, it may be the case that the buyer did not become the owner either. However, the buyer does control the good and therefore he is the possessor of the good (in good faith), even though he has not become the owner. Another example of a possessor who is not the owner is a thief. The thief has factual control over what he stole. But theft is not a way to obtain ownership, and therefore the thief is merely the possessor (in bad faith), but not the owner.

Detentorship

Possession must be distinguished from *detentorship*. A detentor also exercises factual control over a good but not on behalf of himself; he recognizes that he is holding factual control for someone else. The detentor therefore recognizes the right of someone else. This difference is relevant in respect to the possibilities to retrieve an object if it has been taken. Whereas, as we save right above, the possessor can generally retrieve an object with a possessory action, a detentor cannot. Examples of *detention* are when a person has borrowed or leased a good.

Away from the Feudal System

Civil law systems share a basis in *Roman law*. This basis can be found throughout the system of property law, from the classification of objects in land and goods to the rights that can exist in respect of these objects and the way in which these rights are created, transferred, and terminated.

After the fall of the Roman Empire, continental Europe fell under the influence of Germanic law. Germanic law was tribal law, very different from the highly systematized and centrally organized Roman law. It was very fragmented in nature, and each local lord (of a tribe) used his own version. However, what united the Germanic tribes was their system of landholding. Under the influence of this Germanic tribal law, a feudal system came into existence.

A feudal system is not only a system of government but also a system of property law (or better of landholding). In this system, a lord (such as a King) grants feudal rights, known as fees, to a vassal. A vassal might grant a further fee from his own fee to a subvassal, thereby creating a pyramid of landholding.

Feudal System

In this feudal system, property rights and personal rights (or better duties) were closely interwoven. These rights on the land were accompanied by duties of the vassal toward his lord. A fee that was held by a vassal was, on one hand, a kind of property right on the land and at the same time included the duties that the vassal had toward his lord:

To state that a fee was a combination of a property right and a set of duties is in a sense an anachronism. In the Germanic system, in which feudality was grounded, the distinction between absolute property rights and relative personal rights did not exist. Only in retrospect can we say that a fee contained both what we now call a property right and personal duties.

It may be interesting to realize that the distinction between property rights and personal rights was already made in Roman law. However, knowledge of Roman law was lost under the influence of the Germans who had invaded much of continental Europe, and was only rediscovered in the twelfth century.

It was not always clear what exactly the duty of a vassal on the land was. In fact, especially toward the end of the eighteenth century, many vassals were unfamiliar with their rights and duties. The peasants, who were at the very bottom of the feudal pyramid of landholding, complained that they were placed under unfair burdens. Moreover, often only the landlords held documentation of the obligations of the peasants, such as the duty to provide one-tenth of their harvest. These claims were part of the books of grievances or *cahiers de doléances* that the peasants brought with them when they stormed the *Bastille* in Paris in 1789 starting the French Revolution.

French Revolution

The French Revolution meant a change of the system of landholding. On 11 August 1789, the feudal system was abolished, and only in 1804 it was replaced by a unitary system of property law in the newly made French Civil Code. This Code was an anti-feudal document that abolished, for example, all positive duties in property law, such as the duty of farmers to give up parts of their harvest. Moreover, property rights that were previously associated with the feudal system did not reappear in the Civil Code.

The *German Civil Code* of 1 January 1900 makes an even stronger anti-feudal statement. It strictly separates the law of property from the law of obligations and explicitly states that property law must be an autonomous field of private law.

Ownership

Unitary System

Civil law property systems are unitary: there is one system of property law that applies to land and goods alike. A unitary system means that the right of ownership is the same right of ownership regardless of whether it is held on a car or on a piece of land:

This type of system has been in existence since the French Revolution, which caused the abolition of the feudal system of landholding on the continent. Napoleon Bonaparte, who issued the drafting of a civil code for his empire, wanted one single legal system for all objects. His example was followed in the rest of continental Europe.

Definitions of Ownership

Primary property rights are the most comprehensive property rights available in a legal system. In civil law systems that have a unitary system of property law, there is one such right (on tangibles), and that is the right of ownership. Although the right of ownership is defined differently by the various civil law systems, these systems share the idea that the right of ownership is the most comprehensive right.

Art. 544 of the French Civil Code provides the oldest definition of ownership, which is still valid, stating:

Ownership is the right to enjoy and dispose of things in the most complete manner, provided they are not used in a way prohibited by statutes or regulations.

Paragraph 903 of the German Civil Code states:

The owner of a corporeal object can, when this does not interfere with the law or other rights of third parties, do with the object what he wishes and exclude others from interfering. The owner of an animal must, in the exercise of his powers, obey the special provisions for the protection of animals.

Finally, Art. 5:1 of the Dutch Civil Code states:

1. Ownership is the most extensive right which a person can have in a corporeal object.
2. To the exclusion of all others, the owner is free to use the object provided that this use does not violate the rights of others and that it respects the limitations based upon statutory rules and rules of unwritten law.
3. Without prejudice to the rights of others, the owner of the object becomes owner of the fruits the object produces, once separated.

There are, however, also differences between the systems. The French definition of ownership extends to things (*biens*), which includes not only corporeal objects but also incorporeal objects, such as claims. It is therefore possible to own a claim under French law. Suppose that A damaged B's car in a car accident and that A is liable for damages amounting to €2.000 on the basis of tort law, B then has a claim against A for the amount of €2.000. In French law, B would be the owner of this right.

Objects of Ownership

The German and Dutch definitions restrict the concept of ownership to corporeal objects; ownership of a claim is therefore impossible under German or Dutch laws. Therefore, according to German and Dutch law, B would *have* a claim against A but would not *own* this right.

Primary property rights are absolute rights, which means that they can (potentially) be invoked against everyone. Because they are also the most comprehensive rights, an owner can use his right against everyone else. Among others, this means that the owner of a good can vindicate this good. Vindication is a legal action in the civil law tradition by means of which a right holder can reclaim possession of the object of

Vindication

his right. For example, the owner of a stolen bike can reclaim the power over his bike from a thief by way of vindication.

One Right of Ownership

In the civil law tradition, there can be only one right of ownership in respect to an object. If one person holds the right of ownership of a good, then all other persons are not owners. Ownership is therefore a matter of all or nothing, not a matter of degree as it is in common law where different persons can have different titles to a good.

Specific Protection

Property rights, ownership, and other property rights enjoy a special form of protection by the law. This special protection takes the form of specific enforceability, meaning that the duties that follow from the right can be enforced as such.

At first sight, it may seem obvious that legal duties can be enforced, but this is not always the case. Often, if someone does not fulfill his duties, the person to whom the duty was owed can receive monetary compensation for the damages but cannot demand that the duty be fulfilled:

Tort law is a good illustration of this phenomenon. If someone damages someone else's object, the victim can claim monetary compensation, but cannot necessarily require that the damage be undone, or that the act of damaging stops. For example, a water leakage from the upstairs apartment may create damage to the apartment below. A successful action in tort allows a person to claim damages, but not automatically to stop the water flow. In the case of contractual default, the same is the case: the creditor can claim damages, but not necessarily specific performance. There are, after all, situations where performance is difficult or where the debtor really does not want to perform. Think for instance of a soccer professional who does not want to play under any circumstance. Contract law can generally only give monetary incentive to perform. A debtor who really does not want to perform can generally not be forced to do so other than through the payment of money.

Vindication

In the civil law tradition, each property right generally has its own action protecting it. The right of ownership, for instance, is protected by the action that is known as *vindication*. Vindication means that the owner is restored in factual power over the object that she owns. For example, if a thief stole your bike, vindication means that you can claim the actual bike back from the thief.

An action parallel to vindication is also possible in connection with other property rights that involve the factual power over a good. For instance, if a thief stole the bike on which you hold a right of usufruct, you can also claim the actual bike back from the thief.

In common law, only rights relating to land are specifically enforceable; rights relating to chattels are enforced through the law of torts under the tort of conversion. The tort of conversion generally forces the tort-feasor, in this case the person who interferes with someone else's property right, to choose between paying damages or returning the object or ending the interference with it: **Tort of Conversion**

When a thief steals your bike, you may sue the thief in tort and claim damages from him. The thief will then have a choice to pay damages or to return your bike to you.

It should, finally, be noted that property rights are protected not only by property law but also by criminal law. The thief and the person who deliberately destroys someone else's property are liable to be punished.

3.2   **Common Law Property Law**

The unitary system of ownership, according to which the «same» ownership applies to both immovable and movable objects, distinguishes the civil law tradition from the common law tradition that exists in England and Wales. The common law system, as it is applied in England and Wales, comprises two subsystems: common law in the narrow sense and equity. Both have their own version(s) of property rights. In this section, the property law of common law in the narrow sense is discussed. Property law in equity is discussed in ▶ Sect. 3.3.

The common law is the system of customary law that has developed since the Battle of Hastings in 1066. It has two kinds of property law, one for land, land law, and another for «what is not land», personal property law. This division essentially follows the distinction between immovable objects (land) and movable objects (chattels or goods). It is the reason why the common law system of property law is called «fragmented»: **Fragmented System**

The common law of property and the origin of common law are closely related, as William the Conqueror claimed all land in England for himself upon his victory in 1066. From that moment on, all persons held land from the Crown instead of entirely for themselves. Personal property law, i.e. the law relating to movable objects (goods), did not become relevant until the industrial revolution, when movable objects also became of value.

Land Law

Under the rules of common law, the King is the owner of all land; all others hold land from the King in tenure. This is a feudal system of landholding. Under this system, the King could originally determine the content of the right he gave to others, especially the obligations that right holders had to undertake in return for this right to the land.

Because the feudal system was modernized in the course of time, there was no need to overthrow it, as occurred on the continent after the French Revolution. English *land law* is therefore still a feudal system with its own terminology that has developed and been standardized over time:

Scots law also used a similar feudal system, until the Scottish parliament passed the Abolition of Feudal Tenure Act 2000, terminating all feudal rights in 2004.

One of the most recent modernizations of English land law was the Law of Property Act of 1925. With this Act, the legislature sought to limit and standardize the available property rights in respect to land. After this Act, only two types of feudal rights on land remained—«estates» in English legal terminology—which a person can have *at common law*:

- The fee simple absolute in possession, also known as *freehold*
- The fee for a term of years, also known as *leasehold*

Fee Simple

The most extensive right a person can have is a fee simple absolute in possession or, in short, *fee simple*. The fee simple entitles the holder to exclusive possession for an unlimited duration of time.

Term of Years

From the fee simple, the holder can derive a secondary property right in the form of a fee for a term of years or, in short, a *term of years* or *leasehold*, granting exclusive possession to someone else for a limited duration of time:

For instance, X has a fee simple of a piece of land with a house on it. She can grant a term of 5 years on the land with the house to Y. Y will be entitled to exclusive possession of the house, which will give her the right to live in it. For the duration of the term of years X has lost exclusive possession and can therefore not enter the land without Y's permission. After the 5 years have passed, Y's fee will have ended, but X's fee, which is for an (almost) unlimited time, still continues. This means X regains exclusive possession of the house.

Personal Property Law

The feudal estates of freehold and leasehold do not apply to *chattels* (by and large, movable objects). There is a newer system of property law, personal property law, that applies to chattels (goods) and *choses in action* (among others, claims):

In English personal property law goods are known as chattels, after the word 'cattle'.

In personal property law, the primary right is called «title». **Title**
Title, short for «entitlement», is the right of exclusive possession to a chattel. It is the most extensive entitlement to a chattel a person can have. For instance, if Thomas holds title to a book, he, and he alone (exclusivity), is entitled to control what happens to the book.

There is a complication, however, and this has to do with the so-called *relativity of title*. Relativity of title means that it is possible that more than one person is entitled to the same chattel. If several persons who are all entitled to the same good all claim possession over the good, the person with the stronger entitlement will receive possession. The comparison between two titles is always relative: the one title is stronger than the other. However, the title that wins out in one competition may lose in another competition. It is possible that another person with a still better right might come along and claim possession over the current possessor:

Suppose that Thomas holds title to a book, but that Andy claims to have a better title. In fact, Andy claims and is able to prove that Thomas borrowed the book from him. As a result of the evidence Andy will have a better title than Thomas. Suppose, moreover, that Andy himself had borrowed the book from his sister Susan. Susan will therefore hold a better title than Andy. However, as long as Susan doesn't claim her title, Andy can continue with possession of the book.

This is different in the continental system, according to which only one right of ownership can exist on a good. There is therefore no relativity of title in civil law systems:

Let us have another look at the case of Thomas, Andy and Susan, to see how that would be analyzed under a civil law system. Andy borrowed the book from Susan. This leaves Susan as the owner of the book, and makes Andy into a detentor of the book. Andy has no right to the book itself, but a personal right against Susan to use the book. Susan cannot vindicate the book from Andy on the basis of her ownership as long as Andy has this personal right against her. But a new owner (if Susan sold the book) might vindicate the book from Andy, since Andy's personal right only can be invoked against Susan. Thomas is also a detentor, this time based on his personal right against Andy. Andy cannot claim the book from Thomas because of this personal right, but arguably (there are some complications) Susan might vindicate her book from Thomas, since Susan still owns the book and Thomas only has a right against Andy, which cannot be invoked against Susan.

Trusts

Equity is a second system of law that corrects the strict application of the common law. Equity is important to property law as it is the origin of trusts. In a *trust*, management powers and enjoyment rights relating to property are separated and divided between a manager (trustee) and one or more beneficiaries (beneficiary owners):

A trust is very useful to manage property, for example to decide on what happens to your property after death, giving certain goods to your children, but others to charity. Another example is to manage money or shares in another (off-shore) jurisdiction.

4   Primary Rights

Generally, the right of ownership (in civil law) or the fee simple or title (in English law) is the most extensive right to use a thing or an object. It grants the holder of the right the most extensive entitlement to use it.

Limitations

Of course, this does not mean that the holder may do everything; there are limitations. For instance, the holder of a primary right of a monument cannot alter it without permission from the (local) government: monuments are normally under control of the State to ensure that they keep their valuable state. Other examples are that the purpose for which a building is used may not be changed from commercial to residential (to change a building from a shop into an apartment building) without a special permit and that the person entitled to a piece of land can only build on it with a building permit:

These are all examples of how private law rights are limited by rules of public law. However, the permission to (ab)use an object one owns may be limited on the basis of private law too. Around 1900, a discussion raged in French legal doctrine about what an owner is allowed to do with his properties. The liberal French author on property law Demolombe argued that the owner could do with his object of ownership whatever he wished. This would include that the owner of a famous painting, say a

Degas, would be permitted to destroy it by setting it on fire. Although other liberal authors agreed with Demolombe at that time, disagreement is certainly possible and this raises the question about the scope of the ownership of things that are of value not only to the holder, but also to the rest of society.

5 Secondary Property Rights

Property rights other than ownership are known as secondary property rights. There are two types of these secondary rights: (1) secondary property rights to use and (2) secondary property security rights. They comprise of permissions and/or competencies (powers) that would normally belong to the holder of the primary right but that can be exercised by the holder of the secondary right instead of, or next to, the holder of the primary right.

5.1 Secondary Rights to Use

Secondary rights to use are property rights that entitle the holder to use the object for a limited duration of time. Generally, there are two types, one for a short(er) and one for a longer duration of time.

Secondary rights to use for a shorter period tend to be   Usufruct
more extensive in content. The best example is the right of *usufruct*. A right of usufruct is the right to use and enjoy an object that is owned by someone else. The secondary right of usufruct therefore comprises of the permission to use and enjoy the object of the owner, who no longer holds this permission himself. The owner now holds «bare ownership», signaling that he has given away his permission to use and enjoy the object. This secondary property right entitles a person to use an object as if he were the owner, usually for the duration of his life:

For example, it can be the right to have a painting, owned by someone else, in your house for the remainder of your life. This situation is usually created upon death of one spouse in a family to allow the longest living spouse to enjoy the painting without any heir, children or stepchildren interfering. The holder of a right of usufruct can continue to use the object of his right even if the owner of the good sells it. Because the usufruct rests on the object and is not a personal right against the person who granted it, the right 'follows' the object (droit de suite).

Servitude

ServitudeSecondary rights to use for a longer period of time generally have less extensive content. An example is the right of servitude. A right of servitude can be created on one piece of land for the benefit of another piece of land. A typical example is the right of way, which allows the owner of the one piece of land to walk (or drive) over the other piece of land, usually that of the neighbor. Such a right is, for example, useful to reach a nearby road or to ensure an escape route in case of fire.

The right of servitude limits the ownership of the land on which the servitude runs. The owner is normally allowed to exclude everyone else from his land but now agrees to no longer exclude the right holder of the servitude when he or she is exercising his or her right.

The right of servitude is created on the land. The effect of this is that when the right of ownership of the land is sold and transferred to someone else, the new owner is still bound by the right of servitude.

5.2   Property Security Rights

Property security rights are created to secure the payment of a monetary claim. They are usually created on an object on which the debtor of a claim has a primary right:

The best example of a secondary security right is a right of hypothec (or, in the common law, of mortgage). This is a secondary security right that an owner of a house (or land) grants to a bank or other creditor in exchange for financing the acquisition of the house (or land).

There are two main types of secondary security rights:
1. The right of pledge, which can be created on most movable objects (for instance, jewelry or cars) and on particular kinds of rights
2. The right of hypothec (or mortgage), which can be created on immovable objects (land and all that is attached to it, like houses) and on some special movable objects (e.g., ships or airplanes)

Secondary property security rights break the equality of creditors rule, also known as paritas creditorum. When creditors claim money from a debtor, they are generally treated equally.

Suppose that A owes €1.000 to B and a further €3.000 to C. If everything goes well, A will pay both of his creditors. However, if A does not have enough money to pay both B and C, what will happen then? If A pays one creditor and lacks the money to pay the other, the other has bad luck. This creditor still holds a claim against A but will probably not receive his money. However, as long as there still is some money, the claims of B and C are equal in rank; this means that B and C are entitled to amounts of money from A's estate in proportion to their claims. In this example, this is 1:3. It is, for instance, not the case that the older claim prevails over the younger one:

Paritas creditorum

It is the function of the legal institution of insolvency to secure a correct division of money if a debtor cannot pay all of his debts.

A consequence of this principle of equality is that the chance that a creditor will receive his money depends on the claims of other creditors. Most creditors do not find that a comfortable situation and may therefore be unwilling to allow credit. Because credit strongly facilitates commercial transactions, and the unwillingness to allow credit hampers these transactions, the law recognizes the phenomenon of security.

A property security right is held by the creditor of the claim, usually a bank, and will break the *paritas creditorum* rule by giving the holder the power to take possession of and sell the object of the right, to transfer the primary property right of the debtor to a new owner, and to satisfy the debt from the proceeds. Any surplus must be paid back to the debtor:

Property Security Right

For instance, Joan bought a house and for that purpose borrowed €150.000 from the bank. As security for this loan she creates a right of hypothec on her house, in favor of the bank. If Joan does not repay the money in time, the bank may evict Joan from the house, take possession of the house, sell it at an auction to satisfy the outstanding debt by means of the proceeds. Suppose that Joan still owes €100.000 to the bank and that her house brings in €140.000 at the auction. Then the bank can take €100.000 from the proceeds and must return €40.000 to Joan. If the house only brings in €80.000, Joan must still pay the bank €20.000.

Secondary security rights also give the holder of the right priority in insolvency. Holders of personal rights will be treated equally in insolvency: *paritas creditorum*. However, holders with a secondary right for security may claim their money before the creditors who hold only personal rights:

Priority

Suppose that Joan not only owed €100.000 to the bank but also €50.000 to a friend. If there is no hypothec to secure any of these loans and the house is sold to satisfy the creditors, the bank will receive 2/3rds of the proceeds, and the friend 1/3rd, proportional to the claims they had against Joan (paritas creditorum). However, if the bank has a right of hypothec, the proceeds of the house will first be used to pay the bank. If the house brings in €80.000 the bank will receive all that money and Joan's friend will receive nothing. If the house brings in €140.000 the bank will receive €100.000 and the friend €40.000. (This example assumes that there are no other creditors and that Joan has no money, but only the house).

6   Principles of Property Law

Property law systems in Europe differ widely, especially at the level of detailed rules. However, all systems of property law must deal with the same issues, and they approach these issues similarly. This approach is based on principles and rules of property law, which will be dealt with in this section.

6.1   The Principle of *Numerus Clausus*

Property rights exist in land or goods and are not merely directed toward one or more concrete persons; they can, in principle, be invoked against everyone. For this reason, it is undesirable that individual persons (including «legal persons» such as companies with limited liability) can make up such strong rights by themselves, if only because they would thereby bind other persons who were not involved in creating these property rights:

Imagine that A could create a property right on his land, with the content that everyone should pay the owner of this piece of land an annual amount of €50. This would make A rich very quickly indeed.

Therefore, only a limited number (numerus clausus) of property rights are recognized. The property rights in this exhaustive list are the only types of property rights that persons can create.

6.2   The Principle of Specificity

A second principle of property law is the principle of specificity. A property right is a right on a good or on land, and it should be clear in respect of precisely which good or land the property right is created. It is, for instance, not possible that a jeweler can own «four golden rings» without being clear precisely which rings are owned by the jeweler:

The importance of the principle of specificity becomes clear if one considers what would happen if this principle were not respected. Suppose that the jeweler needs money and wants to create a right of pledge on his golden rings. In order to do so, he must give the rings to the holder of the right of pledge. If it is unclear which rings the jeweler owns, it is not possible to comply with this condition for creating a right of pledge. If the jeweler hands in four random golden rings, the creditor might end up with rings that belong to a third party, who has nothing to do with either the jeweler or the holder of the right of pledge.

A consequence of the principle of specificity is that so-called fungible objects, which occur in masses, such as grain, sand, and also money, can generally not be the object of individual property rights if they are mixed with other objects of the same kind:

If Jane brings money to the bank to put it in her savings account, she loses ownership of this money, because in the bank it is mixed with money from other persons and can no longer be identified as the money of Jane. Although Jane has an individual bank account, this is merely an administrative status representing Jane's rights on the money in the bank. Jane only has a claim against the bank to return to her the same amount of money (plus possible interest) that she deposited in the bank. A practical consequence is that if the bank becomes insolvent, Jane has to compete with all other creditors for a share in the remaining money. She cannot take out 'her' money, because there is no money that belongs specifically to her.

Specificity is, finally, also important because property rights end if the things or objects on which they rest cease to exist. This only makes sense if property rights have specific objects.

The principle of specificity is under pressure nowadays because immaterial «things», such as money in bank accounts, claims, and virtual objects in online computer games have become more and more important and valuable. It would be useful to allow property rights on them, but—as can easily be understood—immaterial things are less easy to identify than material objects.

6.3   The Principle of Publicity

If property rights potentially affect everyone, it is important that everyone can know who has which property right. If you want to buy a house, it is essential to know whether there is a hypothec (or mortgage) on the house. The holder of the hypothec can, under certain circumstances, sell off the house to satisfy his claim from the proceeds. Because of the *droit de suite*, this property right can be invoked against anybody holding the house and therefore also against new owners. If this is the house you recently bought and if the debts for which the house is sold are not your own debts, it is rather painful. Therefore, property rights should, in principle, be publicly knowable. The way in which this demand for publicity is satisfied differs for real estate (land and what is built upon it) and movables.

Land

In respect to land, publicity is realized through a land registry:

When Adam sells his land to Beatrice every legal system would require an authentic deed, drawn up by a notary or other official, that contains the agreement of transfer between the parties. Let us assume that in this case the deed is drawn up by the notary Clovis and sent in for registration.

Negative Systems

There are generally two types of registration systems. On one hand, there are registration systems that operate on the basis of a simple registration of *deeds*, i.e., official documents created by a notary:

When the deed drawn up by the notary Clovis is received by a deeds registry, a date and timestamp is placed on the deed. The registrar sees that the deed was drawn up by an official notary who has the capacity to draw up deeds. The deed is then registered under the heading of the piece of land it concerns.

Such *cadastre* systems are called negative systems because the registrar registers the deed with only a marginal check of the formal validity of the contents. They are used in French law (*cadastre*) and in Dutch law (*kadaster*).

Positive Systems

There are also «title registry systems». They are known as positive systems because the registrar actively checks the content of the deeds offered to him. After this thorough check, the registrar updates the registry, which contains not a set of deeds but exact information about who holds which property law entitlement (title) to which piece of land:

When the deed drawn up by the notary Clovis is received by a title registry, a date and timestamp is placed on the deed and the registrar starts his or her investigations into the validity of the deed. He or she will check the parties, the piece of land concerned and retrace the steps made by the notary Clovis. When the check is completed (this can take up to 3 months), the results of the deed are registered: Beatrice will be identified as the new owner.

This positive system of land registry is used in German law (*Grundbuch*) and in English law (Land Registry). In English law, registration has only become mandatory in the last years. Therefore registration of land will only occur henceforth when land is transferred between parties or passed upon inheritance. A full registration system will result over time.

Movable Objects

There are many movable objects, and it is impossible and undesirable to maintain a register which includes every movable object (e.g., for every spoon and every fork in your kitchen) and who has which property right on it. Happily, movable objects are most of the time—but certainly not always—owned by the person who actually has them in his possession. Therefore, when a person holds factual control over an object, this is a signal to the world that this person is exercising a property right. In the case of movable objects, publicity of ownership takes the form of possession.

When a property right on a movable object is transferred, this is usually also done by the transfer of possession. In that way, it is made public that the property relations have changed:

There are some complications here, depending on whether a legal system works with a consensual or with a tradition system. More details will be presented in Sect. 7.2.1.

6.4   The *Nemo Dat* Rule

The *nemo dat* rule holds that nobody can transfer a property right that he did not have himself in the first place. The name of this principle is an abbreviation from the longer Latin phrase *nemo dat quod non habet* (nobody can give what he does not have). A person who owns a thing can transfer the full ownership of it, but the holder of a mere right of usufruct

Competence to
Dispose

may be able to transfer the right of usufruct but cannot transfer the full ownership of the object.

The *nemo dat* rule is implemented in the requirement that a person transferring a property right must have the competence to dispose of that right. When the competence to dispose is lacking, this person cannot transfer the right to someone else.

Although the competence to dispose is closely connected to the property right itself, they are not identical. The normal situation is that the holder of a property right is competent to dispose of it and nobody else. However, sometimes the holder lacks this competence, for instance, if she is in a state of insolvency. Moreover, sometimes someone other than the right holder is (also) competent to dispose of a right, such as the holder of a right of pledge who can transfer ownership of the object under pledge if he has to sell the object for the payment of a debt:

If Bank B holds a pledge on Adam's car, and Adam defaults on his payments, the bank will have the right to take possession of the car and sell and transfer the car to someone else. When this happens, Adam will lose his competence to dispose to the bank. Bank B will now be able to dispose of the (ownership of the) car and sell and transfer it to someone else.

6.5   Prior Tempore Rule

The rule *prior tempore, potior iure* (earlier in time, more powerful as a right), which stems from Roman law, determines that older property rights trump newer rights. This is very important in case there is a conflict between several property rights, such as when there is more than one hypothec on one piece of land. Then the holder of the older hypothec will get paid first from the proceeds of the land, and the holder of the second right comes after the first hypothec holder (but before the creditors who do not have a property right on the land). The same holds for the right of pledge:

Adam has granted a right of pledge on his car to Bank B. However, he has also granted another right of pledge on that same car to Bank C. This creates a problem now that Adam can no longer pay either bank. Bank B and Bank C each claims to have priority over other creditors and seeks to take possession and sell and transfer the car to satisfy their claims with the proceeds of sale. However, only one of the banks will be able to do so.

Property law solves this problem with the *prior tempore* rule. The creditor with the older property right has priority over the creditor with the newer right. Bank B holds the older property right (pledge) and may therefore exercise the right of pledge. Bank C must wait to see if there is anything left of the proceeds of sale after Bank B has satisfied its claim:

It should be noted that with regard to these left-over proceeds, Bank C has priority over other creditors who do not have a security right. For this reason it makes sense for a creditor to accept a second pledge (or hypothec, for that matter) on an object.

The *prior tempore* rule is specific to property law, as personal rights generally compete against each other with an equal status (*paritas creditorum*).

7   Creation, Transfer, and Termination of Property Rights

A large part of property law provides rules on how property rights can be created, transferred, and terminated. These rules are also known as operative or interface rules, as they determine how property rights behave and how we interact with them.

7.1   Creation

All property rights, both primary and secondary rights, must have come into existence at some time. In this section, we only discuss some of the ways in which primary property rights can be created.

A primary property right can originate when an object   Occupation
that previously belonged to no one is found and taken into possession by the finder. This is called *occupation*. This may, for instance, be the case when someone catches fish in open waters or shoots a wild bird.

A property right can also come into existence when a new   Creation
object is created out of a previously existing object. When sufficient labor has been invested in the new object, the person who provided the labor will become holder of a primary right over the new object:

For instance, if someone knits a sweater out of wool, this person becomes the owner of the sweater. However, it is doubtful whether someone who makes a coin out of a piece of gold that belonged to someone else becomes the owner of this coin. In this case, the value of the gold in the coin may be higher than the added value resulting from minting the coin.

Mixing

In case of mixing of two or more objects, a new primary right will arise. Depending on the type of mixing, the new primary right will be shared by the parties previously holding primary rights on the objects that mixed or by one single party:

If money from different persons is collected in a bag, the total amount probably belongs to the original owners together.

Accession

However, if land and bricks with different owners are joined to build a house, the owner of the land will become the owner of the house. This happens by operation of the principle of accession: that which belongs to the land becomes part of the land.

Prescription

Finally, a property right can also be acquired by possession, i.e., the exercise of factual power for oneself, for a long period of time. If after a long period of time the holder of primary right has not objected or taken legal action against the «adverse possession», the possessor will acquire a primary property right of the possessed thing by what is known as prescription. This rule exists to create legal certainty. It is important that discrepancies between the factual situation (possession) and the official legal situation (the title) do not exist for too long. In the long term, the legal situation is adapted to the factual one. So if A is in possession of the piece of land of B for a long duration of time (say 30 years), A becomes the owner of that piece of land and B loses his right of ownership:

When the possessor is in good faith, meaning that he sincerely thought he could exercise a right, the prescription period will generally be shorter then when this is not the case. Possession in good faith can for example occur if someone bought a good from a person whom he rightfully, but mistakenly, took to be the owner. A thief would be a typical example of a possessor in bad faith.

7.2   Transfer

Transfer and Publicity

If a property right is transferred, two requirements must be met. The easiest one is that it must be clear between the *transferor* (the person who transfers) and the *transferee* (the person to whom it is transferred, also known as *acquirer*) that the former has lost the property right and that the latter has acquired it:

An example in which this demand is not met is the following. A and B agree that B will have the book that now belongs to A. One day B visits A at her home and sees the book lying on the table. B puts the book in his suitcase and takes it home. It is possible that B assumes that he has become the owner of the book, but A knows nothing about it. Such 'transfers' are not desirable, and it is unlikely that the law will recognize these events as valid transfers of ownership.

To the extent that only the relation between transferor and transferee is concerned, it would suffice that they both agree that the property right has passed from one to the other. However, the interests of third parties are often involved in the transfer of a property right:

Suppose that A has a claim against C for an amount of €10.000. A agrees with B that from now on, B will have the claim, but they do not say anything to C, who still thinks that she owes money to A. C pays €10.000 to A, but now B claims that C should pay that amount to him. Another example: A transfers the right to a box with golden rings to B, but the box remains on A's premises. Later a money lender visits A, lends A €2.000 and takes the box with rings as object for a right of pledge. B tells the money lender that he will vindicate the rings, because they belong to him. The money lender fears that he will lose his security right.

To avoid problems like those in these examples, it is desirable that third parties know that a transfer of property right took place. In this connection, the principle of publicity plays a role. According to this principle, it should be known to the public at large who is the holder of a property right. If this is known, problems like the ones mentioned above are less likely to occur. To make this known, the requirements for the transfer of a right aim to ensure that the effects of the transfer will be known to the public at large or at least the persons to whom it concerns.

In Europe, there are two main ways in which the transfer of property rights can occur. Both systems can be understood from the need to «publish» the transfer, and their difference can be seen as an outflow of different ways to manage the publicity requirement. One is the consensual system; the other is the transfer system. We will discuss both briefly and only in connection with the sale of a material object.

The Consensual System

A consensual transfer system merely requires consensus to transfer a property right between the seller and the buyer. This means that the conclusion of the contract of sale will transfer the property right from the transferor to the transferee or acquirer:

For instance, if a customer buys a loaf of bread in the bakery, the sales contract makes the customer the owner of the bread immediately. In theory, the customer has already become the owner even before the bread was handed to her. The baker is under an obligation to give the bread to the customer, as the customer is already the owner because of the contract. More important is the consensual nature of transfer in the following case: A sells his car to B, but will only deliver it tomorrow. During the night, the car is stolen. Will B's insurance have to pay? According to a consensual system, the answer is 'yes', because B immediately became the owner of the car, even though he did not actually have possession yet.

The consensual system is used in France, Belgium, and England. However, these countries distinguish between movable and immovable objects. In the case of *movable objects*, the buyer becomes the owner immediately upon conclusion of the contract.

In the case of *immovables*, the property right is also transferred, but this transfer will only have effect between the parties. Only when the contract in the form of a deed—an official document—has been registered will the transfer of the property right also have effect against the rest of the world:

A sells his house to B, but the registration of the deed still takes a few days. Within this short period, A sells the house for a second time, now to C. The second deed is registered before the deed of the first sale agreement was registered. C has now become owner of the house, because the transfer based on the first sale contract only worked against C after the deed was registered. Because the sale contract between A and B had immediate effect between these two parties, B could evict A from the house immediately after the sale contract was entered into, even before registration of the deed.

The Tradition System

A tradition system requires, besides a contract of sale, a special act to transfer the property right. This property-transferring act, especially concerning movables, was known as *traditio* in Roman law, which is why these systems are called «tradition systems»:

Germany and the Netherlands are countries in which a tradition system is in use. England also uses the tradition system for land and for the transfer of chattels not based on a sale agreement (e.g. barter, which is exchange of goods for other goods or services).

A contract of sale in a tradition system therefore serves as the starting point for the transaction but in itself does not have effect in property law. The contract is known as the *title* for the transfer in these systems:

This title, which is the reason why a property right must be transferred, should not be confused with the title one can have in an object, and which is comparable to (some variant of) ownership.

The title does not necessarily have to be a contract of sale. It can also, for example, be a donation (gift).

7.3   Termination

Property rights can be created and transferred, but they can also be terminated. There are generally two ways in which a property right can end.

The first possibility is that the object on which the property right rests is destroyed or ceases to exist independently. Ownership of a car will end when the car is completely destroyed by fire. Land can stop existing, if, for instance, it is permanently flooded or when a large meteor hits and destroys the land. Then there is nothing left to own for the land owner, and ownership ends. Claims can stop existing if the corresponding duty has been fulfilled or if the claim was waived by the creditor.

The second possibility is that the property right on an object ends, even though the object itself continues to exist. One way in which property rights can cease to exist is when they are *waived* or *abandoned* by the right holder. Abandonment of rights is usually possible for movable objects and claims but not easily for land. If a fisher who has captured a fish and in that way became owner of the fish lets the fish go, ownership of the fish is terminated. If B is under an obligation to pay A €100 and A tells B that he does not have to pay anymore, then the claim of A against B has been waived and has perished.

Property rights can also be terminated by operation of law. This happens, for instance, if the title on a piece of land is lost because of prescription. If a piece of land belonged to A, but B used the land as if it was his own for a long period (say 30 years or more), and if A did not protest or undertake any legal action, A loses his title to the land. Normally B would gain the title.

A right of usufruct usually ends if the holder of this right dies, and a leasehold (a fee for a term of years) ends if the term has passed.

Finally, in most legal systems, a property right can also be terminated by agreement between the parties involved in the right. If A is the owner of a piece of land and B is the owner of the neighboring land, who in this capacity enjoys the right of servitude that he may cross A's land, A and B (officially the owners of the two pieces of land) can end this right of servitude by mutual agreement.

8   European Union Property Law

After the overview of property law in the sections above, it is time to look forward to the development of property law. In the European Union, there is an increasing debate on the need to create uniform rules of private law for the European Union's internal market. The starting point of this debate is the assumption that the internal market cannot function properly without common rules of private law, mostly contract law but increasingly also property law:

Imagine an EU citizen buying objects online from another EU Member State. An important question that needs to be answered is when the buyer receives the primary property right over this object, as the holder of a primary right generally also bears the risk if the object is lost before it arrives. If the primary right is transferred upon conclusion of the contract, as in a consensual transfer system, the risk is with the buyer. If delivery, i.e., the transfer of possession is needed to transfer the primary right as in a tradition system, the risk is with the seller.

The European Commission therefore seeks to investigate possibilities to create common rules for the internal market. However, creating these rules is much more difficult in property law than in contract law. Changes in property law are threatened to be wholesale instead of piecemeal because changes in one part necessitate changes «everywhere».

Moreover, because of the importance of property law to a legal system in general, as the basis for other areas of law such as taxation, succession, marriage, and insolvency, changing these rules is controversial and always politically sensitive.

Even if the political will exists to change property law systems to create uniform rules for the EU's internal market, it will be difficult to decide what would be the best rules. In this respect, mixed legal systems may be of help. Mixed legal systems are legal systems that combine multiple legal traditions in a single legal system. In Europe, a combination of common law and civil law systems can provide interesting insights. Property law scholars therefore often look at the law of Scotland, which combines the English common law (not equity) and the French civil law traditions. Another very important mixed system is South African law, which combines Roman Dutch law (which is unwritten civil law from the seventeenth century brought to South Africa by the Dutch settlers) and English common law (again, not equity). These legal systems may offer inspiration for the further development of common rules for the European Union.

Because there are so few and minor similarities between the European systems at the technical level, any decision for harmonization will result in a requirement for many of the legal systems to change their technical rules of property law. Nonetheless, there are several European initiatives that are worth mentioning. For many years, there has already been a debate on the creation of a European right of hypothec, a secondary property security right on land and houses that could be used to finance the acquisition of land and houses in Member States more easily.

Moreover, a debate is ongoing about the creation of a European security right on movables and claims, which would create a uniform European system that can be enforced throughout the EU.

Finally, EU rules on wills and succession, as well as rules on marital property law, are in development, which should enable international couples to choose the legal system that will be applicable to their marriage or succession.

Recommended Literature

Van Erp JHM (2006) Comparative property law. In: Reimann M, Zimmermann R (eds) The Oxford handbook of comparative law. Oxford University Press, Oxford, pp 1043–1070

Van Erp JHM, Akkermans B (2010) European Union property law. In: Twigg-Flesner C (ed) Cambridge companion to European Union private law. Cambridge University Press, Cambridge, pp 173–186

Van Erp JHM, Akkermans B (eds) (2012) Ius Commune Casebooks for the Common Law of Europe, Text and Materials on Property Law. Hart, Oxford

5

Tort Law

Jaap Hage

© Springer International Publishing Switzerland 2017
J. Hage et al. (eds.), *Introduction to Law*, DOI 10.1007/978-3-319-57252-9_6

1   What is Tort Law?

Sometimes events cause damage. For example, a car accident causes bodily harm to the persons involved and material harm to the owners of the cars. This harm, from the legal point of view, is called «damage». A soft drink that has stood too long in the sun may explode and cause damage to bystanders who are subsequently injured. Slander on the Internet can cause psychological harm to a school girl, which may be translated into material damage (the costs of the psychologist who treats her) and immaterial damage (the suffering of the girl who does not dare to meet her school friends anymore).

1.1   Liability Law

Liability law deals with the conditions under which someone who has suffered damage can claim compensation for this damage from someone else. Examples of persons who might claim damages (compensation of suffered damage) on the basis of liability law are:

- The victim of a bar fight whose face had to be treated by a doctor
- The school girl who was the victim of slander on the Internet
- The client of a bank who suffered a loss on his stock portfolio, because the bank did not sufficiently warn him for the risks of a certain kind of investment
- The student who had to re-sit his exam after other students had illegally acquired copies before the exam was taken
- The car owner whose car was damaged in an accident
- The owner of a school building that was set on fire by a 6-year-old pupil
- The victim of an exploding bottle of soft drink that stood too long in the sun

Contractual Liability and Tort Liability

Liability for someone else's damage often occurs in a contractual setting. For example, the window cleaner who damages the window he cleans will normally be liable for the damage of his client on the basis of contract. The law deals with this kind of liability under the heading of contractual liability.

The rules for this contractual liability are similar, although not identical, to the rules for liability outside contract (extra-contractual or tort liability). This chapter mostly deals with the rules for extra-contractual liability, which go by the name of «tort law».

The field of liability law is governed by the demands of two different kinds of justice: corrective and distributive justice. These two kinds of justice are discussed in ▶ Sect. 2, preceding the rest of this chapter.

Justice

The main rule in liability law is that damage must be borne by the person who suffered it in the first place. If a house collapses as result of an earthquake, the house owner must normally bear this damage himself. The main exception to this rule is when the damage can be attributed to an act of somebody else. The other person has caused the damage, and if he did this intentionally or negligently, he must for that reason compensate it. We then speak of fault liability. Most of the above examples illustrate this kind of fault liability. Fault liability will be discussed more extensively in ▶ Sect. 3.

Fault Liability

There are a number of situations in which the damage is not the result of an act at all or is the result of a circumstance where the agent did not act intentionally or negligently. In some of these situations, the law nevertheless imposes liability on someone other than the direct victim. Examples are that parents are liable for the damage caused by their young children or that the possessor of a defective object (e.g., a bottle of soft drink that explodes when exposed to direct sunlight) is liable for the damage if the danger is realized. We then speak of strict liability. Strict liability exists when the law assumes there is liability, but does not base it on a fault of the person who must pay damages. There are several kinds of strict liability, which will be discussed more extensively in ▶ Sect. 4. This section also briefly highlights alternative mechanisms for the distribution of damage over society.

Strict Liability

Both in the case of fault liability and of strict liability, the damage is shifted from the person who suffered it to somebody else. Sometimes there is reason not to shift the damage to one or more specific persons but rather to distribute it over a larger part of society. One reason for doing this is that the damage is too big to be borne by individual persons. Think, for instance, of the damage resulting from a nuclear disaster. Another reason is that the existence of a certain kind of damage is the responsibility of a larger set of persons. In this case, it is in the interest of victims that all members of this set contribute to the compensation of that damage. An example would be that car drivers collectively create the risk of car accidents, and therefore it makes sense to hold them collectively responsible for compensating the damage that results from the use of cars. Damage funds and (mandatory) insurance are mechanisms that distribute the costs of the damage over larger parts of society; they are discussed in ▶ Sect. 5.

Mechanisms for the Distribution of Damage

Limitations

If somebody has the obligation to compensate damage, either on the basis of fault liability or of strict liability, there is a need to determine who can claim compensation and exactly which kinds of damage must be compensated. The law also recognizes several grounds for limiting the liability for somebody else's damage, such as causation and contributory negligence, and these grounds will be the topic of ▶ Sect. 6.

1.2   Tort Law

The expression «tort law» suggests that tort law is a homogeneous field of law, with a few rules regulating the compensation for all kinds of damage. In reality tort law can be applied to very heterogeneous topics, such as bodily harm, manslaughter, insult, libel, infringement of privacy, trespassing land or home, damage to goods, violation of copyright, unfair competition, poor infrastructure, unhealthy food, and so on. What all these situations have in common is that an event causes damage to a victim and there may be reason to let someone else compensate it. For the rest, however, there seems to be little similarity concerning the abovementioned situations.

The Common Law of Torts

It would be possible to develop distinct rules for each different situation. These rules could be fine-tuned to the various kinds of cases and the differences between them. Actually this was the case for English law; it developed rules for several kinds of torts. For this reason, the rules about the different situations were originally called the «law of torts», in the plural. The persons who commit torts are called «tort-feasors».

The very expression «tort law» is derived from the common law tradition. The word «tort» is originally French and stands for «wrong». A tort is a wrongful act which is ground for a legal action for damages.

However, stemming from the *Donoghue v Stevenson* case, a development has started in English law in which one particular tort, the tort of negligence, has come to dominate the field.

Donoghue v Stevenson [1932] AC 562
On August 26, 1928, Ms. May Donoghue visited a bar in Paisley, Scotland. The owner of the bar poured part of a bottle of ginger beer on top of her ice cream. After Ms. Donoghue had eaten some of the ice cream, her friend poured on the remainder of the ginger beer. In doing so, a snail in a state of decomposition came out of the dark-glass bottle. Ms. Donoghue later contracted gastroenteritis from eating the ice cream mixed with the ginger beer, and therefore she wanted to be compensated financially by Stevenson, who had manufactured the bottle. She

claimed that Stevenson owed a duty of care to protect her from this damage. This case between Ms. Donoghue, who allegedly suffered damage from consuming the contaminated ginger beer, and Stevenson, who produced this bottle, has become a classic of tort law.

Someone commits the tort of negligence if they breach a legal duty of care owed to another person and their interests and if this breach resulted in damage to that person. The dominance of this kind of liability has changed the «law of torts» into «the law of tort»; however, the field of tort law still exhibits the traces of the old situation in which there were separate rules for the different torts. Although the tort of negligence may be the most important one, other torts such as trespass still exist.

In the civil law tradition, there are not as many torts as far as legislation is concerned. However, in applying relatively few rules, judge-made case law has differentiated various kinds of wrongful acts.

Civil Law

For instance, in the case of intentional causation of damage such as physical mistreatment, liability is more easily assumed than in case of an accident. The liability for inherently dangerous activities also tends to be greater than for events where the cause of the damage is by way of coincidence. These distinctions cannot be found in original legislation but are based on case law.

Since relatively few rules have been interpreted differently for different kinds of wrongful acts, case law in the civil law tradition created a greater differentiation than appears to exist on the basis of legislation only. The result is that in tort law the difference between the civil law and the common law tradition is mainly one of style.

2   Two Kinds of Justice

During the fourth century BC, the Greek philosopher Aristotle wrote a treatise on ethics in which he distinguished two kinds of justice: corrective justice and distributive justice.

Corrective justice (also called «compensatory justice» or «retributive justice») involves rectifying something that has gone wrong. A typical example is the justice that is involved in the proper punishment of criminals or the compensation of the damage that one person caused to another.

Corrective Justice

As the name «corrective justice» suggests, the idea behind this kind of justice is that a wrong must be corrected. In the case of the punishment of crimes, it may not be clear what this involves precisely. However, in the case of damage, it is relatively easy. The damage must be remedied, that is, the person who suffered the damage must be brought to the same position he or she was in before the damage occurred. For example, if Jane stole Cathy's necklace, she must return the necklace or – if that is not possible anymore – give Cathy the value of the necklace in money.

Typically the person who must restore the situation to its previous condition is the one who disturbed it. This means that there must be an act that caused the damage and that this act must be attributable to the person who is held liable for the damage. If Jane stole Cathy's necklace, the theft can be attributed to Jane, and she is the obvious candidate to compensate the damage.

In cases of corrective justice, the liability to compensate depends on the wrongness of the act that caused the damage. If Carrefour opens a new supermarket in a town, thereby causing damage (loss of income) to the owner of the local Spar supermarket, Carrefour will typically not be liable for the damage on the basis of corrective justice, because free competition allowed it to open a new supermarket.

The liability based on corrective justice is typically fault liability. This does not mean that there is no liability in law if there is no fault, but such liability must have other grounds than corrective justice, for example, distributive justice.

Distributive Justice

Distributive justice is involved in the distribution of some «good» or «bad» over a group of persons. A classic example is the distribution of a cake over a number of children, but other examples are the distribution of wealth over society, of taxes over taxpayers, of pollution rights over polluters, and – most important for our purposes – of damage over society.

The idea that damage can be divided may seem strange at first sight, because damage seems to fall on persons in an arbitrary fashion. That may be the case, but as soon as the compensation of damage is considered, it becomes a matter of justice whether and how the damage will be compensated and who will bear which damage. If the question is dealt with as a matter of corrective justice, compensation is used as a means to restore the distribution that existed before the damage occurred. Under distributive justice, compensation does not necessarily restore the status quo, but can be used to achieve a fair distribution of wealth over society. For example, distributive justice may demand that damage is distributed over all tax payers, as when the damage caused by an earthquake is compensated from a government fund that is filled with money from taxes. It may also demand that the damage caused by car drivers is paid by their insurance companies and therefore make insurance compulsory for all car owners. (See ▶ Sect. 5.)

3 Fault Liability

Fault liability exists when one person is liable for the damage caused to another because the former wrongfully caused the damage of the latter.

Examples of fault liability are the liability of: Examples

— The thief for the damage caused by his theft

— The seller of hot chocolate who serves the drink too hot, for the burns caused to the buyer

— The car driver who drives too fast in a residential area, which makes it impossible to stop in time for a child that inadvertently crosses the road, for the injuries of the child

— The supervisor of the financial sector who does not close down a bank with insufficient financial means for the losses of the bank's clients

3.1 The Common Law Approach

English tort law contains mostly rules that require an intentional or negligent act by the liable person. A tort is intentional if the agent performed the unlawful behavior on purpose.

An example is the tort of trespass. Trespass against land takes place if somebody directly and on purpose interferes with land that is in possession of somebody else. Trespass against a person takes place if somebody directly and on purpose causes an injury to a person or threatens to do so.

The most important tort, especially after the landmark case of Negligence Donoghue v Stevenson, is the tort of negligence. In general, there are four conditions which must be satisfied for liability under the tort of negligence:

1. There must have been a duty of care.
2. This duty must have been breached.
3. There must be damage.
4. This damage must have been caused by the breach.

In this section, we will only focus on the question when a duty Duties of Care of care exists. The notion of a duty of care is used in the common law to describe the range of persons, their relationships, and the kinds of damage for which compensation can be claimed. Criteria to determine whether a particular person or organization owes a duty of care toward another are a central topic of tort law. It is not very easy to say something in general about this issue. An attempt to do so nevertheless is found in the Learned Hand Formula.

Learned Hand Formula

In 1947, in the case of *United States* v *Caroll Towing Co.*, the American judge Learned Hand formulated a rule of thumb to determine what standard of care would be required by a ship owner to ensure that a ship does not break loose of its mooring ropes:

The owner's duty ... to provide against resulting injuries is a function of three variables:
1. The probability that she will break away;
2. The gravity of the resulting injury, if she does;
3. The burden of adequate precautions.

The basic idea is that a balance must be struck between the costs of precautionary measures and the costs of accidents. The «costs of accidents» are the product of the costs of a «normal» accident and the probability that such an accident will occur. If the costs of a precautionary measure are less than the expected costs of the accident, this precautionary measure is required, and a breach of duty exists if such a measure is not taken.

Judge Learned Hand has become a legend, because he did not confine himself to this analysis but went further and gave it a «scientific» twist by summarizing it in the formula: «if the probability be called P; the injury L; and the burden B; liability depends upon whether B is less likely than L multiplied by P: i.e. whether B is less than PL». This formula has become known as the «Learned Hand Formula».

The Learned Hand Formula can be used to determine whether a duty of care exists. This is of course a crucial step in determining whether somebody breached a duty of care and is as such liable for committing the tort of negligence. Its practical relevance is, however, disputed.

In England, the counterpart of the Learned Hand formula is the «neighbor principle», which was formulated by Lord Atkin in the Donoghue v Stevenson case. According to this principle, one must take reasonable care to avoid acts or omissions which could be reasonably foreseen as likely to injure a neighbor. Neighbors are persons who are so closely and directly affected by an act that one ought to have them in contemplation when directing one's mind to the acts or omissions called into question.

The threefold mention in the formulation of this principle of what is reasonable gives this neighbor principle a wide scope of application. The drawback, however, is that the wide scope gives poor clues as to when a duty of care actually exists.

3.2   The Civil law Approach

The civil law approach to tort law differs from the common law approach in that the basic rules for tort liability are formulated in statutes and that these rules appear to be relatively uniform. However, because statutory rules have to be interpreted in case law, the actual situation does not differ greatly from that of common law.

In general, the following two conditions hold for the existence of fault liability in the civil law tradition:

1. There must be an intentional or negligent act or an omission that violates a legally protected right or interest of another person.
2. The unlawful act or omission must have caused damage of a type which qualifies for compensation.

The various civil law jurisdictions differ in the manner in which they specify what counts as such a violation of a legally protected interest. The French *Code Civil* keeps it simple, with two provisions:

Code Civil, Article 1382
Any act whatever of a person, which causes damage to another, obliges him by whose fault (faute) the damage was caused to compensate it.

Code Civil, Article 1383
Everyone is liable for the damage he has caused not only by his act, but also by his negligence or by his carelessness (imprudence).

The *Code Civil* is not very specific about which acts lead to liability. This is different with the German *Bürgerliches Gesetzbuch*. The following central provision gives an example:

Bürgerliches Gesetzbuch § 823
1. A person who intentionally or negligently, unlawfully injures the life, body, health, freedom, property, or another right of another person, is obliged to compensate the other party for the damage arising there from.

2. The same duty arises for a person who infringes a statutory provision intended to protect another. If, according to the contents of the statute, an infringement is possible even without fault, the duty to compensate only arises if the case of fault.

The Dutch *Burgerlijk Wetboek* compromises between the abstraction of the *Code Civil* and the concreteness of the *Bürgerliches Gesetzbuch*:

Burgerlijk Wetboek, Article 6:162
1. He who commits a wrongful act against another, which can be attributed to him, is obliged to compensate the damage suffered by that other as a consequence thereof.
2. An act counts as wrongful if it is a violation of a right, or if it is an act or omission contrary to a legal duty or to what is socially acceptable according to unwritten law, unless there is a ground of justification.

Different as these provisions may be, they have in common that they protect individual rights and interests against both intentional and negligent violations.

4   Strict Liability

Strict liability exists when somebody is liable for damage that was not caused by his or her own wrongful act. It is possible to distinguish two kinds of situations:
1. Liability for damage caused by someone else's act (▶ Sect. 4.1)
2. Liability without a tort-feasor for damage caused by a defective or dangerous thing or activity (▶ Sect. 4.2).

Strict liability requires a specific basis in legislation or case law; there is no general liability for damage caused by somebody else's act or damage caused by a defective or dangerous thing or activity, in the way that there is a general liability for damage caused by one's own unlawful acts.

4.1   Liability for Damage Caused by Other Persons

Cellar Hatch, HR 05-11-1965, NJ 1966, 136
Mr. Sjouwerman was an employee of the Coca-Cola Company. He made a delivery to 'De Munt', an Amsterdam pub. He left the

cellar hatch of the pub open whilst making his delivery. Mathieu Duchateau was a customer having a beer at 'De Munt'. He fell through the open cellar hatch when he was on his way to the men's room, and he had to be taken to hospital. Mr. Duchateau claimed compensation from the Coca-Cola Company, adducing that Mr. Sjouwerman had not taken sufficient precautions because he left the cellar hatch open.

Why would the Coca-Cola company be liable for the fault of Mr. Sjouwerman? There is both a brief and a long answer to this question. The brief answer is a description of the law as it actually is, while the longer answer addresses the issue of why the law is what it is. The brief answer is that according to the law of many jurisdictions, including Dutch law, employers are liable for damage that is negligently caused by their employees in the course of their employment. This is called «vicarious liability».

Vicarious liability

If Mr. Sjouwerman was negligent, the Coca-Cola company as his employer would therefore be liable for the resulting damage.

The longer answer addresses the question why someone should be liable for damages caused by other persons. In many jurisdictions, strict liability does not only exist for employers with regard to their employees but also for parents with regard to their children. The first observation in this situation is that a person who is liable for damages caused by someone else must have a special relation to this person. Normally, this is a relationship where one has the ability to influence the behavior of the other. An employer has this relationship with his employee, and parents have this relationship with their children.

There are two possibilities for liability in this situation, depending on whether the employers or the parents did something wrong themselves. If the employer or the parent did something wrong, for instance, a lack of supervision, they would be liable for their own faults, and not for the faults of their employees or children.

In Germany, this form of fault liability is the way in which employers can be liable for the wrongs of their employees and parents for their children. In England, such fault liability is the basis on which parents and teachers may be liable for damages brought about by their children and pupils, respectively.

In most legal systems, the basic requirements for employer liability are:

1. The employee must have been at fault, which means that he acted intentionally or negligently.
2. The employer must have had sufficient power of direction and control over the employee's activities.
3. The harm must have been caused in the course of the employment.

Century Insurance C v Northern Ireland Transport Board ([1942] AC 509)

Davison was employed by the Transport Board as driver of a petrol tanker. While petrol was being pumped from his truck into the underground tank of a petrol station, he lit a cigarette and threw the match on the ground. This caused a fire and finally an explosion which resulted in significant damage to property.

Was his employer vicariously liable for Davison's conduct? Did Davison act in the course of his employment in lighting his cigarette? The Court of Appeal found that the driver was acting in the course of his employment. The House of Lords upheld the judgment of the Court of Appeal. One of the lords, Viscount Simon, put it this way:

Davison's duty was to watch over the delivery of the spirit into the tank, to see that it did not overflow and to turn off the tap when the proper quantity had passed from the tanker. Waiting and watching was part of his duties. That is why his act – throwing the match on the ground - was within his course of employment. The course of employment broadly comprised all acts done concomitantly to the accomplishment of the tasks which were entrusted to the employee.

Deep Pocket Theory

Placing liability on someone other than the tort-feasor also has an advantage for the victim who suffered the damages, namely, that she is protected against insolvency of the tort-feasor. Parents tend to have more money than their children, and employers are often wealthier than their employees. They are also usually insured against liability. The idea that if the circumstances allow it, liability should be placed where the money is, is known as the «deep pocket theory».

There are also other reasons for making employers and parents liable. One is that the employer sometimes benefits from the torts of the employee – e.g., speeding to arrive faster to serve the next customer. As such, it is fair to make the employer liable for the negative consequences.

Another reason is that the liability of employers and parents makes it possible to take this liability away from employees and children, for whom the damages might not be bearable.

All of the mentioned reasons illustrate that liability for damage is not always a matter of restoring the situation before the damage occurred by the person who is held responsible for creating the damage. Sometimes it is a matter of distributive justice and of policy considerations that give content to this kind of justice.

4.2   Liability Without Tort-Feasor

It happens quite often that an event causes damage and that this is not due to someone's intentional or negligent behavior. In that case the principle that everyone has to bear his own damage plays a central role. However, there are a number of cases in which the law requires that the damage should be shifted to somebody other than the victim. These cases have in common that the person who becomes liable is somehow either responsible for, or profits from, the fact that there is a possibility of faultless damage. Typical examples concern damage brought about by animals or by objects which are dangerous by nature or defective.

By keeping an animal, the keeper creates the risk that this animal will cause damage. As such, there is reason to hold the keeper of this animal liable when the actual damage was caused, even if the keeper did not do anything wrong. Similarly, the owner of a car creates the risk that the car will cause damage, even if the owner is not driving or at fault in a particular case. Cars make society more dangerous, and this is a reason to hold car owners liable. They profit from these danger-creating objects, even when they do not act intentionally or negligently.

Whereas fault liability relates to the obligation to pay damages for wrongful behavior on the side of the tort-feasor, this link between liability and fault is not present in the case of strict liability. As for deciding between fault and strict liability, it is necessary to first establish the criteria on which the choice is to be determined. When we are dealing with the liability for defective products, for example, there are reasons in favor of strict liability. These reasons are that strict liability may offer:

Reasons for Strict Liability

- More protection for the injured party
- An incentive for improving safety
- Better options for insurance
- Fewer problems in determining liability, which saves procedural costs

Differences Between
Countries

There are no general rules for strict liability. Every rule of strict liability has its own requirements, and there are substantial differences between countries with regard to the question which kinds of strict liabilities are recognized. We have already seen that English law hardly recognizes any strict liabilities. France on the contrary recognizes many kinds of strict liability – including strict liabilities for holders of motor vehicles, for custodians of dangerous or defective things, and for the owners of animals. Here, fault liability has become relatively less important in cases of personal injury and property loss.

5   Mechanisms for the Distribution of Damage

Sometimes the law chooses not to leave damages with the victim, nor does it shift the burden to another person. It rather distributes the damage over society, either as a whole or in part. In this connection, we will take a look at two such mechanisms: insurance and damage funds.

5.1   Insurance

Tort law regulates the shift of damage from the original bearer of the damage to somebody else. This other person or organization may be someone who caused the damage intentionally or negligently (fault liability) or someone who is responsible for another person or for a dangerous or defective object regardless of whether they acted intentionally or negligently (strict liability). This last kind of liability may seem unfair, but this seeming unfairness is often mitigated by insurance, a mechanism for the distribution of damage over a larger group of persons. People who insure themselves against damage pay a premium to an insurance company and receive in return the right to be compensated for the kinds of damage against which they insured themselves. Typical examples are health insurance and home insurance.

Many kinds of insurance are voluntary but some are mandatory. Car owners typically have to insure themselves for their liability to victims of accidents in which their cars are involved. This kind of mandatory insurance may be combined with strict liability. The result of this combination of strict liability and compulsory insurance is that the damage of accidents in which cars are involved is distributed over all car owners. In this way car owners, as a collective, pay for the damage which occurs as result of the introduction of cars into society. Those who profit from the benefits of cars must pay for their drawbacks.

5.2   Damage Funds

Another mechanism for the distribution of damage over society is damage funds from which damage to individual persons or groups of persons can (in part) be compensated. For example, Article 3 of the European Convention on the Compensation of Victims of Violent Crime imposes on member states who are parties to the convention the duty to compensate by and large the nationals of member states who fall victim to intentional crimes of violence, who have suffered bodily injury or impairment of health, or are the dependents of persons who have died as a result of such crimes. Moreover, the Council of the European Union has issued a directive relating to compensation for the victims of crime (Council Directive 2004/80/EC of 29 April 2004). If the states pay this compensation from tax money, the damage of the victims is distributed over all tax payers.

Another example is the Canadian Environmental Damages Fund. The money for this fund stems from, among others, fines and court orders and is used to benefit the environment and pay for the restoration of damage. This fund follows the principle that the polluter pays; the compensation for the damage to the environment is not distributed over all tax payers but rather over those forced by the government to contribute to the fund because they are guilty of pollution.

6   Limitations

The main rule in connection to damage is that everybody bears his or her own damage. Liability of others is the exception, and exceptions tend to have limitations. Apart from the general requirements for fault liability and strict liability, these limitations concern:

- The persons who can shift their damage to somebody else (► Sect. 1)
- The defense that the damage should also be attributed to the person who suffered it (► Sect. 2)
- The kinds of damage that can be shifted (► Sect. 3)
- The extent to which damage can be shifted (► Sect. 4)

6.1   Who Can Shift Their Damage?

If somebody is in principle liable for damage that results from an act or omission, or from some other event for which they are (strictly) liable, this does not automatically mean that everybody who suffered such damage can claim compensation. Only those persons whose interests are protected by law can claim compensation.

For instance, a football player tackles his opponent in an unlawful manner. The opponent is injured, and because the tackle was extraordinarily unfair, the person who made it must compensate the damage of his opponent. Suppose that the victim of the tackle was the best player of his team and that as a result of the tackle his team lost the match. An outsider who had placed a bet that this team would win loses money. Can she ask for compensation of this lost money? No, she cannot, because the rule that forbids unfair tackles is there to protect potential victims of such tackles against bodily harm, but not outsiders who happen to place bets on the outcome of football matches.

6.2   Contributory Negligence

Somebody who is liable for damage caused by negligent behavior can sometimes avoid being liable for all the damage by pointing out that part of the damage can be attributed to the negligent behavior of the victim.

For instance, a person who violated a traffic rule and thereby caused an accident may be liable for less than the victim's full damage if he can show that the victim could have avoided the accident if only he would have paid more attention.

In such a case, we speak of «contributory negligence» as a reason to divide the damage over the tort-feasor and the victim in proportion of the way they each contributed to the damage.

6.3   Recoverable Damage

Not all kinds of damage qualify for compensation in connection with all kinds of damage-causing events. Some kinds of damage lend themselves better to compensation than others, and some kinds of damage will be compensated to a greater extent than others. This differentiation between kinds of damage is made explicit in the Principles of European Tort Law (PETL).

The Principles of European Tort Law are nonbinding rules, drafted by a group of lawyers, aimed at finding the common core of tort law.

Article 2:101 of the PETL provides a definition of recoverable damage: damage according to the PETL consists of material or immaterial harm to a legally protected interest.

What constitutes a protected interest is subsequently indicated in:

Protected Interest

Article 2:102 PETL:
1. The scope of protection of an interest depends on its nature; the higher its value, the precision of its definition and its obviousness, the more extensive its protection.
2. Life, bodily or mental integrity, human dignity and liberty enjoy the most extensive protection.
3. Extensive protection is granted to property rights, including those in intangible property.
4. Protection of pure economic interests or contractual relationships may be more limited in scope. In such cases, due regard must be had especially to the proximity between the agent and the endangered person, or to the fact that the agent is aware of the fact that he will cause damage even though his interests are necessarily valued lower than those of the victim.
5. The scope of protection may also be affected by the nature of liability, so that an interest may receive more extensive protection against intentional harm than in other cases.
6. In determining the scope of protection, the interests of the agent, especially in liberty of action and in exercising his rights, as well as public interests also have to be taken into consideration.

► Sections 2 and 3 make clear that the protection of the human body and mind goes further than the protection of property rights such as rights in material goods, copyrights, and patents.

A person who is wounded in a car accident may also begin to suffer psychosomatic effects, such as a change in character, weakness in mental performance, speech disturbances, paralysis, and reduction in libido. The German Bundesgerichtshof (April 9th, 1991) decided that if these defects could be attributed to the accident (which was probable), they should be taken into account in determining the amount of immaterial damages which could be compensated.

The protection of purely economic interest does not extend far. An example of a purely economic interest would be the loss of income suffered by a driver (e.g., travelling salesmen) who was caught in a traffic jam caused by a car accident. The chances are slim that the tort-feasor who caused the car accident will also have to pay for this pure economic loss.

If a person is injured and as a consequence cannot work for some time, the damage is not a purely economic interest anymore, since it is connected to a noneconomic interest, namely, physical integrity. The compensation of such damages is handled under the category of bodily integrity and therefore tends to be allowed more easily.

Losses of Third Persons   In the Draft Frame of Common Reference (DCFR), a project led by the German professor Christian Von Bar and partly financed by the European Commission, we find a special provision for «Loss suffered by third persons as a result of another's personal injury or death».

Book VI, Article 2:202:
1. Non-economic loss caused to a natural person as a result of another's personal injury or death is legally relevant damage if at the time of injury that person is in a particularly close personal relationship to the injured person.
2. Where a person has been fatally injured:
    Legally relevant damage caused to the deceased on account of the injury to the time of death becomes legally relevant damage to the deceased's successors;

    Reasonable funeral expenses are legally relevant damages to the person incurring them; and
    Loss of maintenance is legally relevant damage to a natural person whom the deceased maintained or, had the death not occurred, would have maintained under statutory provisions or to whom the deceased provided care and financial support.

Comparable provisions can be found in many jurisdictions, either in a civil code or in the case law.

6.4   Causation

Even if the victim and the kind of damage qualify for compensation, it is still possible that the damage will not be shifted. This is the case if the damage was not caused by the act or event on which the claim for compensation was based. It seems obvious that damage which was not caused by such an event does not qualify for compensation.

For instance, if somebody causes a car accident, this person does not have to pay for the damage of an unrelated person who happens to have lost his job.

However, sometimes there is a causal link from a damage-causing event to a particular damage, and yet this damage is not attributed to the event in question. That may, for instance, happen if the causal link is too long, or too unlikely, or if there was an intervening act. An example that illustrates all three possibilities is the following:

Fireman Pierre participates in an illegal strike and does not extinguish a fire in a house that was assigned to him. The house burns down completely. The house owner is not insured and must move to another smaller house. His wife does not like the new house and divorces him. Their children need psychological care because of their parents' divorce, and the mother, who had to pay for this care, demands compensation from Pierre. Pierre may not be liable for the costs of the psychological care, first because the chain from his unlawful act to the costs is too long, second because the consequence is rather unlikely (nobody could have predicted those costs), and third, the divorce may be considered to be an intervening act which interrupts the causal chain between the strike and the costs for the psychologist.

7 Conclusion

Liability law consists of rules that specify whether and under which circumstances exceptions are to be made to the basic rule that everybody bears his own damage. One major category of exceptions concerns situations where one person intentionally or negligently causes damage to another person. In such a case, fault liability requires that the former, the tortfeasor, compensates the damage of the latter. The situation that existed before the tort must be restored as much as possible, at least financially.

The other major category can only be defined negatively. It concerns cases where some person is liable for damage of somebody else, even though he did not intentionally or negligently cause that damage. These cases represent strict liability (in one of the variants adopted in the legal systems). Strict liability may concern damage caused by animals or by dangerous or defective objects. It may also concern damage caused by a third person for whom the liable person is held responsible. Where the rules for fault liability are by and large the same in most civil law and common law countries, there are major differences between countries where the rules for strict liability are concerned.

Recommended Literature

Van Dam C (2013) European tort law, 2nd edn. Oxford University Press, Oxford

Van Gerven W, Lever WJ, Larouche P (eds) (2000) Tort law, common law of Europe casebooks series. Hart Publishing, Oxford

Criminal Law

Johannes Keiler, Michele Panzavolta, and David Roef

© Springer International Publishing Switzerland 2017
J. Hage et al. (eds.), *Introduction to Law*, DOI 10.1007/978-3-319-57252-9_7

1 Introduction: The Nature and Function of Criminal Law

Crime and criminal law arguably constitute omnipresent topics in our society. Issues of criminal justice and criminal policy often feature prominently in political discussions and election campaigns. Citizens demand security from their governments and criminal law seems one suitable tool for the task of providing it.

Humans have always construed societies dependent on some social order and have developed rules to assure the continuity of that orderly society and to protect its members. Crudely put, criminal law can be defined as a body of rules by which the State prohibits certain forms of conduct because it harms or threatens public safety and welfare and that imposes punishment for the commission of such acts.

Already early Babylonian law as well as the Roman Twelve Tables and the Ten Commandments of the Christian Bible included rules on crimes such as theft, adultery, rape, murder, etc. However, it would be a fallacy to believe that contemporary criminal law is still confined to these traditional and most prominent forms of wrongdoing. In modern society the realm of criminal law has been considerably extended and nowadays also covers a multitude of fields spanning from environmental and economic crimes to tax and traffic offenses, and more.

Two prominent features of criminal law distinguish it from other branches of law. On the one hand, criminal law deals with so-called public wrongs as opposed to private wrongs (with which civil law is concerned). Crimes are socially proscribed wrongs which concern the community as a whole. This fundamental principle also shows itself if one compares criminal law with civil law cases. A criminal law case is between the whole political community, the State or the people, and the defendant. It expresses a hierarchical relationship between the State and the individual who is called to answer for his wrongful and blameworthy behavior. Conversely, civil law cases take place between two equal parties, and it is up to the person who was wronged to seek legal redress. *Crimes as Public Wrongs*

Furthermore, perhaps the most important difference to other branches of law is that a violation of the rules of criminal law commonly triggers the imposition of public censure and (severe) punishment. However, the imposition of criminal punishment constitutes a severe encroachment on an individual's freedom and autonomy and should therefore not be imposed lightly and only as a last resort (*ultima ratio*). *Punishment and Censure*

A popular folk conception of criminal law takes a victim-centered view and perceives criminal law as an instrument of retaliation. By means of criminal law, the perpetrators of (heinous) crimes receive the punishment they deserve for their criminal deeds. However, such a view is oversimplistic and forgets that criminal law is also and perhaps more importantly an instrument of both social control and control of governmental power. It protects not only society against crime but also the human rights of citizens, including criminals, against a too intrusive State.

Criminal law influences and regulates behavior in a way we see fit in our society. This is done by limiting and protecting freedoms at the same time. Criminal law creates freedom for human beings by protecting important interests, for instance, property rights. On the other hand, it limits freedoms by closely circumscribing their scope and boundaries. Criminal law protects property by prohibiting unlawful appropriation, theft, for instance, but also circumscribes the scope of the usage of this property by proscribing that no other human being wrongfully ought to be harmed by it.

Criminal Law: Between the Sword and the Shield

In the light of the foregoing it becomes apparent that criminal law has two functions which require delicate balancing. On the one hand, it is a tool to maintain public order and control deviant social behavior; on the other hand, its function is to canalize and circumscribe the application of coercive measures and punishment in legally determined channels that respect basic human rights. Thus, criminal law functions on the one hand as a tool of the State against its citizens to control deviant behavior and on the other hand as a tool of the citizens against repressive State powers. In other words, criminal law has both a crime control function (sword) as well as a safeguard function (shield) in our democratic society.

Questions

After this brief introduction to the nature and function of criminal law, this chapter sets out to discuss a number of central questions of criminal law and criminal procedure. The first question, addressed in ▶ Sect. 2, is how we can or ought to decide which conduct should amount to a criminal offense in a liberal society. Subsequently, in ▶ Sect. 3 we will dwell on how the most salient feature of criminal law, i.e., the imposition of punishment, can be justified.

The approaches of criminal justice systems can at first sight seem quite diverse, but one may wonder if it is nevertheless possible to unearth some basic structure of crime. ▶ Sect. 4 will therefore try to answer the question as to what the basic structure of a criminal offense looks like. In ▶ Sect. 5 we will subsequently discuss which objective elements need to be fulfilled in order for criminal liability to arise. The sixth question to be answered relates to the mindset or state of mind with which a person needs to act in order for criminal liability to arise. Must it always be one's purpose to achieve a certain goal, or will sometimes inadvertence also suffice for imposing criminal liability? These questions will among others be discussed in ▶ Sect. 6. Afterward we will turn to liability negating circumstances. Will killing another human being, stealing, or destroying property always and inevitably lead to criminal liability, or does criminal law perhaps also accept exceptions to the legal commandment: Thou shall not kill or steal? This will be the topic of ▶ Sect. 7.

As this is an introductory chapter on criminal law, we focus only on some concepts and doctrines related to the criminal liability of one single perpetrator, like in the example given above. We have purposely left out any questions regarding the more complex scenario of the liability of multiple perpetrators, such as accomplices and others that contribute to the realization of an offense.

The last sections of the chapter deal with the law of criminal procedure. ▶ Sect. 8 addresses the question what interests are at stake in the criminal process. ▶ Sect. 9 seeks to answer the question of what the basic structure of the criminal process looks like, while ▶ Sect. 10 discusses how the criminal justice systems can be categorized according to their features. ▶ Sect. 11 revolves around the cornerstone principle of the presumption of innocence and explores what it means for an individual to be presumed innocent. The chapter will end with some brief concluding remarks (▶ Sect. 12).

2   Which Conduct Ought to Be Criminal?: The Criminalization Debate

It has been explained above that among others criminal law is a mechanism for the preservation of social order. A fundamental preliminary question in this connection is which forms of conduct should rightly be dealt with by means of criminal law? To criminalize a certain kind of conduct is to declare that it amounts to a public wrong and that therefore it ought to be avoided. To provide a pragmatic incentive to adhere to its rules, criminal law uses public censure and punishment as a sanction to rule violations. The consequences of violating criminal norms are so onerous and severe for citizens that the decision to criminalize conduct should never be taken lightly and should always require the careful consideration of a variety of competing interests and factors. Failure to do so may not only lead to overcriminalization – it is, for instance, a criminal offense now in the Netherlands for a person under 18 to possess or consume alcoholic beverages in public places – but it may also create an oppressive criminal justice system.

Unfortunately there exists no ready-made formula by which we can determine whether or not criminal law should be used in a certain situation. There is no single master principle from which the content of criminal law can be derived. The range of actual and potential crimes is simply so wide and varied that this seems unattainable. In practice we will therefore have to accept that the boundaries of criminal law are not fixed but are rather socially, historically, and politically determined. Consider, for instance, that adultery and witchcraft were once well-established criminal wrongs, while it was at the same time considered to be legally impossible for a husband to rape his wife. Since then the views of society and accordingly the law have drastically changed. Nevertheless it remains important to identify interests that are generally thought to warrant the use of criminal law and refine notions such as harm and wrongdoing which usually influence and inform the criminalization debate within criminal justice systems.

The Minimalist Principle

Fundamental in this connection is the minimalist principle, which holds that criminal law should only be used as a last resort (*ultima ratio*). Morality, social convention, peer pressure, but also civil (law of tort or contract) and administrative law are other (informal) techniques of control. In many instances it seems preferable to leave the enforcement of certain forms of behavior to those techniques. The State's most powerful weapon should be used scarcely – Thor's hammer was simply not meant to drive nails!

The Principle of Individual Autonomy

A further important principle within the criminalization debate is that of *individual autonomy*. The principle is central to most liberal political theories and essentially holds that citizens should be free from undue State powers in making their own choices and should be the masters of their own fate. This arguably limits the creation of offenses based on paternalistic grounds, i.e., offenses where the State deprives citizens of individual choice, supposedly for their own good. Many drug offenses (including alcohol and tobacco laws) are, for instance, often based on paternalistic considerations.

The Principle of Welfare

However, the principle of autonomy is certainly not absolute. Besides issues such as whose autonomy should function as a yardstick (e.g., the autonomy of men and women, the rich or the poor, respectively), it is evident that a citizen will never be able to fully exercise his/her autonomy if the State fails to create the necessary conditions for the exercise of autonomy. Certain collective goals and interests, such as environmental protection, economic and financial stability, and food and product safety, are pivotal in a society and therefore also warrant protection by criminal law.

This line of thought often finds expression in the *principle of welfare*, which emphasizes the social context in which the law must operate. It gives weight to collective goals and interests such as protecting the environment we live in or maintaining law and order in society. The principle of welfare and the principle of individual autonomy should however not be perceived as opposites but rather as connected and mutually interdependent principles. They deserve careful consideration within the criminalization debate. When do the needs of the many really outweigh the needs of the few? While there clearly can be conflicts between the two principles, they can also cooperate. If the principle of individual autonomy is taken to require that people are free to and can peruse their own goals (positive liberty), the principle of welfare may work toward the same end by protecting common facilities (e.g., schools), structures (e.g., unemployment or pension schemes), and systems (e.g., the tax or criminal justice system), from which citizens benefit.

In any case, the central notion and starting point of any criminalization debate is the *harm principle*. In the words of John Stuart Mill: «[…] the only purpose for which power can be rightfully exercised over any member of a civilized community, against his will, is to prevent harm to others.»

The Harm Principle

The principle was initially designed to prevent the criminalization of conduct exclusively based on moral or paternalistic grounds. Conduct which may be immoral (such as adultery), but which is not harmful to others, should not be the concern of criminal law, so the argument runs. However, the problem is that the notion of harm is a very flexible one. How can we define harm properly so that it retains a critical and limiting dimension? It seems obvious that if we define harm as «harm to society», almost any conduct could fit under this definition.

The counterpart to the harm principle can be found in *legal moralism*. It seems evident that criminal law has close ties to morality. Crimes such as murder or rape arguably criminalize moral wrongdoing and are therefore almost universally condemned. One may therefore wonder if the simple fact that a certain conduct is considered morally wrong is in itself already sufficient to criminalize it.

Legal Moralism

In practice morality is certainly influential for the criminalization of some forms of behavior. Consider, for instance, the offenses of bestiality (a.k.a. animal sex), disturbing a funeral, or desecration of graves, which are arguably to a large extent founded on moral values. Yet, reliance on morality is inherently problematic for a variety of reasons. First, we would need to determine which morals are to guide the criminalization debate: liberal morals, communist morals, or the morals of the church or other religious groups? Second, moral values are subject to constant changes and are therefore problematic to guide the legal debate. For many years public nudity was, for instance, prohibited as it was considered immoral, but nowadays in Europe nudity, for instance, on beaches hardly raises eyebrows anymore. In addition contentious issues such as abortion, prostitution, and euthanasia are the subject of a diverse and shifting debate in modern multicultural societies, which makes it doubtful that morality will always provide a good compass to explore the limits of criminal law.

The principles outlined above all deserve careful consideration and should guide and inform the political debate with regard to the creation of new offenses. Unfortunately in practice it is often political opportunism as well as moral outrage and panic in society, rather than a carefully balanced principled approach, that drives the creation of new offenses.

3   Theories of Legal Punishment

Since punishment involves pain or deprivation of some fundamental rights (e.g., freedom), its intentional imposition by the State requires justification: what could justify a State in using criminal law to inflict burdensome sanctions upon its citizens when they violate certain legal rules? In the philosophical and political debate, one may distinguish two main types of theories of punishment: utilitarian and retributive. On purpose we leave out some mixed or hybrid theories and theories that give alternatives to criminal sanctions, like restorative justice.

3.1   Utilitarian Theories

Consequentialism

According to Jeremy Bentham's classical utilitarianism, laws should be used to maximize the happiness of society. This means that punishment can only be justified if the harm that it prevents outweighs the harm it creates through punishing the offender. The State should therefore only inflict as much punishment as is needed to prevent future crimes. Utilitarian theories are «consequentialist» in nature; they are all forward-looking theories of punishment as criminal sanctions are only justified when they have beneficial consequences, like deterrence of criminal behavior. If the realization of such future-oriented goals fails to occur or has more negative side effects, a utilitarian justification for punishment may be absent.

Major utilitarian rationales for punishment are *individual deterrence* and *general deterrence*. Individual or specific deterrence punishes an offender in order to prevent the same person from re-offending. General deterrence uses the threat or example of punishment to discourage other people from committing crimes. A recent example of an attempt at general deterrence is that most European systems have significantly increased the penalties for driving under the influence of alcohol in order to deter citizens from drunk driving. {Deterrence}

In discussing whether punishment has a deterrent effect, critics point out that the high recidivism rates of persons sentenced to prison are evidence of a lack of effectiveness of individual deterrence. There are also some limits to the effect of general deterrence. This theory assumes that human beings are rational, autonomous individuals who are always able to calculate the risk of being caught and convicted for the commission of an offense. Critics consider this to be an unrealistic view, arguing that most people remain law abiding, not because they fear criminal sanctions, but as a result of moral inhibitions and socially accepted norms of conduct. Moreover, some crimes, such as sexual offenses and crimes committed under the influence of drugs, can hardly be deterred as their perpetrators do not rationally weigh the benefits versus the costs before breaking the law.

Another utilitarian rationale for punishment is rehabilitation. The object of rehabilitation is to prevent future crime by giving offenders the necessary treatment and training that enables them to return to society as law-abiding members of the community. We may think here of programs that will teach prison inmates how to control their crime-producing urges, like the tendency to abuse drugs or alcohol or to commit sex crimes (e.g., pedophilia). Part of a classical rehabilitation program is usually that an offender will be released on probation under some conditions. {Rehabilitation}

3.2   Retributive Theories

The counterpart to utilitarian goals of punishment is retribution. According to retributive theories, offenders are punished for their crimes because they *deserve* punishment.

Crime Deserves Punishment

Where utilitarians look forward by basing punishment on social benefits, retributionists look backward at the crime itself as the rationale for punishment. According to retributive theories, there is an intrinsic moral link between punishment and guilt. Punishment is therefore primarily a question of responsibility for the crime committed (just desert) and not of beneficial consequences. One of the best-known ancient forms of retributive thinking can be found in the *lex talionis* of Biblical times: «an eye for an eye, a tooth for a tooth, and a life for a life». One should be punished because a crime has been committed, and the punishment should be proportional to the seriousness of the offense and the degree of culpability of the offender: «Let the punishment fit the crime» captures the essence of retribution.

Justice or Vengeance?

The main criticism against retribution is that the fundamental question why an offender deserves to be punished in the first place is not that easy to answer. Retribution may reflect a basic intuition of justice – what goes around comes around – but it may in fact be nothing more than a rationalized desire for vengeance. In short, how can we prove this alleged moral link between crime and punishment? Is it not strange to believe that the moral balance disturbed by an evil act (crime) can simply be restored by inflicting upon the offender another evil (punishment)? Some retributionists attempt to answer this question by viewing the offender as a person who has taken an unfair advantage of others in society by committing a crime and by assuming that punishment restores fairness. If society would allow a person who violates the law to continue to enjoy the illegal benefits, he would be given an unfair advantage over citizens who do obey the law.

Others argue that punishment is justified because retribution is society's way of expressing and communicating through the apparatus of criminal law a moral disapproval of certain transgressions. Punishment thus functions as a means of societal condemnation and denunciation.

To conclude this section, we should note that there is no such thing as an ultimate theory of punishment. In practice the modern European conception of punishment is a pragmatic combination of utilitarian and retributive theories. However, it is interesting to see that the last three decades, there is a revival of retributivist thinking, of the idea that the justification of punishment lies in its intrinsic character as a deserved response to crime. However, much depends also on the nature of the crime. For instance, the punishment of economic crimes, like tax fraud, is more motivated by deterrence than by retribution.

4   The Structure of a Crime

4.1   The Actus Reus and Mens Rea Dichotomy

Although penal laws differ greatly from country to country, it is nevertheless possible to discover on a doctrinal level some striking similarities among different criminal justice systems. It seems, for instance, to be a general principle of law that the attribution of liability generally requires an analysis of two aspects. Each crime can be split into an *actus reus*, the objective element of a crime, and a *mens rea*, the mental or subjective element of the crime. The offense of murder is, for instance, often defined as the intentional killing of another human being. In this case, the *actus reus* consists of killing another person, while the *mens rea* element of this offense requires that the perpetrator did so intentionally.

In order to be liable for murder, a perpetrator needs to fulfill both the *mens rea* and the *actus reus* requirement. This legal demand often finds expression in the famous Latin phrase *actus non facit reum nisi mens sit rea,* which can loosely be translated as «an act does not make a man guilty unless his mind is (also) guilty».

This important dichotomy in criminal law arguably stems from the distinction between the objective or tangible side of a person's conduct, which is susceptible to objective assessment, and the intangible, subjective side of a person's conduct, i.e., his state of mind, which is not. Furthermore, as modern criminal law has its roots in the tradition of the Enlightenment, the very effort to distinguish between objective and subjective elements of criminality rests on the old Cartesian conception that human beings consist of two separate elements, i.e., a mind and a body.

In order to be held criminally liable, the elements generally need to be present simultaneously, as a person cannot be held liable in a liberal society for conduct which he did not intend and at most contemplated (thoughts are free). This basic distinction between *actus reus* and *mens rea* is however not a hard and fast one, and it should be kept in mind that the two notions are best viewed as conceptual tools under the umbrella of which a multitude of different doctrines are pigeonholed. The *actus reus* element is generally considered to include the doctrine of conduct, including omissions, as well as the doctrine of causation (see ▶ Sect. 5). The different gradations of intention, recklessness, and negligence are frequently discussed under the heading of *mens rea* (see ▶ Sect. 6).

4.2   The Bipartite Structure of Crime

Criminal liability is often assessed according to a certain structure or framework. Legal theorists have developed two distinct ways of thinking about the internal structure of criminal offenses. Common law courts have traditionally followed a bipartite structure, simply distinguishing between objective (external) and subjective (internal) aspects of crime. Thus, the framework for assessing liability in this case simply requires that the two basic elements of a criminal offense, i.e., *actus reus* and *mens rea* are fulfilled.

Although the bipartite system offers the convenience of theoretical simplicity, it also has some inherent shortcomings. For one, it fails to account for the entire range of defenses that are grouped under the categories of justification and excuses. Notions such as self-defense or insanity show many complexities that cannot easily be analyzed as part of either *actus reus* or *mens rea*.

A related but nevertheless distinct problem is that this approach seems to conflate the concept of *mens rea* with (moral) blameworthiness. The two concepts arguably denote different things, however. A person could have fulfilled the *actus reus* of a criminal offense with the corresponding *mens rea* but still escape liability due to the absence of blameworthiness. Just think of a person who fatally stabs his wife with a knife. From an objective point of view, the *actus reus* and *mens rea* requirements of murder seem clearly fulfilled here. The defendant killed another human being (*actus reus*), and he did so intentionally (*mens rea*). However, whether he can also be blamed for this offense is an entirely different question. It is, for instance, conceivable that the person at the time of the offense suffered from delusions as an unexpected side effect of his multiple sclerosis medication, which would raise doubts as to his (personal) blameworthiness.

4.3   The Tripartite Structure of Crime

Many civil law systems, such as those of Germany and the Netherlands, have developed an entirely different framework for assessing criminal liability. According to the prevalent tripartite structure of crime, the assessment of criminal liability takes place in three stages. In stage one it needs to be assessed whether or not the legal elements of the statutory offense definition (including both *actus reus* and *mens rea*) have been fulfilled. In the second stage, the wrongfulness (*Rechtswidrigkeit*) of the conduct in question is assessed, while the third stage is devoted to assessing the blameworthiness of the defendant (*Schuld*). Thus, the issues in the tripartite framework of criminal liability line up in the following way:
1. Fulfillment of offense definition (*actus reus* and *mens rea*)
2. Wrongdoing
3. Blameworthiness

When it can be proven that a person has committed an act that falls within the definition of an offense, the presence of wrongdoing and blameworthiness is generally assumed. Only if exceptional circumstances present themselves wrongdoing or blameworthiness might be negated. A successful justificatory defense may, for instance, deny wrongdoing, while a successful excusatory defense is sought to deny blameworthiness (see also ▸ Sect. 7).

One critical feature of the tripartite system deserves emphasis here. In the bipartite framework of the common law, the ordering of the elements is not important. One can consider issues bearing on *mens rea* either before or after those related to the *actus reus*. In the tripartite system, on the other hand, the order is crucial. The offense definition needs to be evaluated first, followed by the requirements of wrongdoing and blameworthiness. The three are logically connected. A certain conduct can only be considered wrongful if it first fulfills the offense definition. Moreover, conduct can only be considered blameworthy if it is found to be wrongful. In other words, in the tripartite system there can be wrongdoing without blameworthiness, but there can never be blameworthiness without wrongdoing.

From a comparative perspective, an interesting question in this context is how the bipartite and the tripartite structure can be reconciled. The differences seem great on first sight, but matters may become clearer once we come to realize that the common law concept of *mens rea* carries a descriptive as

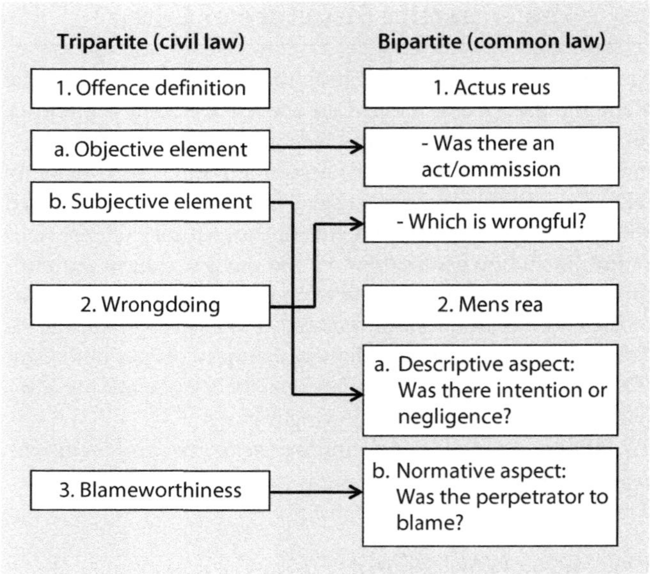

Fig. 7.1 The bipartite and tripartite systems

well as a normative connotation. On a descriptive level, *mens rea* simply refers to the question whether intention or negligence according to the offense definition can be established.

However, on a normative level, the term *mens rea* carries overtones of (moral) blameworthiness and refers to the question whether the offender can be blamed for his conduct. In the tripartite structure, the concept of *mens rea* in the first stage of the evaluation scheme is thus reduced to its purely descriptive connotation, while the normative aspect of the concept has been forged into a separate assessment category (stage 3). Likewise, the notion of wrongdoing is in common law systems often implied in the concept of *actus reus* which is often seen to require that the conduct in question was in violation of the law and thus wrongful. From a comparative perspective, the picture that emerges is that of **◘** Fig. 7.1: the bipartite and tripartite systems.

5   Actus Reus: Commission Versus Omission

It has already been indicated that under the label of *actus reus*, a variety of different doctrines are subsumed. One fundamental notion is the doctrine of conduct, also often referred to as the «act requirement». The doctrine of conduct traditionally plays an important role in establishing and describing general preconditions for liability. It has close ties to the principle of individual autonomy which constitutes a cornerstone of any liberal criminal justice system. The conduct requirement aims to ensure that the law treats citizens as responsible subjects, capable of rational choice, rather than objects of arbitrary State coercion. Holding people liable, for instance, because of their race, religious, political or sexual orientation, or their political affiliations, even though they did nothing wrongful, would not only fail to respect citizens' autonomy but would furthermore make the application of criminal law an arbitrary and oppressive enterprise. Therefore, all penal systems generally agree that the imposition of criminal liability requires at the very least some form of conduct, controlled by the perpetrator.

5.1 Offenses of Commission

However, the act requirement has caused some doctrinal frictions, because of the long-standing practice of defining action by looking at its superficial outward manifestation: the movements of limbs. Traditionally action in criminal law has been defined as «willed bodily movements». This theory is based on the dualistic concept of man as creatures of *animus* (mind) and *corpus* (body). In other words, the animus, i.e., the human will, is seen as the cause of physical action as willed bodily movements. The problems with this definition are manifold. First, the reliance on the joinder of movement and will presupposes a human being as the origin of action. However, in modern society many legal systems also impose punishment on corporations or other organizations for wrongdoing committed by these «legal entities». Just think of a company which intentionally pollutes the groundwater in order to cut costs. The conduct of these legal entities clearly does not fit into the description of conduct as willed bodily movements.

On a more philosophical level, further issues arise. The first one is nicely encapsulated by Wittgenstein's observation: [...] «when 'I raise my arm', my arm goes up. And the problem arises: what is left over if I subtract the fact that my arm goes up from the fact that I raise my arm?» It seems that we can only perceive the will by witnessing it in action. We thus end up in a definitional circle. We can only objectively perceive action and subsequently explain the action as a manifestation of the agent's will. According to this theory, action is thus assessed in a vacuum, disconnected from its social ramifications. This leads to questionable outcomes, as not nature alone determines what an act is but also the social context in which it occurs. Furthermore, it is arguably not the will that distinguishes mere movement from action but rather social definition. Many systems have therefore started to move away from the definition of action as willed bodily movements and nowadays adhere to a social theory of action in which action is interpreted in the social context in which it occurs. Meaning is not fixed; it is socially defined, so it is argued. The movement of a hand can thus in one context be interpreted as a greeting and in another as a threat.

5.2 Criminal Omissions: Liability in the Absence of Action

Be that as it may, the shortcomings of the «willed bodily movement definition» become particularly apparent in the context of omission liability. While in paradigmatic cases criminal conduct will undoubtedly involve bodily movements such as shooting, stabbing, stealing, etc., there are certain situations where liability may also arise out of a failure to act. Think, for instance, of a mother who omits to feed her child, leading to its starvation. It seems clear that criminal censure would be in order here, but adhering to a definition of action as willed bodily movement would imply that no liability can arise in the case of inaction.

Nevertheless, virtually all criminal justice systems accept that certain failures to act can give rise to criminal liability, albeit to different degrees. An omission can in this connection loosely be defined as a failure to act in situations in which the law would have required the perpetrator to act in a certain way. Liability for omissions always presupposes that the perpetrator in question violated a duty of care (toward the victim). For example, if a parent fails to feed her or his children, this may count as a criminal omission.

6 Mens Rea or the Subjective Element

Next to an *actus reus*, the objective element of a crime, most offenses require a *mens rea*, the mental or subjective element of a crime. Take, for example, the offense definition of manslaughter in Article 287 of the Dutch Criminal Code: «a person who intentionally takes the life of another is guilty of manslaughter». The taking of life is the actus reus of the crime, and the required intention as to that conduct is the necessary mens rea.

The term «*mens rea*» covers different subjective elements in order to distinguish relative degrees of fault, reflecting a difference in the reproach directed against the defendant. The exactly required *mens rea* standard may vary from crime to crime, but generally the more serious crimes require the strict *intention* requirement, while less serious offenses require a less culpable state of mind like *negligence*: Different Subjective Elements

Take for example homicide. Homicide can be committed intentionally or by negligence. It is reasonable that someone who really wants the death of the victim is considered more culpable than someone who causes the death of another by his carelessness.

Accordingly, people can be punished much more severely for intentional crimes than for negligence crimes.

Regarding the demarcation of the different subjective elements, the continental civil law systems, such as those of Germany and the Netherlands, distinguish only two major kinds of *mens rea*: intention and negligence. The English framework includes a third subjective element in between intention and negligence, which is called recklessness. Recklessness covers dangerous risk-taking and bridges the gap between the most serious and the lowest degree of *mens rea*. As we will see below, civil law systems bridge this gap by broadening the traditional concepts of intention and negligence.

6.1   Intention

Intention (or *dolus* in Latin) is considered the most serious kind of *mens rea* in all legal systems. Intention consists of knowing and wanting. Accordingly, the elements of intention can be distinguished in a cognitive part on the one hand and a volitional part on the other. Both elements are required, but depending on which of those aspects dominates, we can distinguish two main forms of intention: direct intent (*dolus directus*) and indirect intent (*dolus indirectus*).

This form of intent is characterized by a strong volitional element, where the consequence of an intention is actually desired. It is what we would consider to be intentional conduct in an everyday meaning: Direct Intent

For example, John shoots at Mike with a firearm because he wants to kill Mike. Whether he succeeds or not – John may happen to be a poor shooter, or the shot may not be lethal – John *desires* the death of Mike and is therefore acting with direct intent. The focus is on the will of the agent to bring about a certain result. And if Mike would as a matter of fact survive his wounds, John would still be liable for an attempt to homicide.

Indirect Intent

By contrast, indirect intent is characterized by a strong cognitive aspect and exists where the agent *knows* his conduct will *almost certainly* bring about the result, which he does not actually desire or primarily aim at.

For example, John burns down his villa in order to collect the insurance money for the building, while knowing that his 90 year old grandmother is still upstairs sleeping in her bedroom. John may not actually want the death of his grandmother – it is not his purpose to kill her – but her death is nevertheless an almost certain side-effect of his actions. Therefore, John directly intends the arson and indirectly intends to kill his grandmother.

Intent Is Not Motive

It is essential to realize that intention is in itself value-neutral and has nothing to do with motive. Intentionally killing a person refers to exactly that and not to killing because of an additional evil motive. Only in exceptional cases, e.g., hate crimes, the offense definition is drafted in such a manner that intent must relate also to a specific motive, e.g., racism, which confirms that the intent itself is indeed neutral.

To illustrate the general rule, take the example of Mark who blows up his wife's car to collect the life insurance money. His direct intent is to kill his wife and his motive is purely financial. This is however quite irrelevant to determine the required *mens rea*. He could have killed his wife for another reason, without this changing his direct intent. Arguably, his motives should be taken into account in the punishment, but not in the determination of intent.

Sometimes, the motive for committing a crime may even be considered morally praiseworthy.

Take for example the case where a son gives his mother an overdose of sleeping pills, intending to kill her because she is afflicted with terminal cancer which causes her terrible suffering. Some people would say that this man's motive is not bad at all and depending on the legal system it may even be relevant for making the decision on whether or not to prosecute this offence. However, there is no doubt that the son acted with direct intent.

6.2   Conditional Intent Versus Recklessness

The most problematic question regarding the required *mens rea* is what we should do with those actors who did not want the result or where it cannot be proven that they knew their conduct would almost certainly bring about the result:

Imagine that John gets involved in a bar fight and in the heat of the moment hits Mike several times on the head with an empty beer bottle. Mike loses consciousness and a few hours later he dies from his injuries. What should we do with John, accused of manslaughter, who argues that he did not want to kill, but merely to injure the victim? In such a case there can be no criminal liability based on direct or indirect intent. Neither would negligence really define John's actual state of mind, which is rather a case of taking a serious risk that the victim will die (as a consequence of being hit with a bottle) than mere carelessness.

An adequate protection of legal interests against dangerous risk-taking demands an additional subjective element in between negligence and (in)direct intention. Most continental legal systems have solved this problem by distinguishing a third type of intention next to direct and indirect intent, called conditional intent (*dolus eventualis*).

This form of intent can be defined as the conscious accep-   Conditional Intent
tance of a possible risk. *Dolus eventualis* is thus said to consist of:
1. A cognitive element of awareness of a risk
2. A volitional element of accepting the possibility that this risk would materialize

This lowest form of intention differs considerably in culpability in comparison to the other two forms, as the agent only knows about a risk that may materialize, but takes this risk for granted and acts anyway.

Think of a case where John shoots at Mike, but being a poor shooter he kills Mike's girlfriend Alice instead who is walking next to him. It is clear that John did not want the death of the actual victim, and neither did he know that it was almost certain that she would be hit by the bullet. Nevertheless, he was aware of the risk and accepted the possible but undesired consequence of Alice's death.

Recklessness

Common law systems, such as the English system, do not know the concept of conditional intent. They tend to apply a separate *mens rea* requirement for risk-taking, in between intent and negligence, called recklessness. Recklessness denotes the conscious taking of an unjustified risk.

An important difference between conditional intent and recklessness is that the latter does not require the volitional element of acceptance. It only needs to be proven that the defendant was aware of a risk, which was, in the circumstances known to him, unreasonable to take. Whereas conditional intent focuses on the *attitude* of the defendant (accepting the risk or taking it for granted), recklessness focuses on what he knew, his *awareness*. Cases of risk-taking that would not lead in continental legal systems to a liability based on conditional intent could therefore lead to reckless liability in England.

For instance, take the example of the two construction workers who dig a hole and fail to take the appropriate safety measures. If they omit to do this while believing that no one would fall in the pit, and someone gets injured anyways, this could in England be considered reckless behavior. However, in Germany or the Netherlands this bad risk taxation can hardly be defined as conditional intent. What is lacking here is the volitional element of *dolus eventualis*, i.e. the acceptance of the risk. In other words, only if they would have reconciled themselves with the risk that someone could get hurt – instead of just believing nothing bad would happen – would there be conditional intent. Now, according to Dutch and German law, there is only a form of negligence.

6.3 Negligence

Negligence (*culpa*) is the most normative form of *mens rea* and is primarily based on a violation of the required duty of care which causes a result prohibited by criminal law. Negligence may be expressed in many different ways. The use of terms as «carelessness» and «lack of due care» or «lack of reasonable care» all indicate that negligence is required as a condition for criminal liability.

Most continental legal systems distinguish between conscious and unconscious deviation from the required duty of care. When the agent wrongfully does not consider the consequences of his conduct, this is called unconscious negligence. The agent is not conscious of a risk, but he should and could have been aware of it.

By contrast, when the agent is aware of a risk, but assumes that the result will not occur, this is called conscious negligence. This may sound a lot like conditional intent, but the main difference is the agent's attitude toward the risk; in case of «mere» conscious negligence, the agent is conscious of the risk but nevertheless trusts in the good outcome. He does not take this favorable outcome for granted but still thinks everything will be all right.

Since English law already accepts a third form of *mens rea* called «recklessness» and distinguishes recklessness from negligence in the form of awareness of the risk, it does not recognize a concept such as «conscious negligence». Negligence in England is always unconscious or inadvertent negligence, as it reflects a culpable *failure to be aware* of the unreasonable risk entailed in one's conduct. This means that cases of risk-taking that in the Netherlands and Germany would lead to a liability based on conscious negligence could lead to liability for recklessness in England.

The above example of the construction workers illustrated this. Their conscious deviation of the required standard of care amounts to recklessness in England and conscious negligence in the civil law systems.

Keeping in mind the above comparison of *dolus eventualis* with recklessness, we may conclude that recklessness may cover both cases of conditional intent and conscious negligence.

Conscious and Unconscious Negligence

Negligence in English Law

7   Justifications and Excuses

Even if it is clear that a person's conduct fits the definition of an offense, the question may come up whether he is liable to be convicted for that offense. Criminal law provides certain circumstances (defenses) that take away the criminal liability of the perpetrator. In general we distinguish between justifications and excuses. This dichotomy is widely accepted in the continental legal systems and is also becoming more important in England.

The most fundamental rationale of the distinction is that a justification negates the wrongfulness of the act, whereas an excuse negates the blameworthiness of the agent. This clearly

Negating Wrongfulness and Blameworthiness

coincides with the second and third tier of the tripartite structure of a crime (see again ▶ Sect. 4.3). The dichotomy of justifications and excuses enables a nuanced communication regarding the reason why the defendant should not be held criminally liable. Whereas the acceptance of a justification denies that what the defendant did was wrongful in the eyes of the legal order, the acceptance of an excuse makes clear that what he did was wrong but that he cannot be personally blamed for his conduct.

Criminal law recognizes a wide range of justifications and excuses which can be put forward by the defendant. In this section we only briefly discuss the justification of self-defense and the excuse of insanity.

7.1   Self-Defense

The paradigmatic justification is self-defense, also called necessary defense. Illustrative is the following legal definition of self-defense in Section 32 of the German Criminal Code:

1. He who commits an act which is required as necessary defense, does not act unlawfully.
2. Necessary defense is the defense which is required in order to fend off an imminent unlawful assault from oneself or another.

Imminent and Unlawful Attack Despite differences in development, most legal systems distinguish similar criteria for self-defense. The first requirement is that there is an imminent and unlawful attack.

The requirement of imminence means that the defendant cannot wait any longer for the official authorities to protect his interest. The difficulty lies in determining the limits of this temporal element. On the one hand, self-defense may only be performed at its earliest when danger is already close (no preemptive strike). On the other hand, it may be performed only as long as the attack continues; otherwise it would be retaliation.

The requirement that the attack was unlawful expresses that self-defense is really a fight of right against wrong. It serves to exclude from the defense, for example, situations wherein the perpetrator is being arrested by the police.

The defense must of course pertain to a legitimate interest, such as a person's life, liberty, body, and property. It is important to note that the legal interests of a third party may also be defended. Necessary defense is therefore perhaps a better label for this justification than *self*-defense.

A second requirement for justification on the basis of self-defense is that the defense must be a capable and necessary means to repel the attack. The use of force in self-defense seems to be only necessary when there are no reasonable alternatives, such as firing a warning shot into the air. Generally speaking, this also implies that if there is a possibility to retreat or to get help, one should use it.

Necessity

Imagine a situation where John is attacked at his door by his angry neighbor. Instead of hitting his aggressor, he should simply close the door.

This third requirement assesses the relationship between the offense committed and the amount of harm likely to be suffered by the defendant if he had not intervened with force. It is about weighing the interests of the aggressor against those of the defendant. In principle, the least intrusive means which are still effective should be chosen, taking into account all the circumstances, such as the nature of the force used and the seriousness of the evil to be prevented:

Proportionality

The person who shoots dead a pickpocket who just took his wallet can normally not invoke justified self-defense because shooting the pickpocket dead is not proportional to stealing a wallet.

It is however not required that the defensive force must be exactly in proportion with the attack. As long as the force used was not a *disproportionate* response to the attack, the defendant will be justified. This can be grounded in the reproach that can be made against the aggressor and because the defendant cannot be expected to make a perfect weighing of interests in an urgent situation.

7.2 Insanity

The most popular excuse is insanity. Article 39 of the Dutch Criminal Code gives a good illustration of this defense:

He who commits an act for which he cannot be held responsible by reason of a defective development or medical disorder of his mental capacities is not criminally liable.

Rationale of the Defense

The main rationale of the insanity defense is that it guarantees that those who are not responsible for their actions are not punishable. In all legal systems the insane defendant will therefore be compulsory admitted to and/or treated in a mental hospital. By framing insanity as an excuse, the State may impose measures upon these perpetrators of wrongful acts. As long as the danger remains and treatment is necessary, the defendant can be detained in a mental hospital. This brings about that by pleading an insanity defense, the defendant risks to be deprived of his freedom for an indefinite time. Not surprisingly, most defendants view these measures as a punishment worse than prison.

Requirements

The conditions of an insanity defense essentially require that the offense should be attributable to the mental disorder. This means that first of all, it needs to be established that the defendant was suffering from a relevant mental disorder at the time when he committed the offense. Almost all disorders that are medically recognized, such as psychoses, neuroses, personality disorders, can qualify under the defense. Secondly, it is required that the mental disorder has substantially impaired the defendant's capacities to be held responsible. Depending on the legal system, cognitive, evaluative, and volitional capacities can be distinguished. Thirdly, there is the question whether there may be reasons against attributing the offense to the mental disorder, such as prior fault of getting in a situation where the defendant lost his mind. One may think here of drug use or other forms of intoxication leading to a psychosis.

Diminished Capacity

In cases where the defendant's capacities have been impaired by the disorder, but not to the extent of legal irresponsibility, courts can decide to take into account the partial impairment of the pertinent capacities as reason for mitigating the punishment. These cases of «diminished capacity» are much more common than the application of the complete classification of insanity.

8   Criminal Substantive Law and Criminal Procedural Law

The rules of substantive criminal law determine the conditions for criminal liability and the possible sanctions for crimes committed. What then if the criminal law is violated? The answer is straightforward: the culprit can be punished for the crime he committed. However, establishing whether somebody committed a crime is not easy.

Convicting a person for a crime is a serious matter, given the harsh consequences it bears on a man's life in terms of punishment and social stigma. This is why a decision of guilt must only be taken after the most careful assessment. The function of criminal procedure is not solely to convict the guilty but equally, if not predominantly, to distinguish the innocent from the guilty. Procedural rules identify the steps for accurately establishing if criminal law was breached and if an individual (the accused) can be deemed culpable for the breach and consequently punished.

Since it is the entire society that bears an interest in the prosecution and punishment of crimes and criminals, the State is directly involved in the criminal process. At its origin, the criminal process was an action brought by an alleged victim against an alleged perpetrator. However, as time went by, everywhere law evolved toward a centralized system of State prosecution, where the State authorities are given the powers to investigate and act against the alleged offenders.

State Involvement

In some countries, e.g. England, Spain and Germany, it is still possible for a victim to bring a private criminal prosecution.

The evolution toward State prosecution happened for different reasons. The first reason, based on the assumption that a crime always offends and threatens the society as a whole, is that the monarchs and the citizens felt that the essential interest of a secure society should not be not left in the hands of single untrained individuals. The second reason is that the array of punishable offenses widened over time to include crimes that offend society at large and not just one of its individuals. This includes crimes against public order, crimes against the economy, and crimes against the environment. The last reason is that private victims often did not have the resources to take up the task of investigating and prosecuting their offenders.

Discovering crimes and criminals is essential to ensure the well-being and tranquility of society, but crimes are not always immediately visible. It is for this reason that the powers conferred by the State to its competent authorities are larger and more pervasive than those available to any private civil litigants. This triggers a tension between security and liberty or, put in other terms, between crime control and protection of rights. The coercive and intrusive powers given to State authorities to discover and prosecute crimes encroach upon the liberties of individuals, whether or not they are suspected of a crime.

State Powers

For instance, home searches, interceptions of communications and surveillance measures restrict the privacy of their targets. Arrests and personal searches encroach upon the personal liberty of suspects.

The criminal process carries a natural imbalance because at the earlier stage of the proceedings, one of the two sides (the prosecution) is given a wider array of powers to pursue its goals than the opposing party (the accused). In most, if not all, countries, there are some coercive/intrusive investigative means that are available only to State authorities and not to private individuals. This is more or less inevitable because State authorities need to discover crimes. Furthermore, the criminal investigations often start against unknown individuals, simply on the suspicion that a crime was committed, and this requires that State authorities be given the power to acquire knowledge of the alleged crime before the accused is identified. The structure of the criminal process is of course intended to remedy this natural imbalance between parties as much as possible.

9   The Basic Structure of the Criminal Process

Although criminal procedure differs significantly from country to country, it is possible to observe a general common structure of the criminal process. The criminal process displays two main stages: the investigation (or pretrial) phase and the trial phase.

9.1   Investigations

Once the suspicion of a crime comes to the attention of the law enforcement authorities, they conduct investigations in order to find out if an offense has been committed and to unveil all relevant circumstances (the suspect, the *actus reus*, the *mens rea*, mitigating or aggravating factors). Everywhere the police have the primary role in the investigations, but in several systems it acts autonomously, while in others under the direction and supervision of the public prosecutor, or – in some cases – of the investigating judge.

State authorities can take different investigative measures in order to shed light on the original suspicion: questioning of suspects and witnesses, searches, interceptions of communications (wiretappings), scientific examinations, etc. If the State authorities deem the original suspicion to be unfounded, the case is dropped or dismissed. If they instead come to the reasoned belief that a crime has been perpetrated, a formal allegation is drafted (indictment), and the case is taken to trial, where the hypothesis of guilt built by the investigators is tested.

9.2   Trial

At trial, an impartial court (a single judge, a panel, or a jury) decides whether the accused (more appropriately called «defendant» at this stage) is guilty of the alleged crime(s). In essence, the trial revolves around the statement of facts and law contained in the indictment, and it must answer the following question: is that statement true or false? If the charge described in the indictment is deemed to be true, the defendant is found guilty and is then sentenced; if it is found to be false, the defendant is acquitted. The decision is taken on the evidence available, which must be carefully assessed in its probative value.

Save for a few exceptions, the trial is public. According to modern standards, justice must not only be done, but it must also be seen to be done. The publicity of the trial constitutes a prevention of abuses; it is a form of social control on the criminal process in that it induces self-restraint on the parties and adjudicators and allows society to appreciate the correctness of the final decision.   *Public Trial*

The trial also serves as a remedy to the imbalance of powers between the State and the individual during the investigations. During the investigations, most of the evidence is collected in the absence of the suspect, and sometimes the suspect is even unaware that he is under inquiry. While during the investigations the suspect has little or no opportunity to oppose the prosecution's thesis, at trial the accused has a possibility to properly rebut the allegations by producing evidence and arguments in her favor. A proper defense requires that defendants have clear knowledge of the allegations brought against them and of the evidence on which they are grounded and that they be given an adequate chance to discredit the prosecution's proposition. At trial, the accused can challenge the prosecution with equality of arms.   *Equality of Arms*

10   Adversarial or Inquisitorial?

Apart from the general structure, the systems of criminal justice differ from State to State. These differences reflect the historical roots, political and socioeconomic structures, and cultural traditions of the national States. Several attempts have been made to classify the different systems into homogeneous groups. A popular distinction between procedural systems identifies two major models, corresponding to two legal traditions: the adversarial or accusatorial systems and the inquisitorial or non-adversarial systems. While the Anglo-American systems of the common law tradition belong to the adversarial family, the civil law systems of Continental Europe are by contrast usually labeled as inquisitorial.

Adversarial

The dichotomy is built around some selected traditional features of civil law and common law countries. In this regard, the traditional common law systems are taken to be characterized by the fact that the process consists in a dispute between two parties – the prosecution and the defense – in front of a passive court. The trial involves a battle of evidence and arguments between the accuser and the defendant in front of a jury of 12 laymen. Witnesses are cross-examined directly by the parties. Evidence collected out of court during the investigations is inadmissible, save for some limited exceptions. The trial is presided over by a career judge who introduces no evidence. At the end of the parties' arguments, the presiding judge summarizes the cases to the jurors and poses them the relevant legal questions. The jury returns a verdict of innocence/guilt without giving reasons for it.

Inquisitorial

By contrast, the traditional inquisitorial continental system would be characterized by the fact that the State authorities were charged with the duty to investigate on any suspicion of a crime. The investigations are conducted in a formal and official manner by a career judge, called the investigating judge. All the results of the investigations are recorded in a *dossier*, which the investigative judge would then hand over to the trial court. At trial, the parties have the right to bring additional evidence and to present their arguments. However, since the trial court could rely on the investigative evidence previously obtained and could even collect further evidence on its own motion, the role of the parties is marginal. The judge would conduct the examination of witnesses, while the parties could at most suggest some questions to be put to the witnesses. The trial court gives reasons for its decisions.

Differences

Adversarial and inquisitorial systems are based on two different kinds of fact-finding. An inquisitorial system empowers a neutral investigator to collect all relevant evidence available, while an adversarial system relies on the agonistic approach of the parties and on the assumption that the clash of opposing views will show which of the two versions – the thesis of the prosecutor or that of the defense – is more credible. The risk that the parties of an adversarial dispute will not offer the judge some crucial information to solve the case is equivalent to the risk that the active judge of the inquisitorial system might overlook some crucial information. In the adversarial model, the parties will present evidence and arguments favorable to their position, but they equally adduce all the available elements against the reconstruction of the other party. Both models equally strive for the discovery of the truth, and they both consider it a miscarriage of justice when the outcome of the criminal process reaches a factual conclusion that later proves different from what happened in reality.

It should be kept in mind that the opposition between adversarial and inquisitorial systems can hardly be used to characterize contemporary systems. Several of the historical traits of these systems have now disappeared or have been mitigated. In several continental countries, the investigative judge has been abolished, and where he survived, his role is mostly limited to the investigations on the most serious crimes (whether *de jure* or *de facto*). Nowadays, in most continental countries, the burden of the investigations for the majority of crimes lies on the public prosecutor and the police. In common law countries, the rules prohibiting the use of investigative evidence have been relaxed, while the judges are given some powers to introduce evidence *motu proprio* and thus to play a more active role if necessary.

Although the classic dichotomy between inquisitorial and adversarial systems still retains some importance for understanding certain cultural and theoretical features of each of the two traditions (common law v. civil law), it is important to acknowledge that the borrowings between the two have been so extensive that it is no longer possible to classify any of the criminal justice systems in Western Europe as wholly accusatorial or wholly inquisitorial. Today, the opposition between the adversarial model of a dispute and the inquisitorial model of official inquiry represents two poles of a theoretical spectrum. Each national system can be characterized as being more or less adversarial, depending on the role that the parties have in the trial compared to the position of the judge and on the importance played by the findings of prior investigations on the outcome of the trial.

Furthermore, an important move toward harmonization derives from supranational law. After the Second World War, a number of international instruments have entered into force, with a view to ensuring a better protection of human rights. These instruments place significant limitations on the possibility for States to freely shape their criminal justice systems, and they have led to a growing convergence of the different national procedures. All European countries are bound by fundamental human rights embodied in international conventions, particularly in the European Convention on Human Rights (ECHR). The latter instrument has proved to be

Supranational Law

particularly stringent, thanks to the enforcement assured to its provisions by the European Court of Human Rights (ECtHR). The Convention and the large body of ECtHR case law have had a significant impact on the shape of national systems, even to the extent that they have created a blueprint of European principles of the criminal process.

11   Basic Principles of Criminal Justice Systems

11.1   Tension Between Security and Liberty

As mentioned, the criminal process revolves around a continuous tension between security (of the society as a whole) and liberty (of the individuals within society). It constantly strives to find a balance between these conflicting interests. The more emphasis is put on crime control – coping with a high crime rate or reducing the crime rate and, in general, keeping society safer – the fewer safeguards will be provided to the individuals. If the main accent is put on the need to ensure a due process that minimally restricts the rights of people, the repression of crime might become less efficient. To some extent, rights and safeguards are burdensome and time-consuming: by requiring the State authorities to act under a higher number of constraints, they slow down the criminal process and reduce the number of trials and convictions. Moreover, by placing a series of burdens and hurdles on the actions of the prosecuting authorities, the procedural safeguards increase the chance that a guilty individual may escape punishment. At the same time, they reduce the likelihood of an error against the defendant and limit the impact of the criminal process on the life of possibly innocent individuals.

The ideal solution would be to protect the rights of individuals and the accuracy of the fact-finding process adequately without sacrificing the efficiency and the effectiveness of the repression of crimes. In real life, it is however impossible to have both, hence the traditional dilemma: is it preferable that ten guilty persons escape or that one innocent suffers? The answer to this question is offered by a general principle of liberal tradition that is embraced by all international covenants, explicitly affirmed in Article 6 Section 2 ECHR and largely accepted by all European systems: the presumption of innocence.

11.2   Presumption of Innocence

The presumption of innocence is the cornerstone of the criminal process. An individual is considered innocent and must be treated as such until a decision of guilt is passed against him.

The presumption of innocence is not a prediction of outcome that the defendant will most likely be found to be not guilty. It is instead a purely normative command that is created exactly for the purpose to counterbalance and neutralize the more natural assumption of guilt arising out of criminal proceedings. The presumption of innocence demands that a person is treated and considered as innocent until an accurate finding of guilt has been made. The mere fact that someone is a suspect does not authorize the authorities to treat that person differently from any other non-accused persons. Nature of the Presumption

The presumption of innocence is also intended to remedy the imbalance between the parties in the early stage of the criminal process. As seen above, during the investigations, the State authorities are given strong powers to discover crimes and offenders and may act under a veil of secrecy. There is no equality of arms between the two conflicting sides during the investigations. The presumption of innocence tries to cure this imbalance in two ways:

1. By establishing that a person be treated as an innocent, which entails that in principle a person's liberty should not be unduly prejudiced by the investigative action and findings
2. By imposing that a person be considered as an innocent, which requires that prosecuting authorities reach a high standard of proof in order to obtain a conviction

There are two direct corollaries of the presumption of innocence. The first consists in a procedural rule applicable at the trial stage in the judgment against the defendant: the defendant can be considered guilty only if his guilt has been proved beyond reasonable doubt (*in dubio pro reo*). As a consequence, the prosecution bears the burden to prove all of the elements of the alleged offense. In dubio pro reo

The second corollary of the presumption of innocence is that the personal liberty of a suspect cannot be unduly restricted before a verdict of guilt is passed. This does not mean that the personal liberty of the suspect can never be limited before the trial decision. Pretrial detention is possible in some circumstances. For instance, if the police catches Pretrial Detention as an Exception someone red-handed, they arrest him. The police may also decide that they want to apprehend the suspect in order to interview him out, or of fear that he might flee or commit dangerous acts. What the presumption of innocence demands is that a person should not be kept in detention simply because he is suspected of a crime. The restriction of the suspect's liberty should be limited to a minimum, confined to those situations where it is essential for ensuring a proper course of the proceedings or avoiding a danger to society and assisted by strong safeguards.

11.3   Fair Trial and Proportionality

Closely tied to the presumption of innocence is the principle of fair trial. Convicting the guilty cannot come at any price. The function of the criminal process is not just to reach a correct verdict but also to do so in a manner that generates public confidence in the court's work. Every accused in criminal trial shall have his case adjudicated in a just manner. Under the label of «fair trial» (or «due process») fall a number of safeguards whose array varies from country to country. The common core of the principle includes the right of the accused to a public trial in front of an independent and impartial judge and the right to defense. The accused must be given the opportunity to properly oppose the allegations against him.

This entails the right to receive legal assistance from a counsel. The criminal trial is a very technical matter: there are fine-grained legal distinctions that are not easy to grasp and can be crucial to the outcome of the case. Building an effective defensive strategy compatible with the procedural rules requires adequate knowledge and skills; finding evidence, questioning witnesses, and addressing and persuading the courts are all activities that require experience and preparation. Hence, all defendants can elicit a counsel to assist them in the preparation and conduct of the defense.

The right to defend oneself also includes the right not to cooperate with prosecuting authorities: the accused has a right to remain silent, which means that he should not be compelled (by law or by the prosecuting authorities) to make statements that could turn out to be detrimental to his case.

The right to defense incorporates also the possibility to discredit the evidence offered by the prosecution by confronting the incriminating witnesses.

The fair trial safeguards are also applicable during the investigative stage, at least insofar as this is compatible with that earlier phase. In particular, the rights to legal assistance and to remain silent apply not only to defendants at trial but also to suspects during the investigative phase.

11.4 Proportionality

The main principle concerning the investigation stage is the principle of «proportionality», which entails that State authorities should not make arbitrary use of their coercive and intrusive powers. For instance, searching a house in a case of drunk driving is clearly disproportionate just like searching all the houses of a city to investigate a robbery. Widespread interceptions of telephone conversations should not be tolerated even for discovering serious crimes.

Investigative measures cannot be used lightly or for purposes other than unveiling the elements of a particular offense. Given their intrusion upon individual liberties, the investigative means should be rigorously proportionate to the legitimate ends. Coercive or intrusive action should be allowed only when and insofar as it is strictly necessary to investigate a specific offense.

The principle of proportionality is often a component of the principle of legality (in procedural law), according to which it is up to the law to set out the conditions under which State authorities are allowed to take investigative measures. In many cases, however, it also operates as an autonomous principle, respect for which by the investigating authorities can be ensured by subsequent judicial review. This is, for instance, the case with coercive measures (like pretrial detention) and, in some countries, even with intrusive investigative measures (like interception of communications): the person who suffered the deprivation of liberty or the intrusion can apply to a judicial authority in order to have the restriction scrutinized as to its legality and proportionality with the investigative need and the standard of human rights protection.

12 Conclusion

In this chapter we have identified some basic concepts of substantive and procedural criminal law. We have seen that at the outset of any discussion regarding criminal law, a decision needs to be made as to which forms of conduct rightly ought to be considered criminal and how the subsequent imposition of punishment can be justified (in a given society). The choices made on this fundamental level will strongly determine the general attitude and stringency of a criminal justice system. Although every European country has its own legal culture, each system may be understood as a «local» answer to some «universal» questions that constitute the doctrinal foundations of criminal liability.

One of these fundamental questions is how to conceptually relate the objective and subjective elements of a criminal offense. In other words, how to connect the act requirement, which is related to the principle of harm, with the requirement of a specific state of mind, which is related to the principle of guilt? We have seen that common law systems, such as England and Wales, use a bipartite structure of a crime, whereas most civil law systems, such as Germany and the Netherlands, prefer three rungs on the ladder of criminal liability. On the one hand, this striking difference has definitely its consequences for the categorization of certain concepts, such as blameworthiness, or for the differentiation of defenses, but on the other hand, one should not forget that the practical outcomes may not always be that different. Nevertheless, conceptual distinctions are sometimes of great importance as they may reflect fundamentally different choices regarding the conditions of criminal liability. A good example is how the English system uses a more fine-grained tripartite system of fault instead of merely distinguishing intention from negligence, which has resulted on the continent in often unclear and debatable distinctions between the lowest form of intent and the highest form of negligence.

In the last part of the chapter, we have focused on the enforcement of substantive criminal law through the criminal process. The purpose of the process is to officially establish the guilt of an accused with the related consequences and also to ensure that innocent people are not unduly convicted. We have seen that different legal systems are based on different historical models and cultural traditions. Nevertheless all systems present a common bipartite structure (investigations and trial), and they share some common general principles. All of the basic principles of the process concern the protection of individuals (suspects, defendants, or third parties) in front of the State's power to enforce the criminal law. No matter what function we ascribe to the substantive provisions of criminal law, a democratic State must ensure that the criminal enforcement does not run counter the liberties of the individuals. A crime-free society with no liberties remains a worse choice than a society affected by crime but able to enjoy its natural freedoms.

Recommended Literature

Ashworth A (2002) Serious crime, human rights and criminal procedure. Sweet & Maxwell, London

Bohlander M (2009) Principles of German criminal law. Hart Publishing, Oxford

Damaska MR (1991) The faces of justice and state authority (revised edition). Yale University Press, New Haven/London

Delmas-Marty M, Spencer J (eds) (2005) European criminal procedures. Cambridge University Press, Cambridge

Horder J (2016) Ashworth's principles of criminal law, 8th edn. Oxford University Press, Oxford

Keiler J (2013) Actus reus and participation in European criminal law. Intersentia, Antwerpen

Keiler J, Roef D (eds) Comparative concepts of criminal law. Intersentia, Cambridge

8

Constitutional Law

Aalt Willem Heringa

© Springer International Publishing Switzerland 2017
J. Hage et al. (eds.), *Introduction to Law*, DOI 10.1007/978-3-319-57252-9_8

1   Introduction

Law and State

Law is closely connected to the State, on one hand because the State creates most of the law and on the other hand because the State itself is regulated by the law. From a historical point of view, it was the increasingly effective and tightly organized State—whether it was a city-state, a principality, a kingdom, or an empire—that succeeded in imposing law upon its citizens. This trend is illustrated by the development of criminal law as a separate branch of law, next to private law. States started to monopolize violence and the suppression of crimes, and to prosecute crimes as offenses against the State, rather than as offenses against the victims. In this way States drastically reduced the rates of violence between individual people, clans, and tribes. Through this monopolization of law enforcement, States promoted pacification, improved legal certainty, boosted productivity, and facilitated peaceful commerce between people.

Constitutional Law

As a counterpart to this State monopolization of law enforcement, we expect that the State itself be organized and regulated by the law and that rulers exercise their power in accordance with legal norms, rather than arbitrarily. The branch of law that regulates the State is called *constitutional law*. Constitutional law contains rules on the organization of a State, on the powers that State organs possess, and on the relations between these organs (institutional law). Moreover, it provides fundamental rights that protect the legal position of the individual against the State: human rights law, judicial review, and—as an offshoot—administrative law.

What Do States Do

The primary role and rationale of States is to provide peace, order, and stability (foreign affairs, defense, police). Gradually States have expanded in what kind of activities they undertake such as in infrastructure and education. In this way, since the introduction of the universal suffrage, expectations of the State have increased. For instance, many of us expect the State to provide protection for the needy, young, and elderly and to provide for a clean environment, roads, jobs, decent working conditions and proper wages, a sewage system, schools, culture, health care, and (sustainable) energy. In response to these increased expectations, States have expanded their activities and out of necessity expanded powers and budgets. How and to which extent States have expanded their activities and have intervened in society is a matter of policy, or politics. Obviously, some choices have to be made with regard to the activities States undertake and with regard to the powers and budgets—and therefore also taxes—that States need for these tasks. How these choices are being made, by whom, and through what procedures are the primary domain of constitutional law; yet the outcome of the decision-making processes is politics.

However, constitutional law sometimes restricts politics from making specific choices. For instance, clauses in some European constitutions restrict the powers of parliaments from creating a budget deficit that is too big or a State debt too large. These constitutions include those of Germany, Switzerland, Poland, and Spain. In Italy and Austria, proposals have been launched to this effect, and under the new 2012 Fiscal compact between most EU Member States, they have even agreed to introduce a (constitutional) provision to that effect.

Other examples are that:
- The European Convention of Human Rights, Protocol 1, Article 1, in protecting the right of free enjoyment of property, limits the conditions under which States can nationalize properties.
- EU law imposes economic choices such as free competition, upon the Member States.
- The rules of the World Trade Organization do not permit the inhibition of trade or the financial support of exporting industries.

1.1 Sources of Constitutional law

In most States, the most important constitutional rules have been laid down in a central written document. This document is typically called a *constitution*, but it may also carry different names, such as *basic law, charter,* or *regulation of State.* Because of their fundamental nature, written constitutional documents almost always provide that they can only be amended through difficult, special procedures often involving special majorities. This feature is called «entrenchment», and an entrenched constitution is generally called «rigid». Entrenchment is meant to make changes in the constitution harder to accomplish than changes in ordinary law. As a result, a constitution will reflect a larger majority and be more protective of minorities or minority interests. Some constitutions even define some parts of the constitution as non-amendable!

The Constitution

An amendment of the Polish Constitution, for example, requires a two-third majority in the lower chamber of parliament and an absolute majority in the Senate, and in some cases a referendum may be prescribed to confirm the amendment afterwards. Normal laws, by contrast, in principle require a simple majority in the lower chamber, and the senate may usually be overruled if it objects to a law.

All States have a constitution in the sense of a set of rules that govern the State, but some States—with the UK as the best example—do without an official document, a written constitution. They do however have a constitution. The constitutional rules are then exclusively found in ordinary laws, customs, and case law. If a State does not have a written constitution, its constitution will typically not be entrenched, but rather «flexible». The constitutional norms may be changed by «ordinary» laws.

Other Constitutional Legislation

However, even if a State has an official written constitution, constitutionally relevant rules are often also found in ordinary laws, in case law, or in customs.

Ordinary laws that tend to have constitutional significance are, for example, election laws, rules of procedure of parliaments, laws on the organization of the court system, or laws stipulating the establishment and powers of regional or local governments.

Case Law

Case law may be constitutionally relevant where courts lay down rules with a «constitutional» relevance, such as the UK doctrine of parliamentary sovereignty or the US doctrine of judicial review, or when courts are called upon to interpret the meaning of the constitution or when they establish fundamental rules and principles with constitutional significance in practical cases.

Customs

Customs often play a role in the internal proceedings of parliaments, such as the composition of parliamentary committees or the panel of parliamentary chairmen. They may also play a role in the process of government formation. Of course, customary rules differ significantly between States; what is a custom in one State is explicitly regulated in another and may simply not exist in a third.

Treaties

In quite a few States, international law, specifically treaties, can also be considered to be an important part of national law, more so when a State has adopted a *monist* system in recognizing treaties as part of domestic law (France, the Netherlands). But also in *dualist* systems (UK, Germany), in which international law must be transformed into domestic law before it can be applied, international treaties do play an important role. We can point here to the European Union treaties (see ► Chap. 10) and to the European Convention on Human Rights. The importance of the former is self-evident; the latter has strongly influenced the national protection of human rights and has served as an instrument for national courts to exercise judicial review (see ► Sect. 3.8).

1.2   Three Themes

In this chapter, several topics of constitutional law will be addressed. They will be structured in three major themes. The first theme, «State Power Established», discusses in ► Sect. 2 the State and the source of its sovereignty or authority to rule. The second theme, «State Power Constrained», considers the ways in which the power of the state is limited. This includes the division of the State's power among its organs (or between branches of government) and among its territorial entities, the limits on State action as they result from the protection of human rights, and the power of the judge to determine whether State action is lawful or unlawful. This theme is dealt with in ► Sect. 3. The third theme, «State Power Democratized», relates to the ways in which the power of the State is exercised or controlled by the people. It is the topic of ► Sect. 4.

2   State Power Established

In this section we discuss three issues that are related to the powers of a State. ► Sect. 2.1 deals with two conditions for statehood. These conditions are elaborated in ► Sect. 2.2 about sovereignty. ► Sect. 2.3 finally deals with the relation between a State and the people that inhabit its territory.

2.1   Statehood

A State is an organization that is able to control a certain territory and the people living in it. This control is both in the sense of exercising powers and maintaining law and order inside its own borders and in the sense of defending it against the outside world. Statehood is not an all-or-nothing matter: not all States meet the two conditions to the same extent. Some States are internally weak and have their authority

Two Conditions

disputed. Some States provide a low protection to their citizens or do not (or hardly) provide for internal security or the general interest. Sometimes this even goes so far that we can conclude that there is a situation of anarchy, civil unrest, or even civil war.

The ongoing Libyan civil war which initially led to the end of the Gaddafi regime and is still prevalent would be a case in point. The civil war in Syria is another example.

Some States simply do not manage to exercise effective internal control and the monopoly of force. Strictly speaking, they do not meet the criteria of statehood: they are called «failed States».

An example would be Somalia in its current situation.

Recognition

One possible criterion for statehood is whether a potential State is recognized by the «international community» of States. This would mean that most or all other States engage in diplomatic relations with the State in question and that the potential State is accepted as a member of an international organization, such as the United Nations. However, we have to be careful here. Sometimes a State can function as a State and exhibit many, if not most, of a State's features but still not be recognized as part of the international community.

An example would be the island of Taiwan, which is not recognized as a separate State because of pressure from China, which claims that Taiwan is part of that country. Kosovo also lacks recognition by quite a few other States. It is not a member of the UN, though it was accepted to participate in the 2016 Olympic Games.

Secession

A major problem in connection with statehood is how to cope with parts of a State that wish to secede and become an independent State of their own. Examples in recent history are Kosovo, the Crimea, and South Sudan. Given internal sovereignty as a prerequisite of a State, a State must exercise internal domestic control and possess the power to stop or prevent civil unrest or secessionist and revolutionary movements. This demand is obviously not met if secession is ongoing. In such cases, it depends on the extent and proportionality of the power used by the seceding «State», the legitimacy of the secessionist movement, and possibly also other arguments of international politics, if and how the international community will deal with the recognition of the new State entity. A right to secession may not exist under the domestic law of the land, but secession may eventually still be the effective outcome with international recognition as the result. When a State does not appear to be able to enforce its national constitutional claims to unity and non-secession, secession and the birth of a new State may be the consequence. We may then say that a (new) people has legitimized the birth of a new State.

Some civil wars do not lead to the effectuation of secession (the nineteenth-century American civil war); some secessions do appear rapidly and without devastating force (the Crimea). The latter secession is highly disputed in the international community, however.

2.2   Sovereignty

The two features related to statehood (the capability to exercise domestic control and the capability to defend its territory against foreign intrusions) are considered to be two aspects of sovereignty, namely, *internal sovereignty* and *external sovereignty*. The consequences of sovereignty are normative, relating to competences, powers, and in general the authority possessed by the State. However, the conditions for sovereignty are also factual, relating to control over a territory.

A State may have sovereign powers but still be hindered from exercising them for reasons of international politics, trade relations, (financial) resources, the role of financial markets, or lack of military powers.

The word «sovereignty» is also used to denote the source of a State's coming into being or legitimacy, as in the phrase: the sovereignty of the people. Finally it is used to indicate the highest internal power within a State where ultimate internal power resides, as in the UK: the sovereignty of parliament. All these different meanings may sometimes be confusing and call for the careful use of the concept.

A State's internal sovereignty is foremost a constitutional issue, as the ultimate authority in a State is defined by constitutional law. Sovereignty in that sense is the ultimate source of authority in a particular territory, and it is where the authority of the State originates. If an official is able to lawfully impose obligations upon citizens, for example, the obligation to pay a tax or to perform military service, there must be something that distinguishes the official imposing the obligation from the citizen receiving it. The official must have a right or entitlement to rule. Lower ranking officials such as tax inspectors

Internal Sovereignty

or policemen will cite the authority they received from their superiors. These superiors act on the basis of regulations, which in turn are enacted on the basis of laws. At some point, there must be an ultimate superior, the source from which all State authorities trace their own power to rule: the sovereign.

The tax inspector's individual order to pay a tax may, for instance, be based on an administrative regulation on how to issue such orders; the regulation in turn is based on the tax code, which is a general law regulating tax rates; the tax code has been adopted because the constitution allows the lawmaker to impose taxes. Who, then, made the constitution, and what gave the creator of the constitution the right to empower the lawmaker to impose taxes?

The People

Monarchs, such as emperors or kings, may argue that they derive their authority from God, including the power to make constitutions if they so decide. An enlightened audience will find such claims implausible, however. In modern times, the idea has gained ground that the ultimate legitimization of State authority lies with the people. In many Western constitutions, reference is explicitly made to the people as the origin of the written constitution and as the source of the powers of the State.

Often the preamble, which is a declaratory introductory statement, makes clear on whose authority a constitution is enacted. The US Constitution's preamble famously starts out with the words: «We, the People…». The French Constitution's preamble also makes explicit that the text is written from the point of view of the people. Other constitutions, such as the one of Bulgaria, contain an article in the text itself which proclaims that all public power emanates from the people.

As a result, in systems that are based on popular sovereignty, the people are bound by laws that are made on the basis of a constitution that was enacted in the name of («by») the people itself.

External Sovereignty

The external aspect of sovereignty relates to the mutual relations between States. The basic idea is that a sovereign State is independent of other States and that other States are forbidden to meddle into the internal affairs of a sovereign State. The idea that States are sovereign in this sense has been anchored in Article 2, Section 1 of the United Nations Charter, which states:

The Organization and its Members, in pursuit of the Purposes stated in Article 1, shall act in accordance with the following Principles.

The Organization is based on the principle of the sovereign equality of all its Members […].

Several facts and recent developments have jeopardized the classical notion of external sovereignty of States. We will deal with these in ▶ Sect. 2.3.

2.3   Nation States

Some States have a very long history; others are a more recent invention. When it is said that some States have existed for many centuries, this does not mean that their government structures have existed that long. However, when people share some common characteristics, such as skin color, language, physical build, etc., and have a (long) common history, it gives them a feeling of a shared past and a common identity. Such a group of people is called a *nation*, and a State that is inhabited by such a nation is called a *nation-state*.

> Nations

Where such unifying factors do not exist spontaneously, States can make an effort to create more unity. A national flag, a national anthem, or a national currency can play a role in this connection. Sometimes States find unity in a hereditary monarchy. In the international sports arena, States are represented by national teams.

Here we can spot differences. The UK, for instance, has a national anthem and flag and had a combined Great Britain team for the recent Olympic Games. However, in other sports competitions, teams represent each of the four participating State entities: Northern Ireland, Scotland, Wales, and England.

Many (19) European countries have surrendered their former national currency in favor of the euro. Yet the European Union (EU) is not a State, and neither is the European Monetary Union. These are international organizations, established on the basis of international treaties between the Member States. The EU displays many features of a State, such as the exercise of internal and external powers. The EU has a diplomatic service and the High Representative for Foreign Affairs, and the EU can conclude treaties with other (non-EU) States and international organizations. Internally, the EU has many powers, which have been transferred to it by the Member States. Most significantly, what the EU is lacking are defense powers and police powers. Moreover, international affairs must be agreed unanimously. State-like features such as a national anthem and a flag do exist but are not laid down in the foundational treaties.

> The European Union

Many feel that the EU cannot be a nation-state since the EU is not founded upon one people. They claim that far-ranging powers and their democratic exercise can best (or only) be organized in the setting of a true State with an identifiable people/nation. Can the EU in itself even be called a sovereign entity? No, since it is not the master of its own constitutional development: it is not the master of the treaties. This role is kept by the 28 Member States (27 after the effectuation of the Brexit). The EU's powers have been transferred to it by these States and can ultimately, by amending the treaties or by leaving the EU, be taken back. However, it is accepted that the Member States by transferring to the EU parts of their sovereign powers, some of them even exclusively, now share the exercise of their sovereign rights with the EU. Some would therefore argue that the sovereignty of the Member States is now, and in some domains, severely restricted.

Globalization and International Integration

8

Sovereignty is an important concept that underpins national constitutional systems, but in reality (de facto) it may also become something of a fiction in the real life of the modern world. This is to mean that sovereignty formally exists but that the exercise of sovereign rights is factually restricted. A State may be externally sovereign, but its internal policy making may in fact be controlled, for instance, by a dominant neighboring State or in order to obtain trade benefits or energy or access to transport corridors. Yet even apart from such cases, international cooperation and integration between States make it difficult to argue that all public power emanates from the people or another internal source of sovereignty. International cooperation, and the creation of permanent international organizations that comprise several States, is increasingly necessary. Technological progress in the area of transportation and communication has made it more and more irrelevant where goods and services are produced, a trend captured by the term *globalization*. Private actors operate increasingly on an international scale (financial institutions, Apple, Google, Starbucks) and require joint international efforts for regulation.

Treaties

In order to permit the undertaking of rights and obligations with foreign States (the exercise of external sovereignty), a national constitution may allow the government to sign international agreements, while providing that, before they can enter into force, the national parliament must vote on them or the people must approve them in a referendum. If an international agreement would be in conflict with the constitution, the constitution may have to be changed before the approval for such an agreement is given. Unanimity among States usually governs the conclusion of international agreements; however, as we witness in the context of the EU, the subsequent application may be the subject of majority decision-making. As a whole, States accept the binding nature of international commitments against their will because they benefit from being a part of a greater territorial scope.

There are many power differences between small, weak, or poor States, on one hand, and large powerful, or rich States, on the other hand. Whether we like it or not, the USA and China have a greater impact on international politics because of their sheer economic size and military power than small, poor, and less-developed States. Apparently some States are more sovereign than others.

Power Differences

3   State Power Constrained

Traditional functions of States include the provision of external defense and an internal police force that can maintain the law. In order to exercise sovereignty effectively, a State must be powerful. It must be able to keep a grip on the use of violence within its territory. It must have what the German sociologist Max Weber (1864–1920) called the *monopoly on violence*: only the State may use coercion against individuals. Other organizations may not, and they can be prosecuted as criminal gangs if they do; individuals seeking self-justice to avenge crimes are prosecuted themselves.

An absolute ruler, or despot, may succeed in imposing law upon his citizens but is essentially lawless himself. In fact, this is the origin of the expression «absolutism»: an absolute ruler is *legibus absolutus*, which is Latin for «free from laws». There are no legal constraints upon the absolute ruler, who may regulate, tax, prosecute, torture, and kill his subjects as he pleases: from on-the-spot executions on a whim to veritable genocides. This is still largely true for dictatorships today, and it was certainly true for early States that were able to *impose* laws but that were themselves not *bound by law*.

Absolutism

The influential English philosopher Thomas Hobbes (1588–1679) famously argued that it takes a Leviathan—a centralized government authority appearing like a terrifying giant—to keep people from inflicting misery upon each other (see also ▶ Chap. 15, Sect. 6). However, nowadays, we expect the State itself to be organized and regulated by the law as well. This is an aspect Hobbes did not emphasize, but later scholars of liberal humanism and the Enlightenment stressed this point forcefully and successfully.

Constitutional law subjects the State itself to constraints. Its power may be distributed between different territorial subunits, such as regions, so that the central authority does not

Limitations on State Power

have an exclusive grip on all State power. Its power may be distributed among various organs, so that it does not wholly rest in any one organ. It is even possible that when an organ does possess power to make choices, some choices may simply be prohibited by constitutional law.

3.1   Territorial Division of State Power

One way for constitutional law to curb State power and to prevent its concentration is to spread it over smaller territorial units and to create regional and local governments that exercise State power for their respective units. At the local level, the typical territorial subunit would be the municipalities: towns and cities. The more prominent entities are found at regional level: districts, provinces, or— somewhat confusingly—individual States within a larger federal State.

The USA comprises, as the name suggests, «States»; Mexico and Brazil also comprise States as regional entities. Germany is made up of *Länder*, a term which is also translated as «States». Yet, federal systems may also use other names for their subunits: *Cantons* in Switzerland, Provinces in Canada, Gemeenschappen and Gewesten in Belgium; Australia comprises both States and somewhat less powerful territories.

The major distinction between States in terms of their internal territorial distribution of power revolves around the question of whether they are unitary States or federations.

Unitary States

In a unitary State, all State powers ultimately reside in one central government authority. There may be local or regional authorities, but in a unitary State any such local and regional decision-making powers are granted by central laws. This means that the central government authority may again retract these powers without institutionalized involvement, let alone consent, of the local or regional governments themselves.

In the Netherlands, which is a decentralized but unitary State, provinces and municipalities have their own local regulatory and executive powers. Their autonomy in local affairs is protected by the constitution, but the exact extent of provincial and local powers is laid down in national laws. If the State wants to retract these powers, and give them to its central organs instead, it can do so by changing the relevant laws or by deleting local autonomy from the constitution. The provinces and municipalities themselves will have no formal say in either of these changes.

Federations

In a federation, State powers are divided between the organs of the central State (the federal level) and the organs of the subunits (the regional level). This division is enshrined in the constitution itself, not in ordinary central laws. The involvement of the regions in any changes of this division of powers, if even allowed under the constitution, is highly relevant as this protects the regions against possible restrictions of their powers.

The regions in a federation can exercise the powers that they have in their own right. Even where the federal level is competent to make laws that cover the entire national territory, in many federal States the regions are involved in the federal law making process as well.

The most common way for regions to be involved in federal lawmaking is through an upper chamber in a two-chamber federal parliament. Such a senate would represent the regions as such, as fully or largely equal parts of the federation. In the US Senate each state has the same number of members, namely, two, whereas the States' representation in the House of Representatives depends on their population size.

Regional participation in federal lawmaking would also be guaranteed in the constitution, as would be the region's involvement in any change to that constitution.

The USA and Germany are federal States, and in both cases the federal constitution can only be changed with the involvement of the regions. In Germany the States are involved through an upper chamber which must act by a supermajority of two-thirds; and some amendments of the constitution, for example, the abolishment of the federal character of the State, are expressly forbidden. In the US, constitutional amendments must in addition be approved by a supermajority of the States themselves. This makes it difficult to redistribute regional and federal powers especially with the goal to centralize powers, and it makes it impossible to sideline the regions in such an endeavor.

To summarize: we speak of federalism (1) when a State is divided in territorial subunits, (2) which possess constitutionally protected powers, (3) which do participate in constitutional amendments, (4) are represented on the federal level, wherein (5) an independent arbiter decides on conflicts of federal-State competences, and (6) finally federal laws do prevail over State laws and must be applied in all subunits.

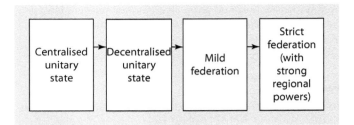

◘ Fig. 8.1   From centralized State to strict federation

Confederations

In a confederal structure, the participating entities effectively remain sovereign States in their own right. One or more of the features of federalism is then missing, such as the supremacy of federal law, or the presence of a constitutional court. The decision-making process in a confederation typically requires unanimity and is restricted to limited issues. A confederation may in fact be so loose that it would not actually be called a State.

The Confederation of 1781, the construction that preceded the modern Union of the USA, was based on a looser association of the individual States, and on a greater preservation of the States' sovereign rights.

While the juxtaposition between the unitary State and the federation is convenient, it should be noted that unitary States can feature different degrees of centralization of power. Federations can preserve the prerogatives of their regions to a larger extent (USA) or to a lesser extent (Austria). Unitary States can become federations (Belgium), and federations can also centralize and become less federal and more unitary (Russia, when regional governors were centrally appointed rather than locally elected). The result is a sliding scale, as depicted in ◘ Fig. 8.1.

3.2   Functional Division of State Power

The same State power that is beneficial when used in a proper way can also be threatening for the people who are the State's subjects. As famously stated by the English politician Lord Acton, in 1887: «Power tends to corrupt, and absolute power corrupts absolutely».

As noted above, Thomas Hobbes advocated a strong central government with unified powers in order to effectively pacify the population. However, several theorists, including

John Locke (1632–1704) and Montesquieu (1689–1755), have proposed functional divisions of State power.

Here we will focus on the idea put forward by Montesquieu, who distinguished three functions of the State, namely:

1. The creation of general legal rules by means of legislation
2. The practical implementation and execution of these rules: administration
3. The application of rules to decide disputes in individual cases: adjudication

State Functions

Montesquieu argued that these three functions ought to be kept apart and should be assigned to three separate branches of the State: the legislature, the executive, and the judiciary. Moreover, each branch would have to stay within its domain. Thus, the courts must only decide in actual cases and should not make general rules; the legislature must not execute the law or rule in individual cases; and the executive has only to execute the laws made by the legislature and must abide by decisions made by the courts.

A law passed by parliament, acting as the legislature, may, for example, provide that heirs can inherit the property of a deceased person and be issued an inheritance certificate (a provision in the civil code) and also that they must pay an inheritance tax (a provision in the tax code). The government, acting as the executive, then goes on to actually issue the certificates (through the civil registrar) and to collect the tax (through the tax inspector). If several heirs argue over their entitlement to the inheritance, the issue may be resolved by a civil court; if an heir argues that he or she should be exempt from the inheritance tax, the issue may be resolved by an administrative court.

This view of Montesquieu has become known as the Trias Politica, after the three bodies that fulfill the three separate State functions. In many States, we find these three branches of government, albeit in different shapes and forms and with slightly different definitions of their respective powers.

Trias Politica

The US Constitution provides a clear example of a Montesquieuvian separation of powers model:

- Article I stipulates that Congress is the legislature.
- Article II defines the President as (the head of) the executive power.
- Article III establishes the Supreme Court and enables the establishment of subordinate federal courts.

Many other constitutions, such as the one of Iceland, are less doctrinal in their numbering but still refer explicitly to legislative, executive, and judicial tasks as distinct functions.

Even the constitution of the Vatican acknowledges that these three functions can be distinguished, even though all three of them are in fact exercised by the Pope.

In Western democracies, the legislative function is typically assigned to the directly elected parliament, although not necessarily on an exclusive basis.

Sometimes the legislature is defined as parliament and the Head of State acting together, such as in Iceland or the UK. Legislative powers may be exercised by regional authorities in federal systems, or international organizations of which a State is member, or by the people themselves in a referendum. Even where legislative power lies with parliament proper, the executive typically takes the initiative to introduce new laws and secure their adoption. Sometimes even the institutional separation between the parliament and the government is blurred: in France, government members cannot be parliament members at the same time, whereas in the UK government members actually *have to be* members of parliament, and they sit on benches in the parliamentary plenary hall among the other members.

3.3   Independent Courts

The aspect of the separation of powers that is probably the easiest to imagine, much more so than the separation between parliament and government, is the independence of the courts and of the judges sitting in the courts. The guiding principle, which is also enshrined in Article 6 of the European Convention on Human Rights, is in particular to ensure that trials are conducted fairly and that neither a court nor its judges can be abolished at whim or be dismissed. Appointment for life may be one of such mechanisms to ensure that the government cannot put pressure on judges to decide one way or another or otherwise interfere with the administration of justice.

Elected Judges

Another way of trying to secure this principle is the election of judges by popular vote so that they are answerable to the community and do not depend on the government for appointment or reappointment.

The majority of US States feature elected judges, even though US federal judges are appointed rather than elected.

In Europe, the notion of elected judges is usually met with distrust since the emphasis is put on the judiciary's professionalism rather than on popularity. As a matter of fact, election campaigns for judgeships tend to stress the candidates' strict stance on crime, which in the long run can drive up incarceration rates (the number of prisoners per 100,000 inhabitants) to excessive levels. However, there is no fundamental reason to object to the election of judges, and it may well be seen as a strong democratic and anti-paternalistic safeguard.

Where judges are appointed, independence can be ensured in a number of ways: judges may be appointed for life, which means that they cannot be removed very easily and will not need to cater to the interests of the incumbent government, or they may be appointed for a limited but long period of time and without the possibility of a second term, which is again designed to remove incentives to please those who may reappoint the judges.

Appointed Judges

The judges at the European Court of Human Rights used to serve renewable 6-year terms; since 2010 they have been serving nonrenewable 9-year terms.

Apart from being independent, courts and judges must also be impartial in two senses. First, they should not have any interests in the outcome of a case, not be related to any party in the case, and not have had an earlier involvement in the issue at hand (objective impartiality). Second, they must have an open mind and not be (or be seen as) more favorable to one party than to the other (subjective impartiality).

Impartiality

All court decisions (apart from appeal to a higher court) may not be ignored or set aside by the legislature or executive and therefore are binding upon the parties and are loyally executed.

Finality

3.4 Parliaments and Governments

Compared with the independence of the judiciary, the separation of the legislature and the executive, i.e., typically parliament and government, is less straightforward. According to the doctrine formulated by Montesquieu, the legislature creates laws, while the administration executes them. In this view, the executive would be the servant, or agent, of the legislature. In reality, the issue is more complicated. In lawmaking in parliamentary systems (see below), the parliament generally follows the agenda of the government where policy and proposals for laws are concerned.

The actual tasks of the administration go beyond mere execution of the laws created by the legislature. Administrations are also prominent in formulating and drafting legislative proposals. In Western democracies, most (if not all) policy making is carried out by the government. In doing so, the government relies on the expertise of its civil service. For the realization of its policies, the government actively seeks the approval of desired legislation in parliament. Policies are implemented and executed not only by means of legislation but also in many other ways: by taxation, by subventions and subsidies, by market supervision, or by the building of roads, harbors, and schools.

Doctrinally it may be true that the legislature creates a tax law and the government goes on to collect the tax. In fact the usual scenario would be that the government calculates how much revenue is needed to finance desired spending and may decide that rather than cutting spending or incurring debt it is necessary to raise taxes. Depending on the national system, it then requests the adoption of a new tax by parliament or directly submits a new draft tax law to the parliament.

Parliamentary Systems

A crucial factor affecting the form of government–parliament relations is whether the system is parliamentary or presidential in nature. In a parliamentary system, the head of the executive (administration)—usually a prime minister—comes to office (or at least stays in office) as long as he is supported (or at least tolerated and not voted out of office) by parliament (or at least the lower chamber of parliament). The effect is that the *government is accountable to parliament* rather than to the Head of State. In a monarchy the King or Queen, or in a republic the president, may appoint a prime minister. In this case, they do so either after the prime minister has already been elected by parliament or, again, with a view to the creation of a stable government, with enough support in parliament.

However, while the government depends on the parliament to stay in office, the modern reality in parliamentary systems is that a prime minister who enjoys majority support in parliament is able to not only guide the executive but also to demand loyalty from the majority (party/parties) that keep him in office when he puts forward a legislative proposal.

Presidential Systems

In contrast, in a presidential system, the head of the executive (whether he is called President or something else, such as Governor) has his or her own mandate, which is independent from parliament, and is usually based on elections. In such a case, the head of the executive does not rely on parliamentary confidence to stay in office. Furthermore, members of parliament—who are directly elected as well—are not compelled to support the head of the executive. Their fates are not entwined or at least to a much lesser extent.

For example, US governors, the government leaders in the US States, are directly elected. The US President is elected formally by indirect popular vote via an electoral college, but this has de facto all the features of a direct election and ensuing mandate.

France and also other States such as Romania or Russia feature a semi-presidential system. They have a directly elected Head of State who has executive powers (the presidential aspect), as well as a Prime Minister who is accountable to parliament and can only remain in office with parliamentary support (the parliamentary aspect).

Semi-presidential Systems

Other republics may have presidents and prime ministers too; if these presidents have only ceremonial roles and no executive powers, the system is still considered parliamentary. Examples of such systems are Germany, Italy, or Israel, where executive power is held by the respective Chancellor or Prime Minister. South Africa has a mixed system: the president also relies on parliament.

> **Main Forms of Government**
> *Parliamentary systems*
> - The head of the executive relies on the confidence or tolerance of parliament to enter or stay in office.
> *Presidential systems*
> - The head of the executive is elected independently from parliament and may not be dismissed for reasons of lack of confidence.
> *Semi-presidential systems*
> - A directly elected Head of State and a Prime Minister who is accountable to parliament share executive power.

3.5   Checks and balances

In its pure form, the Trias Politica doctrine envisages separation of powers. An added feature to prevent the abuse of power and to prevent a concentration State powers is to build in mutual checks and controls. This is called *checks and balances*.

Forced Cooperation

Under the US Constitution, federal judges are appointed by the President, but this appointment is subject to the approval of the Senate. In the lawmaking process, the Senate and the

House of Representatives jointly adopt legislation but the President may veto it, which may in turn be overruled by supermajorities in the House and the Senate.

Another possibility to ensure the prevention of the abuse of power, and a situation where all power is concentrated in one hand, is to spread the decision-making process over different actors (organs/institutions). An example is the ordinary legislative procedure of the European Union. If European laws are to be made, a proposal must be submitted by the Commission which has the sole right of initiative. This proposal must then be voted upon by both the Council of Ministers and the European Parliament (see also ▶ Chap. 10, Sect. 4). This requires the making of compromises and the impossibility for one institution to push through its will.

Obvious advantage of the systems of checks and balances and the requirement to cooperate is the need to seek the other organs' approval and find compromises; an obvious downside is the possible delay and slowing down of policies and deadlocks.

Judicial Review

A very important check on the political institutions of parliament and government is judicial review, whereby courts check the legality of acts created by these institutions.

A court exercising judicial review might rule that the collection of a tax by the government was not covered by the tax code, for example, because the tax code provided for a tax exemption in a particular case under which the applicant falls, and that the tax has therefore been collected unlawfully.

Arguably, the ultimate power of judicial review is constitutional review, whereby a court checks whether legislation adopted by parliament itself is lawful in the light of what the constitution provides.

A court carrying out constitutional review, if it is competent to do so, might rule that the tax code itself is unconstitutional, for example, because it imposes a higher tax on women than on men, whereas the constitution prohibits discrimination based on sex. Thus, even if the collection of the tax took place in accordance with the law, it would still be unlawful because its legal basis was unlawful, and in this case unconstitutional.

3.6   The Rule of Law

The overarching constraint from constitutional law on the State is the rule of law itself. It is hard to define what exactly the rule of law means because interpretations differ. In a broad sense, the rule of law may include such sweeping notions as fairness, inclusiveness, independent adjudication, accountability, or transparency. It also has the qualitative meaning that the law must not only be legal but also reasonable, compatible with human rights, and fair. In a narrow sense however, it means that:

— The State rules through law.
— The State itself is ruled by law.

The first aspect means that the exercise of power must be performed by methods that comply with minimum standards to prevent arbitrariness. For example, laws that are enforced against citizens should at the very least be published before they are enforced. It also means that the proper procedures have been followed in making the law and that the law was made or executed by the competent authorities.

The second aspect means that the State and its organs are only allowed to perform particular tasks if they have been given the power to do so by law and to the extent that these tasks are allowed by law. Thus, State action requires a legal basis: the State may not legally act unless it is authorized by written law; an idea known as the principle of legality.

Legality

This principle plays an important role in both criminal law and administrative law. As the requirement of a legal basis, it also functions in European Union law.

The opposite is true for private citizens: they may do everything unless it is prohibited by law. Even where the State is authorized to act, it remains bound by the law in the performance of the action itself.

A policeman cannot stop vehicles on the road unless he is authorized to do so by law. Further, this policeman·cannot open citizens' private letters as this would violate the fundamental right to freedom of correspondence.

And even where powers actually have been given, they can only be exercised in accordance with the purpose for which they have been given. This is called the prohibition of abuse (or misuse) of power, or of *détournement de pouvoir*.

The mayor of a town may decide on the granting of building permits, but he may not refuse a permit just because the applicant belongs to a political party which he opposes.

The notion of the rule of law is largely a common law notion. In civil law systems, reference is often made to the *Rechtsstaat* or *État de Droit*. This is a State «under the law», which generally means that the State is bound by legal norms, respects the separation of powers, abides by human rights, and has a full-fledged independent judiciary.

3.7   Fundamental Rights

A very important way to curb the State's power, and to protect the individual against it, is to commit the State to respect fundamental human rights.

National Instruments

The codification of fundamental rights goes back many centuries. An important historic example—even though we have to acknowledge that this document did not cover all human beings—was the *Magna Carta* (1215), a document in which King John of England accepted limitations to his arbitrary power.

It contained, for instance, the rule that no «freeman» could be punished except through the law of the land.

The English Parliament again insisted on the codification of individual rights in the Bill of Rights 1689. Two other more recent historical documents are of particular importance. One is the revolutionary 1789 French *Declaration des droits de l'homme et du citoyen*, which heralded the overthrow of the absolute power of monarchs on the European continent. The other is the *Bill of Rights*, which was added in 1791 to the US Constitution. Subsequent modern constitutions, particularly in the twentieth century, also reserved prominent chapters for human rights catalogues. Combined with the power of courts to strike down laws that conflict with the constitution and its human rights catalogue, where such power exists, these bills of rights proved to have a great political and legal significance.

International Instruments

In addition to national codifications of fundamental rights, international instruments protecting human rights have been adopted as well, including the Universal Declaration of Human Rights of 1948, and regional instruments such as the European Convention on Human Rights of 1950, or the

European Union's very own bill of rights, the Charter of Fundamental Rights of 2000, which became legally binding in 2009. These and many other international human rights instruments underline the importance attached by the international community to build mechanisms through which States may be held accountable for human rights violations.

The actual interpretation of fundamental rights is not always easy. The rights are formulated in a necessarily broad manner so that it is up to the authorities, and often in the last resort to the judge, to determine what is allowed and what is not in real-life circumstances.

Consider in this respect the principle of equality or non-discrimination, which prescribes the equal treatment of people in equal circumstances, and the difficult questions that can arise from its application:

- Is the wearing of head scarves an infringement of the equality principle (where it is imposed on women only), or does banning head scarves from public life constitute an infringement of the equality principle (where other types of headgear are not banned)?
- Is it a violation of the principle of equality to further the societal equality of minority groups by according them preferential treatment over majority groups via so-called affirmative action?

Or consider the possible reversals of recognized fundamental rights:

- Does the freedom of religion only entail the right to freely practice one's religion, or does it also include the right not to be bothered by other people's religion, in cases where crucifixes are displayed in schools?
- Does the right to life only entail protection from unlawful killing by the State, or does it also include the right to end one's own life and to seek the assistance of a physician for that purpose (euthanasia), in cases where the law prohibits assistance to suicide?

Even where the scope of a fundamental right as such is relatively clear, it may still be that the right has to be balanced against a public interest:

- How to balance the right to privacy (which may include the right to have private conversations on the phone and to keep personal genetic information out of the State's hands) against the public interest of fighting crime, including terrorism (which may require phone tapping and the establishment and use of DNA databases)

Interpretation of Fundamental Rights

— How to balance the right to family life (which may include the right to not be forcibly separated from family members) and the public interest to implement immigration policies, in case one family member is to be expelled from the country for being an illegal immigrant?

Fundamental rights are found in many legal systems, but the interpretation and application of the rights often differ between the systems.

For example, in some systems free speech is upheld even in cases where the speech is intemperate, because the right as such is linked to the open and unimpeded political process and is perceived to require the most far-reaching protection in a democracy. In other systems, certain expressions such as hateful propaganda are deemed to be a threat to the functioning of the democratic system itself, including its human rights values, and are excluded from the protection that freedom of speech otherwise accords.

The successful invocation of fundamental rights in court may trump democratically legitimized public choices, which makes the issue relatively sensitive. Constitutional and treaty human rights can therefore be seen to facilitate courts in exercising checks on legislatures and executives. Furthermore, a tendency can be observed, where more and more claims are phrased as human rights arguments. Where classical civil and political rights focused on preventing the State from interfering with individual liberties, for example, by not torturing people or by not exercising censorship, more recent social and economic rights are phrased in a way that calls for State action to pursue certain goals. Thus, the right to education or health care would require the State to provide for schools and hospitals. Even more recent third-generation rights include legal claims to things like a clean environment. This certainly does not make the task of public authorities, especially judges, any easier. Human rights issues, in many instances, make for quite complex and sensitive issues, as we noted above.

3.8   Judicial Review

Problematic Nature

Constitutional review of legislation by courts, where it exists, means that judges have the power to check whether a law is in compliance with the constitution. This exercise, which is for reasons of brevity usually referred to simply as judicial review, is not entirely unproblematic. After all, it means that judges overrule the will of the lawmaker and impose policy choices on society through their own interpretation of what the constitution supposedly means. Judges enjoy neither the proper legislative power nor the democratic legitimacy of an elected parliament. And yet, a case can be made that judicial review is a necessary, or at least a useful, institution to have.

Reasons for Judicial Review of Legislation

First, judicial review of legislation can be an element in the checks and balances between State organs. The judiciary then acts as a check upon the legislature. The idea that courts must check upon the legislature has not remained undisputed, however.

Checks and Balances

In the UK, the notion of the supremacy of parliament implies that the will of the legislature cannot be questioned by the courts.

In the Netherlands, it is the lawmaker who is entrusted with respecting the Constitution when making laws, not the judge.

In France, judicial review was not possible until 2008, when the Constitution was changed to allow judges to refer questions of constitutionality to a special organ, the Constitutional Council. Before that, the separation of powers was taken to imply that judges should be separated from lawmaking and therefore should not question the validity of laws.

A second rationale for judicial review is that it upholds the supremacy of the constitution and thereby, in systems based on popular sovereignty, protects the will of the people itself, as is expressed in that constitution.

Will of the People

This was the reasoning in the 1803 US Supreme Court decision in the famous case *Marbury v. Madison*: it is clear that the Constitution is higher in rank with respect to ordinary laws and that judges are obligated to let the Constitution prevail over such ordinary laws if the two are in conflict, due to the fact that Congress had passed a law that violates the Constitution.

A third argument is based on the assumption that courts, situated at a certain distance from politics, are more inclined to protect individuals and minorities against majorities that control lawmaking institutions and that a democracy must also protect such minorities.

Protection of Minorities

Decentralized Systems

A very fundamental organizational distinction regarding judicial review is whether any court in the system can carry out the review, or if it is the domain of one special constitutional court. In a decentralized system, the constitution is a norm that all judges must uphold whenever they are asked to apply a law whose validity they doubt. The power of judicial review is that it is linked to the regular jurisdiction of all courts, which must resolve conflicts of norms before resolving disputes between parties.

The judicial review system in the USA is strictly decentralized: there is nothing special about the Supreme Court, other than the fact that it is the highest in the federal judicial hierarchy.

The Nordic countries in Europe also have a decentralized system of judicial review, although courts there tend to be more restrained and to yield to the preferences of parliament.

In a decentralized system, assessing the validity of a law vis-à-vis the constitution is not perceived as fundamentally different from deciding on a conflict between two laws or between a law and lower regulation.

Centralized Systems

In centralized systems, as they apply in most of Southern, Central, and Eastern Europe and beyond, ordinary judges must refer questions regarding the constitutionality of laws to a constitutional court, which then has the sole power to quash them. This model allows for a concentration of constitutional expertise and for the imposition of specific requirements and procedures for the appointment of constitutional judges who are, after all, entrusted with a delicate task.

In Germany, each of the two legislative chambers—the *Bundestag* and the *Bundesrat*—elects half of the judges at the Federal Constitutional Court. That is different from the appointment procedure for judges at all other federal courts. In Belgium, a fixed number of judges at the Constitutional Court must be former members of parliament.

Types of Review

The power of constitutional courts can go far beyond judicial review in cases referred to them by ordinary courts. For next to this *concrete* review, which arises from actual adversarial court proceedings between parties, some constitutional courts may also engage in *abstract* review. In that case, officeholders such as the government or members of parliament may claim that a law is unconstitutional even though it is not being applied in a concrete case. If judicial review is considered sensitive or controversial, it is surely abstract review that will attract most controversy. After all, here it cannot be said that judicial review is an inherently judicial task. Unlike the resolution of any other conflict of norms, here a court is expected to pronounce itself in a context that normal judges are not confronted with and to rule in the abstract. Nevertheless, where judicial review is cherished as a powerful counter-majoritarian instrument for checking on the lawmaker and for upholding the constitution, abstract review is certainly not misplaced.

European Union

Judicial review also exists in the European Union. It is exercised by the Court of Justice of the European Union (CJEU): a centralized system. The domestic courts must refer legal disputes that raise questions about the interpretation and validity of EU rules to the CJEU for a binding ruling. For EU Member States, EU law is supranational law, which must be applied by the domestic courts even when this implies setting aside domestic law. This has certainly had a large impact on domestic perspectives on the inviolability of domestic law.

Judicial Review by Specialized Courts

Constitutional judicial review can have many features when put in the hands of special courts: we draw attention to four of them:

1. When a question arises about the unconstitutionality of a statute in a case pending before a court, the court may/ must refer the case to the constitutional court and await its ruling on the constitutionality of the statute [France (since 2008) and Germany].
2. Members of parliament may refer a statute to the constitutional court to check for its constitutional validity even after it has been adopted. The court has to rule on the constitutionality of a statute in the abstract without the statute having been applied in a concrete case (France— this review only takes place before a law adopted by Parliament entered into force—and Germany).
3. Individual citizens may file a complaint with the constitutional court, arguing that their individual rights have been violated by State organs (Germany).
4. Constitutions or statutes may empower a constitutional court to rule on «other» constitutionally important issues such as election disputes (France, Germany), the prohibition of political parties (Germany), or conflicts between political agents, such as between the chambers of parliament or between a minority in parliament and the majority/government (Germany).

Judicial review is a potentially powerful instrument. In many States, it has led constitutional courts to deal with far-reaching issues, such as whether social security or tax laws should be set aside because of discriminatory aspects. Judicial review has also tackled several moral issues in relation to constitutions, such as the right to an abortion, the possibility for homosexuals to get married, and the protection of the rights of citizens to peacefully demonstrate and associate. As a result, there is an ongoing debate about the scope of the powers of constitutional courts, which addresses issues such as

- How does a constitutional court interpret the constitution?
- To what extent should the constitutional court accept the judgment of Parliament?
- How does a constitutional court cope with judgments that might have a huge financial impact (as might be the case in the domain of taxation)?
- How does the court deal with politically sensitive issues, such as the constitutionality of the health-care system (decided in 2012 in the USA) or the constitutionality of the European rescue fund for the euro (Germany)?

4   State Power Democratized

«Democracy» means «rule by the people». Historically, the term had some negative connotations, as it sometimes implied anarchy or mob rule. Today, however, the term «democracy» has universally a positive connotation. Democracy implies also that:

- The government is installed to rule the people because it is in the interest of the people to have a government in the first place.
- This government pursues the interests of the people rather than its own.

Under a democracy, the idea is that the government rules with the consent of the governed, or at least that the government is established with the support of the people and has regular confirmation of that support, or else should not be in power. As a form of government, democracy is endorsed around the world. States are either democratic or if they are not, they usually claim to be democratic. In the latter case, they may argue that the regime actually represents the interests of the people even if it did not get elected or if elections were not free and fair.

One should always be suspicious if a republic advertises its democratic character by calling itself «Democratic Republic» or «People's Republic».

The case for democracy is indeed compelling because one might think that it helps in aligning government choices with the citizens' preferences, which then maximizes the well-being of the greatest number of people. Or at least it helps in conveying the message that the government is based on collective choice and promotes policies that serve the general interest. Also, regular elections ensure that the government remains accountable to the people and that the risk of abuse of power is minimized because rascals can be voted out of office. Further, the transition of power is bloodless because it is regulated in a universally accepted peaceful procedure.

Effects of Democracy

4.1   Direct and Indirect Democracies

Democracy is a system of government where public power lies with, or emanates from, the people. If the democracy is direct (lies with the people), the State power is actually exercised by the people themselves. If the democracy is indirect (emanates from the people), the power is exercised by the people's representatives.

Direct Democracy

In hunter-gatherer societies, the members of a band could easily assemble around a campfire to discuss public affairs, such as where to move next or how to deal with individual misbehavior. Communal decision-making was very immediate. In constitutional terms, it is a form of direct democracy as the constituents who make up a society decide by themselves and for themselves. Later, urban societies, notably the Athenian democracy, also reserved crucial decision-making powers to the general assembly of citizens. This still occurs in Swiss villages and cantons.

There are two major problems with the practicality of direct democracy. One has to do with the complexity of the decisions that need to be taken. In organized societies, gains in productivity are achieved by division of labor, which in turn compartmentalizes society. Meanwhile, the reduced rates of violence between people, and the rising living standards resulting from productivity gain, facilitate population growth. In turn, this growth increases the complexity of society. In increasingly large and complex societies, assuming they are still to be organized according to democratic principles, decisions also become more complex. This may extend to the point where ordinary citizens cannot grasp the full extent of the implications that every particular decision could have.

Complex Decisions

Logistics

This leads to the other problem: the logistical organization of democratic decision-making in societies made up of millions of people is complicated. This is especially the case if such decision-making is not supposed to be limited to casting a vote but should also include collective consultation and an exchange of opinions.

Furthermore, one would need rules to prevent the abuse of powers by direct democratic majorities and human rights violations, as well as definitions of who participates, in what procedures, and under what criteria, as well as about the execution of policies and possibilities of redress, judicial review, etc. These issues however do also apply to representative democracy.

Representative Democracy

To deal with the increasing size and complexity of decision-making, representative or indirect democracy becomes a viable alternative to direct democracy. In a *pure* representative democracy, public power is exercised by a ruler, or group of rulers, who have been elected or appointed by the ruled. For the duration of their term of office, the rulers are not subject to dismissal by the ruled, and their decisions may not be overturned by the ruled themselves. As the French scholar Montesquieu wrote in 1748:

As in a country of liberty, every man who is supposed a free agent ought to be his own governor; the legislative power should reside in the whole body of the people. But since this is impossible in large States, and in small ones is subject to inconvenience, it is fitting that the people should transact through their representatives what they cannot transact by themselves.

Challenges

The implementation of a representative democracy creates a number of challenges that are addressed by means of constitutional law:

— It should be decided how the rulers are elected or appointed.
— A system needs to be devised to regulate how powers are distributed among various rulers and how the offices relate to one another.
— Fundamental consideration should be devoted to the question of how to prevent abuses of power by the rulers. After all, there is no guarantee that those in power will not seek to perpetuate their power, at which point the system becomes neither representative nor democratic.

Controls against the abuse of power are indeed vital. As the American revolutionary and drafter of the US Constitution James Madison observed in 1788:

> If men were angels, no government would be necessary. If angels were to govern men, neither external nor internal controls on government would be necessary. In framing a government which is to be administered by men over men, the great difficulty lies in this: you must first enable the government to control the governed and in the next place oblige it to control itself. A dependence on the people is, no doubt, the primary control on the government; but experience has taught mankind the necessity of auxiliary precautions.

A powerful check on the government in a representative democracy is the introduction of elements that are taken from direct democracy. In an otherwise representative democracy, direct democratic elements can take two main forms: the recall election and the referendum. A recall is a popular vote to dismiss an already elected officeholder before the term of office has expired.

Recall

In Western systems, recalls are typically found at regional and local levels rather than at national level.

Famously, Arnold Schwarzenegger became governor of the US State of California in a recall election to oust the incumbent governor Gray Davis in 2003.

A recall is a deviation from the principle of representative democracy in that powers are delegated for a fixed term and that the electoral sanction is the refusal to reelect an officeholder. A referendum, however, deviates from the principle that decisions are taken by the rulers or representatives on behalf of the governed. Instead, the approval or continued effect of a certain decision is subjected to a popular vote.

Referendum

Sometimes a referendum vote is used not only to correct decisions taken by the legislature (asking for a yes or no of a legislative decision—corrective referendum) but also to enable the people to adopt a new and original proposal to become law, bypassing the legislature. States may opt for both possibilities or pick one of them.

Evidently, referenda need to be subject to procedural checks, such as the circumstances in which a proposal is considered to be adopted or rejected (e.g., whether it is because a majority of the votes have been cast or there is a majority of the people in favor, defining the threshold needed to table a referendum, what subjects may be excluded from a referendum, etc.).

The modern use of «referendum» derives from a Swiss practice to adopt agreements between the *cantons*, or constituent regions, whereby the agreements would be subject to a referral ('ad referendum') to the people of the *cantons* themselves before they could enter into force. To this day Switzerland is the Western system most famous for its frequent reliance on referendums.

To some, referendums constitute the purest form of the democratic legitimation of a decision, guaranteeing the explicit consent of the governed and forcing rulers to align their own preferences with the preferences of the population they represent. Others might point out that most decisions are too complex to be determined in a simple «yes or no» fashion and that populations tend to be generally change-averse so that necessary reforms are made more difficult.

Forms of Referendum
Mandatory referendum
- For certain types of decisions, a referendum is required. Examples include constitutional amendments, which in some States must be approved by referendum.

Optional referendum
- For certain types of decisions, a referendum can be, but does not have to be called. Examples may include a popular vote on whether or not to join an international organization.

Binding referendum
- The outcome is binding: a rejected proposal cannot enter into force; it has to be approved.

Consultative referendum
- The outcome indicates the preferences of the voting population, but the government may deviate from it nonetheless.

Initiating referendum
- The referendum initiates a new bill or proposal.

Corrective referendum
- The referendum is held to support or block a law already adopted by parliament.

4.2   Election Systems

A representative democracy is not the only form of democracy, and in fact it may not even be the fairest one. Montesquieu himself saw the merit of the Athenian way of appointing certain (though not all) magistrates by lot from among those who would volunteer to put their names in a lottery drum. Election-based systems were seen as having an aristocratic tendency as rich and influential elites would monopolize power, whereas lots would ensure a healthy rotation in office. Nevertheless, in the Enlightenment-inspired eighteenth-century revolutions in America and France, the lot was discarded; both because it was impracticable and because a higher value was accorded to the idea of consent of the governed, which cannot truly be expressed via lot but which is expressed well through elections.

Who is allowed to vote? Throughout history, several restrictions have been applied on the franchise, that is, the right to vote. In Western democracies, the franchise is in principle universal, as the most important limitations of the franchise have been overcome, namely:

Franchise

- The exclusion of women's right to vote
- The exclusion of the right to vote for slaves or serfs
- The exclusion of the right to vote for persons not fulfilling certain property or taxation requirements

However, in the contemporary world, certain limitations do exist or persist, notably the exclusion of minors through a minimum age limit, the exclusion of soldiers, the exclusion of convicted prisoners or persons with a prior conviction, the exclusion of foreigners, and the exclusion of nationals living abroad.

The translation of votes into seats in a representative assembly generally follows one of two possible models, although hybrids do exist. One model is the majoritarian system, where a candidate is elected if he receives a defined majority of votes. A country may, for instance, be divided into many small districts, each of which elects one parliamentarian.

Majority Systems

In a plurality system, the candidate with the most votes (more than any of the other candidates) is elected.

Plurality Systems

In an absolute majority system, a candidate will need more than half the votes.

Absolute Majority Systems

If only one person is to be elected nationwide, such as in presidential elections, the system is necessarily majoritarian, but even then a plurality or an absolute majority or even higher supermajorities may be required.

The French President is elected with an absolute majority of votes, and if no candidate achieves this in the first round then a run-off between the two strongest candidates determines the winner.

The German President is elected (by an electoral college rather than by the people) by absolute majority, but if after two rounds no one musters an absolute majority, then in the third round a plurality suffices.

The US president is elected by an absolute majority of members of the Electoral College (not necessarily equaling an absolute majority of the votes), and if no one reaches that threshold, then the fallback procedure is a special election by the House of Representatives.

Benefits

Generally, a major benefit of the majoritarian systems is the link between members of parliament and the constituency where they are elected. This is thought to give citizens access to their representatives and makes them directly accountable to the district.

Also, it is mostly majoritarian systems that have the tendency to lead to clear and workable majorities after elections (because of voting behavior that favors two big parties, who alternate in size). This enables a distinct government and a majority in parliament and allows for effective governing because it makes cumbersome coalition negotiations after elections less likely.

Proportional Representation

The other main model for election systems is proportional representation (PR), whereby the share of seats in the assembly is proportional to the share of the votes. Thus, roughly speaking, 20% of votes will translate into 20% of seats for a political party. In a purely list-based system, political parties then go on to fill their seats with candidates from the lists that they had established before the elections.

Benefit

Generally, the benefit of a PR system is the representation of many political sentiments in society; the idea of parliament here is to mirror the composition of the population in parliament.

Downside

The downside, however, is that the parliament may be fragmented into too many political parties, which may make the formation of stable government coalitions more difficult. The imposition of a threshold will limit the fragmentation of the parliament, as only parties obtaining a minimum share of the vote (such as 5%) are entitled to seats, yet this is at the cost of the parliamentary representation, as it leaves a share of the voting population unrepresented. Some countries have opted for a system of bonuses: extra seats for the largest party in order to create a workable majority and coalition government.

The choice, as authors have put it, is therefore between certainty and clear and effective governing, on one hand, and a representative parliament with negotiations between majority-seeking parties, on the other hand. In practice, many States have sought variations of the two systems in order to try to benefit from the advantages of both approaches, such as multimember districts or alternative voting, wherein voters number candidates according to their preference.

5   Final Comment

In practice, electoral systems show the narrow link between politics, political parties, and constitutional law. We have noted before that politicians and politics decide the many choices left open by constitutional law. Here we note that political parties are very much involved in elections and the effects and outcome of elections. Constitutional law cannot be fully understood without a comprehension of politics, the political situation, and history. Similar constitutional systems may have different effects and lead to different outcomes and stability or success than others. Legal instruments may be copied, but political practice, political parties, political culture, customs and the interplay with other legal and constitutional institutions, and (legal) education are a lot more difficult, if not impossible to copy, and yet these other aspects codetermine the success or failure rate of a constitutional model. In time, a constitutional model may have to change in its political and factual *modus operandi* due to changed circumstances. Sometimes institutions remain the same in name but change drastically in how they operate.

The British Queen may be the Head of State and possess a variety of prerogative powers, but this description does not do justice to constitutional law and politics in the UK, which sets out that the Queen operates as the Queen in Parliament and that she may only act upon the recommendation of the Prime Minister.

The study of constitutional law therefore shows, as have the many examples given in this chapter, that what is required is a comprehension of constitutional law in action and an understanding of the mechanisms of power, control, accountability, personality, and non-state agents such as political parties.

Recommended Literature

Ginsburg T, Dixon R (eds) (2011) Comparative constitutional law. Elgar, Cheltenham
Heringa AW (2016) Constitutions compared, 4th edn. Intersentia, Antwerpen

Administrative Law

Chris Backes and Mariolina Eliantonio

© Springer International Publishing Switzerland 2017
J. Hage et al. (eds.), *Introduction to Law*, DOI 10.1007/978-3-319-57252-9_9

1   What Is Administrative Law

1.1   From Police State to Welfare State

In everyday life, many things are not organized by private parties but by public authorities. To drive your car to school or university, you must have a driving license. While driving, you use public roads and cross traffic lights. You also pass sites where public authorities have permitted the operation of industrial facilities, while other areas have been designated as residential estates. Hopefully, the use of dangerous substances in industrial production processes is sufficiently controlled. If you study abroad, your certificates have to be recognized, and you probably need a residence permit. Public authorities (who deal with a country's administration) play a role in all these matters. In order to be able to perform their tasks, public authorities (also described as administrative body or executive) need money. Raising taxes or other financial contributions is an important task for the administration too.

In the nineteenth century, the tasks of the State were mainly limited to maintaining law and order within the country and defending its territory against attacks from abroad. The idea behind this limitation was that public authorities should refrain from interfering with the rights and freedoms of citizens as much as possible.

After the industrial revolution, the tasks of the State shifted toward providing community services and distributing wealth among its citizens. This process was enhanced after several economic crises and, in particular, World War II. The tasks of the administration were no longer just defense and the maintenance of public order but also the provision of public goods and services.

For instance, the State now grants social security benefits and sponsors theaters.

The nature of the State has changed from «police State» to «welfare State».

More recently, tasks like monitoring the quality of foodstuffs and food production, as well as the implementation of an immigration and naturalization policy, have also been added to the responsibilities of the administration.

In all these fields, administrative bodies perform public duties and exercise certain powers. To do so, there have to be administrative authorities and civil servants. They must be equipped with the power to raise taxes or to stop your car if you drive too fast. In making use of these powers, the administrative authorities are guided and bound by procedural rules and substantive requirements that serve to protect the interests of all parties concerned. When the administrative authorities use their public powers, they can interfere with your rights and interests. Therefore, there must be legal remedies available to protect your rights and interests against the possible abuses of the administration.

Topics of
Administrative Law

Administrative law is mainly about
- Administrative authorities and their civil servants
- How administrative authorities get public powers
- Procedural rules for the use of public powers
- Substantive requirements administrative authorities have to take into account when using their powers
- Objection procedures and judicial protection against administrative action

1.2   Multilayer Governance

In any State, there are several levels of administrative decision-making. Besides national ministries, regional authorities of different kinds and municipalities, as well as other local bodies, fulfill important administrative tasks. The organization and structure of such authorities, their competences, and their dependence or independence from national authorities differ considerably between countries. This is owed to differences in the organization of the national State (centralized or federal) and to different traditions and cultures.

In France, for instance, national authorities have quite strong powers to control and influence the *regions*, whereas in Belgium, many administrative competences are concentrated in the *gemeenschappen* and *gewesten (regions)*, and the competences of the central government are very limited.

In Germany, the *Länder* enjoy (limited) sovereignty; they are subjects of international law and therefore competent, within certain boundaries, to conclude international treaties with other States. The division of tasks and competences between the federation and the *Länder* is laid down in the German Basic Law (*Grundgesetz*) and hence can only be altered by amending the *Grundgesetz*.

In a unitary State like the Netherlands, the provinces can be merged or totally dissolved through an act of parliament. Their tasks and competences are much more limited than those of the German *Länder*.

In 2007, Denmark abolished the 14 existing *Amten* and introduced five regions instead.

Together with the division of public powers between several territorial entities (central government, region, municipality), most countries have authorities specialized in certain subject areas, which often require specific technical knowledge and equipment. Examples are the British Environment Agency and the Dutch Water Boards (*waterschappen*).

Administrative tasks and competences are not only divided between several layers of administrative authorities within a national State. Nowadays, many administrative tasks are performed jointly by European and national authorities. Regional and national authorities often cooperate closely with the European Commission and European agencies. Examples of such cooperation can be found in the area of food safety and air traffic safety and in the designation of nature reserves that together form a European ecological network. Hence, administration is no longer a purely national affair but rather a joint venture of the European, national, and regional authorities. This is referred to as multilayer governance.

1.3   **Various Instruments and Powers to Protect the General Interest**

In order to serve the general interest, the administration has various *instruments*—i.e., juridical and factual acts—at its disposal to put its policies into effect and to bring about legal consequences for individuals. The legislator can empower the administrative body to issue general rules, and it can also give the administrative body the competence to grant subsidies or permits and to take decisions in individual cases. In some cases, in order to achieve certain policy goals, the administrative body needs to perform factual acts.

For example, municipalities install litter bins and flower tubs to enhance streets and public places.

In continental legal orders, a fundamental difference exists between competences under public law and competences under private law. In brief, public law competences are those competences that are exercised exclusively by public authorities. Therefore, competences under public law are competences that private law subjects (citizens, enterprises) cannot have, like the right to raise taxes or the right to issue residence permits to foreigners. Administrative authorities can have both kinds of powers. Besides competences under public law, which are typical for administrative authorities, private law

Competences

acts, such as concluding a contract for the construction of a bridge, can also serve the general interest.

1.4 The Administration Within the *Trias Politica*

In the chapter on constitutional law, we already quoted Lord Acton, who in 1887 very aptly summarized the need for a division of power as follows: «Power tends to corrupt, and absolute power corrupts absolutely».

Trias Politica

To avoid too high a concentration of power, the competences of the government must be divided between legislature, administration, and judiciary. According to Montesquieu's doctrine of the *Trias Politica*, the administrative (or executive) branch of power should be separate from the legislative and the judicial branches. In an ideal model of the democratic *Trias Politica*, the legislator is chosen by and is responsible to the people. The administration receives its powers only from the legislature. It executes these powers and is controlled by independent courts. See ◘ Fig. 9.1.

All European legal systems offer the possibility to go to court to challenge both juridical and factual acts of administrative authorities. The courts can check whether the executive remains within the limits imposed by law. In a system with a thorough distribution of powers, the competences of the judiciary are limited. Mainly, courts may control whether the administrative body has acted within the confines of the competences attributed to it and the rules imposed upon it by the legislature. In any event, the courts are bound by the law and may not deviate from the decisions of the legislature. The

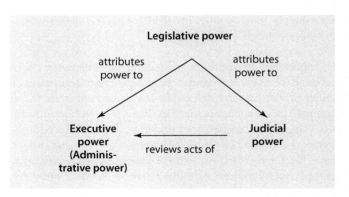

◘ **Fig. 9.1** *Trias Politica*

executive is hence situated between the legislature, from whose acts it derives all its competences, and the judiciary, which controls whether the executive has remained within the confines of the law.

Take, for example, the construction of a new power plant in an industrial area. The legislator has laid down the requirements to be fulfilled in order to obtain an environmental permit and planning permission, both of which are necessary if you want to construct such a power plant. Environmental law prescribes the procedure of decision-making and provides some general conditions. The administration applies the environmental statutes and follows the prescribed procedure, investigates and weighs all relevant interests, and determines the concrete conditions for the operation of the power plant. It issues the permit and afterwards monitors whether the operator complies with the conditions attached to it. If requested to do so, the courts assess whether the administration has correctly followed the procedural rules and applied all relevant legislation and whether all interests have been properly considered.

1.5 Questions

In the modern social welfare State, the public authorities are involved with almost every aspect of the daily life of individuals and in every area of society. The issues that administrative law deals with can be divided into two main categories. One category concerns the powers that administrative authorities need in order to fulfill their tasks and the conditions attached to such powers. It concerns what is called the *instrumental function* of administrative law.

The other category concerns the *safeguarding function* of administrative law. It deals with the protection of the rights and interests of citizens and of private organizations against the use of administrative power.

These two functions of administrative law correspond to two sets of questions that administrative law has to answer. The first set has to do with the rules that bind the administration in the execution of its tasks. The first question in this connection is when an administrative body has the power to act in a particular matter. This question is addressed in ▶ Sect. 2. The second question in connection with the instrumental function of administrative law concerns which rules bind the administration if it has the power to act in a particular matter. This is the topic of ▶ Sect. 3.

The second set of questions has to do with the supervision that the judiciary exercises over the administration. The first two questions in this connection are to what extent the judiciary is competent to review the acts of the administration and what it can do if it finds that the administration did not remain with the limits of the law. These two questions are the topic of ▶ Sect. 4, which also addresses two views on the function of administrative justice. Supervising the administration is a specialized task, and most countries have specialized judges to perform this work. This leads to a technical question of great importance; namely, when does an issue belong to administrative law and fall under the competence of these specialized judges? This question is addressed in ▶ Sect. 5. ▶ Section 6 deals with the question of which persons can address the court when they think that the administration has done something wrong. Can everybody complain about every mistake, or should one have some kind of interest in the matter? ▶ Section 7, finally, discusses the remedies that are available in case a court finds an administrative decision to be mistaken.

2   Public Powers: Rule of Law and Legality Principle

In order to pursue public goals and general interests, the administrative authorities receive certain competences from the legislator. We will now deal with the left half of the *Trias Politica* scheme. See ◘ Fig. 9.2.

The principle of the rule of law underlies administrative law in all European legal systems. It can have slightly different meanings across European legal systems, but its essence is always that the administration is, at all times, bound by the law. The allocation and execution of powers are regulated by

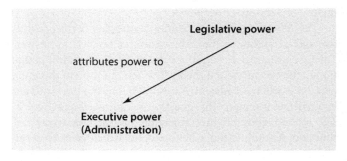

◘ **Fig. 9.2** Attribution of power

law, and the administration must refrain from violating the law, including the basic rights of individuals.

A special requirement of the rule of law is the legality principle. Generally, this principle requires that the administration's competence to act must have a basis in legislation. The legislature should confer competences upon the administration to perform public duties and provide it with the power to interfere with the legal position of individuals. Administrative statutes hence provide for the legality of administrative acts. In this way, the legislature endows the administration with the necessary instruments to put its policies in various areas of society into effect and to serve the general interest.

Moreover, legislation should also set limits to the powers conferred upon the administration. Above all, this means that the administration is not allowed to use its competences for a different purpose than that for which they have been conferred.

Take, for instance, the power of the mayor (in the Netherlands) to restrict the right to demonstrate in order to ensure public safety and order. The mayor may not prohibit demonstrations merely because he does not agree with the political statements of the demonstrators or the aim of the demonstration. The administration may not divert its competence from the purpose other than that which the legislator intended when creating the competence.

The French call this the prohibition of *détournement de pouvoir*. Both the legality principle and the closely related prohibition of *détournement de pouvoir* bind the administration to the legislature, as the democratic representation of the people.

Legality Principle

Détournement de Pouvoir

3 Procedural Rules and Substantive Requirements for the Use of Public Power: The General Principles of Administrative Law

3.1 Rationale of the General Principles: Preventing Abuse of Discretionary Power

As was mentioned above, the range of tasks and competences of the administration in various areas of society has grown enormously over the past decades. As a consequence, the administration's power to interfere with the rights and obligations of individuals has also increased. Administrative competences have grown not only in quantity but also in quality: compared to former times, administrative authorities today do not only have more powers to regulate various policy areas and to interfere with the rights of individuals; they also enjoy greater freedom in exercising these powers.

Tax Law

How substantive the conditions for the use of public power are differs from one field of law to another. Tax law, for instance, prescribes exactly which percentage of your income has to be paid in income tax and what may be deducted from your income before taxes are calculated. Tax officers thus have relatively little leeway to weigh diverging interests when taking their decisions. They have, in other words, little discretionary power.

Land-Use Plans

On the contrary, when a regional or municipal council draws up a plan for the use of land and decides whether a particular area will be designated as a residential or industrial estate or whether it is protected as a nature reserve, the statutory provisions empowering the administration to make this decision contain few concrete requirements. Much is left to the administration, which should investigate all interests involved in the concrete case, weigh these interests, and take a decision. Because the legislator is unable to regulate in detail which decision should be taken by the administration in any given case, administrative authorities enjoy more discretionary power. Therefore, the rights and duties of individuals who are affected by the land-use plan are not regulated concretely in legislation.

Fundamental Rights

Whenever the administration must take decisions in concrete cases, it is not only bound by the conditions and limits explicitly mentioned in the applicable general rules. It also has to respect the fundamental rights of those affected by the decision, and it must take general principles of administrative law into account.

When investigating an enterprise (enforcement of administrative law), an inspection agency has to respect the fundamental right of protection against arbitrary interference of home and may not enter a dwelling without the permission of a judge. Furthermore, when entering the dwelling, the agency has to take the interests of the owner into account and has to act carefully in order to keep any impairment of his rights to a minimum (general principle of proportionality).

It was especially the need to prevent the abuse of highly discretionary powers that caused the evolution of general principles of administrative law. The function of these principles is to control the administration, to set limits to administrative action, and to provide generally applicable safeguards against the abuse of administrative competences.

To some extent, one could say that the general principles of administrative law compensate for the frequent lack of concrete conditions and limits in the general rules that bind the administration. Moreover, with reference to the original idealistic model of the *Trias Politica*, one could say that this shift in function from legislation to general principles has caused a shift of power from the legislator, who is unable to formulate sufficiently concrete conditions and limits in specific legislation, to the courts, which can review the use of discretionary administrative powers by applying the general principles of administrative law.

Supervision by the Judiciary

3.2   Which Are the Most Important General Principles of Administrative Law?

Originally, the general principles of administrative law were developed in case law. Nowadays, however, there is a tendency in European legal systems to codify them, i.e., to lay them down in (general) statutory legislation. All European legal systems recognize more or less the same general principles of administrative law, although they may go under different names in different systems. The principles that are common to most European legal systems are:
1. The impartiality principle
2. The right to be heard
3. The principle to state reasons
4. The prohibition of *détournement de pouvoir*
5. The equality principle
6. The principle of legal certainty
7. The principle that legitimate expectations raised by the administration should be honored
8. The proportionality principle

Besides these principles, the European and national courts have acknowledged further principles that often can be understood as subcategories of the above-mentioned eight common principles and will not be dealt with here. In applying these principles to the acts and decisions of the administration in individual cases, the courts try to ensure that, even though the administration has certain discretion, some legal limits are imposed on the administration in the exercise of its powers. Applying the general principles of administrative law protects the rights and interests of individuals against the abuse of public power and against an overemphasis on the general interest when public power is used.

Procedural Principles

Some general principles of administrative law are more of a procedural (or formal) nature, while others are more substantive. The procedural principles address the decision-making process and the way in which the interests of individuals are taken into account during this process. The first three principles mentioned above have a mainly procedural character. In every decision-making process, the administration has to act impartially.

For instance, the mayor and aldermen of a municipality should not favor members of their political party in deciding which construction firm will be granted the building of the new city hall. When preparing a decision, the administration must investigate all relevant interests and hear all persons possibly affected by the decision. If somebody applies for a building permit, the neighbors should be given the opportunity to state their views. When the decision is published, the authority should state the reasons that were decisive for the decision. It will not do if a province only informs an enterprise that it will not be granted an environmental permit without giving any explanation.

Substantive Principles

The latter five principles mentioned above may be qualified as substantive principles. Substantive principles impose certain requirements on the administration with regard to the content of the decision or measure.

As already mentioned above, authorities may use their public power only for the purpose for which it has been conferred on them (prohibition of *détournement de pouvoir*).

If in a regulation, a competence to control vehicles is delegated to ensure traffic safety, the police are not allowed to use this power to stop cars in order to search for a murderer.

Decisions of the administration should (among others) be clear and understandable (legal certainty). Furthermore, they generally should not have any effect on events that occurred before the decision was published (no retroactive effect; this is another aspect of legal certainty).

For instance, the tax authorities should not suddenly modify the interpretation of tax rules, thereby retroactively attaching tax duties to events from the past that used to be tax-free.

The decisions should not treat people unequally without having a legitimate reason to do so (equality principle).

If one restaurant owner is allowed to have seats on a terrace in front of the restaurant, another restaurant owner who is in a similar situation should also be allowed to have them.

Administrative decisions should not negatively affect the interest of people more than is necessary to achieve the envisaged goal and should not lead to a clearly disproportionate result (proportionality principle).

If the administration establishes a violation of the rules on playing loud music in a bar it would be disproportionate to close the bar immediately. It can give a warning, though, and take measures if the violations continue.

Furthermore, if the administration raised legitimate expectations that a certain decision would be taken, it should, if possible, honor such expectations.

If a competent public officer informs a citizen that she will receive unemployment benefits because she satisfies all the conditions, and this citizen rents an apartment in the expectation that she will receive these benefits, it will not be easy to refuse the benefit because after all it turned out that the conditions for the benefit were not satisfied.

4　Judicial Review of Administrative Action

As we have seen, the rule of law means that the executive is bound by the law that governs the exercise of a specific power. Furthermore, the executive has to respect fundamental rights and must apply general principles of administrative law.

However, administrative bodies are not infallible, and it is possible that they act in an unlawful manner.

This would, for instance, be the case if they use a power for a purpose other than that for which it was conferred, e.g., where a building permit is refused because the mayor does not want a political enemy to become his neighbor (*détournement de pouvoir*).

An administrative body can also act unlawfully outside the sphere of its public law powers. This is the case, for instance, when it closes a bridge for maintenance for a period which is unnecessarily long and is to the detriment of the shop owners in the neighborhood (violation of the principle of proportionality) or when it discriminates in accepting tenants for houses owned by the city (violation of the principle of equality).

The questions then are as follows: who can do something about this, what can be accomplished, and how can it be accomplished? These questions are the subject matter of the current and following sections.

4.1   The Power of the Judiciary to Review Administrative Acts

The judiciary receives its power from the legislator. See ◻ Fig. 9.3.

If we look at the task of the judiciary within the structure of the *Trias Politica*, we deal with the relation between the judicial and the executive powers (see ◻ Fig. 9.4).

To what extent does the judiciary have the power to review acts of the executive? We have seen that the answer to this

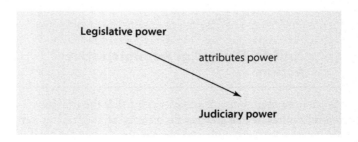

◻ **Fig. 9.3**   Attribution of judiciary power

....

Executive power ← ——————— **Judiciary**
(Administration)   reviews   **power**

◘ Fig. 9.4   Judicial review

question is, to a large extent, dictated by the doctrine of separation of powers and the way this doctrine is given shape in the form of the *Trias Politica*. The judiciary has the task to control the functioning of the executive, but in doing so it should remain within its own sphere and not take over the tasks that are assigned to the administrative body. We will see that this theoretical division of tasks is not always easy to implement in practice.

The actual implementation of the *Trias Politica* differs widely between national legal orders and deviates substantially from the theoretical ideal model. In practice, the legislator is often unable to describe the power conferred upon an administrative body in more than very vague terms and therefore grants broad discretionary powers to the administrative authorities. In such a case, in order to come to a decision, the administrative body has to identify all interests involved, balance them, and decide which interest will be given priority and to what extent. The outcome of this process therefore depends on the weight that the administration chooses to attach to each interest, within the framework conditions set by legislation. As the conditions prescribed by law are often quite vague and general, it is, to a large extent, not the legislator who decides about public rights and duties but the administrative body itself. Hence, administrative authorities do not only execute legal provisions, norms, and standards provided by legislation but also determine these norms and standards autonomously.

For example, environmental legislation by no means prescribes the permissible amount of emissions of hazardous substances to the air, or effluents to the water by industry. The reason is that the determination of this quantity largely depends on the circumstances of the individual case. The kind of industrial process in question, the age of the installation, the geographical conditions and the existence of recently developed environmental techniques all play a role. Because legislation by its nature deals with general rules, the executive is in a better position than the legislature to evaluate the details of concrete cases. For that reason, legislation mainly prescribes that the operator of a certain installation has to apply for an environmental permit. It is then up to the administrative body to attach conditions to the permit, which specify limits with regard to air pollution or the discharge of substances.

Limitation of Administrative Competences

In many countries, administrative courts assess not only whether the administration has remained within its competences but also whether it has adequately investigated and weighed all relevant interests and used its powers appropriately. However, which decision serves the public interest best is, first and foremost, not a legal matter, but a policy choice. Therefore, the decision must be based on a general framework set by the elected legislature. The decision in concrete cases is left to the executive, which obtains a competence to act from the legislature and is bound by the general framework. The courts, however, have no role in this; their task is merely to check whether the executive has remained within the limits of the law.

The principle of legality imposes limits on the competences of the administrative body. Fundamental rights and several general principles of administrative law (see ► Sect. 3) guide the process of identifying and weighing the diverse interests that must be considered in administrative decision-making. Whether the administration has remained within its competences and whether it has observed these rights and principles in taking its decision are legal questions. Therefore, they can and must be examined by a court if an applicant requests a judicial review of the decision. However, whether the most suitable and advisable decision has been taken is a matter of policy, not a legal question, and hence is up to the executive. The legal question of whether all relevant interests have been taken into account and the outcome of the weighing is not disproportionate and the political questions as to which decision is preferable are narrowly related, which makes the task of the administrative court a difficult one.

How exactly the powers between the legislator, executive, and judiciary are distributed and where the boundaries between these three functional entities of a State can or should be found are ongoing and vividly discussed topics within each democratic State. Each country finds its own, to quite an extent, different answers to these questions.

4.2   The Function of Administrative Justice

The view on the main purpose of administrative justice influences which individuals have access to the courts in administrative affairs and which remedies can be obtained by judicial review of administrative actions. Therefore, we must first answer the question of what the *function* of administrative justice is before we discuss who can challenge administrative action and what can be achieved by doing so. The answer to this question differs substantially between national legal orders.

In the UK, the very existence of administrative law as a separate branch of law has always been controversial, and for a long time its existence has been denied. According to the nineteenth century British constitutional scholar Albert Venn Dicey: «the words «administrative law» are unknown to English judges and counsel, and are in themselves hardly intelligible without further explanation».

United Kingdom

Dicey's views on administrative law have been very influential and meant that until quite recently there was no formal separation between private law and administrative law in the UK. The executive was subject to common law, and administrative disputes were dealt with by the ordinary courts and decided on the basis of the same rules that also govern the disputes between private actors.

Consider again the example of a refusal to grant a building permit, inspired by the wish of the mayor not to have his political opponent as a neighbor. If the opponent filed a claim against an administrative body, this was originally treated in the UK analogously to a claim of one private actor against another for unlawful behavior.

The last years, however, have seen the emergence of separate judicial bodies for administrative matters and of special rules applicable to the executive (◨ Fig. 9.5).

In continental Europe, there are, broadly speaking, two main views of the function of administrative justice. It is, however, almost impossible to find them in their pure form. Rather, «elements» in the different jurisdictions are found, which may be traced back to one view or the other.

Continental Europe

The first view of administrative justice, which, for instance, is to a large extent characteristic of the French system, is based on the notion of *recours objectif*. According to this view, the main aim of judicial protection against administrative behavior is to check whether an administrative body has acted law-

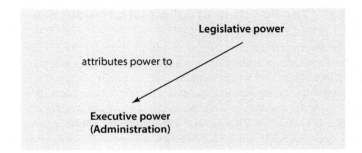

■ **Fig. 9.5**   Attribution of power

fully and within the scope of its powers. Judicial review thus mainly serves a public interest, namely, the interest that the executive should not act unlawfully. Of course, it is an individual who brings a claim before the court, and he or she does so in order to protect his or her own interests. And yet, in the view of *recours objectif*, this individual acts, in a way, as an «instrument» to allow the court to check the legality of the administrative behavior. The protection of the applicant's legal sphere is thus a by-product of the judicial review process, not its main objective.

In the *recours objectif* view, the political opponent of the mayor who challenges the refusal of a building permit functions primarily as an instrument of the public interest that makes the administration use its competences for the purposes for which they were given. A possible «by-product» would be that the opponent also gets his building permit.

The second continental view on administrative justice, which characterizes, for instance, the German system, is based on the notion of *recours subjectif*. According to this view, the aim of judicial protection against administrative behavior lies not so much in the check on the executive but in the protection of the individual's legal position. The primary task of a court that reviews administrative action is therefore not to determine whether the administration has acted lawfully but rather to determine whether the legal position of private actors has been violated. Of course, these two aims may partially overlap in some situations, but, as we shall see below (▶ Sect. 6), this is not always the case.

Consider again the example of a refusal to grant a building permit, inspired by the mayor's wish not to have his political opponent as a neighbor. If the opponent challenges this refusal before a court, he does so in order to protect his rights. Under the doctrine of *recours subjectif*, this would be the primary function of this lawsuit. That the administration is forced to comply with the demands of legality would merely be a welcome «by-product».

5   Organization of Judicial Review in Administrative Dispute

Regardless of the way in which a certain legal system understands the function of the system of administrative justice, most systems feel that there must be a way to control the actions and omissions of the executive. However, the way in which this system of control is organized varies greatly throughout the legal systems. In the following sections, we will explain the main variations in the systems of administrative justice and their rationales. In this connection, several factors need to be taken into account.

5.1   Preliminary Objection

The first factor to be taken into account is the existence of a system of preliminary objection with the administrative authorities.

Some countries, such as Germany, have traditionally opted for a system of compulsory preliminary objection. Before a claim may be brought before an administrative court, individuals must first ask the public administration to review the administrative measure that allegedly violates the individuals' legal positions.

Other countries, such as France, also use the system of objection, but they do not consider raising an objection as a necessary prerequisite for access to court. Other countries, finally, do not have a system of preliminary objections, and individuals have no way to complain about administrative action to an administrative body. Where this is the case, individuals can only appeal against administrative decisions in court or, as we shall see below, before other types of quasi-judicial bodies.

The aim of the system of preliminary objection is to ease the workload of the courts and to make sure that violations by the authorities are remedied in a speedy and efficient way. Furthermore, some legal systems allow an administrative body to change the measure challenged in an objection procedure: this might be impossible for the courts because of the doctrine of separation of powers and is therefore an advantage vis-à-vis judicial proceedings, at least from the perspective of an individual. The disadvantage of this system, however, might be that it is the administrative body that will have to rule on the alleged unlawfulness of its own actions. Therefore, in such cases, at least some doubts can be cast on the likelihood of the administrative body «changing its mind» and admitting its own error. This is why many legal systems adopt some «control mechanisms» such as the possibility to install an external advisory committee during the objection procedure (as is the case in the Netherlands) or to have a hierarchically higher administrative authority take a decision on the objection procedure (as is the case in Germany).

5.2   Specialized Administrative Courts

The second factor that can play a role in the categorization of the courts' systems is whether administrative matters are dealt with by specialized branches within general courts or by separate specialized courts. There are systems such as Germany that opt for review by specialized courts of administrative matters, while systems such as the Netherlands (in the first instance) or the UK opt for a review by specialized branches within the general courts.

While it is not unthinkable that there could be no separate courts or separate branches for administrative disputes, this setup is highly unlikely given the complexity of administrative law.

Because of the complexity of administrative issues, which range from environmental law to migration law to spatial planning law to many more, many legal systems have opted for the creation of specialized administrative courts for some specific areas. For example, Sweden has environmental courts, and Austria has courts for migration and asylum matters.

Similar to specialized courts, but not completely comparable to courts, are Tribunals, which are typical for both the UK and the Irish administrative legal systems. Tribunals are quasi-courts, and they fulfill a role that is similar to that of a court. However, they are highly specialized; there are Tribunals for social security and for environmental matters and also for matters relating to milk quotas only! Moreover, disputes are resolved not only by «real» judges, i.e., persons with a legal education, but also by lay people with a specific background in the subject matter of the dispute.

In a way, one could say that what happens before a Tribunal is a hybrid between court proceedings and a preliminary objection before the administration.

The advantage of this system is the concentration of expertise in the Tribunal and the fact that there are very few procedural hurdles for applicants. It is quite easy to access Tribunals, and this ensures that individuals always have a forum that will hear their complaints. At the same time, however, one could argue that, while Tribunals are applicant-friendly for their informal nature, this feature might sometimes go to the detriment of individuals; for example, in many Tribunals legal representation is not compulsory. This creates a very low threshold for applicants to access the Tribunals because they do not need the help of a lawyer, but this rule might in the end go to the disadvantage of those without representation because they will not be able to accurately present the point of law they wish the Tribunal to take into consideration.

5.3   What Is an «Administrative Dispute»? The Public/Private Divide

If a legal system decides, as the vast majority does, to assign «administrative disputes» to either a specialized court or to a specialized branch within ordinary courts, it is faced with the question of what an «administrative dispute» actually is.

This question may seem quite straightforward for certain cases. Few would doubt, for example, that a claim against an order for the demolition of a building is an administrative dispute, as this measure represents the core of what administrative law is about: the possibility for the public administration to limit the legal sphere and the rights or interests of an individual in the name of the public interest.

The delineation of what an administrative dispute is, however, becomes more complicated when, for example, an administrative body has concluded a contract with a building company for the construction of a bridge. Does the matter then fall within the competence of the administrative courts because the public administration is one of the parties to this contract? Or should this matter be reviewed by the ordinary courts since, after all, the subject matter of the controversy is a contract between two entities and hence, in principle, a private law juridical act?

Legal systems have adopted different solutions to this issue. Some legal systems, such as the British one, focus on the

Agent

agent: here, every dispute will be qualified as an «administrative dispute» if the challenged action has been carried out by a body «exercising public law functions», regardless of whether the action constitutes a private law juridical act or a public law juridical act. So, if the London police department buys new police cars, this can lead to an administrative dispute.

Action

Other legal systems, such as the Dutch one, focus not so much on the nature of the agent (i.e., the administrative body) but on the type of action that is at stake. Typically, these legal systems would assign only public law juridical acts that are not the creation or modification of rules to the jurisdiction of the administrative courts, while private law juridical acts (e.g., contracts) and the creation of rules would fall under the jurisdiction of the ordinary courts.

In the Netherlands, a claim concerning a building permit can be brought before the administrative branch of the ordinary courts, but not a sales contract, nor a complaint about the content of a local regulation.

Focusing on the action, however, may lead to different results in different countries. In the Netherlands, the criterion is whether the action is a written decision of the administrative body for a concrete case based on a public law competence. The determining criterion in France is not whether the act is a written decision but whether the action in question can be qualified as a public service that is carried out on the basis of a public power.

In France, similarly to the UK, even a claim regarding a contract between an administrative body and a private individual may be qualified as an «administrative dispute». This would, for instance, be the case if the administrative body is, with that contract, carrying out a public service such as the provision of bus services between two villages.

6   Standing

Once it is established that a matter is an «administrative matter» and it falls within the jurisdiction of a certain kind of court (be it a general administrative court, a specialized administrative court, or a specialized branch for administrative matters within the ordinary courts), an individual should seize a court of this kind if he or she wants to challenge the administrative action. However, having selected the appropriate kind of court does not necessarily mean that the claim will actually be dealt with. Before being able to plead their case before a court, potential applicants have to show that they have «standing». The concept of standing is linked to the idea that there should be some kind of «link» between the applicant(s) and the subject matter of the action.

Legal systems understand and qualify this necessary link in very different ways. In some situations, there is little disagreement between the legal systems. For example, if the applicant is the addressee of an administrative measure (because an order for demolition is directed toward the building of which he or she is an owner), it can hardly be doubted that there is a clear link between his or her legal sphere and the contested measure.

The existence of this link becomes progressively more blurred if one thinks, for example, of a father challenging the amount of disability benefits received by his teenage son or a taxpayer challenging a local tax imposed upon all residents of a municipality or a resident of a city challenging a measure that imposes the closure of a certain street or an environmental NGO challenging the decision to open a nuclear plant in certain area where very rare birds nest.

For such situations, legal systems establish the necessary link in essentially two main ways, using the concept of either «interest» or «right». This choice is not accidental, but it is (at least traditionally) connected to the different conceptions of *recours objectif* and *recours subjectif* (see ▶ Sect. 4.2). Legal systems that adhere to the conception of *recours objectif* will typically have quite liberal standing rules. If the aim of the system of administrative justice is to check the objective legality of the administrative action, it is in the interest of the legal system itself that a rather loose link between the applicant and the contested administrative action suffices for the applicant to have access to a court.

This link is the concept of «interest». In order to have standing, the applicant will only have to prove that he or she has an «interest» in the legal situation affected by the administrative action. This means that not only the addressee of a measure will be able to prove standing but also whoever can show that the consequences of the administrative action are of interest to him or her.

For example, in case of a challenge against a license to open a nuclear plant, standing would be granted, in an interest-based legal system, not just to the individuals living around the affected area but also to environmental NGOs who wish to protect citizens or the environment in general.

Conversely, legal systems that are based on the idea of *recours subjectif* often only grant standing to an individual where he or she can successfully demonstrate that the contested administrative action affects his or her rights.

This means that it will be much harder, in the example made above, for environmental NGOs to bring a claim before a court, given that they will hardly be able to show that their own rights have been affected.

However, this correlation between «interest-based» standing and *recours objectif* on the one hand and «right-based» standing and *recours subjectif* on the other hand is currently no longer that clear. While it is still the case that in systems with a right-based approach to standing the proceedings can be characterized as *recours subjectif*, there are also many systems with an interest-based approach to standing which adhere to a *recours subjectif* conception (such as the Netherlands).

The rather restrictive approach to standing which is present in legal systems adopting a *recours subjectif* approach should not be judged in isolation. As we will see (▶ Sect. 7), this restricted admittance to the courts goes hand in hand with relative extensive powers for the courts once the claim is declared admissible.

7   Remedies

Of course, one files a lawsuit not only for being dissatisfied with the behavior of the public administration but also because one wants a certain result. These demands, in technical terms, are called «remedies» or «actions.» Some remedies are so inherent to the idea of judicial protection against the acts of public authorities that they are to be found in every legal system. Some others are only available under certain circumstances or with some restrictions or are available not before the administrative courts but only before general courts. If the latter is the case, this means that an applicant is forced to make that demand before an ordinary court even if the respondent is an administrative body. If, for example, someone in Germany wants to hold a public authority liable because it acted unlawfully and wants to claim compensation of the damage that occurred from this unlawful action he has to file a suit at German civil courts, notwithstanding the fact that the party being sued is a public authority.

The range of remedies available to administrative courts in the different legal systems does not vary accidentally but is to an extent the consequence of the rationale underlying the systems of administrative justice. If a system adheres to the view of a *recours objectif*, then it will typically grant courts only the powers that are strictly necessary to eliminate the illegal administrative action. If a system embraces the idea of *recours subjectif*, it will provide the courts with more extensive powers, as the aim of the claim is seen in the protection of the individual's legal sphere.

7.1   Annulment

When an applicant complains about an allegedly unlawful restriction of his or her legal sphere by the executive, the appropriate remedy (and the most «typical» one in the systems of administrative justice) is annulment. The applicant will typically make this demand (or, in more technical terms, bring this action or ask for this remedy) against an administrative decision that restricts his or her legal sphere. Then he will ask the competent court to deprive the contested measure of its effects.

Annulment is the equivalent in administrative law of what is called «avoidance» in private law. Annulment is only an option if the unlawful behavior of the executive consisted of a juridical act, because factual acts cannot be annulled.

An action for annulment may also be brought against a decision to deny a particular request. When this is the case, this only means that the measure (such as the denial to grant a license to open a restaurant) is annulled. It does not mean that the administrative body has been ordered to grant the license. It is even less likely that the court will grant the license itself.

7.2   Performance

Many legal systems allow individuals to ask the court to force an administrative body to issue a certain measure or to perform a certain activity, such as to repair a road, to pay a subsidy, and also to perform on its contractual obligations. For this purpose, many legal systems grant courts so-called injunctive powers. These are typical powers provided to courts in a legal system with the *recours subjectif* conception, as these powers are aimed at protecting the individual's legal position and not merely at restoring the objective legality of the administrative action. However, these powers are not completely uncontroversial: they may conflict with a certain understanding of the *Trias Politica*. Giving courts the power to issue (more or less) detailed binding orders to the executive may be regarded as an interference of the judicial power into the realm of the executive and hence a potential breach of the principle of separation of powers. The necessity to keep courts and administration separate from each other and the idea that courts should not act as administrators have induced the legal systems that provide for this «injunctive» power to surround it with certain yardsticks.

In France and in Germany, for instance, courts are allowed to issue orders to the administration, but these orders may only have a specific content if there is only one way in which the administration may act. This is the case, for example, if there is no question about the amount of social security benefits that a person is entitled to. Then the court may order the administration to grant the benefits at that amount.

In all other cases, i.e., with discretionary decisions, courts are allowed to order the administration to act (i.e., to reopen the decision-making proceedings) but not to direct the content of the action.

While this choice is undoubtedly respectful of the principle of separation of powers, it is certainly not the most efficient one, given that the issue will have to go back to the administration, which will have to start the decision-making proceedings anew. How to increase the effectiveness of judicial protection without violating the principles of the *Trias Politica* is a much-debated issue in many countries.

8   Conclusion

Administrative law mainly deals with the relationship between the executive and private persons and/or organizations. In a democracy, an administrative body is strictly bound by law. First, it needs powers to be assigned to it by means of legislation. According to the rule of law (legality principle), all competences of administrative bodies that interfere with the legal position of individuals must derive from legislation.

Second, in performing a task, an administrative body is bound by the specific rules that govern this task and more generally both by the fundamental rights of the private persons and organizations that are affected by the administrative actions and by the general principles of administrative law.

The judiciary has the task to check whether the executive remains within the limits imposed on it by law. Notably, separation of powers means that it should not check whether the decisions taken by an administrative body and its other actions are the optimal ones. This kind of evaluation of the administration's work belongs to political bodies that are democratically legitimated. Courts can check whether an administrative body complied with the law, by checking whether the administrative body had the power to perform a task, and whether it obeyed the rules and rights that govern the execution of the tasks of the administration.

The precise procedures by means of which courts can check on the executive differ from country to country. An important factor in this connection is whether a country has a *recours objectif* or a *recours subjectif* view on the function of administrative justice. In legal systems adhering to the first view, quite some persons and organizations will have standing, but the powers of the courts to provide remedies are more limited. In legal systems adhering to the second view, it is just the other way round.

Recommended Literature

Bok AJ (2005) Juridical review of administrative decisions by the Dutch administrative courts: recours objectif or recours subjectif? A survey including French and German law. In: Stroink F, Van der Linden E (eds) Judicial lawmaking and administrative law. Intersentia, Antwerpen

Kuennecke M (2007) Tradition and change in administrative law. Springer, Berlin

Schwarze J (2006) European administrative law, 2nd edn. Thomson/Sweet, Andover

Seerden RJGH (ed) (2012) Administrative law of the European Union, its member States and the United States, 3rd edn. Cambridge, Intersentia

The Law of Europe

Jaap Hage

© Springer International Publishing Switzerland 2017
J. Hage et al. (eds.), *Introduction to Law*, DOI 10.1007/978-3-319-57252-9_10

1   Early History and Overview

Schuman initiative

The European Union (EU) is the outcome of a series of events that were initiated by the Second World War. After this war ended, politicians both on and off the continent saw cooperation within Europe as a means of lessening the chances of another war breaking out. Some saw the creation of a European federation as the way to accomplish this, but a full-blown federation, the «United States of Europe», was a bridge too far.

Against this backdrop of events, which divided Europe into East and West, a 1950 initiative by the French Foreign Minister Robert Schuman found fertile soil. Schuman proposed that Franco-German production of coal and steel as a whole be placed under a common «High Authority», within the framework of an organization open to the participation of other countries in Europe. This proposal was inspired by the desire to improve relations between France and Germany and to prevent a new war between these two countries by combining their coal and steel production. Since coal and steel were crucial resources for warfare, uniting the production of these two resources would make a new war between the involved countries less likely.

To cut a long story short, the Schuman initiative led to the creation of the European Coal and Steel Community (ECSC) in 1952 with the Treaty of Paris. There were six participating States: the German Federal Republic (West Germany), France, Italy, the Netherlands, Belgium, and Luxembourg. In 1958, the six States that founded the ECSC also founded the European Economic Community, the EEC, by means of the Treaty of Rome. In 1992, the ECSC and the EEC (and Euratom, an organization of minor importance) were joined by means of the *Maastricht Treaty* or the *Treaty on European Union (TEU)*. This treaty was followed by other treaties that reorganized the EU, with the Treaty of Lisbon (2007) as provisional terminus.

2   Sources of EU Law

Primary EU Law

The law of the EU can be divided into two main categories. On the one hand, there are the treaties upon which the EU was founded. The most important treaty for the EU in this regard is the Treaty of Lisbon. In this treaty, the Treaty on European Union and the Treaty on the Functioning of the European Union were given their present form.

It is important to distinguish between treaties as European legislative instruments and treaties as texts containing law of Europe. The former treaties, including the treaties of Rome, Maastricht and Lisbon, are legislative tools by means of which the Treaty on European Union and the Treaty on the Functioning of the European Union as law-containing treaties were created, or modified.

On the other hand, there is the law that was created by the EU itself. There are three main ways in which the EU, through its institutions, can create binding legal effects, namely, by means of regulations, directives, and decisions. Together with the case law of the Court of Justice of the European Union, they form what is called secondary EU law. Moreover, the EU can also give nonbinding recommendations and opinions (Article 288 of the Treaty on the Functioning of the European Union, TFEU).

Secondary EU Law

Regulations contain rules, just like «ordinary» legislation. They have general application and are binding and directly applicable in all Member States. This means that they directly create rights and duties for individual persons and organizations in the Member States.

Regulations

An example is Council Regulation No 2531/98 of 23 November 1998 concerning the application of minimum reserves by the European Central Bank (ECB).

Directives are a special type of legislation, directed to the Member States, obligating them to bring about a legal situation conforming the contents of the directive in their national law. In a sense, directives contain rules, but the EU does not directly impose these rules. It is left to the Member States to implement them in their national systems.

Directives

An example is Directive 2004/38/EC of the European Parliament and the Council of 29 April 2004 on the right of citizens of the Union and their family members to move and reside freely within the territory of the Member States.

By using a directive, rather than regulating an issue itself, the EU provides the Member States with the opportunity to make a national regulation that fits in the existing legal system. In light of the principle of subsidiarity, this is a preferable way of organizing the EU legal order. At the same time, directives tend to be so specific that EU citizens and companies can count on directive-based law to be practically the same across other European Member States.

For example, Article 5 of the abovementioned Directive on the rights of Union citizens reads: The right of all Union citizens to move and reside freely within the territory of the Member States should, if it is to be exercised under objective conditions of freedom and dignity, be also granted to their family members, irrespective of nationality. For the purposes of this Directive, the definition of 'family member' should also include the registered partner if the legislation of the host Member State treats registered partnership as equivalent to marriage

Decisions

Where regulations are meant to be general, decisions are typically meant for specific cases. A decision is binding, but decisions that specify their addressee only bind that addressee.

An example is the decision of 24 May 2004 of the Commission in a proceeding against Microsoft, because Microsoft had, amongst others, made the availability of the Windows Client PC Operating System conditional on the simultaneous acquisition of Windows Media Player (2007/53/EC).

3   Main Institutions of the EU and the ECB

The EU consists of several smaller organizations. The more important ones are the Commission, the European Parliament, the European Council, the Council of the European Union, the Court of Justice of the European Union, the Court of Auditors, and the European Central Bank.

The Commission

The Commission is the institution within the EU that has the promotion of the general interest of the Union as its official task. To fulfill its central role in legislative procedures, the Commission must ensure that the treaties and other EU laws are applied. It has an important role in EU policy making.

The seat of the Commission is in Brussels. The Commission is led by its President, a function that is presently fulfilled by Jean-Claude Juncker. To fulfill its many tasks, the Commission avails over a bureaucratic apparatus of around 24.000 members (in 2012).

Originally, every Member State of the EU had at least one representative in the Commission, but the number of Member States has increased greatly, and Article 5 TEU determines that the number of Commissioners in principle equals to two-thirds of the number of Member States. However, Commissioner posts are still divided over the Member States, currently with one Commissioner for every Member State. Commissioners are not representatives of their States: they are there to promote the general Union interest.

The Commission must answer to the European Parliament, and the Parliament must sanction the Commission's appointment and has the power to dismiss the Commission.

The European Parliament (EP) has its seat in Brussels and Strasbourg. The parliament has three main functions: *(The European Parliament)*
- It is involved in the legislative process.
- It must approve the annual EU budgets (Article 314 TFEU).
- It supervises the Commission.

The current 751 members of the European Parliament (MEPs) are directly elected by voters in the EU Member States. The MEPs form groups in the EP along political lines rather than on the basis of the countries from which they stem. For example, the EP has large groups of Christian-Democratic (European People's Party) and Social-Democratic politicians (Progressive Alliance of Socialists and Democrats).

The Council of the European Union consists of ministers from the Member States. Which ministers are included depends on the issue that is at stake. If, for instance, the Common Agricultural Policy (CAP) of the EU is being discussed, the ministers of agriculture will represent their national governments in the *Agriculture and Fisheries Council*. When monetary issues are at stake, the ministers of the treasury are the obvious participants in the *Ecofin Council*, while ministers of justice typically participate in the *Justice and Home Affairs Council*. Note that the Agriculture and Fisheries Council, the Ecofin Council, and the Justice and Home Affairs Council are all instantiations of the same EU institution, the Council of the European Union. *(The Council of the European Union)*

The main responsibility of the Council of the European Union is to take policy and legislative decisions, often in cooperation with other EU institutions. As the Commission is not as well staffed as national governments are, much of the real execution of EU policies must take place through the apparatus of the Member States. The Council of the European Union functions as an intermediary between the world of Brussels and the national governments.

Where the task of the Commission is to promote the general interest of the Union, the members of the European Council represent their national States in negotiations and decision-making that determines the general course of development of the EU. *(The European Council)*

The members of the European Council are the Heads of State (or Heads of Government) of the Member States; they are usually prime ministers, sometimes presidents. These Heads of State are supplemented by the President of the European Council (not a Head of State) and the Chair of the Commission (Article 15, Section 2 TEU). The current President of the European Council is Donald Tusk.

The President of the European Council should not be confused with the President of the European Commission.

The European Council meets at least twice in every 6 months. These meetings are called the «Euro Summits».

The Court of Justice of the European Union

The EU has its own judicial tribunal called the «Court of Justice of the European Union» (CJEU). This court is seated in the city of Luxembourg.

The tasks of the CJEU are manifold, but two important ones are:

1. To give preliminary rulings concerning the interpretation of the TEU and the TFEU and the validity and interpretation of acts of the institutions, bodies, offices, and agencies of the EU (Article 267 TFEU). If a national court of a Member State must decide a case where, for instance, the interpretation of the TEU or the TFEU is at stake, it must ask for a decision from the CJEU about the proper interpretation of these treaties. Such a decision is a preliminary ruling.
2. To review the legality of legislative acts intended to produce legal effects vis-à-vis third parties by the Council, the Commission, and the European Central Bank, other than recommendations and opinions, as well as the acts of the European Parliament and the European Council (Article 263 TFEU).

The European Central Bank

Together with the national banks of the Member States which have the Euro as their national currency, the European Central Bank (ECB) has the main responsibility for the monetary policy of the EU (Article 282 TFEU). Its primary task is to maintain price stability (Article 283 TFEU). In practice this means that the ECB strives for a limited amount of inflation within the Euro countries.

4   The Ordinary Legislative Procedure

If an EU rule creates the competence to make EU legislation, it also specifies which legislative procedure is to be followed. The procedure that is usually adopted is the «ordinary legislative procedure», which is described in Article 294 TFEU. In this procedure, the Commission, the Council, and the European

Parliament must cooperate in order to create new legislation. If these three institutions agree, the procedure is quite simple:

1. The Commission submits a proposal to the European Parliament and the Council.
2. The European Parliament adopts its position and communicates it to the Council.
3. If the Council approves the European Parliament's position, the act concerned is adopted in the wording that corresponds to the position of the European Parliament.

If the Council and the European Parliament disagree, the legislative proposal may be sent back and forth several times between these two institutions and the Commission. The decision-making procedure within the Council may change from unanimity to qualified majority voting, but in the end, the Council and the European Parliament must agree if a legislative proposal is to be adopted.

The brief remark above that the decision-making procedure within the Council may change from unanimity to qualified majority voting deserves separate attention, because it marks a significant transfer of power from the Member States to the EU. After a crisis during the 1960s (the «empty chair crisis»), it was established that the decision-making procedure for the Council of the European Union would allow every Member State to veto a decision. It guaranteed to every Member State that EU legislation could not be imposed upon it against its will.

In the ordinary legislative procedure, which was only adopted under the Lisbon Treaty of 2007, it is possible to overrule a Member State. Although nationals of the Member States participate in these two institutions, Member States do not have a say in the Commission or in the European Parliament as these nationals do not act on behalf of their home States. Therefore, if a Member State wants to block legislation, it must do so in the Council. However, the ordinary legislative procedure makes it possible to overrule individual Member States in the procedure with qualified majority voting.

Qualified Majority Voting

Article 16, Section 4 TEU

As from 1 November 2014, a qualified majority shall be defined as at least 55% of the members of the Council, comprising at least 15 of them, and representing Member States comprising at least 65% of the population of the Union.

A blocking minority must include at least four Council members, failing which the qualified majority shall be deemed attained.

5   The Internal Market

The process of European integration, of which the EU is the outcome, started as a process of economic integration. However, the functions of the EU are no longer limited to the promotion of economic integration through free trade. The following quotation from the Treaty on European Union illustrates the ambitions of the EU well:

Article 2 TEU
The Union is founded on the values of respect for human dignity, freedom, democracy, equality, the rule of law and respect for human rights, including the rights of persons belonging to minorities. These values are common to the Member States in a society in which pluralism, non-discrimination, tolerance, justice, solidarity and equality between women and men prevail.

Article 3 TEU
1. The Union's aim is to promote peace, its values and the well-being of its peoples.
2. The Union shall offer its citizens an area of freedom, security and justice without internal frontiers, in which the free movement of persons is ensured in conjunction with appropriate measures with respect to external border controls, asylum, immigration and the prevention and combating of crime.
3. The Union shall establish an internal market. It shall work for the sustainable development of Europe based on balanced economic growth and price stability, a highly competitive social market economy, aiming at full employment and social progress, and a high level of protection and improvement of the quality of the environment. It shall promote scientific and technological advance.

    It shall combat social exclusion and discrimination, and shall promote social justice and protection, equality between women and men, solidarity between generations and protection of the rights of the child.

    It shall promote economic, social and territorial cohesion, and solidarity among Member States.

    It shall respect its rich cultural and linguistic diversity, and shall ensure that Europe's cultural heritage is safeguarded and enhanced.
4. The Union shall establish an economic and monetary union whose currency is the euro.

5. In its relations with the wider world, the Union shall uphold and promote its values and interests and contribute to the protection of its citizens. It shall contribute to peace, security, the sustainable development of the Earth, solidarity and mutual respect among peoples, free and fair trade, eradication of poverty and the protection of human rights, in particular the rights of the child, as well as to the strict observance and the development of international law, including respect for the principles of the United Nations Charter.

The EU performs many tasks, including foreign, monetary, environmental, agricultural, and fishery policies. Here we focus on one of them, the creation and maintenance of the internal market. Free trade between countries is good for at least two reasons. Firstly, free trade economically benefits all parties involved in this trade:

Suppose that there are two car manufacturers. One of them builds a certain kind of car for €9,000 and is prepared to sell it for €10,000. The other can only make the car for €10,500 and will sell at €11,000. We assume that all other conditions and circumstances are the same. If there is free trade, a potential customer will buy the car for €10,000, thereby stimulating the first car manufacturer to continue making cars. Both the seller and the buyer profit from this deal. The second will not sell his car and will therefore not be stimulated to build more cars. However, if the buyer and the second seller are in the same country, while the first seller is in a different country and for that reason is prohibited to sell the car to the potential buyer, the buyer must pay €1,000 'too much'. Moreover, the expensive car manufacturer will be encouraged to continue producing cars, even if he cannot do so efficiently. Free trade stimulates the creation of products by those who can do so most efficiently, and promotes that consumers do not have to pay more than what is necessary. The money they save can be used to buy something else, thereby stimulating the economy even more.

Secondly, if there is intensive trade between two countries that benefits the inhabitants of both countries – and we have seen above that it does – it is less likely that the two countries will wage war against each other. Both reasons are good reasons to have a single internal market within the EU, where potential traders are not hindered by boundaries between countries.

To stimulate this single internal market, the EU has proclaimed the «four freedoms»: the free movement of goods, persons, services, and capital.

Free Movement of Goods

The EU uses several approaches to encourage the free movement of goods. One of them is to *prohibit quantitative restrictions* on trade or – in general – movement of goods between EU Member States.

Quantitative restrictions on imports and all measures having equivalent effect shall be prohibited between Member States. (Article 34 TFEU)

Another is the *prohibition of customs duties* on the transportation of goods from one Member State to another. Article 28, Section 1 TFEU states it as follows:

The Union shall comprise a customs union which shall cover all trade in goods, and which shall involve the prohibition between Member States of customs duties on imports and exports and of all charges having equivalent effect, and the adoption of a common customs tariff in their relations with third countries.

Another approach to facilitate the free movement of goods is to ban *other measures* that may hamper this movement. Such measures may, for instance, concern the specific characteristics of a good that tend to differ from one country to another.

Cassis de Dijon (CJEU Case C-120/78)
The German firm Rewe-Zentral AG wanted to import a fruit liqueur from France, which was named 'Cassis de Dijon'. The firm applied to the *Bundesmonopolverwaltung für Branntwein* (a section of the German Federal Ministry of Finance) for a permit to import this liqueur, but the permit was refused. The reason for the refusal was that the marketing of fruit liqueurs such as Cassis de Dijon is conditional upon a minimum alcohol content of 25% in Germany, whereas the alcohol content of the product in question, which is freely marketed in France, is between 15% and 20%. According to the CJEU this was not allowed because it violated the precursor of the present Article 34 TFEU.

Free Movement of Persons

For economic integration between different countries, a single internal market for goods is required, but it is also important that persons can move freely from one country to the other and are allowed to provide services in countries other than from where they originate. The free movement of persons and of services is meant to safeguard these possibilities within the Union. The core provisions of the TFEU that deal with the free movement of persons are as follows:

Article 45 TFEU:
1. Freedom of movement for workers shall be secured within the Union.
2. Such freedom of movement shall entail the abolition of any discrimination based on nationality between workers of the Member States as regards employment, remuneration and other conditions of work and employment …

Article 49 TFEU:
Within the framework of the provisions set out below, restrictions on the freedom of establishment of nationals of a Member State in the territory of another Member State shall be prohibited. Such prohibition shall also apply to restrictions on the setting-up of agencies, branches or subsidiaries by nationals of any Member State established in the territory of any other Member State.

Freedom of establishment shall include the right to take up and pursue activities as self-employed persons and to set up and manage undertakings …

EU law does not only contain a freedom to move but also a freedom to provide and receive services. In principle, residents of one Member State are allowed to provide services in another Member State:

Free Movement of Services

Article 56 TFEU
Within the framework of the provisions set out below, restrictions on freedom to provide services within the Union shall be prohibited in respect of nationals of Member States who are established in a Member State other than that of the person for whom the services are intended …

If goods and services are to be distributed freely within the EU, it should also be possible to move capital from one Member State to another as if the goods and the services cannot be paid for, the freedom to move them across borders loses much of its value.

Free Movement of Capital

The free movement of capital is the most controversial among the four freedoms. In the original Treaty of Rome, which foresaw only a customs union to begin with, there was only an obligation to move toward integration of the capital

market. Of course, some sort of further economic cooperation is necessary to create a single capital market in which
there can be free movement of capital. The Maastricht Treaty
therefore also included the first real article on the free movement of capital, now firmly enshrined in the TFEU:

Article 63 TFEU

1. Within the framework of the provisions set out in this chapter, all restrictions on the movement of capital between
Member States and between Member States and third countries shall be prohibited.
2. Within the framework of the provisions set out in this
chapter, all restrictions on payments between Member
States and between Member States and third countries shall
be prohibited.

6   Enlargement

The precursors of the EU, the ECSC and the EEC, started with
six Member States: Belgium, the German Federal Republic
(West Germany), France (including Algeria), Italy,
Luxembourg, and the Netherlands. In 1962 Algeria became
independent of France and left. In 1973, the number of
Member States increased to 9 with the accession of Denmark
(including Greenland), Ireland, and the United Kingdom.
After becoming democracies, Greece followed in 1981 and
Portugal and Spain in 1986. When Greenland gained inde-
pendence from Denmark in 1985, a referendum was held and
it decided to leave. The *Deutsche Demokratische Republik*
(Eastern Germany) joined the *Bundesrepublik Deutschland*
(West German Federal Republic) in 1990 and also became
part of the European Community. In 1995 Austria, Finland,
and Sweden joined the EU, and from that moment on, the
enlargement process quickened with the additions of Estonia,
Greek Cyprus, Hungary, Lithuania, Malta, Poland, and
Slovenia. Slovakia and the Czech Republic joined in 2004;
Bulgaria and Romania followed in 2007 and Croatia in 2013.

Apart from the exit of Algeria and Greenland in 1962 and
1985, respectively, both countries that had never decided to
become members of the European Community themselves,
the size of the EU has only increased since its start as the ECSC
in 1958. Most likely this will change since the population of
the United Kingdom decided in a referendum that the country
should leave the EU. This «Brexit» will be the first case of a
country leaving the EU after having voluntarily joined it.

7   EU Law and National Law of the Member States

In the Member States of the EU both national law and law that belongs to the EU stipulate compliance. This raises the question of how EU law relates to the national law of the Member States. The (precursor of the) CJEU answered this question in two groundbreaking decisions.

The first decision was taken in the *Van Gend & Loos* case (CJEU Case C-26/62). It dealt with the question of whether the legal subjects of Member States could derive rights from EU law.

Van Gend & Loos

The Van Gend & Loos company imported a chemical substance from Germany into the Netherlands. According to the Dutch law that was valid at the time, this import was to be charged with an import duty. However, according to the EEC Treaty, new duties on transborder transport of goods within the EEC were not allowed. Article 12 of the Treaty of Rome, through which the EEC was founded (now replaced by Article 30 TFEU), reads:

Member States shall refrain from introducing between themselves any new customs duties on imports and exports or any charges having equivalent effect, and from increasing those which they already apply in their trade with each other.

The question was whether Van Gend & Loos could invoke this prohibition against the Dutch State before a Dutch court. The CJEU was consulted in this case by a Dutch court (the «Tariefcommissie») to provide a preliminary ruling on the content of EEC law. The CJEU had to answer, among others, the following question:

Whether Article 12 of the EEC Treaty has direct application within the territory of a Member State, in other words, whether nationals of such a State can, on the basis of the article in question, lay claim to individual rights which the courts must protect.

As part of its answer to this question, the CJEU wrote:

Legal Text
The objective of the EEC Treaty, which is to establish a common market, the functioning of which is of direct concern to interested parties in the community, implies that this treaty is more than an agreement which merely creates mutual obligations between the contracting states. (...)

In addition the task assigned to the Court of Justice under Article 177, the object of which is to secure uniform interpretation of the treaty by national courts and tribunals, confirms that the states have acknowledged that community law has an authority which can be invoked by their nationals before those courts and tribunals.

The conclusion to be drawn from this is that the community constitutes a new legal order of international law for the benefit of which the states have limited their sovereign rights, albeit within limited fields, and the subjects of which comprise not only Member States but also their nationals.

Independently of the legislation of Member States, community law therefore not only imposes obligations on individuals, but is also intended to confer upon them rights which become part of their legal heritage. These rights arise not only where they are expressly granted by the treaty, but also by reason of obligations which the treaty imposes in a clearly defined way upon individuals, as well as upon the Member States and upon the institutions of the community.

From this fragment it becomes clear that EU law can give nationals rights (and impose duties upon them), *independently of national legislation*. Moreover, in case this was not sufficiently clear, the CJEU added that these rights do not only arise where they are expressly granted by the Treaty but also arise by reason of the obligations that the Treaty imposes in a clearly defined way upon individuals, as well as upon the Member States and upon the institutions of the EU.

Costa/ENEL

While the CJEU decision in the *Van Gend & Loos* case was already revolutionary, the CJEU added to it in its decision in the case between Flaminio Costa and ENEL (CJEU Case C-6/64). In this case, the question arose whether EU (EEC) law could be set aside by later national legislation. In this connection, the CJEU wrote the following:

Legal Text

By contrast with ordinary international treaties, the EEC Treaty has created its own legal system which, on the entry into force of the treaty, became an integral part of the legal systems of the Member States, and which their courts are bound to apply.

(...)

The integration into the laws of each Member State of provisions which derive from the community, and more generally the terms and the spirit of the treaty, make it impossible for the states, as a corollary, to accord precedence to a unilateral and subsequent measure over a legal system accepted by them on a basis of reciprocity. Such a measure cannot therefore be inconsistent with that legal system. The executive force of community law cannot vary from one state to another in deference to subsequent domestic laws, without jeopardizing the attainment of the objectives of the treaty.

The obligations undertaken within the framework of the treaty establishing the community would not be unconditional, but merely contingent, if they could be called in question by subsequent legislative acts of the signatories.

It follows from all these observations that the law stemming from the treaty – an independent source of law – could not, because of its special and original nature, be overridden by domestic legal provisions, however framed, without being deprived of its character as community law, and without the legal basis of the community itself being called into question.

The decision for which the Costa/ENEL case has become famous affirms that States cannot override the law of the treaty by means of later national legislation. If they could, the resulting law might vary from Member State to Member State, and the obligations undertaken through the treaty would become conditional on not being derogated from by a later national law.

8 Subsidiarity and the Requirement of Legal Basis

In the *Van Gend & Loos* and *Costa/ENEL* cases, the CJEU claimed solid ground for EU law as a legal order in itself, the rules of which apply directly in the Member States and override the national rules. However, while the EU may have powers that prevail over those of the Member States, they are only in those fields in which the Member States have transferred those powers to the EU. If the EU is to perform juridical acts and change the legal positions of Member States and their nationals, it must like all other legal agents have received the appropriate competency. By limiting this competency, the Member States can limit the powers of the EU institutions and try to control the transfer of powers from the Member States to the EU. The limitations of the powers of EU institutions take the shape of two demands on the exercise of these powers that were imposed on the EU in the treaties:

1. Powers can only be exercised within the limits of the competencies conferred upon the Union (Article 3, Section 6 TEU).
2. The use of these competencies is governed by the principles of subsidiarity and proportionality (Article 5, Section 1 TEU).

Legal Basis

This means that the EU has only those competences that were attributed to it and no others. This is essentially the principle of *legality*, which holds in general in public law. In its application to the EU, it is sometimes called the demand for legal basis.

Subsidiarity

Moreover, the EU should only use its powers where it can perform a task better than the Member States could do themselves. For example, the EU should only limit the use of alcohol if a central regulation would be more effective than national regulations. This is the principle of subsidiarity.

Proportionality

Moreover, the EU should only act if the:
1. Adopted measure is suitable to achieve the desired end.
2. Measure is necessary to achieve this end.
3. Measures it takes are not worse than the problem it wants to address with this measure.

Together, these three demands fall under the principle of proportionality. The demand for a legal basis in combination with the principles of subsidiarity and proportionality together limit the powers of the EU and impose a limit on the amount of powers that the Member States have transferred to the EU.

9   Towards an Ever-Closer Union or Not...?

The Treaty on European Union, signed in Maastricht in 1992, represented a substantial step in the direction of European integration. According to Article A, Section 2 of the treaty:

This Treaty marks a new stage in the process of creating an ever-closer union among the peoples of Europe, in which decisions are taken as closely as possible to the citizen.

Article B mentions the objectives of the EU, which are, among others:

- To promote economic and social progress which is balanced and sustainable, in particular through the creation of an area without internal frontiers, through the strengthening of economic and social cohesion and through the establishment of economic and monetary union, ultimately including a single currency in accordance with the provisions of this Treaty;
- To assert its identity on the international scene, in particular through the implementation of a common foreign and security policy including the eventual framing of a common defense policy, which might in time lead to a common defense;

- To strengthen the protection of the rights and interests of the nationals of its Member States through the introduction of a citizenship of the Union;
- To develop close cooperation on justice and home affairs; …

As these quotations illustrate, the parties to the Maastricht Treaties had high ambitions. These ambitions had already existed for a long time. During the Second World War, Spinelli and Rossi coauthored the *Ventotene Manifesto*, a document that contained a plea for a European federation. The creation of the ECSC may have created the impression that this plea would become reality. However, in 1954 the French National Assembly blocked the ratification of treaties for a European defense community and a European political community. A real transfer of powers from the national States to a central European body turned out to be a bridge too far. Defense and politics, in particular foreign relations, were too sensitive an area. Instead the EEC was created in 1957, an organization with a mixed supranational and intergovernmental structure.

The two words «intergovernmental» and «supranational» stand for a built-in tension in the ECSC and all later European organizations. On one hand, the organizations were meant to further the national interests of the Member States. This is the intergovernmental perspective on organizations, including the EU. The role of the Council of the European Union and even more explicitly of the European Council can best be understood from this intergovernmental perspective. On the other hand, the EU is seen as a means to further the common interests of its citizens, including peace and economic prosperity. From this supranational perspective, the EU transcends the Member States and their national interests. The roles of the European Commission, the European Parliament, the CJEU, and the ECB are best understood from this supranational perspective.

Article A, Section 2 of the treaty of Maastricht still emphasized the movement of the EU toward an «ever-closer union». This idea of an ever-closer union became more and more problematic for some Member States and their inhabitants. We can already see a reflection of this in the text of Article 3a of the TEU, which was inserted through the Lisbon Treaty. Section 1 emphasizes that the EU will not have more competences than were explicitly conferred upon it:

In accordance with Article 3b, competences not conferred upon the Union in the Treaties remain with the Member States.

Supranational vs. Intergovernmental

Section 2 explicitly declares that the EU should respect the national identities of the Member States, including their responsibility for their own security:

The Union shall respect the equality of Member States before the Treaties as well as their national identities, inherent in their fundamental structures, political and constitutional, inclusive of regional and local self-government. It shall respect their essential State functions, including ensuring the territorial integrity of the State, maintaining law and order and safeguarding national security. In particular, national security remains the sole responsibility of each Member State.

Euroscepticism

In 2016, voters in the United Kingdom surprised many by supporting the withdrawal of the United Kingdom from the EU: the Brexit. Others were not surprised but saw this step back as a desirable one: the EU had in their eyes taken too many powers from its Member States and should either return many of its powers or should be given up altogether. Below we take a closer look at this so-called Euroscepticism and its causes.

9.1   Spillover and Spillback

An important idea in the history of the EU is that the development of the European institutions would be guided by a phenomenon called «spillover». In general, spillover means that the full realization of one thing requires the realization of some other thing.

The general idea is well illustrated by a pyramid of glasses. There is a continuous stream of water into the glass at the top and once this glass is full the water flows over into the glasses at the second layer, until the glasses at this layer are full and the water flows over to the glasses on the third layer, ... and so on.

When applied to the EU, spillover means that the realization of full cooperation in one field requires other forms of cooperation. For instance, in order to have a fully functional internal market, the impediment of different monetary currencies and continually changing exchange rates should be set aside. The main function of the introduction of the Euro was to accomplish precisely this. However, a shared currency is only possible if there is a common economic policy, including social security and taxation. More generally, the idea is that the functions fulfilled by States are not independent from each other and that cooperation in the performance of one function «spills over» into cooperation in the performance of other functions.

This might mean that European cooperation, which started on a relatively small scale, is bound to grow through more and more cooperation into a fully fledged European federation. The projected trajectory toward an ever-closer union with spillover as the driving force is known as the *Schuman method* of integration, after the French minister whose address laid at the foundation of the ECSC and later the EU. It might also mean that if cooperation and integration in one field necessitates cooperation and integration in another field, and if the latter would be deemed undesirable, the former would be deemed undesirable as well. The same force that drove the integration of Europe may also drive it back if the final outcome is not considered to be acceptable. For example, if the free travel of persons through the EU is not considered acceptable, perhaps the existence of a completely open common market is not acceptable either. Spillover may mean that European integration is an all-or-nothing matter. And where some have hoped that it would turn out to be all – a full European federation – others see this as a reason to completely abandon the project of European integration. In this way, spillover would turn into spillback.

9.2   Euroscepticism

What might cause Euroscepticism if European integration has obvious advantages such as diminished chance of war and economic prosperity? It is likely that rather than one single cause, there are three main factors that play a role: the EU is more of a common market than of a community of European citizens, the EU has grown (too fast) too large, and the EU suffers from a democratic deficit.

The EU started very much as a project to create a common market with free trade between Member States and borders that were open to the movement of goods, services, workers, and money. Attempts to make it a real community of European citizens are relatively recent and arguably less developed than the internal market. In this way, it is telling that the free establishment of workers received a higher priority than the avoidance of social dumping, the movement of labor to places where it is cheapest because of lower costs for social security. It is similarly

Market Instead of Community

telling that the main task of the ECB is to maintain a low level of inflation, rather than to promote job creation. People who have the impression that their jobs are moved to other parts of Europe where production is cheaper and who worry because their national governments are urged by the EU to limit budgetary deficits and therefore to invest less in job creation are prone to blame the EU, even if this blame may be unjustified.

Enlargement

After the collapse of the iron curtain that separated East and West Europe, the number of Member States of the European community increased quickly. In 1950, when it all started, there were only six Member States. In 1995 there were still a mere 15 Member States, while the present number – discounting the imminent Brexit – is 28.

This steady enlargement has had major implications. First, the member States have become more diverse, with division lines between the North and the South and also between the East and the West. These differences lead to different views on how to handle, for instance, the financial (debt) crisis or the refugee crisis. Second, the larger number of Member States has made decision-making within the EU more difficult, and measures such as QMV have become crucial to avoid deadlocks. When it comes to the modification of the founding treaties of the EU (the TEU and the TFEU), things are even more difficult; treaty revisions have to be ratified by all Member States. If Member States have a referendum as part of their internal procedure, the majority of the population of a single Member State is able to block a treaty revision. Although this may be seen as a sign that European decision-making is still democratic, the fact that a relatively small number of people can block changes in the primary EU Law may be a cause of dissatisfaction.

Democratic Deficit

It is sometimes claimed that the EU suffers from a «democratic deficit». However, it is not always clear what is meant by that. The citizens of the EU can vote for the members of the EP, and the ability of EP to influence European affairs has increased over the course of time. For example, the EP plays a crucial role in the ordinary legislative procedure, and it can send the Commission home. Citizens of the Member States have often the opportunity to use national voting procedures to influence their governments behavior within European institutions, such as the EU Council and the Council of the European Union. Moreover, through their national parliaments, citizens can also influence the ratification of treaties in which the EU is involved.

Yet, correctly or not, people often have the feeling that they have no influence on what is going on in «Brussels». This may in part be explained from the fact that people are often little aware of what is being decided in the European institutions, let alone of the role that their representatives play in this connection. The powers that European citizens may have are not experienced as such, and that gives many the feeling that they cannot influence what goes on in the EU; decisions are taken over their heads.

In a sense, this is just one manifestation of the distance between politics and the citizenry which is also experienced in national settings. However, because Europe is much bigger than the individual Member States and perhaps also because European issues often receive less publicity than national affairs – although this cannot be said about the debt crisis and the refugee crisis – the distance between politics and the citizens is perceived more acutely.

An additional factor here may also be that citizens identify less with «Europe» than with their home countries or regions. Moreover, still another factor is that governments sometimes want to limit the influence of their citizens on their European politics, perhaps motivated out of fear that their citizens make wrong decisions because of a lack of knowledge or understanding.

No matter whether the democratic deficit is real or merely imaginary, and no matter what causes the feeling that such a deficit exists, the perception of a democratic deficit is likely a cause of Euroscepticism.

Whatever may explain Euroscepticism, the phenomenon exists, and it exerts its influence in European decision-making. It has been seen in the rejection through popular referenda of the European Constitutional Treaty in 2005, the impossibility of creating a common European policy to deal with the refugee crisis, and last but not least the majority vote in the United Kingdom to leave the EU. At the moment of writing this chapter, the European Union is in turmoil, with great uncertainty concerning how, and perhaps also whether, to continue the project of European integration. The European Union has known more crises, and often it has come out of them stronger. However, as the saying has it, the past does not contain guarantees for the future.

Recommended Literature

Barnard C (2013) The substantive law of the EU. The four freedoms, 4th edn. Oxford University Press, Oxford

Craig P, De Burca G (2011) EU law text, cases and materials, 5th edn. Oxford University Press, Oxford

Nugent N (2011) The government and politics of the European Union, 7th edn. Palgrave MacMillan, New York

Tax Law

Marcel Schaper

© Springer International Publishing Switzerland 2017
J. Hage et al. (eds.), *Introduction to Law*, DOI 10.1007/978-3-319-57252-9_11

1 What is Tax Law?

1.1 Defining Taxes

Taxes are compulsory, unrequited payments to government. The law obliges a person to give money to the government without receiving anything specific directly in return. Taxpayers only enjoy a general benefit of their involuntary gifts; taxes pay for the institutions, infrastructure, and policies that the government provides to society.

User charges and service fees, such as highway tolls or passport fees, are considered nontax revenue. These charges and fees are normally only due when an individual requires a specific service or a good offered by the government as consideration. The amount of the charges and fees are roughly proportional to the cost to government of providing the services or goods.

It is sometimes difficult to distinguish taxes from nontax revenue. The best example is social insurance. Social insurance contributions may be qualified as nontax revenue because persons receive future benefits for their contributions in the form of social insurance payments. The level of the payment also often depends on the period during which an individual made contributions. Notwithstanding, participation in the social insurance system is usually compulsory, and persons perceive no real difference between paying contributions or income taxes.

1.2 The Taxing Power

Tax law is public law because it governs legal relations between private persons and the government as such. Tax law is often considered a field within administrative law. There are two areas of tax law: *substantive tax law* (which lays down the criteria of taxation, who is taxed, for what, for how much, where, and when) and *procedural tax law*, which regulates formalities on how the tax liability is assessed and collected, defines taxpayer rights and obligations, and states provisions concerning the powers of the judiciary for settling disputes between the taxpayer and the tax administration.

The tax system is a mix of different taxes (▶ Sect. 3). In many States, each tax is regulated by its own substantive law. A general tax law is most often used for definitions that apply throughout the tax system and for issues of procedural tax law.

Taxation as law

Limitations to the Taxing Power

The power to impose and collect taxes is normally granted to the government by the constitution. Tax laws may be enacted by the central government as well as by regional and local governments. The division of taxing powers between levels of government applies not only to unitary and federal States but also extends to supranational organizations like the EU.

The differences between the taxing powers of the United States and the European Union are particularly striking. The federal government as the highest level of government in the United States has enacted laws on income taxes but not on goods and services taxes. Whereas the States share the power to collect income taxes with the federal government, there is no universal federal goods and services tax in the United States. In contrast, goods and services taxes are harmonized throughout the European Union by EU legislation. There is no comprehensive legislation on income taxes at the EU level. Income taxes remain a reserved competence of the Member States. The European Union also cannot collect any taxes directly, except from its own civil servants. The Member States transfer a part of their national tax revenue to the EU budget.

The taxing power is not only created by the constitution, but it is also limited by the general principles of law and fundamental rights that the constitution protects. The principles of legality and equality are the major constitutional limitations to the taxing power. The taxing power is further balanced by assigning different tasks to the three branches of government. Legality, equality, and balance of powers should be upheld as guiding legal principles of a good tax system.

Legality

The legality principle prescribes that only the law may impose tax obligations. Taxation therefore requires a legislative act. This fundamental principle of representative democracy is also known as «no taxation without representation». Although one might view taxation as encroaching upon property rights, taxation is also necessary for the government to be able to maintain a justice system to protect property rights.

Equality

The principle of equality prohibits arbitrary taxation devoid of reasonable foundation. In the field of taxation, the legislature nonetheless enjoys a wide margin of appreciation in assessing whether and to what extent differences in otherwise similar situations justify a different tax treatment.

In Burden v United Kingdom [2008] ECHR 356, the European Court of Human Rights ruled that there was no violation of the prohibition of discrimination in the case of two sisters who had lived together all their lives in their parent's home. The sisters were afraid that they could not pay the substantial inheritance taxes on the house when either sister would die. The Grand Chamber held that the cohabiting sisters could not be compared to a married couple or civil partners who would pay much less inheritance taxes.

The legislative branch of government decides on the existence and the design of tax laws, but the executive branch carries out their enforcement. The tax administration as a part of the executive branch is responsible for the collection of taxes. The judiciary settles disputes between the tax administration and taxpayer. In many States, the legislature delegates competence to the executive to issue interpretative decrees and implement regulations for tax laws. This bypassing of parliament on substantive tax matters is thought to be necessary to allow the government to respond quickly to changes in economic situations and taxpayer behavior.

Balance of Powers

A domestic taxpayer of the Netherlands who earns foreign income may request a reduction of Dutch taxes on that foreign income to avoid double taxation. Article 38 of the General Tax Act leaves it to the Minister of Finance, without a requirement to involve parliament, to set the rules and conditions under which such relief is granted by an administrative decree.

2   Goals of Taxation

2.1   The Three R's of Taxation

To understand tax law, one first needs to define its objectives. Taxation serves three goals. We call these the three R's of taxation:
- Revenue
- Redistribution
- Regulation

Unsurprisingly, the main goal of taxation is to raise revenue to finance government expenditures. Redistribution of wealth and regulation of behavior are generally considered secondary goals but may even be the primary goals for some specific taxes. The extent to which a tax pursues these goals may differ, and the government must always make a trade-off between the three R's. Any political discussion about the size and the tasks of government has consequences for the design of the tax system in terms of these three goals. A political position that favors «small government» (e.g., a libertarian view) would advocate low tax revenue and little regulation through the tax system. A political position that favors egalitarian outcomes and solidarity (e.g., a social democratic view) would support using the tax system for redistribution of wealth.

2.2   Revenue

Raising revenue through taxation invariably means that persons need to transfer some of their income or wealth to the State. Taxation thus inherently reduces welfare. It is generally accepted that high taxes have a negative impact on economic growth. Nonetheless, taxpayers are willing to accept significant taxes in return for good government. Higher taxes, however, increase the likelihood that taxpayers put additional effort into tax management strategies to on their tax expenditures (▶ Sect. 7.3). Therefore, higher taxes do not necessarily result in more tax revenue. Beyond a certain level of taxes, any further increase in taxes leads to a greater loss in revenue due to taxpayers deciding to stop earning income or increased tax management strategies in the forms of tax avoidance and tax evasion.

Behavioral Responses   Taxes influence economic decisions and so trigger behavioral responses. Taxation has effects on the basic economic choices between work and leisure and between consumption and saving. In this way, distortions in economic choices lead to social costs. For instance, a tax on labor income increases wage costs for employers and so impacts employment. Further, value added taxes increase the cost of goods and services and so determine the quantities bought and sold by consumers and producers.

Deadweight Loss   Social costs of taxes arise because of behavioral responses. These negative impacts on welfare in addition to the cost of the tax are called the «deadweight loss» or «excess burden» of taxation. An efficient tax system raises revenue while minimizing the deadweight loss. Consequently, neutrality is a desirable design characteristic of a good tax system. A neutral tax system ensures that persons make decisions based on their economic merits and not because of their tax consequences. However, the goals of redistribution and regulation demand taxation to be non-neutral regarding some persons and choices of behavior. That means that some decisions become more economically favorable due to their tax benefits, whereas other decisions become less favorable in comparison after discounting their tax consequences.

Specific taxes (excise duties) are levied on cigarettes and alcohol. Smoking and drinking damage your health, increase the costs of health care to society, and are therefore considered socially undesirable behavior. Excises moderate the likelihood that people start and maintain these bad habits. The excise raises the price of smoking and drinking (it «internalizes» the cost to society—the costs to everyone else—into the private costs of the consumer) and so reduces demand for cigarettes and alcohol.

These activities may also be directly regulated, e.g., by a prohibition on the sale of alcoholic beverages to underage children and by smoking prohibitions in public places.

2.3   Redistribution

The extent to which the tax system should redistribute income and wealth between the rich and poor—its progressivity or regressivity—is a question that divides politics. Although it is best to assess the progressivity of a tax system as a whole, it may nevertheless be helpful to understand how individual taxes contribute to the distribution of income and wealth within society.

Progressivity

Thomas Piketty (1971) is a French economist who published the book *Capital in the Twenty-First Century* in 2013. The central thesis of his work is that when private wealth grows faster over the long term than the general economy (this has become known as the formula r > g), wealth will concentrate («the rich get richer»). Very unequal distribution of wealth may cause social and economic instability. Piketty therefore advocates a progressive tax system that takes more from wealthier persons. This view has received both acclaim and criticism from other economists.

Differential taxation, according to which not everybody pays an equal amount of taxes, redistributes income and wealth between taxpayers. The ordinary approach is to impose higher taxes on more advantaged persons and no or lower taxes on less advantaged persons. Differential taxation of this kind is called «progressive taxation», and it results in income and wealth positions becoming more equal after taxes as compared to before tax positions. In contrast, regressive taxation—the average tax rate decreases with higher income or more wealth—increases inequality between taxpayers. Taxation is proportional if the tax liability as a percentage of total income or wealth is equal regardless of the size of income or wealth.

Progressive, Regressive, and Proportional Taxation

Assessing the progressivity of a tax should be done in real terms. A tax that is equal in law may be unequal in effect. Take taxes on alcohol and cigarettes, for example. These are equal in amount for everyone who drinks and smokes, but they tend to hit less advantaged persons harder because their consumption of alcohol and cigarettes makes up a larger portion of their income or wealth. They are therefore regressive taxes.

When assessing the redistributive impact of a tax, the government must always carefully consider on whom the tax burden ultimately falls: the incidence of the tax. The statutory

Incidence

bearer of the tax is the person who is legally responsible to pay the tax (legal incidence). That need not be the same person whose welfare is, intentionally or unintentionally, ultimately affected by the tax (economic incidence).

Direct vs. Indirect Taxes

When legal and economic incidences normally coincide for the same person, the tax is a direct tax. This is the case for personal income taxes. Indirect taxes are those which legal and economic incidence likely falls on different persons: the statutory bearer of the tax generally tends to shift the burden of the tax to another person.

Entrepreneurs are legally responsible to pay VAT to the government. However, since the VAT is included as a part of the price of goods and services sold, the economic burden of the tax mainly falls on the consumers of the goods and services. Consequently, the VAT is an indirect tax.

2.4   Regulation

Taxation triggers behavioral responses, because persons consider the financial consequences of the choices that they make. Mindful of these economic effects of taxation, the government may steer peoples' behavior to choices that stabilize the general economy and foster growth. The government can also regulate specific choices and activities by stimulating socially desirable behavior (through decreased taxation) and discouraging undesirable behavior (through increased taxation). While some view these value judgments as tax paternalism, there is significant regulation through taxation in many States.

Examples of fiscal stimulation are the mortgage interest deduction for residences, a child credit, and lower tax rates on income from environmentally friendly investments.

3   The Tax Mix

The Tax Base Distinction

The tax base is what is taxed. While nearly everyone and everything will be subject to one or more taxes, we can make a broad distinction between different taxes in the tax mix according to their tax base. The three main kinds of taxes are:
1. Taxes on income (▶ Sect. 4)
2. Taxes on goods and services (▶ Sect. 5)
3. Taxes on property (▶ Sect. 6)

Taxes on income consider the personal and family circumstances of the taxpayer, in addition to the total amount of income earned. Income tax laws therefore require answers to nonfinancial questions like: is the taxpayer married; does the taxpayer have children; and, did the taxpayer make special expenditures for illness? Because they take account of the individual characteristics of the taxpayer, income taxes are also called personal taxes or *ad personam* taxes (Latin for taxes «directed to the person»).

Taxes on goods and services ordinarily do not consider the personal situation of the taxpayer and impose a charge to tax with exclusive regard to the nature and the value of each individual taxable transaction. Goods and services taxes are therefore often labeled as transaction taxes or *in rem* taxes (Latin for taxes «on things»).

4   Taxes on Income

Taxes on income were introduced in the United States and Europe during the last half of the nineteenth century. The first modern income tax was introduced in the United Kingdom to fund the Napoleonic war. Similarly, in the United States, the direct cause was the need to pay for the Civil War. In Europe, income taxes have been raised significantly to pay for the costs of the two World Wars.

4.1   What: The Definition of Income

In defining the tax base for income taxes, one fundamental question arises first: «What constitutes income?»

Historically, income is theoretically defined according to the accretion and source concepts of income.

The first approach to defining income is the accretion concept or Schanz-Haig-Simons concept of income. Under this very broad concept, income is the net accumulation of the taxpayer's wealth over the year. A taxpayer's wealth changes because the taxpayer consumes or saves his or her income. Consequently, income under the accretion concept is defined as the sum of the market value of all consumption (everything bought) and the change in the value of property rights over the year (the value of property at the end of the year subtracted with the value of property at the start of the year, i.e., everything saved).

The source concept of income defines income more restrictively as the market value of all gains from specific and stable sources of income. A source of income generally exists if a taxpayer actively participates with some product of labor and capital in an economic market with a reasonable expectation to derive an economic gain. This includes participation in the economy as an employee, as an entrepreneur, or as an active investor. It typically excludes hobby activities and transactions between family and friends as taxable activities.

It is easy to understand the distinction between the two concepts of income with the classic apple and tree analogy. The accretion concept considers all economic gains: all apples that fall from the tree are considered income but also the change in value of the tree itself. Under a source concept of income, only the apples are tax relevant and are considered income. The existence of the tree is merely the precondition for earning income. This is the reason why many States that follow a source concept of income have not taxed capital gains on private investment property for a long time and have only done so after express changes to their income tax laws. The capital gain on disposition (the increase in market value compared to the historical cost price) was not considered income because the source of income itself, namely, the investment property, was alienated. Further, gains that do not have a source, such as lottery winnings or personal injury awards, are traditionally not regarded income under the source concept.

4.2   Who: Subjective Tax Liability

Taxes on income are levied from persons. Any income tax law therefore needs to define the taxpayer by answering the question about the subjective liability to tax: «Who is liable to pay income taxes?»

The unit subjectively liable to pay tax may be one or more persons. There are two theoretical extremes and a hybrid definition of the tax unit. The first extreme is that income taxes are assessed individually without regard to the family circumstances of the taxpayer. Under this system, a taxpayer is taxed on his or her personal income, and the tax position is not affected by the presence and income of family members. The second extreme is the exact opposite, namely, that income taxes are assessed with regard to the total sum of income of the family (however defined). Such a system would, for example, impose taxes on the total joint income of a married couple, and it would make the partners jointly liable to pay tax. Under a hybrid system, the tax is assessed individually and returns of married couples are filed separately, but the family circumstances and the income of other family members are considered in some way.

The aggregation of the income of married partners and their joint liability for income tax purposes has been found by courts to violate the equality clause of the constitutions in, among other States, Germany, Ireland, Italy, and Spain.

4.3   When and What: Objective Tax Liability

After we have established whose income is subject to taxation, we need to ask a question about the objective liability to tax: «What amount of income will be taxed at what moment in time?»

Three elements determine the objective liability to tax:
1.   Timing
2.   Taxability
3.   Reductions

The most important principle of timing for income taxes is the realization principle. The norm is that income becomes taxable only when it is realized. Realization events traditionally include the moments when consideration has been received, when funds have been made available or settled, when a legal claim to income becomes recoverable and collectible, when property has been sold or disposed of, or at any moment when the law deems that income has been realized by way of fiction. However, the timing of taxation of realized income may be deferred into the future. We then say that the law grants a «deferral». **Timing**

Realized and taxable income may be exempted from tax. Exemptions apply to income that is principally taxable according to the concept of income. The law requires an explicit provision to that effect. If taxable income is not specifically exempted, it is subjected to tax. **Taxability**

Exemptions are prevalent in occupational pension plans taxation. When an employer contributes to a pension plan on behalf of an employee, that contribution normally constitutes income from employment for the employee. However, many States exempt these contributions and only tax the employee when he or she receives pension payments from the plan. Also, the return on investment by the pension plan is normally exempted from tax. The most prevalent system is therefore EET, meaning that contributions are exempt, returns on investments are exempt, and pension payments are subjected to tax. TEE systems tax contributions but exempt returns on investment and pension payments. The third system, ETE, only taxes the returns on investment.

Allowances and deductions reduce the amount of taxable income. Allowances are fixed or varying statutory amounts that reduce taxable income. Most States provide for at least a **Reductions** «basic» or «personal» allowance that keeps a minimum subsistence amount of income free of tax. Such an allowance thus functions as a threshold above which income becomes subjected to tax. Married couples' allowances and child allowances are also often granted. The regulatory goals that a legislator aims at achieving with providing allowances differ between countries.

Business and Professional Deductions

Some deductions are business and professional expenses that a taxpayer has incurred while carrying out income-earning activities. These expenses are thus directly linked to taxable revenues. Accordingly, they reduce taxable income and are thus recognized as such by the law as deductions. Business and professional expenses are not deductible when they are made for a capital purpose, e.g., when an enterprise buys a machine to use for production. However, the enterprise or professional may deduct depreciation expenses in each year to take account of the reduction in value of a capital asset.

Suppose that a shop receives a total revenue of €300,000 from sales of goods. To sell those goods, the enterprise has bought them from a manufacturer at a cost of €150,000. The shop is established in a rented space in a shopping mall. An annual rent of €15,000 is due to the owner of the shopping mall. The enterprise also employs a sales assistant for an annual wage of €20,000. The property and equipment owned by the shop has depreciated €5,000 in value over the year. To finance the activities of the shop, a loan was received from a bank at a principal amount of €10,000 over which the bank charges interest at 5% per year. Total revenues are €300,000. Business deductions amount to a total of €190,500 (€150,000 cost of goods sold + €15,000 rent expenses + €20,000 wages +€ 5,000 depreciation expenses + €500 interest expenses). The taxable income of the enterprise is therefore €109,500.

Personal Deductions

Deductions for personal expenses, like buying groceries, are not allowed. Personal expenses are rather considered to be a consumption of income. Some deductions for personal expenses are however recognized, including charitable gifts, expenses related to chronic medical conditions, and alimony payments. The reason for their deductibility is regulatory or is in consideration of the negative effect of these personal expenses on the taxpayer's ability to pay.

Suppose that the entrepreneur of the previous example has given €500 to charity. This personal expense will further reduce his or her taxable income to €109,000.

Some expenses are explicitly made nondeductible or are limited in deductibility. Bribes, penalties, and fines cannot normally be deducted, even though income from illegal activities may be subject to tax. So-called mixed expenses that are made in the course of a business, but which also relate to the personal situation of (or might carry an advantage for) the taxpayer, are limited in deductibility. This applies, for example, to commuting expenses or to expenses for business-related entertainment.

Limitations to Deduyctibility

One way to pragmatically deal with the deductibility of expenses occasioned by the exercise of employment is to deny their deductibility altogether. Alternatively, a legislator could choose to allow the employer to reimburse the employee free of tax for any expense that the employee has incurred while exercising his or her employment and of which the employer believes such expense was necessary and reasonable for business or professional purposes.

4.4   How Much: Tax Rates and Credits

Once the law has given answers to the questions who is taxed, when, and for what amount of income, we can ask the final substantive question: «How much taxes are due?»

Tax rates are applied to the taxable income. Many States apply a progressive schedule of rates with lower rates on low-income brackets and higher rates for higher-income brackets.

Tax Rates

A simple example of a schedule with three rate brackets may look like this. The first bracket taxes income up to €25,000 at a low rate of 20%. Suppose that the next €50,000 of taxable income is taxed at a general rate of 30%. This means that the middle class pay at least €5,000 of income taxes in the first bracket and any income exceeding €25,000, but still below €75,000, will be taxed at this 30% rate. The third bracket could be a 40% rate on any income exceeding €75,000. So, a taxpayer with an income of €50,000 falls in the second bracket. He will pay the full €5,000 of taxes of the first bracket and an additional amount of 30% of €25,000 (€50,000 − €25,000) = €7,500 in the second bracket. The total tax on overall taxable income will be €12,500 for this taxpayer.

The distinction between average and marginal rates is essential. The average rate is the total taxes divided by total taxable income. The marginal rate is the tax rate that applies to an additional euro of taxable income. Marginal rates are important since they influence behavioral responses: people think

Average vs. Marginal Rates

«at the margin». Higher marginal tax rates decrease the incentive to earn additional income.

The average rate for the taxpayer in the previous example is 25% (€12,500 / €50,000 × 100%). If the taxpayer would earn €1 more, that additional amount would be taxed in the second bracket at 30%. Therefore, the marginal rate for this taxpayer is also 30%.

Global vs. Schedular Systems

Irrespective of how the general concept of income is defined, any income tax law should address the question of whether all types of income should be taxed in the same manner when setting tax rates. A global system does exactly that: it applies the tax rates to the sum of all items of income, whether they are wages, business profits, private investment income, or of another nature. A schedular system of income taxation makes a distinction between the applicable rates for different items of income.

The Nordic countries (Denmark, Finland, Norway, and Sweden) apply a specific type of schedular system: the dual income system. The dual income system taxes wages, pensions, and other labor income at (higher) progressive rates, but taxes income from capital (such as business profits, dividends, interest income, and rents) at (lower) flat rates.

Flat Tax Systems

In political calls for income tax reform, reference is often made to «flat taxes». Several Eastern European States have indeed introduced such systems. What is usually meant by this term is an income tax system with:
1. A single proportional tax rate
2. No or only a very limited number of deductions
3. A generous basic allowance

In a flat tax system, the average tax rate on pretax income increases as taxable income increases, due to the basic allowance. This means that higher-income earners pay a larger proportion of total taxable income in taxes. Thus, even this «flat» tax system is progressive in effect. The only thing that stays the same is the marginal tax rate on income exceeding the basic allowance. Therefore, proponents argue that flat tax systems are less distortive to the economy.

Tax Credits

Tax credits directly reduce euro for euro the amount of taxes due. Some credits are refundable, which means that the taxpayer may claim a refund for the amount of credit that reduces tax liability beyond zero. The same applies to credits as to reductions: the policy reasons for which States give these tax advantages are multiple and varied.

While income reductions (allowances and deductions) also reduce taxes, the progressivity analysis of income reductions and tax credits is different. A tax credit of €1,000 reduces taxes for everyone with €1,000. It has the same tax value for everyone. However, a €1,000 tax credit takes a relatively larger chunk out of the low taxes of low-income taxpayers, compared to the limited significance it carries to the high taxes of high-income taxpayers. An income reduction of €1,000 through an allowance or a deduction has a tax value that corresponds to the marginal tax rate of the taxpayer. If the last €1,000 of a person is taxed at 25%, an income reduction of €1,000 has a tax value of €250 for that taxpayer. A taxpayer whose last €1,000 of income is subject to a higher rate of 40% enjoys an advantage with a tax value of €400.

4.5 Income Taxation of Companies

Taxes on income are not only imposed on individuals, they are also levied from legal entities, i.e., companies. These income taxes on companies are usually called «corporation taxes».

Companies are creatures of the law: a company can assume legal rights and legal obligations just like individuals. Unlike people of flesh and blood, companies exist only on paper. For this reason, some argue that companies cannot ultimately bear a tax burden. Why then impose income taxes on companies too?

All corporation taxes will be paid by individuals eventually. Corporation taxes, as any taxes, carry deadweight losses, and their burden also manifests as social costs. Corporation taxes will either be shifted to consumers (through price increases of goods and services), to shareholders and other capital providers (by lower rates of return, meaning lower dividends and interest), to employees (by decreased wages), or to management (by decreased compensation). Due to the uncertain economic incidence of the corporation tax, it is generally accepted to be a significantly distortive tax.

The main argument in favor of corporation taxes is pragmatic. It is simply more convenient to collect taxes from one legal entity than to assess all individual owners of the company with a personal income tax on their proportionate share in the company's profits. At the same time, the corporation tax assures that a tax on income is effectively levied, irrespective of the personal tax treatment of the companies' owners, i.e., the shareholders. There is also an element of fairness and neutrality: it does not matter how you run your business—as a sole entrepreneur, in partnership with a business friend, or together with many other investors through a company—the sum of all business profits will subject to income taxation.

5   Taxes on Goods and Services

Taxes on goods and services may come in three basic forms:
- General transaction taxes (e.g., VAT and sales taxes)
- Taxes on specific goods and services (e.g., excises on alcohol, cigarettes, gambling, and energy)
- Taxes on the use of goods (e.g., motor vehicle registration taxes)

Value Added Tax

The value added tax (VAT) is the most important general transaction tax. Almost everyone sees VAT charged on the invoices for goods and services bought. It was introduced in the 1960s and replaced many of the then existing general transaction taxes. Taxes on specific goods and services were actually reduced because of its introduction. The common VAT system in the EU is a result of harmonized laws, but its basic features are not unlike those of other VATs in force internationally.

In Australia, Canada, and New Zealand the VAT is called a Goods and Services Tax.

Basic Features of VAT

Taxable transactions for VAT are the supply of goods and services. Taxpayers are all persons who carry out taxable transactions. VAT does not apply to transactions between persons acting in a private capacity. VAT is charged fractionally as an exact proportion of the price of each taxable transaction in all stages of the production and distribution process up to and including the retail stage. This means that total VAT is collected in portions that correspond to the tax due on the economic value added of each stage in the production and distribution process of goods and services.

The general transaction tax (sales tax) imposed by the States in the United States only applies at the retail stage when goods and services are sold to the final consumer.

Exemptions and Rates

Some transactions are exempted from VAT. These exemptions are due to difficulties in assessing the tax in respect of some sectors (e.g., financial services) or may be a result of regulatory aims. About the latter, the exemption of medical and dental services, for example, aims to guarantee basic access to health care. Many systems provide for more than one rate and thus apply lower rates (sometimes even 0%) on some transactions. Low taxation of foodstuffs and books are well-known examples.

The minimum statutory standard VAT rate in EU is 15% (Article 97 of Directive 2006/112/EC), but almost all Member States apply statutory standard rates of 20% or higher.

Taxpayers are obliged to charge VAT on each taxable transaction, and they should record the VAT on the invoice that they render to customers. Each taxpayer may credit the VAT that is recorded on invoices received (input VAT) against the VAT charged on invoices rendered (output VAT). This invoice-credit method preempts that VAT burdens cumulate over several stages of production and distribution. It effectively makes only the value added in each stage subject to tax. There is usually no credit for input VAT that is attributable to exempted taxable transactions. However, input VAT attributable to transactions that are zero rated is deductible. If a taxpayer paid more input VAT than the output VAT charged in a taxable period, he or she is entitled to a refund from the tax authority.

Invoice-Credit Method

John produces and sells retail goods. In 1 month, John has produced and sold goods for a value of €100,000 to private consumers. Given a standard VAT rate of 20% of the price of goods supplied, John is obliged to record €20,000 in VAT on the invoices he renders to customers. In the same month, John has paid €48,000 inclusive VAT to suppliers for raw materials. On the invoices that John received from these suppliers, VAT was stated for an amount of €8,000. The value added of John's business over the month is €60,000, because the value of input materials was €40,000 and the value of John's output goods was €100,000. Accordingly, VAT for an amount of €12,000 (20% of €60,000) should be due. This corresponds exactly to the balance of €20,000 in output VAT charged and €8,000 in input VAT credited.

6   **Taxes on Property**

Taxes on property may be broadly divided into taxes on property ownership and taxes on property transactions.

6.1   Property Ownership Taxes

Taxes on property ownership are a product of a tax rate and the value of the property held by the taxpayer. If the tax includes all assets and debts of a taxpayer, we qualify this tax as a net wealth tax. Many States impose taxes on specific property, for example, a tax on immovable property.

A special system of property ownership taxation applies in the Netherlands. Until 2017, this system presumed that a taxpayer earns 4% of income from his net savings and investments above a basic allowance of nontaxed wealth. This fixed proportion was used as the tax base, even if the real income was higher or lower. The presumptive income is then taxed with an income tax of 30%. The Dutch system is economically equivalent to a net wealth tax with a 1.2% rate on the value of the taxable property. Legally speaking though, the Dutch tax is a tax on income.

6.2   Property Transaction Taxes

Taxes on property transactions include all estate, inheritance, and gift taxes that become due when property ownership changes from one person to another without consideration, for instance, by cause of death or by gratuitous promise. These taxes are sometimes referred to generally as succession duties.

Estate, inheritance, and gift taxes prevent the accumulation and concentration of wealth in the hands of a small proportion of taxpayers over generations, due to shared background and family relations. The tax takes away a part of the wealth when property ownership changes, usually down the line of the family tree.

An estate tax is levied on the value of the property of the deceased («the estate»). An inheritance tax is levied on the part of the property that an heir receives from the estate («the legacy»). Since it is easy to avoid estate and inheritance taxes by transferring ownership before death, many States also tax gratuitous transfers inter vivos (Latin for «between the living») with a gift tax. Many inheritance and gift taxes impose very low taxes on transfers of property ownership between first-degree relatives, but the rates are higher for more distant family relations.

A special type of property transaction taxes is financial transaction taxes. The financial crisis has increased the demand from society that the financial sector contributes to economic recovery by paying a fair share of taxes. The European Union has therefore proposed to levy a financial transaction tax that should raise substantial revenue and that should also discourage harmful speculation on financial markets. The latter objective is, of course, a regulatory goal to stabilize the economy.

7　Tax Procedure

7.1　Taxpayer Rights and Obligations

Most developed States recognize the following basic taxpayer rights and obligations in laws or regulations.

Taxpayer rights	Taxpayer obligations
Right to be informed, assisted, and heard	Obligation to be honest
Right of appeal	Obligation to be cooperative
Right to certainty	Obligation to provide information
Right to privacy	Obligation to keep records
Right to confidentiality	Obligation to pay taxes on time

In defining the proper rules of conduct between the tax authority and taxpayers, the principles of administrative law are important. In summary, this means that the tax authority should always duly observe that its actions toward the taxpayer are impartial and proportionate.

7.2　Assessment and Collection

The requirement for the taxpayer to file a tax return is the basis of most assessment procedures. This tax return includes all necessary information to establish the tax liability. A tax return is assumed to be correct unless the tax inspector determines otherwise. There are two basic types of assessment procedures:

Assessment Procedures

1. Assessment by the tax authority
2. Self-assessment by the taxpayer

Under the first method, the tax returns filed by the taxpayer are more or less treated as statements of information to the tax authority. The tax authority then uses the information in the tax return, combined with information received from employers, property registries, and banks and other financial institutions, to determine the tax liability of the taxpayer. The tax authority may also request additional information from the taxpayer. The determination of how much tax the taxpayer owes is thus carried out by the tax authority. The taxpayer receives a tax assessment from the tax authority that formalizes the liability. The taxpayer should then remit the taxes owed to the tax authority. This system is used in many States for taxes on income.

Under the second method, the taxpayer himself determines the tax liability when filing the return. Since there is no need for the tax authority to issue a tax assessment, the taxpayer normally also immediately remits the taxes owed upon filing the return. This system is used in many States for taxes on goods and services, but some also apply it to income taxes.

Withholding Tax

A withholding tax is a tax that a third party withholds on behalf of the taxpayer (who is thus the statutory bearer of the tax) from payments that this third party makes to the taxpayer. Any taxes that have already been paid by a withholding procedure may be credited against the tax liability for the same income of the taxpayer. Withholding taxes often apply to payments of wages, dividends, interest, and royalties.

When an employer pays wages to an employee, the employer deducts any wage taxes due on the payment and remits those wage taxes to the tax authority. Although the employee is liable to pay income taxes on the wages, there is no need for the employee to make an actual payment since the tax liability has been fulfilled by reason of the wage taxes previously withheld by the employer.

Penalties

To ensure effective assessment and recovery in compliance with the law, the tax authority can impose penalties if a taxpayer does not comply with taxpayer obligations. These have both a deterrent and punitive function. In many States, the tax authority imposes penalties for the following categories of acts:

- Omission or late filing of returns and forms
- Inaccurate or frivolous filing of returns and forms
- Refusal to disclose information and similar obstructionist behavior
- Omission or late payment of taxes

Criminal Sanctions

Some acts of taxpayers are so wrongful that they are dealt with under criminal tax law. The main example of a tax crime is tax evasion or tax fraud.

7.3   Tax Management

A popular saying goes that nothing is certain but death and taxes. One might add that it is a lot easier to escape taxation than death. Bending the tax law to one's advantage is called tax management. A general principle of tax management is that it is legitimate and lawful to arrange one's affairs as to keep taxes as low as possible. However, there are certain lines in the sand which any taxpayer should observe when engaging in tax management strategies.

If the legislator intentionally creates two sets of rules for similar activities or transactions, the taxpayer may lawfully construct his activities and legal transactions such that the more favorable set of rules applies to his or her situation. Often, the legislator intentionally creates tax-advantaged arrangements, recall the regulatory goal of taxation. The lawful use of options provided by the law is called tax planning.

Due to the complexity of tax laws, it is not always clear whether the taxpayer stays within the distinct collection of legal possibilities afforded by the legislator. The imagination of one legislator is no match to the creativity of many taxpayers and tax intermediaries. That creativity becomes problematic and a legal issue when a legal arrangement is set up with the overriding view to obtain a tax advantage, but any changes in the economic position of the taxpayer are marginal and subordinate to that tax advantage. Such simulations, shams, and wholly artificial arrangements that are void of commercial justification run contrary to the legislator's general intention to reserve tax consequences for real economic transactions and activities.

Michael J. Graetz, a renowned US tax professor, informally defined tax avoidance strategies as deals «done by very smart people that, absent tax considerations, would be very stupid.»

Tax avoidance may be viewed as unethical, but it is not unlawful. However, most States draw the line here and generally respond by closing the legal loophole for the future with additional regulation and specific anti-avoidance rules (SAAR). Many States also apply a general anti-avoidance rule (GAAR) that disallows tax advantages that taxpayers intend to obtain by constructing wholly artificial arrangements.

A GAAR may be expressly laid down in written legislation or construed by courts as a general principle of legal interpretation. The legal effect of a GAAR is usually that the wholly artificial arrangement is ignored for tax purposes, or the construct is reclassified to correspond to a legal arrangement that falls within the aim and purpose of the tax law, but that does not carry the intended tax advantage.

In contrast to tax planning and tax avoidance that take place within the black letter boundaries of the law, tax evasion or tax fraud involves illegal conduct. The evasion of taxes is pros-

Tax Planning

Tax Avoidance

Tax Evasion

ecuted as a criminal offense or crime depending on the type of illegal conduct involved. A simple example of tax evasion is intentional non-reporting of income: taxpayers who earn illegal income often hide it from the tax authorities. Or taxpayers disguise the true, illegal source by reporting it under another legitimate title, thereby effectively engaging in money laundering. Fraudulent fabrication of invoices leads to tax evasion by unlawfully claiming or overstating deductions of expenses that have not been made in fact.

The notorious Al Capone was convicted of tax evasion and was locked up in Alcatraz, whereas he could not be successfully prosecuted for bootlegging and smuggling liquor.

8   Globalization and Tax Law

8.1   International Tax Law

International tax law is the body of law dealing with the taxation of persons and events that have a cross-border element. International tax law concerns specifically rules that prescribe the allocation of taxing powers between States.

Universal vs. Source Jurisdiction

The taxing jurisdiction that a State asserts on domestic persons is universal: it covers all income and wealth, whether derived from domestic or foreign activities and property. The taxing jurisdiction that a State asserts on foreign persons is almost always limited to only those activities and property of the person which are within the national borders of that State. We then say that the income or property should be sourced in that State. Given these basic rules, it is very likely that one State asserts universal jurisdiction on a person, but another State asserts source jurisdiction on the same person.

Person X lives in State R. State R considers X therefore a domestic person and asserts universal jurisdiction on all income of X, wherever earned. Person X works in State R and also in State S. Because person X derives income from activities exercised on the national territory of State S, State S will assert source jurisdiction. Person X will be taxed twice on the income earned in State S: once in R and again in S.

Single Tax Principle

Overlap between the taxing jurisdictions of two or more States on the same person arises easily in any cross-border situation. Consequently, more than one State will create a tax liability on the same person for the same income or property.

This potential overlap is called the problem of double taxation. Double taxation is a major obstacle to international trade and investment. The most important guiding principle of international tax law is therefore that a taxpayer should only once be subjected to taxation on income and property. Single taxation, not more and not less, is the norm.

International rules are necessary to resolve potential double taxation of persons and their income and property. To ensure single taxation, rules on international taxation give answers to the following legal questions:

- When is a person a domestic or a foreign person?
- What is the source of income and property?
- Which methods should States use to relief double taxation?
- Which procedures govern how tax administrations exchange information and cooperate?
- To what extent should domestic and foreign persons be treated equally?

International Tax Rules

The detailed rules of international tax law are laid down in national law but also in tax treaties. Tax treaties are international agreements between two or more States that provide international tax rules to resolve potential concurrences of taxing jurisdiction between the contracting States.

Tax Treaties

There are over 3,000 tax treaties in force worldwide. Most treaties are modeled after the Model Tax Convention on Income and on Capital of the Organization for Economic Cooperation and Development (OECD). The United Nations has drafted a specific model tax treaty based on the OECD Model Tax Convention to govern international tax relations between developing and developed States.

Whereas national tax law creates tax liabilities, tax treaties may only limit these existing tax claims. By limiting the taxing jurisdiction that each contracting State asserts on a person, the total sum of jurisdiction exercised by the contracting States under a tax treaty amounts to single taxation over the person in a best-case scenario. The rules of application and interpretation to give legal effect to tax treaties follow the general rules of international law.

Limiting Function of Tax Treaties

8.2 Tax Problems of Globalization

Historically, taxation addressed domestic economic and social concerns. The process of globalization has reduced institutional barriers to trade and investment in other States.

Outdated International Tax Rules

The mobility of persons has increased too. The current international tax regime was, however, developed when there were significant restrictions on trade, investment, and mobility. These international tax rules are predicated on a permanent physical foreign presence to enable the foreign State to exercise effective taxing powers. However, technological developments and the digitization of the economy have reduced the need for businesses to maintain a permanent physical presence in other States to participate in their economic markets. Globalization and digitization have therefore resulted in the current international tax rules becoming outdated. They are not fit to address the global economic and social concerns of now.

Tax Competition

As States became economically connected through globalization, domestic tax policies increasingly affected international trade and investment flows. States started applying specific tax policies to direct international trade and investment flows to their benefit. States commenced competing by lowering tax burdens to increase the competitiveness of domestic businesses and to attract international businesses. The problem of tax competition thus arose.

Tax competition can be good, because with lower taxes, the negative effects of taxes on the economy also decrease, which is beneficial to global welfare. Tax competition can also be harmful if the tax policies of one State unfairly erode the tax base at the expense of other States' economies.

International Tax Reform

Multinational enterprises are global players. As we have seen, States engage in tax competition with attractive domestic tax rules for international economic activity. Globalization and digitization have made the rise of multinational enterprises possible, but the outdated international tax rules are inadequate to effectively tax the mobile multinational tax base of these enterprises. Because of the combination of these two factors, society has questioned whether multinational enterprises pay their fair share of taxes. Citizens, governments, and nongovernmental organizations all agree on the basic premise that the time has come for fundamental international tax reform.

The G20 and the Organization for Economic Cooperation and Development have engaged in a project, called BEPS (Base Erosion and Profit Shifting) that should lead to fundamental international tax reform. The aim of the project is to enable States to effectively levy a fair share of tax from multinational enterprises, by significantly updating the international tax rules and by better coordinating domestic tax policies.

Recommended Literature

Arnold B, Ault H (2010) Comparative income taxation: a structural analysis. Kluwer Law International, Alphen aan den Rijn

Avi-Yonah RS, Sartori N, Marian O (2011) Global perspectives on income taxation law. Oxford University Press, Oxford

Mirrlees J et al (2011) Tax by design. Oxford University Press, Oxford

Schenk A, Thuronyi V, Cui W (2015) Value added tax: a comparative approach. Cambridge University Press, Cambridge

Smith S (2015) Taxation: a very short introduction. Oxford University Press, Oxford

Thuronyi V, Brooks K, Kolozs B (2016) Comparative tax law. Kluwer Law International, The Hague

International Law

Menno T. Kamminga

© Springer International Publishing Switzerland 2017
J. Hage et al. (eds.), *Introduction to Law*, DOI 10.1007/978-3-319-57252-9_12

1   Introduction

Traditionally, two kinds of law are distinguished. On the one hand, there is national or domestic law, which deals with legal relations within the territory of a single State and with the organization of that State itself. On the other hand, there is international law (sometimes called «public international law»), which deals with the legal relations between States. The sharp distinction between national and international law may have been adequate in the past, but it is no longer clear-cut. It is, for example, a mistake to assume that States are free to adopt whatever laws they like. In Member States of the European Union, a large percentage of domestic laws and regulations currently originates from Brussels. But much of European Union law in turn originates from Geneva, New York, or Nairobi. Whether they are international trade and investment rules, Security Council sanctions or greenhouse emission standards, legal standards are increasingly devised at meetings of international organizations or ad hoc international conferences around the world instead of in domestic capitals.

The interplay of rules and measures stemming from institutions at different levels may be illustrated by the *Kadi* case. The case provides an example of the interplay between the United Nations Charter (under which financial sanctions were imposed on Mr. Kadi), domestic law (under which the sanctions were implemented), EU law (under which the sanctions were first transformed and then nullified), and the law of the European Convention on Human Rights (ECHR), on the basis of which it was decided that Mr. Kadi's human rights had been violated.

Kadi case (C-402/05 P and C-415/05 P)

In 2001 the UN Security Council decided that the assets of Yassin Abdullah Kadi, a Saudi businessman, should be frozen on suspicion that he was financially supporting terrorist activities. The Security Council has established a procedure under which the assets of persons suspected of financing the terrorist activities of Al-Qaeda and the Taliban may be frozen. The identification of suspects takes place behind closed doors on the basis of information provided by intelligence services and there is no trial. Persons that are put on the sanctions list are not informed of the measures taken against them. They simply find out 1 day that they can no longer withdraw money from their bank accounts. Decisions are binding on the Member States of the United Nations, meaning that States are required to implement the sanctions immediately. Article 103 of the UN Charter provides that obligations under the Charter prevail over any other treaty obligations States may have. Within the European Union Security Council sanctions are transformed into EU Regulations and thereby also become binding on EU Member States under EU law.

In various court proceedings Mr. Kadi attempted to challenge the sanctions imposed on him. Initially this was in vain, but in 2008 the Court of Justice of the European Union (at that time known as the European Court of Justice) annulled the EU Regulation imposing the sanctions against him on the ground that he had not been informed of the evidence against him and therefore had not been able to challenge that evidence. Under the law of the European Convention on Human Rights – that has been incorporated into EU law – anyone charged with a criminal offence is entitled to be informed of the charges against him and to defend himself.

The *Kadi* case illustrates another shortcoming of the traditional account according to which international law is merely concerned with the legal relations between States. Although the case concerns the legal position of an individual citizen— a situation traditionally regulated exclusively by domestic law—it nevertheless turns out to be largely governed by international and European law. Apparently, international law is not merely a legal system governing relations between States but rather a legal system that also addresses individual citizens.

In some States, individuals may directly invoke rules of international law (e.g., human rights standards) before domestic courts. Such States are said to have a *monistic* approach to the relationship between international and domestic law. In other States, rules of international law may only be invoked before domestic courts after they have first been *transformed* into rules of domestic law. Such transformation may be carried out, for example, by an act of parliament introducing a human rights standard into the constitution or a piece of legislation. These States are said to have a *dualistic* approach to the relationship between international and domestic law. States are free to choose which type of relationship they prefer as long as they comply with their international legal obligations.

2   Topics of International Law

International law deals with many different topics, which include but are certainly not confined to relations between States. Here are some examples.

War and Peace

One of the oldest fields of international law consists of the laws of war and negotiating peace to resolve conflicts between States. The well-known 1949 Geneva Conventions on humanitarian law with their Additional Protocols and the 1993 Chemical Weapons Convention are international agreements on what are lawful and unlawful means of waging war by States. Nowadays, the United Nations take a central role in safeguarding international peace and security, especially through its Security Council.

The Sea

Shipping and the use and exploitation of the sea also are long-standing topics of international law. Questions addressed by the international law of the sea include the following:

- Which restrictions may be imposed on shipping?
- Which activities are allowed on the high seas and coastal zones?
- Are States permitted to exploit the seabed?
- Which States have fishing rights in a particular area of the sea, and how many fish can they take every year?

Many of these questions are covered by the 1982 United Nations Convention on the Law of the Sea (UNCLOS). UNCLOS also contains provisions on the compulsory adjudication of disputes concerning the interpretation and application of the Convention:

Pursuant to these provisions, the Philippines in 2013 commenced proceedings against China concerning the delimitation of the continental shelf and coastal zones in the South China Sea. In 2016, an arbitral tribunal decided in favor of the claims submitted by the Philippines. Although it is a long-standing party to UNCLOS, China declined to participate in the proceedings or to appear before the tribunal. It stated that the tribunal's decisions were 'null and void' and had 'no binding force' even though UNCLOS clearly provides that decisions by an arbitral tribunal shall be complied with by the parties to the dispute.

The Environment

Environmental issues such as global warming, the emission of greenhouse gases, and the pollution of water and the atmosphere transcend the domain of national States. They are therefore also regulated by treaties negotiated between States, such as the UN Framework Convention (1992) and the Paris Agreement (2016) on Climate Change.

As has become abundantly clear over the last few decades, both trade and finance are no longer issues that can be exclusively dealt with at the national level. The World Trade Organization (WTO), the World Bank, and the International Monetary Fund (IMF), organizations governed by international law, are examples of the crucial role of international law in the sphere of economic and financial relations. The WTO has a highly respected and quickly functioning dispute settlement system under which Member States may challenge protectionist measures by other States. Economic and Financial Relations

Crime and criminals are not confined by national borders. Crimes may have international aspects (e.g., trafficking in drugs), and criminals may move from one country to another to commit their crimes and to escape arrest. The combating of crime therefore requires international cooperation, such as the UN Convention against Transnational Organized Crime (2000), the United Nations Convention against Illicit Traffic in Narcotic Drugs and Psychotropic Substances (1988), and an international organization such as INTERPOL (the International Criminal Police Organization). Crime

Human rights are rights held by individuals vis-à-vis States. The 1948 Universal Declaration of Human Rights proclaimed that human rights are universal, but the text was not adopted by consensus. Byelorussia, Czechoslovakia, Poland, Saudi Arabia, South Africa, the Soviet Union, Ukraine, and Yugoslavia registered their disapproval by abstaining from voting in favor of the Declaration. However, the subsequent UN human rights treaties in which human rights are codified in binding form were very widely ratified by States so that the core human rights have indeed become universally accepted. Human Rights

3   Participants in the International Legal System

(Economic) globalization is the trend toward a single worldwide system of production and consumption disregarding national frontiers. Globalization is driven, on the one hand, by technological innovation (resulting in a dramatic reduction of the costs of moving goods, people, capital, and information across the globe) and, on the other hand, by policy decisions to reduce barriers to international economic transfers. Globalization is therefore both an autonomous process driven by technological progress and a political process Globalization driven by policy preferences of States. It could be slowed down if political preferences change, but it cannot be halted indefinitely because technological progress is bound to continue.

Globalization has a major impact both on the status of the participants in the international legal system and consequently on the contents of international law. It boosts the influence of non-State actors at the expense of the State, the entity that has traditionally monopolized international law. Here are a few examples:

- *International organizations* benefit from globalization because States increasingly transfer competences to international institutions in response to problems that can only be adequately addressed at a global level (e.g., international trade, crime, and civil aviation).
- *Multinational enterprises* benefit from globalization because the liberalization of international trade and foreign direct investment enables them to conduct their activities and serve markets wherever this is most profitable.
- *Nongovernmental organizations* benefit from globalization because the Internet and social media help to undermine the traditional governmental monopoly of information. At the same time, these media make it easier to mobilize people and campaign against governmental abuses;
- *Individuals*—at least the lucky ones—benefit from globalization because traveling and studying abroad have become much easier and cheaper. As a matter of fact, individuals who are less well-off—such as peasants who are forced to compete on world markets—may be confronted with the negative consequences of globalization.

3.1   States

Expanding Circle of States

Although international law goes back thousands of years, the current system of international law is usually traced back to the peace of Westphalia (1648). The Westphalian peace treaties marked the end to the 80 Years' War between Spain and the Netherlands and the 30 Years' War in the Holy Roman Empire. They signaled the replacement of the long-standing power of the Pope and the Emperor by the sovereign power of independent Nation States. Sovereignty meant that States were henceforth the highest authority both internally (within their own territories) and externally (toward the outside world). They no longer had to respect the authority of the Pope and the Emperor above themselves.

In true Eurocentric spirit, the States that emerged from the Westphalian peace treaties referred to each other as «Christian» States. This indicated that international law was only binding between themselves. In their colonies, they could behave as they pleased toward the indigenous population without—in any way—being restricted by the rules of international law. Slavery, for example, could be lawfully practiced outside the circle of Western States.

When in the nineteenth century Turkey and Japan were considered suitable to join the club, the label of the States to which international law applied was changed to the «civilized» States. In the uncivilized rest of the world, international law remained inapplicable.

In 1945, at the end of World War II, the label was changed once again. The Charter of the United Nations provided that States had to be «peace loving» in order to be admitted as a member of the United Nations. All States that met this— admittedly rather subjective—standard were considered fit to be admitted to the United Nations. Since no State was ever expelled from the United Nations for no longer being peace loving, it implied that international law was henceforth considered applicable to all States without exception.

Statehood and Sovereignty

Ever since 1648, States have been the world's dominant legal entities. The number of States continued to increase as colonies became independent, and States split up into new States (such as the former Soviet Union and the former Socialist Republic of Yugoslavia). When is an entity entitled to call itself a State? This is an important question because statehood entails important legal consequences. A State is entitled to conclude treaties with other States, it can become a member of international organizations, and its sovereignty must be respected. But statehood also entails duties. A State must refrain from settling international disputes by force, and it must respect the human rights of persons within its jurisdiction.

There are three generally recognized criteria for statehood: a defined territory, a permanent population, and a government exercising effective power. Recognition by other States is not a separate requirement for statehood. A State that fails to be recognized by other States is still a State:

Palestine, Kosovo and South Sudan are among the world's newest – although in the case of Palestine and Kosovo still contested – States.

The most fundamental principle of international law is the sovereign equality of States. An expression of that sovereign equality is that all States have one vote at the General Assembly of the United Nations, whether they are a superpower or a mini-State with a few thousand inhabitants, such as the Pacific island States Nauru and Tuvalu. But there are some exceptions to this general rule. The most important is the special status of the five permanent members of the UN Security Council, to be discussed below.

Non-State actors derive whatever international legal status they have from States. States decide which rights and duties non-State actors have under international law. This demonstrates that States are still the leading participants in the international legal system in spite of the increasing importance of non-State actors.

3.2   International Organizations

The term «international organizations» refers to intergovernmental organizations (IGOs), i.e., organizations with States as members. This distinguishes them from nongovernmental organizations, organizations of which individuals are members. IGOs may have a worldwide or a regional membership. IGOs with a regional membership are the European Union and the Organization of African Unity. IGOs with a (potentially) worldwide membership are the United Nations, the World Trade Organization (WTO), and the World Health Organization (WHO).

Attribution of Powers

In order to safeguard the sovereign rights of their members, the competences of IGOs are based on the principle of attribution of powers. This means that they can only exercise the powers explicitly granted to them in the founding charter of the organization. This principle may cause difficulties, however, if an IGO is faced with the need to exercise powers that were not foreseen when the organization was established. Of course, the organization's founding charter can always be amended, but this requires the unanimous agreement of the Member States, which is not always easy to achieve. Even a relatively homogeneous regional organization such as the European Union has found it difficult to muster at all times the unanimity required for repeated amendments of the EU treaty.

Implied Powers

A way out of this difficulty has been provided by the International Court of Justice. In response to a request for advisory opinion from the UN General Assembly (in the Reparation for Injuries Case), the Court observed that IGOs enjoy implied powers, which means that they may exercise the powers that are necessary to achieve the organization's objectives even when these powers have not been specifically spelled out in the organization's founding charter. This means that as long as an action is necessary to achieve the organization's objectives, it may be carried out.

As more and more responsibilities are transferred from States to international organizations, the question may arise whether these organizations are bound by international law in the same way as States. Is the World Bank required to respect treaties on international environmental protection when providing a loan for the construction of a dam in a rainforest? Are the United Nations bound by treaties on the law of armed conflicts (international humanitarian law) when carrying out peacekeeping activities under their command?

IGOs and International Law

Since treaties are the main source of international law, the question whether IGOs are bound by international law depends to a large extent on whether IGOs can become parties to treaties. Generally speaking, only States and not international organizations can become parties to treaties. This is because States are reluctant to treat international organizations on an equal footing with themselves. There are however an increasing number of exceptions to this general rule. More and more treaties provide that not only States but also the European Union as a whole can become a party:

IGOs and Treaties

For example, proposals have been made for the EU to become a party to the European Convention on Human Rights. This would mean that EU decisions will fall under the scrutiny of the European Court of Human Rights in Strasbourg; it will be able to check whether they are in conformity with the European Convention on Human Rights.

The 1949 Geneva Conventions on international humanitarian law are still not accessible to international organizations. Some years ago, the UN Secretary-General therefore issued a formal unilateral declaration according to which troops acting under UN command would henceforth be bound by the principles of international humanitarian law.

3.3   The United Nations

Among the international organizations that have been created by national States, the United Nations is the most prominent and important. The UN was formed in 1945 first and foremost to prevent the outbreak of another world war. The UN Charter was originally signed by 51 States. It created one main body, the General Assembly, three councils: the Security Council, the Trusteeship Council, and the Economic and Social Council, and the UN Secretariat and the International Court of Justice. The UN Charter also allows the UN authority to create additional committees, agencies, and other subsidiary organs to carry out its mission.

General Assembly

Membership

The United Nations General Assembly (GA) consists of representatives of the Member States. There are currently 193 States in the General Assembly; the latest state to gain UN membership was South Sudan in 2011; membership is granted by the General Assembly upon the recommendation of the Security Council. A veto by the United States has so far prevented Palestine from becoming a UN member.

As noted above, in the General Assembly, each member has one vote regardless of its size, population, or economic power.

It is important to distinguish the UN from a State: the UN does not have a legislature that passes laws that are binding on the Member States. Resolutions issued by the General Assembly are nonbinding recommendations. The General Assembly can also adopt treaties, but these must first be ratified before they become binding on ratifying States.

Observers

A State may also be granted observer status by the General Assembly. An observer State can attend meetings and make statements but has no voting rights. The two current observer States are the Holy See (Vatican City) and Palestine. Numerous IGOs, such as the International Committee for the Red Cross (ICRC), INTERPOL, and UNESCO, have observer status. Regional organizations such as the EU and the African Union also are observers.

Committees and Specialized Agencies

The General Assembly has established several committees as fora for discussion and to provide reports and studies on a wide variety of topics. Most UN committee reports are available at the UN website, ▶ www.un.org, in one of the six official languages of the UN: Arabic, Chinese, English, French, Russian, and Spanish.

Operating under the auspices of the United Nations also is a large network of so-called specialized agencies, some of which are in fact older than the UN itself. They include the International Labor Organization (ILO); the World Health

Organization (WHO); the Food and Agriculture Organization (FAO); the United Nations Educational, Scientific and Cultural Organization (UNESCO); the International Monetary Fund (IMF); the World Bank; the World Intellectual Property Organization (WIPO); and the World Meteorological Organization (WMO).

The Security Council

According to the UN Charter, the UN Security Council's main purposes are to:
- Investigate any dispute or situation that might lead to international friction.
- Recommend methods of adjusting such disputes or the terms of settlement.
- Formulate plans for the establishment of a system to regulate armaments.
- Determine the existence of a threat to the peace or an act of aggression and recommend what action should be taken.
- Call on Members to apply economic sanctions and other measures not involving the use of force to prevent or stop aggression.
- Take military action against an aggressor.

Authority for the UN Security Council to accomplish these tasks is found under Chapter VI (Pacific settlement of disputes) and Chapter VII (Action with respect to threats to the peace, breaches of the peace, and acts of aggression) of the UN Charter.

Economic sanctions available to the Security Council include the suspension of trade, the embargo of goods, boycotts, and the so-called smart sanction of the freezing of individual financial assets, as used in the *Kadi* case mentioned above. Military action can take the form of naval blockade, aerial bombardment, or full-scale military operations as in the first Iraq war and more recently in Libya.

The Security Council has 15 members. Five States, China, France, Russia, the United Kingdom, and the United States, are permanent members, and each permanent member enjoys veto power against the adoption of a Security Council decision. The other ten Security Council members do not have veto power; they are elected periodically by the General Assembly.

Security Council Resolutions are binding upon the UN Member States, and those States must obey those decisions. The UN Security Council can enforce its decisions by imposing sanctions on States that refuse to comply.

International Court of Justice

The International Court of Justice is seated in The Hague to settle disputes in accordance with international law. The Court can only settle legal disputes between States; it is not empowered to decide disputes involving non-State actors. Unlike domestic courts, the Court does not have automatic jurisdiction. It can only settle a dispute if the States concerned have decided to accept the Court's jurisdiction. States can also withdraw from the Court's jurisdiction, for example, if they object to the Court's rulings:

The United States withdrew its recognition of the jurisdiction of the International Court of Justice after the Court had found that the United States had violated the prohibition of the use of force against Nicaragua. France withdrew its recognition of the Court's jurisdiction when it disapproved of the Court's exercising jurisdiction in a case concerning French nuclear tests in the Pacific. Of the five permanent members of the Security Council, China and Russia never accepted the Court's compulsory jurisdiction.

UN Secretariat and Secretary-General

The UN Secretariat's main purpose is the administration of the UN and its employees, including the internal affairs of the UN headquarters in New York and other offices worldwide such as in Geneva and Nairobi and the affairs of the various departments, subsidiary organs, and agencies.

The Secretary-General heads the Secretariat and is the chief administrator of the UN. Candidates for the post of Secretary-General are nominated by the Security Council and appointed by the General Assembly for no more than two 5-year terms.

Secretaries-General have been drawn from a wide variety of States, notably not from countries that are permanent members of the Security Council: Trygve Lie (Norway), Dag Hammarskjöld (Sweden), U Thant (Burma), Kurt Waldheim (Austria), Javier Pérez de Cuéllar (Peru), Boutros Boutros-Ghali (Egypt), Kofi A. Annan (Ghana), Ban Ki-moon (Republic of Korea), and the current Secretary-General, António Guterres (Portugal).

In addition to his administrative duties, various political functions have been accorded to the Secretary-General over the years. UN Charter Article 99 provides:

The Secretary-General may bring to the attention of the Security Council any matter which in his opinion may threaten the maintenance of international peace and security.

Because of this discretionary power, the post of Secretary-General carries with it a great deal of symbolic influence. It depends on the occupant whether this influence is used in practice.

3.4 Multinational Enterprises

A multinational enterprise is a company that has its headquarters in one State and its production or distribution facilities in one or more other States. The resulting octopus-like structure enables multinational enterprises to take full advantage of globalization. They can invest and set up subsidiaries where this is most advantageous, i.e., where the conditions with respect to taxation, labor costs, and environmental protection are least onerous.

States are keen to attract foreign investment from multinational enterprises because this creates jobs, encourages transfer of technology, and generates income from taxation. Governments therefore have a tendency to compete with each other by lowering their standards at the expense of their population and the environment. This process is called the «race to the bottom».

Race to the bottom

Since there are no international minimum standards regulating the conduct of companies, the race to the bottom can go on indefinitely. Proposals to create binding international minimum standards for companies have been discussed at the United Nations for quite some time, but they have met with little support from States and from companies themselves. Although one might assume that «good» companies have an interest in the creation of a level playing field that obliges their competitors to behave properly, this does not turn out to be the case. Some cynics believe that international regulation of corporate conduct will only come about after another major accident that demonstrates the dangers of the current free-for-all system. Until that happens, multinational enterprises are bound merely by the domestic legal systems in which they operate.

3.5 Nongovernmental Organizations

There is no authoritative definition of a nongovernmental organization (NGO). Typically, an NGO is defined negatively by what it is not: not a government, not a political party, not an opposition movement. It usually consists of a group of individuals who aim to achieve certain idealistic objectives: protection of human rights or the environment, abolition of cluster bombs, etc.:

One of the oldest NGOs is the Anti-Slavery Society established in the nineteenth century to campaign for the abolition of slavery.

NGOs have no rights or duties under international law. Like multinational enterprises, they enjoy legal status only under domestic law. For example, the Netherlands branch of Amnesty International is an association established under Dutch law.

Consultative status

IGOs may however decide to grant certain NGOs so-called consultative status. Consultative status enables an NGO to attend meetings, circulate documents, make speeches, and lobby delegates. But NGOs with consultative status have no right to vote, and they may be deprived of their status at any time if the majority of the Member States find that they have abused it, for example, by publicly criticizing States. This illustrates how NGOs remain dependent on States for their formal international status.

Even without formal international status, however, NGOs may have significant impact on international decision making. This is because of their expertise and the fact that they represent important strands of public opinion:

The Ottawa Convention banning landmines would never have been adopted in 1997 without the forceful and sustained campaigning by a worldwide coalition of NGOs. The Rome Statute of the International Criminal Court would not have been adopted in 1998 without very effective campaigning by hundreds of NGOs around the world.

Some States have become so concerned about the perceived influence of NGOs at the international level that they have proposed the adoption of international minimum standards for NGO conduct. No such standards have been adopted so far, however. Because the power and influence of NGOs is much more limited than that of multinational enterprises, the need for the establishment of international minimum standards is less obvious for NGOs than for multinationals.

3.6 Individuals

A century ago, individuals had no rights whatsoever under international law. This meant that governments were free to treat them as they pleased. If a government saw fit to discriminate or even to exterminate a group of its population, no other State could object since there were no international standards prohibiting discrimination or genocide:

This is what happened, for example, during the Armenian genocide in the Ottoman Empire (Turkey) from 1915–1917. Ambassadors from Western countries were fully aware of the massacres that were taking place but they had to turn a blind eye for fear of interfering in the Empire's (Turkey's) internal affairs.

A turning point therefore was the adoption of the Universal Declaration of Human Rights by the UN General Assembly in 1948. The Universal Declaration was itself a nonbinding instrument, but human rights have subsequently been codified in a large number of binding international treaties.

States that are parties to these treaties are required to guarantee the rights contained in them to all persons within their jurisdiction. Individuals who consider that their rights have been violated may sometimes—after exhaustion of legal remedies before domestic courts—complain to international human rights courts or similar international bodies. A State that is violating human rights is acting contrary to its international obligations, whatever its domestic laws or its domestic courts may say. Even in North Korea or in Somalia, international law gives individuals rights that must be respected by the authorities.

It is often forgotten that individuals not only have rights but also have duties under international law, namely, the duty not to commit international crimes, such as genocide, war crimes, and crimes against humanity. These crimes are defined in the Statute of the International Criminal Court and also in ad hoc international criminal tribunals dealing with international crimes committed during armed conflicts in countries such as Yugoslavia, Rwanda, and Sierra Leone. Although only a small percentage of international crimes committed in the world are tried by these international courts and tribunals, their symbolic significance should not be underestimated. This further demonstrates the increasing status of the individual in international law.

Duties Under International Law

4   Sources of International Law

International law still has some of the traits of a primitive legal system, and this is reflected in the doctrine of its sources. While customary law has lost most of its importance in modern national legal systems and has given way to statutory law, in international law it still plays an important role. Examples of rules of customary law are the prohibitions of aggression, genocide, and discrimination.

Article 38 of the Statute of the International Court of Justice mentions four sources of international law:

Art. 38 Statute of the International Court of Justice

1. The Court, whose function is to decide in accordance with international law such disputes as are submitted to it, shall apply:
   1. international conventions, whether general or particular, establishing rules expressly recognized by the contesting States;
   2. international custom, as evidence of a general practice accepted as law;
   3. the general principles of law recognized by civilized nations;
   4. subject to the provisions of Article 59, judicial decisions and the teachings of the most highly qualified publicists of the various nations, as subsidiary means for the determination of rules of law.

4.1   Treaties

Of these four sources, «international conventions», also known as «treaties», and international custom (or customary law) are the most important ones. The central role of treaties follows from a basic principle of traditional international law, namely, that a State is bound only by the rules of international law to which it has specifically consented.

Voluntarism

This principle reflects voluntarism, the idea that a State can only be bound by an obligation after it has given its consent. Voluntarism follows from State sovereignty. Since States represent the highest authority in the international legal system, they are not required to accept any obligations they do not agree with. A State may express its consent to be bound, for example, by becoming a party to a treaty in which the obligation in question is included:

The way in which treaties can be concluded is regulated by the *1969 Vienna Convention on the Law of Treaties*.

A State therefore is entirely free to join or not to join international legal instruments such as the Paris Agreement on climate change. A State may feel under political pressured to join, but it is under no legal obligation to do so. It may also leave a treaty after it has joined, in accordance with the procedure foreseen in the treaty (usually a couple of years after the deposit of the notification of withdrawal). After a State has left a treaty, it is no longer bound by its provisions, but it remains of course bound by any relevant rules of customary international law:

In 2016, Burundi, Gambia and South Africa announced that they would pull out of the Statute of the International Criminal Court and the United Kingdom declared that it would leave the European Union. The UN Charter does not have exit provisions because its founding fathers wished to create an organization with universal membership. Nevertheless, no-one could of course prevent a State from leaving the United Nations. It must be regarded as one of the organization's achievements that no Member State has ever stepped out, even when military enforcement action was taken against it (some States have temporarily suspended their membership).

4.2   Ius Cogens

The traditional voluntarist approach is being undermined by the emergence of *ius cogens* or peremptory norms of international law. Rules of *ius cogens* or peremptory norms are the highest in rank, and they override any contrary international obligations of a State. Examples of rules of *ius cogens* are the prohibition of genocide and the prohibition of aggression. Article 53 of the *1969 Vienna Convention on the Law of Treaties* provides the following description:

Peremptory Norms

A treaty is void if, at the time of its conclusion, it conflicts with a peremptory norm of general international law. For the purposes of the present Convention, a peremptory norm of general international law is a norm accepted and recognized by the international community of States as a whole as a norm from which no derogation is permitted and which can be modified only by a subsequent norm of general international law having the same character.

It follows that a treaty in which two States agree to commit aggression against another State is null and void because it is incompatible with the rule of *ius cogens* prohibiting such conduct. Such a hierarchical structure of norms makes international law more comparable to domestic legal systems in which laws override regulations and constitutional provisions override ordinary laws.

5   Jurisdiction

«Jurisdiction» refers to a State's competence to make and enforce rules in respect of persons, property, or events. Such competence may be exercised in three ways: by way of legislation (by the legislature), adjudication (by the courts), or enforcement (by the police or the armed forces). The law of jurisdiction is an important chapter of international law because it is obvious that conflicts may arise if different States exercise competing jurisdiction over the same persons, property, or events:

Is the European Commission entitled to impose hefty fines on Microsoft and Apple (US companies) for their monopolistic practices worldwide? Are the United States entitled to take sanctions against non-US companies that conduct business in Cuba? Are the Netherlands entitled to prosecute a Rwandan national for her participation in the 1994 genocide?

The traditional starting point for answering such questions is that States exercise exclusive jurisdiction on their own territories. This means that there is a traditional presumption against the exercise of so-called extraterritorial jurisdiction. However, as a result of globalization (including foreign travel and migration, international trade and investment, military enforcement action, environmental degradation, transnational crime and terrorism, and legal and illegal uses of the Internet), States increasingly perceive the need to protect their own interests and the interests of the international community in respect of conduct beyond their borders.

Extraterritorial *enforcement* action (such as an arrest or a drone strike in a foreign country) is still strictly prohibited by international law unless specifically consented to by the territorial State. But *legislation* and *adjudication* in respect of extraterritorial persons or events are increasingly being permitted or even required by international law. This development is driven by idea that such exercise of jurisdiction is allowed if there is a sufficient connection between the State exercising jurisdiction and the person or the event. Whether in a particular situation there is a sufficient connection tends to be determined with reference to several jurisdiction principles:

1. The *active nationality principle* refers to the jurisdiction a State may exercise over persons (including legal persons) that have its nationality. This principle is well established.

2. The *passive nationality principle* refers to the jurisdiction a State may exercise over conduct abroad that injures its nationals. This principle is more controversial, but it is increasingly being included in multilateral treaties aimed at combating terrorism and international crime.

3. The *protective principle* refers to the jurisdiction a State may exercise over persons who threaten its vital interests by preparing a *coup d'état*, carrying out acts of terrorism, counterfeiting currency, or conducting other activities against national security. This principle is not controversial, but it is uncertain precisely which offenses are covered by it.

4. The *universality principle* refers to the jurisdiction a State may or must exercise over certain serious crimes, irrespective of the location of the crime and irrespective of the nationality of the perpetrator or the victim. Unlike the protective principle, the interests protected by the universality principle are those of the international community as a whole. International crimes subject to universal jurisdiction include piracy, war crimes, terrorism, and torture. Although the principle is included in an increasing number of multilateral treaties, its implementation in practice may give rise to controversy because States may object to their nationals—especially their (former) officials—being tried in foreign countries.

5. The *effects principle* refers to the (civil) jurisdiction a State may exercise when foreign conduct produces substantial effects on its territory. Unlike the other jurisdiction principles, this one tends to be relied upon in commercial rather than in criminal cases. The principle originates from US case law but is increasingly accepted also in other countries as a basis for exercising jurisdiction.

6 Characteristics of International Law

How does international law compare to domestic law? Perhaps the overarching difference is that the international legal system is less developed than the average domestic legal system. Accordingly, international law has a limited, although continuously increasing, rule density. This means that many matters are still unregulated and therefore left to the discretion of States. This is the case of course because States are reluctant to give up their freedom of action. The limited development of international law is also reflected in its institutional framework and its enforcement system.

6.1   Institutional Framework

The international legal system still lacks the institutions that are familiar in domestic and regional (European) laws, such as a centralized legislator, a centralized judiciary, and a centralized enforcement system. International institutions, which at first sight seem to play this role in the international legal system, on closer inspection turn out to have a much more limited function. As noted above, the United Nations General Assembly does not have the power to adopt global legislation. It can only adopt nonbinding recommendations. Also, as noted above, the International Court of Justice does not have automatic jurisdiction over disputes between States.

International courts and tribunals exist, but they have no hierarchical relationship to each other. Judgments of the Court of Justice of the European Union, the highest judicial organ of the European Union, cannot be appealed before the International Court of Justice, the principal judicial organ of the United Nations. A person convicted by the Yugoslavia Tribunal cannot appeal to the International Criminal Court. This creates a certain risk of diverging case law, although in practice there are not many examples of conflicting jurisprudence.

6.2   Enforcement

For its enforcement, international law is still dependent on States and on domestic institutions. There is no standing UN police force to enforce compliance with the rules of international law. The International Court of Justice relies on the willingness of States to comply with its judgments. The UN Security Council may authorize the use of force against an aggressor State, but the implementation of such a decision is dependent on a «coalition of the willing», i.e., a group of States willing to make their armed forces available for this purpose.

The International Criminal Court may issue arrest warrants against anyone suspected of having committed international crimes, even against heads of States. This sounds impressive but for the capture of a head of State the Court relies on domestic institutions able and willing to carry out the arrest. For example, in 2009 the Court issued an arrest warrant against Sudan's President Omar Hassan al-Bashir, but he has so far managed to travel to several African countries without being arrested.

7   Trends in the Development of International Law

The emergence of non-State actors, in particular individuals, as participants in the international legal system is having a major impact on the content of international law. It undermines the traditional interstate nature of international law, which is aimed exclusively at the protection of the interests of States. This is reflected in the rise of international *ius cogens*, as described in ▶ Sect. 3.2. Following are some further examples of major developments in international law.

7.1   From Prohibition of Interference in Internal Affairs to Responsibility to Protect

Traditional international law primarily contains negative rules, i.e., standards that impose on States an obligation to refrain from taking certain actions. One example is the prohibition of interference in internal affairs reflected in Article 2 (7) of the UN Charter:

Nothing contained in the present Charter shall authorize the United Nations to intervene in matters which are essentially within the domestic jurisdiction of any State.

The prohibition of interference in internal affairs or matters within domestic jurisdiction is a crucial element of traditional international law because it helps to protect State sovereignty against outside intervention by other States. Accordingly, under traditional international law, it is an internal affair for a government to destroy its environment or massacre its own population. No other government is permitted to intervene or even to express concern.

However, this situation changes when international standards are created according to which States have a duty to respect and protect their natural environment and the human rights of their inhabitants. Any violations of these obligations are then no longer an internal matter of the State in question since these obligations are owed to the other States that are parties to the same convention or that are bound by the same rule of customary international law. Those other States are permitted to insist on compliance with those standards, and they may take legal proceedings against the violating State or even apply sanctions against it to force it to comply with its obligations. What amounts to an internal affair or a matter of domestic jurisdiction is therefore subject to continuous change. In fact, the scope of the notion «internal affair» is continually shrinking.

Under traditional international law, «third» States are entitled but not obliged to take remedial measures against a violating State. Often, third States will have good political reasons to simply look the other way. No government enjoys being told by another government what it should do. The natural tendency is not to criticize the behavior of other States because it increases the risk that a government may itself be at the receiving end of such criticisms in the future.

Responsibility to Protect

According to more recent developments in international law, however, States actually have a duty to respond, at least to serious breaches of international law. They have a responsibility to protect people against international crimes (genocide, war crimes, crimes against humanity, and ethnic cleansing). The «responsibility to protect» principle was formally adopted by the United Nations General Assembly in 2005. The principle entails that States have a responsibility to protect the human rights of their own inhabitants, but if a State fails to comply with this responsibility, the international community has a responsibility to act. Although the principle was included in a nonbinding resolution, it has since been referred to in several Security Council Resolutions that are binding on States, including in Security Council Resolutions imposing sanctions on, and authorizing the use of force against, Libya under Colonel Gaddafi. This obviously is a long way from the prohibition of interference in internal affairs that pertained in the past.

7.2 From Immunity to Universal Jurisdiction

Under traditional international law, the highest representatives of a State (the head of State, the head of government, and the foreign minister) enjoy immunity from criminal prosecution before foreign courts. This means that they may not be prosecuted there for any criminal offense they may have committed. The underlying reason for this principle is that bringing these high representatives of the State to trial before foreign courts would be incompatible with the sovereign equality of States. Since all States are equal, the persons personifying them should not be subjected to the jurisdiction of other States. Moreover, if these high officials could be arrested any time they are traveling abroad, this would undermine the freedom of interstate relations. As a matter of fact, international law does not prohibit—and may even require—the prosecution of these officials in their *own* countries.

More recently, however, States have been adopting treaties that oblige States to prosecute and try certain very serious crimes, such as genocide, war crimes, crimes against humanity, and torture, irrespective of where or by whom they were committed. These treaties, which have been widely ratified, do not make an exception for high government officials. There is therefore a contradiction between the traditional immunity rules and these universal jurisdiction provisions in respect of international crimes. The dilemma sharply arose in the Arrest Warrant Case before the International Court of Justice (Arrest Warrant of 11 April 2000 (Democratic Republic of the Congo v. Belgium), Judgment, I.C.J. Reports 2002, p. 3):

In 2000, a Belgian investigative judge issued an international arrest warrant against Abdoulaye Yerodia Ndombasi, the Foreign Minister of the Democratic Republic of Congo. He was accused of having made a speech inciting genocide against the Tutsi ethnic group. Congo responded by filing an application against Belgium at the International Court of Justice, claiming that its Foreign Minister enjoyed immunity from Belgian jurisdiction. In 2002, the case was decided in Congo's favor. The Court found that as a Foreign Minster Mr. Yerodia enjoyed full immunity and could not be prosecuted in Belgium even for international crimes. The judgment was criticized for failing to properly balance the traditional State interest of immunity for high State officials versus the emerging interest of the victims of international crimes to combat impunity for the perpetrators of international crimes. The criticism was aimed in particular at an observation by the Court according to which high State officials continue to enjoy immunity even after they have retired from office as long as the crimes of which they are accused have been committed in an official capacity.

The dilemma may be solved by assuming that high officehold-ers cannot be prosecuted abroad, even for international crimes, as long as they are in office. But as soon as they are no longer in office, such prosecutions would be possible even for crimes committed in function. In this way, a compromise would be found between two contradictory interests: tradi-tional respect for other States' sovereignty and the emerging wish to bring an end to the impunity of the perpetrators of the most serious crimes.

International criminal courts and tribunals do not face this problem of immunity of high officeholders. Their statutes always specifically provide that they can try anyone irrespec-tive of their official rank:

Accordingly, the Yugoslavia Tribunal has tried former President Slobodan Milošević (but he died before the trial was con-cluded). The Sierra Leone Tribunal has found Charles Taylor, the former President of Liberia, guilty of war crimes and crimes against humanity.

7.3   From Nationality as a Favor to a Right to Citizenship

Another illustration of the traditionally inferior status of the individual vis-à-vis the State in international law is the law relating to nationality. Under traditional international law, a State is entirely free to decide by which criteria and on which individuals it will confer its nationality. It should just make sure not to interfere with the rights of other States. This fol-lows again from the fact that States are sovereign.

One result of this approach is that currently there are some 12 million stateless persons in the world. Such persons experi-ence great difficulty in traveling, and if their human rights are violated, no State will act on their behalf.

Article 15 of the Universal Declaration of Human Rights provides that «Every-one is entitled to a nationality», but this provision is difficult to enforce because the Declaration is not binding on States. No similar provision has been included in UN human rights treaties that have been concluded subse-quently. There are some treaties that attempt to reduce the number of stateless persons, but these have had limited impact. However, as the status of the individual in interna-tional law continues to strengthen, it may be expected that nationality will gradually change from a favor that may be granted or not be granted by States into a right that can be enforced under international law.

8   Concluding Observations

International law is a highly dynamic branch of law. Its content is changing rapidly as a result of globalization and the growing influence of non-State actors. The emergence of these non-State actors on the global scene is having an increasing impact on the procedural and substantive rules of international law because they insist that their interests and their aspirations are reflected. As a result, international law is gradually being transformed from interstate law into the law of the world community. International law now covers practically all topics that are traditionally covered only by domestic law, and it is therefore extremely wide ranging. The study of international law is interesting, also for the nonspecialist, because the comparatively undeveloped nature of the international legal system stimulates reflection on fundamental aspects of the law. Although the international legal system traditionally consists of unrelated rules and institutions, there are some modest indications of an emerging international constitutional order.

Recommended Literature

Dixon M (2013) Textbook on international law, 7th edn. Oxford University Press, Oxford

Evans MD (ed) (2014) International law, 4th edn. Oxford, Oxford University Press

Shaw MM (2014) International law, 7th edn. Cambridge University Press, Cambridge

13

Human Rights

Gustavo Arosemena

© Springer International Publishing Switzerland 2017
J. Hage et al. (eds.), *Introduction to Law*, DOI 10.1007/978-3-319-57252-9_13

1   Introduction

Human rights may be defined as

- rights that every person has;
- by virtue of merely existing; and
- that aim to secure for such a person certain benefits or freedoms that are of fundamental importance to any human being.

Human rights have changed the way we look at law. For a long time, law has been seen primarily as a set of rules laid down by an authority that people are (legally) obligated to comply with. The advent of human rights has added on top of that a set of requirements impinging on the lawmaking authority itself. For the law to be valid, it is not enough for it to be laid down; it must also sufficiently respect and promote the fundamental interests of human beings. This has substantially moralized law, for better or worse, and this change resonates across the whole legal system.

This chapter takes for granted that constitutional fundamental rights and human rights are roughly equivalent because they have the same function, that is, they aim to do the same thing: to protect the basic interests or freedoms of all human beings. However, some would rather emphasize that different ideologies, national identities, and historical developments underlie different systems of human rights protection, which lead to radical differences between these systems. Most international treaties for the protection of human rights and most national constitutions protect the freedom of speech of individuals against State intervention, and from that perspective, they are equivalent. But the interpretation that is given to freedom of speech, the value that is afforded to it, and the exceptions that are made to this right can be seen to depend on ideological divides that underlie the similarities.

For example, as may be seen from the case *Brandenburg v. Ohio*, the United States has an individualistic culture that is tolerant of hate speech. By contrast, as may be seen by the case *Saada Adan v. Denmark* (UN Committee for the Elimination of All Forms of Racial Discrimination), the UN considers that hate speech is dangerous and discriminatory and that it should be criminalized.

The present chapter is divided as follows. First, ▶ Sect. 2 presents an account of the historical development of human rights. Because human rights are not exclusively a legal concept, ▶ Sect. 3 explains how human rights are seen from different disciplinary perspectives. ▶ Sections 4 and 5 describe who benefits from human rights and who is obligated to provide the benefit, respectively. ▶ Section 6 describes the actual rights that are provided by law, and ▶ Sect. 7 explains how these rights may be limited or constrained. ▶ Section 8, finally, explains how human rights are protected.

2   The Historical Development of the Idea of Human Rights

In this section we explore the philosophical ideas and historical developments that led to the present day systems of human rights protection. Given the fact that the idea of human rights has existed, in one way or another, for millennia, it is inevitable that this account can only be schematic.

2.1   Natural Law Background

Historically, human rights can trace their origin to the natural law tradition developed, among others, by the Stoics of Ancient Greece and Rome and philosophers such as Thomas Aquinas (1225–1274). According to the natural law tradition, above positive law there is a higher law that protects all mankind and to which positive law should conform.

This way of thinking was based on the idea that in nature there is an inbuilt order of things with requirements that men should identify and follow. For example, it is fitting for man to procreate, and the law should therefore recognize and protect children. This order of things was thought to be independent of the truths of revealed religion. Under this framework it was thought that, for example, Christians, Muslims, and pagans could all participate through reason in teasing out the requirements of natural law, even if they held different faiths and attributed different origins to nature. Natural law was thought to be a common ground for different cultures and religions. For example, natural law was a basis for claiming that although South American natives were not part of the Christian civilization and did not have access to revelation, they were still owed respect.

Classical natural law lost a lot of persuasive power due to the advent of the scientific world view which sees nature as mechanical and deprived of inherent purpose or meaning, so that it is human beings who have to decide for themselves what needs to be done.

The collapse of the old view led to a modern variant of natural law thinking that retained the idea of a universal higher law from the old tradition but which gave «nature» as such a very minor role to play, emphasizing instead the capacities of free individuals to seek cooperative schemes of mutual advantage. This line of thinking was championed by intellectuals such as Hugo Grotius (1583–1645), John Locke (1632–1704), and Immanuel Kant (1724–1804). These scholars reinterpreted natural law principally in terms of subjective rights that are the prerequisites for the construction of a fair social order. Here the linkage between natural law and human rights becomes clearer because the focus lies on individual rights which enable the exercise of individual freedom.

The natural law tradition found a receptive soil in the American political experiment. In 1789, the United States was the first country to adopt a legally enforceable constitution, with a list of basic rights. The writers of the American Constitution were knowledgeable about the two variants of natural law thinking and appealed to it when drafting the Constitution.

Natural law thinking lost steam in the nineteenth and the first half of the twentieth century. As mentioned, classical natural law was undermined by the advent of the scientific world view, but its fall was further solidified by the rise of Marxism, Darwinism, and Freudianism, which showed that the mechanical view of nature could be used to provide far reaching explanations of topics which were normally thought to be beyond the reach of science. The modern variant of natural law was undermined by the Romantic Movement, which celebrated local cultures, shared sentiments, and particular identities, instead of individual rationality. All these countercurrents to human rights thinking remain influential today.

2.2   Revival After the Second World War

The Second World War allegedly «shook the conscience of mankind» and sparked a renewed interest in the idea that there are universally applicable moral limits to what States are allowed to do with their subjects. Such renewed interest in human rights found expression at the global, regional, and domestic levels.

Global Developments

At the global level, the protection of human rights became a key concern of the United Nations. While the UN Charter, the founding document of the United Nations, makes little reference to human rights, the UN took for itself to promote human rights at the global level, and today the promotion of human rights constitutes one of the three main aims of the United Nations (the others being achieving peace and security, and promoting development).

The United Nation's engagement with human right started with the 1948 *United Nations Declaration of Human Rights*. This non-binding instrument was to be followed by binding treaties, the most general being the *International Covenant on Civil and Political Rights* (ICCPR) and the *International Covenant on Economic, Social and Cultural Rights* (ICESCR), both of which entered into force in 1976.

Regional Developments

Some regions of the world have sought to have a supranational system of human rights protection that is stronger or better adapted to regional peculiarities than that of the United Nations. Three regional systems of human rights protection are notable:

1. The European System of Human Rights Protection, operating out of the Council of Europe (not the European Union) and encompassing most States of geographical Europe, including Russia, Turkey, Georgia, Azerbaijan, and Armenia but excluding Belarus
2. The Inter-American System of Human Rights, operating out of the Organization of American States encompassing almost all States of the continent but with full participation of mostly Latin American States
3. The African System of Human Rights Protection, originally operating out of the Organization for African Unity and now based in the African Union, encompassing nearly all African countries

Less mature initiatives exist in Asia and the Arab region, but their relative lack of development means that citizens of these countries need to rely more on the global UN system or on domestic law.

It is curious that States have found it pertinent to make a variety of global and regional treaties protecting human rights. At first glance, it may be thought that human rights are predominantly a domestic affair. Compare: if a country pollutes the ocean, or imposes excessive tariffs on imports, other countries are affected, but if a country mistreats its own citizens, it is not immediately clear that this will impact other States. This anomaly has been explained in a variety of ways.

First, it has been argued that the international community as a whole is morally concerned with the protection of all human beings. Second, it has been argued that massive human rights violations spill over into wars, and consequently, all States have an interest in ensuring compliance with human rights. From a purely factual perspective, neither of these two claims is wholly convincing.

At the domestic level, the Basic Law of the Federal Republic of Germany of 1949 (eventually the constitution of the reunified German State) was, like the United Nations Declaration of Human Rights, a reaction to the atrocities of the Second World War. The Basic Law served as a model for new constitutions being made all over the world.

Domestic Developments

The first article of the German Constitution reads: «Human dignity shall be inviolable. To respect and protect it shall be the duty of all State authority», and this article is followed directly by a list of fundamental rights. Constitutions typically start by making references to the sovereignty of the people, the shared territory, language, or history. The German constitution is unique for departing from human dignity and rights. Nowadays, most States of the Western world have constitutions that include enforceable bills of rights with roughly the same content as the ICCPR. Even traditional bastions of resistance to the idea of legally entrenched and judicially enforceable human rights, such as the United Kingdom and Canada, have been influenced by this trend. In the case of the United Kingdom, this has been done through the domestic incorporation of regional human rights standards (the Human Rights Act of 1998 incorporated the European Convention of Human Rights into domestic law), while in Canada this occurred through the development of a homegrown bill of rights (in particular, the Canadian Charter of Rights and Freedoms of 1982).

3   The Dimensions of Human Rights

Human rights are not the monopoly of lawyers. Although the present chapter focuses on human rights as a legal phenomenon, the legal dimension of human rights does not exhaust the concept. In principle, one can use human rights in (at least) four different ways, only one of which is, strictly speaking, legal. Human rights are (1) positive law, (2) moral claims, (3) standards for measurement, and (4) a political language. It is important to be aware of these different dimensions of human rights, because such an awareness can help avoid ungainful confusion.

Human rights are a legal reality. From this perspective, they exist because they are created by law, and to know what rights we have, we have to look at the relevant sources of law that are currently in force. Normally the place to look will be the constitution and ratified international treaties.

That being said, human rights also exist as moral claims. The natural law tradition claims that there are rights that apply to all human beings, which precede the positive law and which the positive law must recognize and honor. Such moral claims are relevant for lawyers. They inspire the creation or rejection of legal rights and can be useful for interpreting the legal rights that are found in treaties and constitutions.

Human rights have also become a standard for measuring the development of States. In the field of development there has been some disillusionment with the use of economic criteria as a means for assessing development, and some have claimed that societies should be assessed not by their economic output but by the degree to which they secure the enjoyment of human rights.

The idea of using human rights as standards for development has received imperfect expression in the Human Development Index published by the United Nations Development Program. This index ranks countries in relation to their performance in life expectancy, education, and per capita income. These criteria are supposed to be closer to human rights than to traditional economic analysis. In the twentieth century, economist Amartya Sen (1933-) and philosopher Martha Nussbaum (1947-) achieved academic prominence for conceptualizing human rights as the main component of development.

Finally, human rights are also a tool for social protest. It is said that we now live in a culture of rights. Western society regards matters of human rights as having a much greater importance than all other issues. Due to this, human rights have become a powerful language to frame social grievances. There is the expectation that framing a claim as a matter of rights will make it more effective. This use of rights is independent from the legal and moral dimensions of human rights. Human rights may be effective as a means to frame complaints even if the complaints being made have no clear legal or moral backing.

4   Critiques

For most people in the West, the phrase «human rights» has a positive connotation: human rights are seen to be fundamentally a good thing. Yet not everyone agrees with this. Some believe that there is something wrong with human rights.

Three powerful objections are that human rights are (1) suboptimal, (2) undemocratic, and (3) parochial.

The problem of suboptimality is easy to grasp. Human rights rule out certain forms of behavior because they infringe the rights of individuals. But it is quite easy to think of situations where infringing the rights of an individual will lead to better results overall. While this problem is endemic to rules in general, it is more severe in the field of human rights because human rights are very hard to change.

Fearing an attack like that of September 11, the German Parliament approved a law (the Luftsicherheitsgesetz) that would allow it to shoot down civilian airplanes if they were hijacked by terrorists intent on using the plane as a weapon against civilians in the ground. The German Constitutional Court (see decision *BVerfG, 1 BvR 357/05 vom 15.2.2006*) invalidated this law on grounds that it infringed the rights of civilians in the plane, treating them as mere objects. Many feel that respecting the rights of citizens in such a situation would be suboptimal. It would lead to a loss of life in both the airplane and the building. There was nothing the parliament could do to reject this seemingly suboptimal decision.

Maybe suboptimality is not a big problem. Human rights aim to secure a just society, not an optimal one. But the next two critiques threaten to put in question the justice of human rights.

Human rights are undemocratic in more than one way. First, they authorize courts to ignore or invalidate democratically made legislation because it infringes individual rights. This is not necessarily a bad thing. That something is democratically decided does not obviously make it just or fair. But sometimes it is question-begging to assume that something is owed as a matter of rights and therefore meant for judicial, rather than parliamentary, determination. In these situations, an appeal to human rights removes contested issues from the political arena and hands them over to lawyers.

Returning to the example of the decision of the Constitutional Court against shooting down hijacked planes, it is question-begging to assume that respecting the dignity of passengers of the plane is a matter of rights, while protecting the life of civilians on the ground is not. Both claims can be defended as a matter of rights. In such cases it is worthwhile to ask who is better situated to resolve the polemic in an even-handed manner: judges, a representative body like parliament, or the people on referendum?

Finally there are worries that human rights are not universal, but parochial to the West. The idea here is that it is unfair to impose on non-Western countries normative expectations that have nothing to do with their history and traditions.

Psychologist Jonathan Haidt (1963-) has identified a type of morality he calls WEIRD. The letters stand for «Western Educated Industrial Rich and Democratic». An emphasis on individualistic rights is a core part of WEIRD morality, and maybe such an emphasis makes sense in a WEIRD social environment, but why should it be exported to different social environments where different values hold?

The force of this critique should not be overstated. Even if it turns out that human rights are the product of Western thinking, it may be the case that they are still desirable for non-Western cultures because they provide benefits that are attractive from any cultural standpoint, for example, protecting individuals from State abuse. But if this is the case, arguments will need to be produced to show that human rights are better at doing this than other alternatives that may exist in non-Western societies.

5   The Right Holders

If we are talking about human rights, it seems obvious that the right holder must be a human being, but such simplicity hides pervasive disagreements. Some claim that human rights accrue only to «persons», understood restrictively as human beings in actual exercise of rational capabilities. Others claim that human rights accrue to all human beings, understood in the wide sense as members of the human family, independently of the exercise of rational capacities.

Similarly, one can question whether legal persons (such as corporations) should count as persons deserving human rights protection. On one hand, corporations are mere fictions. On the other hand, it seems that certain rights naturally express themselves through corporations and excluding corporations from protection can lead to gaps in the system. For instance, it is customarily assumed that freedom of press can be exercised by a newspaper company or that freedom of association includes the right to create legal persons.

This particular issue has been resolved differently in different jurisdictions. The European Court of Human Rights grants protection to corporations, the Inter-American Court of Human Rights does not.

Another relevant problem concerns the rights of collectives. Human rights have been traditionally conceived as rights of individuals. Many have thought that such individualism should be tempered by adding a collective dimension to the rights that protect not only the individual person but also the subsistence of a group and its customs.

In relation to various indigenous tribes in South and Central America, the Inter-American Court of Human Rights has recognized at times that there are human rights that these tribes enjoy collectively, especially the right to collective ownership of their ancestral lands. The African Convention on Human and Peoples' Rights takes the same approach, and explicitly recognizes collective rights to development, peace and a healthy environment.

The danger of collective rights is that they may enter into conflict with individual rights, for instance, when the right of a collective to practice its traditional forms of justice implies the endorsement of procedures and punishments considered backward or inhumane.

In some Latin American countries indigenous tribes have gained the right to use and administer their own justice system. Such systems sometimes involve flogging, the death penalty and rudimentary standards of evidence. If human rights are individual rights only, then it is clear that these practices are prohibited. If there exist both individual rights and collective rights, the result is unclear.

6   Duties

6.1   Who Are the Duty Bearers?

The general orthodoxy is that human rights only create duties for the State. Human rights originated as guarantees against State abuse. This orthodox view has been challenged on many fronts. Some argue that due to globalization the State has lost practical control on what happens in its territory. Often non-State entities such as corporations and terrorist groups hold more power than the State, and it is unrealistic to expect underdeveloped countries to keep them in line. This, it is claimed, would justify addressing human right duties directly to these non-State entities. Others worry that due to its focus on States human rights law is insufficiently sensitive to what happens within the private domain of the family.

It is open to question whether these concerns really justify attributing human rights duties to non-State actors. Human rights are very vague standards, especially in contrast to the norms of civil law and criminal law, and, consequently, their application against private parties will be unpredictable and potentially oppressive. It seems more appropriate to use human rights to demand the state to ensure that appropriate civil or criminal legislation is in place.

This strategy has proved effective in the courts. For example, in the case X and Y v. The Netherlands, the European Court of Human Rights found that the failure of the State to have appropriate criminal legislation against child abuse was a human rights violation.

6.2   Types of Duties

It is traditional to distinguish two different sets of rights by looking at the sorts of demands they make on the State. «Negative» or «liberty» rights demand State inaction; «positive» or «welfare» rights demand State action. For example, the right to freedom of speech is negative because it only demands that the State censors no one, while the right to health is positive because it requires the State to provide health care for the sick.

The tension between these two sets of rights was a dominant theme in the drafting of the main UN global treaties for the protection of human rights. The Universal Declaration of Human Rights (UDHR) included both types and at first the idea was to make a single binding human rights treaty with the same content as the UDHR. Nevertheless, first world countries strongly resisted the inclusion of economic, social and cultural rights in a binding treaty, while socialist countries championed their primacy. As a result of this controversy, it was decided to split the rights into two treaties, resulting in the ICCPR and the ICESCR we have today.

The strict division between liberty or negative rights and welfare or positive rights has lost ground. At present it is usually assumed that a single human right may give rise to many duties; some of these duties may be negative and others positive. For example, the United Nations claims that any right may give rise to duties (1) to respect, (2) to protect, and (3) to fulfill.

Duties to *respect* are negative and are complied with by the State by refraining from doing something: from impairing the enjoyment of a right.

Duties to *protect* require the State to take action to prevent third parties from impairing the enjoyment of a right of another individual.

Duties to *fulfill* are positive and require the State to take action (such as aiding, providing, or informing) in order to ensure that somebody enjoys a right that he/she is presently not enjoying.

So, for example, the traditional «negative» or «liberty right» freedom of speech can be though to give rise to:
- A duty to respect, in the sense that the State should not censor speech that criticizes the government
- A duty to protect, in the sense that the State must protect protesters from harassment and intimidation that could discourage speech
- A duty to fulfill, that the State must take steps to encourage pluralism in media

Likewise, the traditionally «positive» or «welfare right» to education gives rise to:
- A duty to respect, that the State should not ban certain children from receiving an education
- A duty to protect, that it should ensure that negative stereotypes do not impede children from getting a good education
- A duty to fulfill, to make public education available for everyone

Positive rights are, nonetheless, not universally accepted. There is a fear that the protection of positive rights may undermine negative rights. For example, if human rights enjoin States to promote pluralism in media and responsible journalism, States may use this as a pretext to censor broadcasters in the name of rights. This objection is very similar to the concern (discussed above) that introducing collective rights may undermine individual rights.

6.3   Getting from Rights to Duties: The Role of Case Law

Generally the treaty law or the constitutional text will provide us with a list of rights, but it will say nothing of the duties that flow from such rights or their scope. Getting from the rights to the duties is never a mechanical procedure. For example, if the right to life prohibits arbitrary killings, it may not be clear what arbitrary means. Moreover, it is debatable whether such a right enjoins the State to take police action to prevent killings from third parties, to prosecute and punish murders, to reduce infant mortality rates, or to do other desirable things.

For the most part, the critical task of specifying what duties arise from rights falls onto judges. For this reason, it may be said that human rights is an area of law that is driven by judicial decisions. This means that even where there is no doctrine of *stare decisis* (civil law jurisdictions, international law) human rights still relies on case law.

7   The Catalog of the Rights

Having discussed who enjoys human rights and who has to protect them, we now need to discuss the rights themselves. Naturally, the international, regional, and constitutional lists of rights are not identical. They have nevertheless broad similarities, and this section will focus first on these similarities by identifying six clusters of human rights that have widespread acceptance. Afterward the section will discuss some controversies relating to what belongs and does not belong in the list of human rights.

7.1   Rights to Integrity of the Person

The right to life and the right to be free from torture deserve to have their own cluster due to their intimate connection to the being whose humanity is being protected.

The right to life prohibits States from engaging in murder and other arbitrary deprivations of life. Because the focus is on *arbitrary* deprivations of life, this right is hedged by a variety of exceptions. For example, the police may use lethal force when it is necessary to do so in order to secure public order, and in some regions, the death penalty is permitted.

By contrast, the right to be free from torture is supposed to be devoid of exceptions. That is to say, the prohibition of torture is thought to be an absolute prohibition. Sadly, the prohibition of torture exhibits in practice a variety of textual «loopholes» that relativize what should be an absolute prohibition.

The United Nations Convention Against Torture, Article 1 defines torture as follows:

For the purposes of this Convention, torture means any act by which severe pain or suffering, whether physical or mental, is intentionally inflicted on a person for such purposes as obtaining from him or a third person information or a confession, punishing him for an act he or a third person has committed or is suspected of having committed, or intimidating or coercing him or a third person, or for any reason based on discrimination of any kind, when such pain or suffering is inflicted by or at the instigation of or with the consent or acquiescence of a public official or other person acting in an official capacity. It does not include pain or suffering arising only from, inherent in or incidental to lawful sanctions. This seems to create a variety of significant gaps. For example, what about pain and suffering inflicted for no purpose whatsoever, or the pain and suffering inflicted by non-State agents?

Violations of integrity rights tend to be considered particularly severe. Most international crimes or categories of crimes, such as genocide, torture, crimes against humanity, or war crimes, involve violations of integrity rights.

7.2   Freedom Rights

Under freedom rights, we cluster those rights that create a sphere of autonomy for individuals, in which the State may not intervene. Freedom rights include, most prominently, freedom of conscience, freedom of religion, freedom of speech, freedom of movement, freedom of association, the right to property, and the right to privacy.

Although they are not as intimately connected with the human being as integrity rights are, they are nevertheless of tremendous importance. These rights are instrumental for the maintenance of a free society, a space where individuals may interact with each other in conditions of freedom and equality, exchange ideas, and form their identities without the intervention of the State. A free civil society is necessary for democracy, and the absence of a free civil society is a mark of totalitarianism.

Despite their importance, these rights are characterized by being subservient to the public good. Almost all freedom rights expressly allow for limitations when the public good is at stake. Such limitations vary from banning television programs that are deemed to be harmful to minors to allowing surveillance of private conversations to stop criminal activities.

Not all freedom rights are subject to exceptions. Freedom of religion and freedom of conscience are generally thought to have an external and an internal aspect. The internal aspect refers to what one believes in one's mind, and the external aspect refers to making those beliefs public. The internal aspect of these rights is generally considered to deserve absolute protection. The law may never legitimately interfere with a person's conscience.

7.3   Political Rights

Strictly speaking, political rights are the right to vote in free elections and to be elected into office. From a broader perspective, it can be seen that most freedom rights have a political dimension. Freedom of conscience protects one's political beliefs, freedom of speech allows one to disseminate them, freedom of assembly allows one to make a political protest, and freedom of association allows one to organize a political party. Usually the importance given to these rights by courts is heightened when they are exercised in a political context.

Even then, it is useful to distinguish political rights, strictly defined, from freedom rights in their political dimension. It is generally accepted that the political rights of being able to vote and to be elected to office can be made available only to nationals but does not hold true for the political exercise freedom rights.

Due to this restriction one could see political rights as an exception to the rule that human rights belong to every human being. To have political rights, one needs a special legal status, that of having a particular nationality or being resident in a particular country. Even then, this should be seen in the light of the presupposition that every person is a citizen of a country and that statelessness is an anomaly. In reality, according to the United Nation's High Commissioner for Refugees (2009), there are some 12 million stateless persons in the world.

7.4   Welfare Rights

Welfare rights refer to a wide set of provisions that, fundamentally, aim at addressing the problem of poverty. The most notable welfare rights include the right to an adequate standard of living, food, water, access to health services, education, housing, social security, and work.

For most of these rights, it is understood that the State must provide benefits for those who are unable to take care of themselves. This means that welfare rights clearly constitute «positive rights» and for this reason they are traditionally objects of polemic. Since the 1990s, there has been a clear trend for increased recognition of positive rights, but it would be premature to say that they have received widespread acceptance.

India and South Africa are leaders in the judicial protection of welfare rights. In the case *People's Union for Civil Liberties v. Union of India & Others* the Indian Supreme Court enjoined the State to provide meals to children attending public schools. In the case *Minister of Health and Others v Treatment Action Campaign and Others*, the South African Constitutional Court ordered the State to make available an antiretroviral drug that prevented mother to child transmission of HIV.

7.5   Equality and Nondiscrimination Provisions

The idea of human rights and the idea of equality are closely connected. Not only do most lists of human right include a right to equality under the law, but also all human rights are supposed to apply equally to all human beings. Human rights instruments tend to be written in an egalitarian language: «everyone shall enjoy freedom of speech», and «no one shall be held in slavery».

But the idea of equality can be cashed out in a variety of ways. Among conceptions of equality vying for legal recognition, two stand out: formal equality and material equality. Formal equality is content with having laws that are neutral and that do not single out any specific class of persons for special treatment. Material equality, by contrast, aims to ensure that persons end up enjoying the same benefits and, to achieve this, is willing to treat certain classes of persons differently, giving them special benefit or burdens. Material equality provisions are meant to overcome the limitations of formal equality which are well captured by the famous quote from Anatole France: «The law, in its majestic equality, forbids the rich as well as the poor to sleep under bridges, to beg in the streets, and to steal bread».

Connected to the idea of equality, we find the prohibition of discrimination. Discrimination is prohibited under human rights law, but what discrimination means is contentious. The traditional approach to discrimination sees discrimination as the intentional belittlement or exclusion of a group that impacts the enjoyment of their rights. The modern approach to discrimination finds discrimination in any difference in the enjoyment of rights, irrespective of whether the difference was brought about intentionally or happened accidentally, as long as that different cannot be rationally justified.

The traditional and modern conceptions of equality and the traditional and modern conceptions of discrimination tend to go together. The traditional notions of equality and discrimination tend to focus on how individuals are treated. The modern notions of equality and discrimination tend to focus on what people end up enjoying. Problematically, making people equal in one sense will make them unequal in another sense. Which dimension of equality should be legally recognized and enforced remains polemical.

For an example, consider the case of religious minorities that are required to work in days that are of religious observance for them. In such cases, it is clear that there is no intent on part of the business owner to belittle or to exclude the employee. The business owner treats his employees equally, but this nonetheless results in heavy burdens for the minority. Canadian courts would consider this to be discrimination. They would simply see that there is a difference in result that is not justifiable because the business could find ways to accommodate the worker and make him more equal (see, e.g., *Supreme Court of Canada, Ont. Human Rights Comm. v. Simpsons-Sears*).

7.6   Fair Trial and Administration of Justice

Finally, we must consider rights that are relevant when one is subject to a judicial or administrative dispute. The rights that fall under this cluster are very diverse. They include the right to a fair trial, the right to an effective remedy, and specific requirements, such as restrictions on the time one may remain under detention without trial. For ease of exposition, we will focus on three functions that these rights, taken as a whole, carry out.

First, they control what the State can and cannot do to a person without passing first through judicial control. For instance, a State cannot criminally punish a person without a trial.

Second, these rights also control the functioning of judges requiring them to follow a procedure that achieves certain levels of fairness and effectiveness. The list of requirements that these rights make is large and varied. For example, judges must come to a verdict within «reasonable time», they must be impartial, they must ensure the equality of arms between the litigants, there must be a fair and public hearing, and in criminal proceedings they must respect the presumption of innocence.

Third, these rights guarantee the very existence of a fair judicial procedure that one can have recourse to when one's human rights are violated. In this way, these rights are both discrete human rights and guarantee for the protection of all human rights.

These rights are often applied, with some variation, to disputes between citizens and the public administration. For example, it may be the case that the revocation of a license as a penalty imposed by the public administration may not be carried out without giving the citizen a fair and public hearing.

7.7   Polemics about the Rights Catalog

The clusters that have been discussed represent widely accepted human rights. But these clusters do not tell the whole story. Today there is an exuberant variety of things for which recognition as human rights is demanded.

Just to give three examples, coffee, tourism, and the internet have all been claimed to be human rights by official bodies. These proposals have not been legally recognized. But somewhat outlandish demands have received legal recognition. For instance Article 7 of the ICESCR proclaims the right of everyone to paid holidays, and Article 12 of the same treaty proclaims the right of everyone to the highest attainable standard of physical and mental health. Clearly, a world without torture is a different sort of concern than a world without unpaid holidays.

Many object to this so-called proliferation of rights which conflates the essential and the nonessential that dilutes the power of human rights as well as its transcultural acceptability. Objectors would claim that for something to be included into the catalog, it must pass a test of rational acceptability. A relevant test may be one of seriousness. Only sufficiently serious interests deserve protection as human rights. Paid holidays with leave may be a nice thing to have, but not essential. Another relevant test may be that of practicability. Taken literally, having everyone reach the highest standard of health would require absurd levels of state intervention. This way of thinking gives the «moral» dimension of human rights a large role to play in constraining the development of the legal dimension of human rights.

But not everyone sees human rights this way. Those who see human rights first and foremost as a tool of political protest would reject efforts to put restrictions to the rights catalog, as this would create a barrier to the political process whereby excluded groups claim to have rights.

8   Rights as Trumps?

Human rights make a claim to hierarchy. They are not at the same level as the civil code, the labor code, the criminal code, or common law (in common law countries). Human rights aim to limit the power of government, to define certain things that the government may never do or that the government must always do, notwithstanding what may be politically convenient at the time. For this role, human rights need to be above ordinary legislation.

Ronald Dworkin (1931–2013) famously described human rights as «trump cards»: when a human right is involved, that right must be honored in spite of any other consideration, including legal rules that do not express human rights, but rather promote economic efficiency or political expediency.

Nevertheless, the promise of rights trumping «ordinary» rules is never truly realized for two reasons. First, when human rights are implemented as legal rights, hierarchy is not always fully recognized. Some constitutions do single out human rights as the highest point of the legal edifice, but others do not make them more important than other parts of the constitution.

The issue is even more complicated in international law. It is unclear whether treaties have a higher rank than domestic constitutions. An international lawyer and a constitutional lawyer are apt to answer the question differently. Furthermore, within international law, different sorts of treaties, whether they formulate human rights or not, share the same hierarchical position, as do other sources of international law, such as custom and general principles. This means that a human rights treaty does not necessarily have to be superior to, say, a free trade treaty, and this makes it difficult for human rights to assert their role as «trump cards» at the international level.

Moreover, most implementations of human rights leave room for valid legal counters. That a right is in play, or appears to be in play, is never a sure win. Invoking a right is never the coup de grace argument that ends the legal dispute. On the contrary, counterarguments must be carefully considered and subtly balanced against rights. Three mechanisms play a role in this connection: (1) conflicts of rights, (2) limitations to rights, and (3) exceptions.

8.1   Conflict of Rights

Invoking a right cannot mean automatic triumph if the other party can also invoke a human right in his favor. This is quite common, as human rights tend to conflict with each other. For example, the freedom of speech of a journalist who aims to publish pictures of a celebrity may be taken conflict with the right to privacy of the celebrity who wishes to remain free from public scrutiny.

Of course, the existence of a conflict depends on the interpretation that is given to the rights. For instance, for the right to freedom of speech to conflict with nondiscrimination, it must first be established that «mere words» can as such discriminate. In this connection the distinction between positive and negative duties becomes particularly important. If rights are interpreted as purely negative demands, many apparent conflicts disappear.

For example, the von Hannover case at the European Court of Human Rights was framed as a conflict between the right to privacy of a celebrity and the right to freedom of speech of a journalist. But if what the right to privacy requires is merely that the State should not breach your privacy –and not to protect your privacy from third parties– then the fact that the journalist's publication will interfere with the privacy of a celebrity is not grounds to speak of a conflict. The State is only under one obligation: not to censor the journalist.

In any case, once a conflict is established, it will fall onto judges to resolve it. Two ways of dealing with conflicts stand out: hierarchy and balancing.

Hierarchy supposes that it can be ascertained that some rights are more important than others so that in case of conflicts the more important right defeats the less important one. This solution is unpopular because the relative importance of rights seems to depend on the facts of the case and cannot be determined beforehand.

Many people think that the right to life is always superior to the right to privacy, but this opinion might not hold in a particular context. Many think that the decision to end one's life is a private matter, and that the State should not interfere with it, even to protect life.

The alternative for solving conflicts is case-by-case *balancing*. Instead of creating an abstract hierarchy independent of the facts of the case in which two rights are in conflict, each individual situation is looked at in isolation, and the judge decides which right is more important *in that scenario*. This solution is more popular than hierarchy but is criticized for the lack of predictability it brings. After all, how can we rely on our rights if we cannot know if they will be balanced out of existence?

An example of this is the so-called freezing effect discussed in the context of the right to freedom of speech: if one is not sure whether a certain speech is protected or not, and the issue is so uncertain that it may lead to protracted litigation, one may simply decide not to express one's ideas, losing the benefits of the right in practice.

8.2   Limitations

Sometimes rights go too far. If complying with rights may cause a great deal of harm to society, there is a point at which one might consider dishonoring the right to protect the common good. The doctrine of limitations of rights can be seen as an escape clause for these situations. Under this doctrine, when certain (presumably rigorous) conditions are met, it can be legitimate not to honor a right.

For example, in the case Leyla Sahin v. Turkey, the European Court of Human Rights found that it was legitimate for the State of Turkey to ban the use of headscarves in education in order to enforce the idea that the State is secular.

At the international level, there is significant consensus on the conditions under which a right can legitimately be limited:
- The nature of the right must allow limitations.
- The limitation must be provided by law.
- The limitation must be restricted to a legitimate goal.
- The limitation must be proportional to the goal.
- The limitation must be of such nature that it is necessary in a democratic society.

With regard to the first condition, it is generally accepted that some rights are truly absolute and cannot be limited. The longer lists of these absolute rights usually include freedom from torture, freedom from slavery, freedom of conscience, and the right to be recognized as a person.

The «provided by law» condition demands that the restriction be general and prospective rather than ad hoc.

The «legitimate aim» condition requires that the restriction be brought about by an actual interest in the common good and not by partial political interests.

The requirement of proportionality is a sort of balancing test; restrictions should not go beyond what is needed to protect the legitimate goal.

The construct of «necessary in a democratic society» aims to capture the broader context of values in which the decision must be taken. Some restrictions of rights that may seem to be proportional might turn out to be unnecessary if we live in a society committed to values of tolerance and equality.

In the case *S.A.S. v. France*, the European Court of Human Rights dealt with French laws that forbade the covering of the face in public. These laws negatively impact certain expressions of piety within Islam. The court found that prohibitions were justified in light of the legitimate aim of promoting French culture. Granting that the prohibition was provided by law, that the promotion of French culture is a legitimate aim, and that the restriction on freedom of religion was proportional to this aim, it is still open to question whether the whole enterprise would be unnecessary in a society committed to tolerance and equality.

Beyond this, many academics argue that while limitations for non-absolute rights are allowed, there is a minimum, an essence of every right that may not be limited under any circumstance. This essence is usually called the «core content» of the right.

8.3 Exceptions

Where limitations on rights can be seen as a way to push back the range of application of a right, sometimes the law explicitly says that the protection granted by the right does not cover something.

Known exceptions in United Nations human rights treaties include the death penalty, as an exception to the right to life, hate speech, as an exception to freedom of expression, and lawful sanctions which may nevertheless cause severe suffering are an exception to the prohibition of torture. Naturally, what counts as «hate speech» or «lawful sanction» is subject to interpretation.

9 Protection of Human Rights

This section discusses two broad ways in which rights may be protected: judicial and nonjudicial.

9.1 Protection by Courts

Because human rights are rights, courts are the natural guarantors of human rights. The judicial procedure for the protection of human rights will normally involve three stages.

The first is a stage of admissibility, where the court has to decide whether the claim satisfies several formal requirements for being considered by the court. If such requirements are not met, the claim is immediately dismissed, without the court giving an opinion on the substance of the case.

These formal requirements vary from court to court. The European Court of Human Rights requires that claims should be made by an interested party, that the claims reveal a prima facie violation of human rights, that claims are made within a certain time period after the alleged violation, and that claims are made with regard to rights enshrined in the European Convention on Human Rights. It also requires that claims show that the applicant has suffered a significant disadvantage and that domestic remedies are exhausted. Whether these requirements are fulfilled or not is analyzed by a panel of one or three judges.

If a claim is found admissible, that does not guarantee that it will be found valid. That second judgment depends on the merits stage of the proceedings. Here, the court will assess the law and the available evidence to determine whether a human right has been violated. This will involve many of the issues already discussed. The court will have to determine which duties flow form the right, and it will have to analyze whether the right being claimed is outweighed by another right or whether it should be subject to limitations.

In the European Court of Human Rights decisions on the merits are usually analyzed by panels of 7 judges, or in cases of high importance, by the Grand Chamber, which is composed by 17 judges. Here the focus is no longer on whether the claim meets formal requirements, but on whether the complainant is right or not.
In analyzing the merits of a rights-based claim, the European Court of Human Rights will often invoke the margin-of-appreciation doctrine. According to this doctrine the court should not venture judgments in controversial moral issues when there is no Europe-wide consensus on the matter. Rather the court should allow different States to come to different conclusions.

If the court determines that a human right has been violated, it passes to the remedies stage of the proceedings. Here, the court will determine which reparations should be granted by the State to the victim of human rights violations. Remedies might include declaratory relief (the idea that the court judgment is a form of moral recognition), monetary compensation, measures of restitution (requirements that the State do certain things), and guarantees of non-repetition.

Traditionally, the European Court of Human Rights has tended to order only remedies of compensation—that is, monetary remedies—and to consider the judgment itself as a form of moral redress. This has been changing: the European Court of Human Rights is becoming much more flexible with regard to the remedies it can award. In particular, the Court has become friendlier to giving order for restitution, for example, requiring the State to free those who are unjustly imprisoned.

Steven Greer (1955-) has made a useful distinction between two models of judicial protection of human rights. The constitutional approach courts focus on giving broad guidelines for justice in society. The individual justice approach courts focus on reparations for individual victims. Naturally every court will have aspects of both, but sometimes one can see that courts favor one approach or the other.

Historically, the European Court of Human Rights has tended to favor an individual justice model, because it allows all individuals to make claims to the Court, and if they win, it provides monetary compensation that eases their troubles, but does not really affect other citizens. By contrast the Inter-American Court of Human Rights has tended to follow a constitutional model. Before a case can go to court, the American Commission has to approve this case. The Commission would only refer to the court cases whose resolution would have wide social significance. Likewise, the remedies ordered by the court have had a tendency to go beyond repairing the individual harm, and to address wider social problems. For example, instead of just compensating a victim of police violence, the court will also require the state to train police officers in human rights.

Of course human rights issues may also arise as an incident within ordinary judicial procedures. Ordinary courts may be called to interpret the civil law or criminal law in a way which furthers human rights or to cease to apply a statutory law because of requirements arising from rights that are protected by the constitution or by international treaties.

9.2   **Other Forms of Protection**

Beyond courts there are a wide range of institutions that are charged with promoting human rights. Examples of this include «expert bodies» like the United Nations Human Rights Committee, political bodies charged with promoting human rights such as the Human Rights Council, nongovernmental organizations such as Human Rights Watch, ombudsmen, and so-called human rights defenders: private individuals who decide to make promoting human rights a big part of their life.

This list involves considerable variety in terms of who is appointed to promote human rights, under what sort of credentials, and what is the behavior expected of him.

Some organs such as the United Nations Human Rights Council are staffed by politicians, and nobody would expect them to be insensitive to their national interest. By contrast, other bodies such as the Human Rights Committee are staffed by experts who are supposedly chosen because of their high moral standing and who are expected to be wholly impartial. Some NGOs are more successful than others, and the most successful ones are granted consultative status in the United Nations.

However, from a legal perspective, what is notable is that none of these bodies has the power to create law: they cannot apply law to individual cases in a binding fashion, and they cannot interpret law in a way that is binding for everyone. Nevertheless they still contribute to the protection of human rights by scrutinizing the behavior of States, identifying the human rights violations that take place and making them public. They can also propose interpretations of human rights instruments that may be useful for addressing social problems.

Is it a problem that these bodies don not have the power to issue binding decision? In the civil law or criminal law that the law is binding means that somewhere down the line, if you disobey, force is threatened or used. But in international law there is no global police force that may swoop down and force states to uphold human rights. Something similar is true for constitutional law. Police action against a recalcitrant Head of State may be impossible, or it may trigger a civil war. Under these conditions, whether a decision is binding or not is not very meaningful, and instead about worrying about the binding character of a decision or its lack thereof, it may be more productive to discuss whether the decision is legitimate and rationally persuasive. The jurist Thomas Franck (1931-2009) proposed this change of emphasis in his influential book *The Power of Legitimacy Among Nations*.

10   Conclusion

Nowadays, it is impossible to approach the law—domestic or international—without reference to human rights, and almost no one is against human rights. Nevertheless, this superficial agreement hides deep tensions. There is profound disagreement on what the human rights are, on which duties they give rise to, and on the proper methods for implementation. Support for human rights must not preclude us from questioning the foundation of rights, their role in the law, and their effectiveness in society. Quite on the contrary, reflection and critical thinking are a vital part of a healthy culture of rights.

Recommended Literature

Alexy R (2009) A theory of constitutional rights (trans: rivers J). Oxford University Press, Oxford

Coomans F, Kamminga M, Grunfeld F (eds) (2009) Methods of human rights research. Intersentia, Antwerpen

Dembour MB (2010) What are human rights? Four schools of thought. Hum Rights Q 32(1):1–20

Forsythe D (2006) Human rights in international relations. Edited by themes in international relations. Cambridge University Press, Cambridge

Griffin J (2008) Human rights. Oxford University Press, Oxford

Moeckli D, Shah S, Saivakumaran S (2010) International human rights law. Oxford University Press, Oxford

Shue H (1996) Basic rights: subsistence, affluence, and U.S. foreign policy. Princeton University Press, Princeton

Tomuschat C (2008) Human rights: between idealism and realism. Oxford University Press, Oxford

Van Dijk P, Van Hoof F, Van Rijn A, Zwaak L (eds) (2006) Theory and practice of the European convention on human rights. Intersentia, Antwerpen

Elements of Procedural Law

Fokke Fernhout and Remco van Rhee

© Springer International Publishing Switzerland 2017
J. Hage et al. (eds.), *Introduction to Law*, DOI 10.1007/978-3-319-57252-9_14

1   Introduction

In law, there are always at least two sides to every issue: parties to a contract often disagree about its interpretation; heirs have different views on the meaning of a will; the public prosecutor holds the evidence to be sufficient, whereas the suspect denies the charges. Even in cases in which only less specific interests like public order are at stake (when it comes to appointing a guardian for a minor, for instance), the persons concerned will probably disagree about the way those interests tend to overrule their private objectives.

If these issues are indeed of a legal character, ideally there will be a best solution in the eyes of the law; ideally, because all stakeholders will have very good reasons to claim that the solution that fits them best is the solution prescribed by law. To decide these matters, a third person or institution is needed. Leaving the decision to one of the parties involved would indeed be unwise. There is little hope that they will choose the solution that would be in accordance with the law instead of serving their own interests. This is a good reason for any social system with legal rules to have some kind of institution to resolve legal disputes by applying the law, instead of making a choice between the interests of the parties.

Alternative Dispute Resolution

There are other good reasons for such an institution. If it would be for settling disputes like the above, this institution would only be necessary if the parties would not be able to solve their disagreements themselves. And indeed, most societies primarily leave it to the parties to find a solution of their own. Maybe somewhat misleadingly this is labeled as «alternative dispute resolution» (ADR), which comes to us in many forms, like arbitration, mediation, and binding advice from—for instance—experts. Other approaches in this vein are *preventative law* (aiming at helping parties to find solutions out of court) and *collaborative law* (where parties even enter a contract enforceable by penalties not to start proceedings).

Speaking of *alternative* dispute resolution is misleading since the genuine way of solving disputes in permissive societies is in fact leaving dispute resolution to the parties themselves. «Primary dispute resolution» would have been a better term. The State institutions that are provided are only there to solve matters people cannot solve themselves. Even the decision to try to find a solution at all is, in most societies, left to the parties themselves, although in socialist settings, State-initiated procedures on behalf of citizens against other citizens are not excluded.

1.1   The Judiciary

Nevertheless, most jurisdictions agree that some decisions should not, under any circumstances, be left to citizens at all. This is especially the case if it is a public policy matter. Family relations, for instance, are defined by law, and it would be a bit odd if we would allow citizens to label themselves at random as the father or mother of someone else. Likewise, if you want to prevent misuse of drastic punishments like imprisonment, it is better to have a State-controlled institution dealing with it, rather than allowing victims setting the level by retaliation.

All these questions are a matter of administration of justice. How can we guarantee that justice will be done in a society in which the law has to be respected by everyone, even the State and the legislature itself? This requirement of the rule of law calls forth the need for an institution that can be relied on as administering justice in accordance with the law in force. This power of deciding on the contents of the law and applying it if necessary is attributed to an institution labeled as «the judiciary» or «the courts».

The way this is done, the scope of the judiciary's powers, and its position within the framework of the State may vary from jurisdiction to jurisdiction and are not even constant within a given jurisdiction. Traffic fines, for instance, were originally a matter of the courts but are now imposed by the administration in most jurisdictions. However, some general principles are generally recognized as suitable or even necessary safeguards for a judiciary that can be relied on as regards respect for the rule of law. These principles can be found in various legal instruments, varying from national constitutions to international treaties and declarations.

Principles

Compare, for instance, Article 10 of the Universal Declaration of Human Rights, Article 14 of the International Covenant on Civil and Political Rights and Article 6 of the European Convention on Human Rights and Fundamental Freedoms (ECHR). These provisions and especially the case law of the European Court of Human Rights (ECtHR) on the latter article allow us to describe these principles in more detail. Case law of the ECtHR is the main source for the concept of a fair trial and related institutional and procedural matters, since it is the only international court that can be appealed to directly by individual citizens complaining about a violation of their rights under the Convention (Article 34 ECHR). This has led to a vast amount of leading case law (► www.echr.coe.int/hudoc), which is accessible in English and French. Some important cases will be mentioned in this chapter.

1.2   Overview

This chapter will first deal with the fundamental principles governing court systems respecting the rule of law. These principles will be divided into institutional principles and procedural principles. This distinction has no legal consequence, but it helps to give a clearer picture of the ways in which safeguards can be obtained.

The principles of independence and impartiality are institutional. They are discussed in ► Sect. 2. Principles with direct consequences for the way legal proceedings are conducted are procedural. They are discussed in ► Sect. 3. The last section of this chapter (► Sect. 4) introduces some general aspects of the administration of justice by courts and court proceedings in general. Court decisions require proceedings, and there are some general aspects to these procedures that are worth remarking on.

2   Institutional Principles

The institutional principles relate to characteristics of the court system itself and are generally considered to be essential for the proper administration of justice under the rule of law. These principles are:

1. Judicial independence
2. Judicial impartiality

2.1   Judicial Independence

The requirement of judicial independence is evident for every legal system that is based on the principle of separation of powers. The balance between the three powers (legislature, judiciary, and executive) is only guaranteed if disputes over the content of law are settled by a power that cannot be influenced by the other powers. This brings the concept of a fair trial (in its broadest sense) to the core of modern, democratic societies. But even apart from constitutional choices, the notions of a proper administration of justice and independence are inseparable. Independence, after all, is equal to the absence of undue influence, thus allowing courts to decide freely on the contents of the law and its just application.

Appointment for Life

Independence itself can be realized in several ways. In many States, the appointment of judges for life is part of this concept. Judges who are appointed for life will not easily tend to give decisions that favor the government out of fear of being fired if they do not. In the same vein, decisions about the recruitment of new judges and their discharge are, in most cases, either the exclusive domain of the judiciary itself or done in cooperation with the central government in accordance with strict procedures. Leaving the appointment of judges to the executive alone will give it a powerful tool to influence the policy of a court, as can be learned from the way Justices of the American Supreme Court are appointed (i.e., by the President). Independence of judges can also be guaranteed by the constitutional requirement to regulate their legal position by statute.

Allocation of money to the judiciary forms a related problem. If the central government itself would take all decisions concerning how budgets for the judiciary are fixed, and how the money is spent, these cash flows could easily be directed in the direction of courts taking the most favorable decisions. To avoid this, an institution like a Council for the Judiciary could be positioned in between the central government and the judiciary, with the task to allocate the budgets and to supervise the quality of the courts' output. Judicial Budget

The notion of «contempt of court» may also be seen as part of the requirement of judicial independence. This notion includes (among other things) that parties, the media, or the public are not allowed to comment on a procedure pending before the court (cases that are *sub judice*) beyond a certain point since these comments could influence the court. Contempt of Court

The notion is—in varying modalities—part of the law of, for instance, the United Kingdom, Cyprus, Ireland, and Malta: jurisdictions in which the courts have the power to take measures (sometimes draconic, like immediate arrest) in case of contempt of court. Although many countries do without this strict form of contempt of court, the belief that some caution has to be observed when giving an opinion regarding pending cases is generally shared.

2.2   Judicial Impartiality

Human rights treaties stipulate not only that tribunals be independent but that they be impartial as well, for obvious reasons. If we want our courts to decide according to the content of the law, they are not allowed to favor one of the parties in any way.

Having to deal with real people and not with computers, we have to bear in mind that even judges might be tempted to disregard their professional obligations. Therefore, judges should Recruitment be carefully selected and schooled. A psychological test could be part of the procedure, as well as interviews and simulations of court sessions with actors. In addition, every candidate should be screened, should be able to present recommendations, and should pass a test.

Remuneration

Guaranteeing impartiality costs money. Judges should not be tempted to take money in exchange for certain decisions because their remuneration is not sufficient to satisfy needs that must be deemed reasonable in relation to their social position. Their salaries should therefore be at least as high as what a private lawyer would gain and preferably slightly higher. Paying less and counting on their magnanimity means asking for trouble.

A fine source for judges' starting salaries can be found in the biannual reports of the European Commission for the Efficiency of Justice (CEPEJ). In Europe, the common law countries remunerate their judges far better, with 4–5 times the national average salary. France and Germany really take risks with only factor 1.1 and 1.0. These figures are food for reflection: what do these differences tell us about the position of the judicature in the State framework?

Exemption

Judges who feel that their impartiality might be questioned in a certain case should exempt themselves, either by following a formal procedure provided by national law or by arranging informally that he or she will not decide the case.

Challenge

If, nevertheless, parties have good reasons to suppose that a judge trying their case is prejudiced, even though he has not exempted himself, national law should provide a procedure to challenge this judge. Of course, this is a sensitive matter since who should decide on a challenge? Although it is evident that only judges should take the decision, it has the drawback that the impartiality of a judge will be judged by his colleagues. To guarantee their neutrality, challenge chambers can be recruited from judges of other courts. The case itself should be stayed awaiting the outcome of the challenge since a potentially partial judge should not be allowed to take any decision before his impartiality has been established.

After a challenge, impartiality is assessed by applying a double test. The *subjective* test should establish whether the judge acts with personal bias, i.e., on a personal conviction that favors one of the parties. According to the *objective* test, «it must be determined whether, quite apart from the judge's personal conduct, there are ascertainable facts which may raise doubts as to his impartiality» (ECtHR 24 May 1989, *Hauschildt v. Denmark*).

Mogens Hauschildt was suspected of a massive tax fraud for which he was taken into detention on remand. The judge who had to decide on orders of further remand in custody also presided over the trial itself. Since the orders of remand were based on an assessment of the evidence against Hauschildt, which had to provide a «particularly confirmed suspicion», the impartiality of this judge became open to doubt and did not pass the objective test.

Safeguarding impartiality also has implications for the private life of a judge. Although most fundamental freedoms are not denied to them, their use of, for instance, their freedom of speech requires some moderation. Strong affiliations with political parties or pressure groups could give rise to doubts about their impartiality and neutrality. Even in their private lives, they should be aware of possible appearances that would undermine their credibility. Playing golf and leaving on holidays with advocates should, in most cases, exclude the handling of cases of those same advocates even if the judge concerned feels completely free to give a judgment in accordance with law.

Private Life

3   Procedural Principles

Procedural principles focus on the proceedings before the courts more than on the organization of the judiciary. These principles should be observed by the legislature, but they can also serve as guidelines for the courts when handling a case. Even parties themselves could be affected since they should not be allowed to frustrate each other's rights to a fair trial. These principles will be discussed under five headings:
1. The right to access to justice
2. The right to a fair hearing—fair trial
3. The right to a public hearing
4. The right to judgment within a reasonable time
5. The right to enforcement of the judgment

Again, this classification does not have legal consequences and treating the right to (for instance) a public hearing as part of the right to a fair trial would not change its scope or meaning.

3.1   Access to Justice

A court system, as perfect as it might be, would be idling if citizens could not get access to it. Procedural codes establishing the most perfect trial imaginable would be useless when they would not open the gates to those who are seeking justice.

Therefore, the right to access to justice is implied in the right to a fair trial even if it is not stated literally in the human rights conventions (ECtHR 21 February 1975, *Golder v. United Kingdom*).

By the 1960s, Parkhurst Prison on the Isle of Wight had developed into a top-security prison. It held Britain's most reputed and dreaded criminals, like «Mad» Frankie Frazer, the Kray twins, and the Yorkshire Ripper. Rules were very tight and visitors were practically not allowed. On October 24, 1969, at 7 pm, an unprecedented prison riot came about. More than a hundred prisoners barricaded themselves in an association room, taking seven prison officers hostage. Syd Golder was falsely accused by one of the wardens of participating and assaulting prison officers. Golder asked for leave to get in contact with his solicitor to commence a civil action for libel, but the answer he received politely informed him that the Secretary of State had considered his petition but had found no grounds to take any action. Golder submitted a complaint to the ECtHR, claiming that his right to a fair trial had been violated. The UK government replied that there had been no trial, so it could not possibly have been unfair. This led the ECtHR to its famous decision that the right to access of justice is implied by the right to a fair trial.

Scope

This calls for a definition of the scope of this right to access to justice since it is obvious that courts are not there to decide on just any matter (like the color of your shoes for the gala dinner). In the introduction to this chapter, we already pointed out that courts are there to settle disputes for those who cannot find an agreement themselves and to decide on matters we do not want to leave to citizens at all. The right to access to justice is therefore usually related to the determination of criminal charges and of civil rights and obligations.

At first sight, this seems to imply that only civil and criminal procedure is affected by this principle. However, since it is such a basic principle, these notions (which are mentioned in the provisions cited in the introduction to this chapter) should be taken in a broad sense. Thus, if private interests of a legal character are at stake, access must be opened to a court, even if the other party is the State itself and not a private person.

Likewise, a right to some sort of judicial review (i.e., the right to annulment of State acts by the judiciary) of certain administrative acts and legislation can be derived from the right to access to justice.

14

Guaranteeing access to justice implies more than just opening a procedure to have a court decide on a matter. Although somewhat trivial, money should be one of the concerns of each jurisdiction in this respect. Going to court costs money, especially if representation in court is obligatory. To start a procedure, in most jurisdictions, a writ of summons has to be served by a bailiff, and court fees have to be paid in court. Attorneys and solicitors are expensive. What should we do with people who cannot afford to litigate? A right of access to justice entails some kind of facility enabling citizens of little means to start proceedings or defend themselves in court. State-sponsored legal aid could be such a facility.

Under Irish law, divorce was impossible, but instead a judicial separation could be obtained by a High Court decree on one of three grounds: adultery, cruelty, or unnatural practices. The ground had to be proven by witnesses, which necessitated legal assistance. Mrs. Airey lacked the money to pay a solicitor and thus could not obtain a judicial separation from her violent and alcoholic husband. The ECtHR found a violation of the right to access to justice, thus also imposing on governments a positive obligation to facilitate this access. However, the Court expressly did not set any standard for dealing with this problem. The cases in which and how access has to be guaranteed will depend on the circumstances (ECtHR 9 October 1979, *Airey v. Ireland*).

A more indirect way to guarantee access to justice can be created by allowing «no cure no pay» agreements, contingency fees, or conditional fee agreements (CFAs). What all these lawyer–client agreements have in common is that they are outcome dependent, freeing the client from (part of) his obligation to pay when the case is lost. The risk of losing money by litigating is then shifted from the client to the lawyer. Some countries have accepted these outcome-related fees with the specific objective to guarantee access to justice. On the other hand, most European countries have limited these agreements in some way to obviate immoral conduct of lawyers, the risk being that under an outcome-related fee agreement, lawyers' own interests will prevail over the interests of their clients.

Another issue in relation to access to justice is the application of formal, procedural law. Procedural law always imposes restrictions on access to court. Such restrictions are even called for by its nature, i.e., the nature of the right of access to justice. Access to justice cannot be unlimited and unregulated, so national law will decide on the procedures to be followed and the time limits, periods, and formalities to be observed. This leaves a certain margin of appreciation since the actual contents of these restrictions are to be chosen and imposed by the national authorities. However, these restrictions

1. May not impair the right of access to justice in its essence (which might be the case if a procedure is only available under conditions that can hardly be met)
2. Must pursue reasonable objectives
3. Must be proportionate to these objectives

Failure to comply with any of these three requirements is labeled as «excessive formalism». Thus, a decision to declare an appeal inadmissible because the number written on the file was erroneous would violate the right of access to justice as a result of excessive formalism even if such a number is required by national law.

Periods for Legal Remedies

A related consequence of the right of access to justice concerns periods and time limits for legal remedies. In every jurisdiction, these time limits tend to be fixed and inflexible. Legal certainty about the status of judgments (i.e., whether they are final or not) is more valued by domestic law than fairness and equal chances. A party who failed to appeal in time will have to bear the consequences of the judgment even if it was legally wrong. However, if the expiration of a period for a legal remedy cannot in any way be imputed to the party concerned, it seems reasonable not to apply these periods in the light of the right of access to justice.

When their father died, the life insurance payment of the Stagno sisters was deposited in their mother's account. Instead of administering this money to the benefit of her daughters, she spent everything. Proceedings were impossible, since the mother was the only one who, according to Belgian law, could represent her minor daughters in an action against herself, which she obviously would never start. A civil action was later dismissed because the limitation period had expired. This constituted a violation of the right of access to justice (ECtHR 7 July 2009, *Stagno v. Belgium*).

3.2   Fair Hearing: Fair Trial

Legal proceedings have to be fair, which means that every party should have a reasonable opportunity to present every relevant aspect of his case to the court. This fairness relates to all parties equally and refers to all stages of the proceedings. If we describe this by the right to a fair hearing, we should bear in mind that «hearing» is not to be taken literally. And if we use the term «fair trial», then we do not mean a trial in its narrow sense of a court session. In this chapter, the right to a fair trial is broken down into six distinct parts:

1. The principle of *audiatur et altera pars*
2. The right to equality of arms
3. The right to be present at the trial
4. The right to an oral hearing
5. The right to produce evidence
6. The right to a reasoned judgment

From its other Latin version—*audi et alteram partem*—it emerges even more clearly that this principle is actually a command to «hear the other party as well», addressed directly to the courts. Courts should hear both parties and give both parties equal opportunities to react to each other's statements. Just hearing the parties is of course not enough; the courts have to consider the arguments put forward as well.

Audiatur et altera pars

The fear for procedures going on endlessly because of this principle is unfounded. Procedural law respecting the principle of *audiatur et altera pars* is allowed to limit the possibility to introduce new statements, in which case there is no need for another round. If a party comes up with new statements when this is no longer allowed, the judge should ignore those. The justification for this is found in the ancient principle that all proceedings should come to an end at some point (*lites finiri oportet*).

Modern procedural law tends to allow only one round of written statements before «going to trial.» That was quite different in the nineteenth century. In England, for instance, the written part of the proceedings could extend itself from the statement of claim to the statement of defense, the reply, the rejoinder, the surrejoinder, the rebutter and the surrebutter. The situation in other countries was not much different.

The concept of this principle of *audiatur et altera pars* extends to everything that is brought to the attention of the court with the aim of influencing its decision. Thus, the parties have the right to comment on submissions of court advisors like the «advocate general» (ECtHR 30 October 1991, *Borgers v. Belgium*).

Sometimes, hearing the defending party might ruin the case of the other party, especially when merely by informing the party of the request would reveal information that should remain secret for some time (for instance, when a creditor seeks permission to attach the debtor's bank account). In those cases, many jurisdictions allow courts to take decisions on the request of one party (decisions *ex parte*) and hear the other party only afterward.

Right to Equality of Arms

The right to equality of arms implies that parties should have equal opportunities in presenting their case. If, for instance, one of the parties is granted the right to hear witnesses, the other party should have the same right. The ECtHR derived from this principle the notion that excluding party witnesses from taking the stand amounts to a violation of the right to equality of arms (*Dombo v. the Netherlands*).

Until 1988, the Netherlands did not allow parties to take the stand. Their testimony was regarded as one sided and not trustworthy as of right. This rule was extended to those persons who could be identified with a party, like the managing director of a company with limited liability. When the company Dombo commenced proceedings against its bank regarding their financial relationship, it had to prove that a contract had been concluded to extend the existing credit arrangements. On Dombo's side this arrangement had been negotiated by its managing director, whereas the bank was represented by one of its employees. Thus the witness of the bank could be heard but not Dombo's. The right of equality of arms was violated, which forced the Netherlands to change its rules of evidence (ECtHR 27 October 1993, *Dombo v. the Netherlands*).

The scope of this principle is slightly controversial. Taken in its sense above, it is strictly procedural. Within the procedure, parties should have equal opportunities, but that does not alter the fact that opportunities are not equally distributed in society. Everyone knows that social and economic differences could favor one of the parties, for example, when a multinational is starting legal proceedings against one of its employees. A more material interpretation of the principle would require a procedural remedy for these social and economic inequalities. Usually, the principle is interpreted in its narrow sense, leaving the circumstances of the parties to substantive law.

Interests shared by many citizens can sometimes be bundled in various ways, thus creating «class actions» against mighty opponents who otherwise would not have to fear anything from their customers (think of trifling claims of consumers not worth going to court that, when bundled, represent a lot of money).

From the right to be heard and the right to react to the statements of other parties, it can easily be derived that every party (in criminal as well as civil cases) has the right to be present when it comes to a court session where his case is discussed. But there is more to it. A party has the right to be present when witnesses are heard; he has the right to be confronted with the other parties, to see the judge, and to be seen by the judge. Physical presence and observation of physical appearances can be of utmost importance for the way a case is pleaded.

Procedural law should take care of, first, safeguarding this right and, second, of formulating exceptions in a careful way. Precise rules governing the summons to a trial should guarantee that these summons will actually reach the party concerned and at least stipulate that hearings have to be stayed if this condition has not been met. Court powers to exclude parties from a court session or to deny them from being present should be limited to interests that are undoubtedly of greater weight. Examples can be found in the mental health of victims taking the stand, in due process, or in State security issues.

The same idea underlying the right to be present at trial (i.e., the idea that a direct confrontation with the court, parties, and witnesses could make a difference) leads to the right to an oral hearing. Each party is entitled to «his day in court» before the judgment is given, and courts cannot decide before having heard the parties in a court session. Face-to-face confrontations are useful or even necessary—is the idea—to bring out truth and to help the courts to reach a just and fair decision.

This «principle of orality» is an ancient concept that is easy to conceive since societies existed long before script was invented. This might be the reason why jurisdictions with a demonstrable tendency to conservatism and traditionalism still embrace this principle in a pure form, including all its consequences. In this vein, everything that is shown to American juries should in principle be read out loud. While this may seem time-consuming to continental lawyers, it is clear that a written statement of a witness can never replace a cross-examination when it comes to getting an idea about the reliability of the witness's declaration. Designing procedure therefore means to strike a proper balance between written and oral forms of procedure.

Closely related is the principle of immediacy. According to this principle, everything on which the court should base its judgment has to be produced in the presence of the court in an oral hearing. Even if the principle of orality is not

Right to Be Present at Trial

Right to an Oral Hearing

embraced, this could mean that written evidence is only allowed to be used in a judgment if it has been read out aloud in the presence of the parties or accused, who had the opportunity to respond and comment on it. The weight of this principle is valued higher in criminal than in civil cases. Accordingly, many jurisdictions order a retrial if a criminal judge has to be replaced, whereas the substitution of judges in civil cases is often (with exceptions, like Germany) merely considered undesirable but without further consequences.

Right to produce evidence

Claims and defenses are in most cases based on alleged facts. If those alleged facts are indeed underpinning what has been put forward but has been disputed (by one of the parties, by the public prosecutor, or maybe by the court itself), the right to a fair trial entails that these facts will be the object of evidence and (following from the principle of equality of arms) counterevidence. In other words, no claim or defense should be dismissed simply because the court does not believe the alleged facts.

Perić had a contract that stipulated that her neighbors would take care of her the rest of her life in exchange of all her property after her death. She claimed termination of the agreement for a breach of contract. The court ordered hearing of witnesses on both sides. However, after hearing the witnesses of the neighbor, the court decided that the case was clear and that Perić's witnesses would not be heard. Obviously, her claim was dismissed. This violated her right to produce evidence (ECtHR 27 March 2008, *Perić v. Croatia*).

Right to a Reasoned Judgment

Losing a case in court is not an enjoyable experience, but it is even worse if you don't know why. Even winning without knowing why is only a mixed blessing. Court decisions should be verifiable and acceptable, the first requirement allowing one to follow the reasoning and the second requirement allowing one to approve of it, if it is in accordance with the law. Courts should therefore give reasons for their decisions.

The way grounds for decisions are given depends on the domestic legal system, legal culture, and legal tradition and on differences with regard to statutory provisions, customary rules, legal opinion, and the presentation and drafting of judgments. In some civil law jurisdictions, for instance, great importance is attached to the fiction that the judiciary can be seen as a unity, speaking with one mouth and giving its unequivocal opinion. All judgments (civil, criminal, and administrative) are in writing, and they give their reasons in full (discussing all essential statements the parties have submitted), but if unanimity is not reached, only the opinion of the majority of the judges is published. The publishing of dissenting opinions is even forbidden and constitutes a criminal offense (secret of the deliberations *in camera*).

Common law jurisdictions follow a system that is different but not incompatible with the principle of a right to a reasoned judgment. In those jurisdictions, judgments are often oral and the written version will not contain any reasons at all, just the provisions of the verdict. On the other hand, common law judges often produce a written opinion on the case, either concurring with the outcome of the case or dissenting from it. These opinions tend to investigate all legal dimensions of the problem at hand without entering into a debate with the submissions of the parties. This approach is understandable against the background of common law, where the development of certain fields of law (like tort law) is left to the courts.

3.3 Public Hearing and Public Pronouncement of the Judgment

An administration of justice that is fair can only exist in an open setting. Public and media must be allowed to witness hearings and to comment on them afterward. This way of public control compels courts to stick to the straight and narrow path of justice since deviations will be noticed, criticized, named, and blamed. Exceptions to this rule (closing the doors) should be formulated with caution.

Art. 6 ECHR allows closing the doors only «in the interests of morals, public order, or national security in a democratic society, where the interests of juveniles or the protection of the private life of the parties so require, or to the extent strictly necessary in the opinion of the court in special circumstances where publicity would prejudice the interests of justice».

In addition, judgments themselves should be given in public. The interest of justice itself is served by public judgments as well since this will help scholars, lawmakers, and courts to develop the law by studying, discussing, and commenting on the reasoning of the courts. In fact, common law could not even exist if judgments were kept secret.

In a modern society, pronouncing every judgment is virtually impossible and at least very impractical. Having regard to the number of cases and the length of the judgments, there is not enough manpower and time to read out loud all judgments. And besides, who would care to come and listen? In European jurisdictions, most judgments are only virtually (by means of a fiction) pronounced in public. In agreement with the spirit of Article 6 ECHR, the pronouncement in public has been substituted by the much more effective right given to every citizen and organization to demand a certified copy of every judgment they are interested in. In addition, the most important decisions are made available on the Internet without charge (as is the case with the ECLI search engine for the whole European Union).

3.4   Judgment within a Reasonable Time

Justice should not only be just; it should be fast as well. Long delays amount to denying justice since in many cases parties cannot go on with their lives (or with their mutual relation) without a court decision. International human rights treaties therefore stipulate that courts should deal with cases «within a reasonable time», thus forbidding any undue delay.

The circumstances of the case, the nature of the proceedings, and the overall course of the procedure determine the reasonableness of an eventual delay. To assess delays, the entirety of the litigation or procedure, including appeal, cassation, and enforcement proceedings, should be taken into account. The circumstances of the case could include the complexity of the matter at hand, the conduct of the parties and the relevant authorities, and what is at stake in the dispute.

In general, in criminal cases, a delay of 2 years for any step is considered to be unreasonably long. This could lead to the inadmissibility of the claims of the public prosecutor or a milder punishment.

In civil cases, a violation of the right to a judgment within a reasonable time will only follow after approximately 10 years, depending on various circumstances. The consequences of undue delay in civil cases cannot be translated to winning or losing a case since both parties will be the victim of the same violation. The best remedy will be damages to be paid by the State.

3.5   Right to Enforcement

Just as a right to a fair trial without access to justice would be meaningless, the same can be said of a right to a fair trial without means of enforcing court decisions. The right of access to justice would be illusory if court decisions are allowed to remain inoperative. Moreover, the enforcement of the decision should lead to a result without undue delay (ECtHR 19 March 1997, *Hornsby v Greece*).

The means of enforcement can vary from jurisdiction to jurisdiction. Some jurisdictions leave enforcement to the parties (with the bailiff as intermediary); other jurisdictions require a separate order allowing the winning party to take more stringent measures (like attachment of salary) against the losing party.

4   Some General Aspects of Procedures

Rules regulating legal procedures change all the time, but it is not only for that reason that studying procedural law can be quite demanding. Procedural rules are mostly interrelated, and their meaning depends on precise and well-defined concepts. That may lead to puzzles (If A has an inheritance lawsuit against B in court C, can this be combined with a claim of B against D living in district E?) that will bring back unpleasant memories of mathematic exams in junior high school.

What could help is having some insight into what kind of rules and regulations those procedural regulations will usually contain. In fact, codes of procedure are mostly about the same things, regardless of the actual jurisdiction. Realizing this will get you on the way to the core of the meaning of all those rules and will also put you on the trail of the traps that you could encounter on your journey through this jungle. This section is therefore devoted to some general aspects of procedural rules.

4.1   Jurisdiction

The judicature always is composed of different courts with different functions. Each of these courts has its specific jurisdiction. The jurisdiction of a court defines the scope of its judicial powers and activities. For the parties, the designated court is the one that is competent to deal with their case. Regulating jurisdiction is inspired by many, and different, considerations.

For instance, regulating jurisdiction might be called for to avoid backlog and congestion of the court system. If parties would be allowed to choose a court at their convenience, probably after some time, popular courts would be overloaded with work. Parties are economic beings and tend to maximize their profits. If *forum shopping* is not discouraged or impossible, it will certainly happen. Regulations regarding territorial jurisdiction (jurisdiction *ratione loci*), dividing the work between

Territorial Jurisdiction

courts of the same level (like district courts), offer a simple and effective solution. However, the right of access to justice will impose some constraints on the choices to be made: distances between courts and the parties' residence should remain reasonable.

Jurisdiction *Ratione Materiae*

Another economic reason to regulate jurisdiction can be found in the advantages of the division of labor. By designating specialized courts, the overall level of their judgments will satisfy higher standards against lesser costs. At the same time, if needed, jurisdiction *ratione materiae* (related to the legal nature of the claim) can be accompanied by special procedural provisions to enable these courts to conduct proceedings more suited to the kind of cases they have to handle.

Jurisdiction *ratione materiae* could also be a matter of «internal separation of powers» within the court system. It is probably better not to mix appeal courts with first instance courts to safeguard the professional distance that is needed to judge impartially about a claim to review a decision of colleagues in another court. It is common usage to refer to these relations between courts as those between «higher» and «lower» courts, but this is, after all, merely a figure of speech.

National Jurisdiction

A fundamental jurisdiction problem is at stake when determining the scope of the powers of all courts in a national court system taken together. This national jurisdiction gives an answer to the question which legal issues can be decided by the national courts at all. For example, if a French citizen is killed by an Australian in Argentina, could this crime be tried by the Criminal Court of Singapore where the perpetrator has been arrested when he came off the airplane? And in the case of two women who married in Belgium, can they get their divorce in a Japanese court? These are all questions of national jurisdiction that can be solved at a national level but are also, in many instances, the subject matter of bi- or multilateral treaties or international regulations.

National jurisdiction is a very sensitive matter since States could refuse to accept each other's views on these questions. That explains why there is a national and an international aspect to it. The national legislature can determine the jurisdiction of its own courts but is limited in its possibilities by international law. In the European Union, for instance, many jurisdiction and recognition issues have been settled in EU regulations. And if there is a free margin of appreciation, States do not always accept the way this margin has been used by the courts of another State, stipulating special conditions for the recognition of foreign judgments. The possibility of enforcement of foreign judgments thus depends on the recognition of these judgments by the national authorities, of course within the framework of the numerous bi- and multilateral treaties that have been concluded regarding this matter.

4.2 Standing

Procedural law imposes restrictions on the possibility to appear in court. Some entities, although existing in some way or another, are not recognized by law as entities with the possibility to start proceedings as a claimant or being summoned into court as a defendant. Some entities, we say, do not have legal standing: they do not qualify as a *persona legitima standi in iudicio*; they do not have a *locus standi*. Animals are a good example. The issue of standing can also depend on the particulars of the case. Generally speaking, a natural person has legal standing, but sometimes he will lack an interest that is sufficient to commence proceedings. All these questions are covered by what is called the «doctrine of legal standing».

Using the word «entity» is unavoidable since lacking standing sometimes implies that we have to do with something rather vague. A neighborhood committee organizing a fancy fair is a good example. Persons working together coordinate their actions, but for most jurisdictions, this does not create shared liabilities or entitlements. The committee will not have legal standing, but the distinct members of the committee do.

On the other hand, jurisdictions might extend the concept of standing—normally reserved for natural and legal persons—to some forms of cooperation. Interest groups and commercial activities can thus be allowed to start proceedings (or have proceedings started against them).

Standing may also depend on the subject matter of the case. He who does not have an interest that is recognized by law will not be allowed to commence proceedings. To express this, often the French adage is used: *Point d'intérêt, point d'action*. Thus in principle it will not be possible to lodge a claim against someone to make him pay his debts to a third party.

Another instance of this rule is related to trifling claims. If the amount of money at stake is too low, the court will not admit the claim. As the Romans said: *De minimis non curat praetor* (the court does not deal with trifling claims).

4.3   Representation by a Lawyer

Procedural and substantive laws can be difficult, which can already be seen from the fact that law is an academic discipline. Allowing parties to conduct proceedings themselves could do much harm to their own interests (missing all the arguments any lawyer would put forward) and to the administration of justice (since much time will have to be spent reacting to pointless motions and elucidating what the layman could have meant with his assertions and claims).

Every jurisdiction will draw a line and will make legal representation at some point obligatory for parties who want to appear in court. Where the line is drawn depends on many factors. One could be the complexity of the procedure, for which reason in as good as every jurisdiction legal representation before the highest court is obligatory. Another factor can be found in the interests at stake.

Legal representation is often monopolized by recognized specialists. This recognition can take the form of providing facilities (access to files, the right to plead, the right to represent clients without proof of power of attorney), but in most countries, the profession is completely regulated and protected by excluding all others from defending clients in court (or even giving legal advice out of court, like in Germany, Italy, and Greece). This has created vast monopolies of professional groups of lawyers. Their names and titles are well known, like the *barristers* and *solicitors* in common law countries; the *avocats*, *avoués*, and *procureurs* in France; and the *abogadi* and *procuradores* in Spanish-speaking countries. They are united in associations with names like the Law Society or the Bar Association. Their existence and proper functioning is of mutual benefit to (the administration of) justice, to the public, and to themselves, because specialization costs money and thus has to be paid for.

The public interest involved in the existence of a capable and competent legal profession has given it a very strong position. In the European Union, for instance, the rules of free competition do not apply to the legal profession as long as it can be assumed that fixed or minimum prices for its services serve the interest of quality. At the same time, the monopoly granted to the profession left it with a strong dependency on choices made by the legislature regarding legal representation. Thus, the profession will always be strongly opposed to any liberalization of the rules on obligatory legal representation.

4.4   Commencement of Proceedings

In all jurisdictions, special attention is paid to the way proceedings can be started. As noted above, the commencement of proceedings is closely linked to fundamental principles of the administration of justice. The way proceedings have to be started determines the scope of the right of access to justice and should also guarantee that the court will listen to both sides, ensuring that the other party (which could also be the accused in criminal proceedings) will somehow get to know what has been submitted to the court.

The first document to commence proceedings is usually highly regulated. In every procedural code, detailed rules will be found with regard to the names of the parties, the grounds of the claim, and the claim itself. That is understandable since the scope of the proceedings will at least initially be determined by this document.

Document Initiating the Procedure

The precise contents of these rules depend on the way proceedings have been shaped. A standard scenario of «claim-defense-oral hearing» will require more detailed grounds than a procedure in which a written reaction to the defense is foreseen. In addition, sometimes formalities have to be observed, like using the right form, sealed paper, and the like.

The first document will have to state the facts of the case and the claim of the plaintiff. Jurisdictions will only differ in the required preciseness of this factual statement. The extensive way of providing a basis for a claim is called «fact pleading». When factual details can be left out (like in the United States), the term «notice pleading» is used.

In addition, mentioning the rules of law on which the claim is based could also be one of the requirements. This might be useful for the defendant or accused since the law is not always clear and could be hard to find. If such a regulation exists, it will certainly not be meant to inform the court about the legal basis of the claim or prosecution. *Ius curia novit*—the court knows the law—is an adage that will almost universally apply. Parties can give their opinion on the law, but the ultimate decisions about its contents will always rest with the court.

Ensuring that the defendant or accused will be informed about the commencement of proceedings is another matter that has to be regulated. The systems followed are diverse. Sometimes this is seen as incumbent on the claimant, who will have to make use of the means of convocation prescribed or facilitated by the law (like recommended letters, electronic summons, summons served by a bailiff or police officers). Another solution is to task State organs with informing the defendant or accused in time.

Informing the Defendant or Accused

Commencing proceedings can be subject to additional requirements, like paying court fees. Some jurisdictions feel that civil justice has to be paid for by the claimant (the polluter pays). England, for instance, is aiming at a court fee

Court Fees

system that will cover all court costs. Some countries even claim a court fee from the defendant, although that is an exception (the Netherlands, Scotland).

At the other end of the spectrum, justice is seen as a fundamental right that should be free for all in all circumstances. Thus, France and Spain do not impose any payment for commencing proceedings or filing a defense. In fact, should we not be grateful to the parties that they submit their conflicts to our courts? Without them, the law could not be developed and specified by our judges. This could provide another reason not to impose too many burdens on the parties.

4.5   The Ordinary Course of Proceedings

At first, this might seem a bit peculiar, but essentially all court proceedings are a journey from the law to the facts. First, a selection has to be made of the relevant rules that apply to the case at hand. In most criminal matters, the rules to be applied are pretty obvious and follow directly from the indictment, but even then, sometimes, some hard nuts have to be cracked. In civil matters, selecting the rules (or relevant case law) is sometimes rather complicated. Once the relevant rules have been established, most proceedings enter into a second stage. In that stage, the facts have to be investigated in order to verify if the rules apply or not.

Trial

In common law jurisdictions, a tricky word has been coined to indicate this second stage of investigating the facts: the trial. The word is tricky since many scholars from the civil law tradition have been tempted to use the word for every court session or oral hearing in court. They thus underestimate the connotations that underlie the term, which is heavily linked with passive judges, jury decisions, cross-examinations, battles of experts, and cunning lawyers who try to bend truth to lies and lies to truth. It is better to set the term «trial» aside for this kind of events.

Pleadings

Before entering the stage of fact finding, the parties will exchange their views on the matter at hand, in most cases already handing in documentary and other evidence. Jurisdictions differ in the way this is organized. Again, rather disturbingly, this phase, normally in writing, is usually designated by the word «pleadings». The word «pleadings» has, because of its resemblance with its singular counterpart, a strong oral connotation for those coming from a civil law tradition. Still, pleadings (plural) are always in writing.

In most common law jurisdictions, the phase of the pleadings is preceded or accompanied by requests for information directed toward the other party. In the United States, this procedure is known as «discovery». It is characterized by drastic powers attributed to the parties' attorneys, who may, for instance, subpoena (summon) witnesses to their office to subject them to an oral examination.

Discovery and Disclosure

In England, the term «disclosure» is used. Disclosure is not as party controlled as discovery, although parties can be forced to release information that is not advantageous for their own case.

In civil law jurisdictions, fact finding by the parties is, as a rule, not part of the standard proceedings but can be achieved by following separate procedures leading to interim orders of the court.

When the pleadings are over, the court comes in to decide on the law (selecting the rules) and to see what factual matters still have to be decided. Usually, the court's decision is laid down in a written interim judgment.

Funnel Model

If no factual matters remain (either because there is no course of action or because all defenses have to be rejected), a final judgment puts an end to the case. Otherwise, «the case is sent to trial», i.e., a factual investigation is ordered.

Civil law jurisdictions use a funnel model to make the transition from the legal stage to the factual stage. All alleged facts are filtered by the court, which will expressly state which facts have to be proven *and* what means of proof is to be used. The costs of fact finding can thus be limited in a significant way.

When fact finding is over, the decision about the facts that indeed have been established has to be made. Some jurisdictions think it is best to leave this decision (at least in certain cases) to a jury, i.e., an assembly of laymen, selected from the population at large. The reasons put forward are twofold: firstly, the layman knows what a fact is when he spots one and is not obfuscated by legal reasoning, and, secondly, justice should be as democratic as possible. Doubts regarding the efficiency of jury trials and the correctness of their outcomes pushed most jurisdictions in the direction of totally abolishing them or at least minimizing the participation of laymen in the administration of justice.

Juries

4.6   Law of Evidence

Material and Formal Truth

Fact finding and deciding on matters of fact are not the same. The rules of evidence are in between. Every jurisdiction regulates, in one way or another, how facts can be proven. Fact finding is always a pursuit of the material truth (i.e., the real state of affairs), but since we can never be sure of what exactly happened in the past, the laws of evidence try to establish standards to exclude uncertainties that are not acceptable in the eyes of the law. In the end, the outcome is the formal, procedural truth that may not coincide with the material truth.

Evidence and Trial

A first category of rules regarding evidence is closely linked to the concept of a fair trial, even at the price of giving up the material truth for higher values. Torturing witnesses or the accused to get the truth out of them could be very effective, but most jurisdictions do not regard this as a valid method of getting evidence. Searches of premises are limited to specified circumstances, and even the way witnesses are examined can be restricted. Exclusion of evidence could be the consequence, although other remedies are used in practice (like reduction of the sentence).

Privileges

Related to this, the law of evidence in many jurisdictions is respectful of the duty of professional secrecy of, for instance, doctors and lawyers. To serve their customers, confidentiality is essential for doctors and lawyers. Patients and clients have to be sure that all information given to their doctor or lawyer is strictly confidential and will not be revealed to anyone else. As a counterpart, the information obtained is sometimes privileged and cannot be revealed in court. Where the line is drawn is different for each jurisdiction.

Means of Evidence

The law of evidence may also limit the means of evidence that are allowed in court. In particular, new technologies are sometimes regarded with distrust. There are still jurisdictions in which photographs and digital media can only be introduced by using detours like an expert's or witness's statement. In fact, the traditional list of acceptable means of evidence only contains witnesses, experts, documents, confessions, and the court's observations. In the French tradition, this can be supplemented by presumptions of fact, inferences made by the court based on undisputed or established facts.

Value of Evidence

Evidence is rarely completely reliable, and in most cases, some extra considerations are needed to choose between the possibilities offered by all means of evidence presented in court. The doctrine of *free evidence* leaves the appreciation of all means of evidence to the court. The court will have to base its decision about the evidence on the scenarios presented by the parties (or the prosecution and the evidence) and the likelihood of each of these scenarios in the light of the evidence that has been produced. The less this appreciation is trusted, the more the judge is curtailed by rules telling him which evidence to discard and which evidence to believe.

A rule found in many jurisdictions is the *unus testis nullus testis* rule, stating that nothing can be proven with only the testimony of one witness. On the other hand, some types of documentary evidence, like deeds written by notaries, often have an imperative probative value.

Evidence in law is not like evidence in mathematics. Proof in law is a matter of excluding other possibilities beyond a certain point, being fully aware that complete certainty about events in the past can never be obtained. Courts therefore developed criteria to set the required level of certainty.

Standards of Assessment

In criminal cases, it is often said that the facts have to be proven «beyond reasonable doubt». That is a high standard, excluding the possibility of a not so exceptional explanation for the same facts other than that the suspect committed the crime.

In civil litigation, the standard of proof is usually the preponderance of the evidence, simply meaning that one party has more proof for its statements than the other party.

Fact finding may be structured when a «burden of proof» model is used. In civil law countries, the rules of evidence indicate which of the parties will have to prove certain statements. Usually, the claimant has to prove all disputed statements on which his claim is based, while the disputed facts underpinning the defendant's defense have to be proven by the defendant.

Burden of Proof

This *onus probandi* is decisive of the outcome of the case. If a party with the burden of proof fails to come up with sufficient evidence, his claim or defense is rejected. The burden of proof can be shifted to the other party in special circumstances when this would be fairer. The rule *negativa non sunt probanda* (negative statements do not have to be proven) could, for instance, imply that the other party has to prove the positive counterpart.

4.7 The Role of the Court and the Parties in Litigation

Both in civil, administrative, and criminal cases, there has to be a certain division of labor between the court and the parties to bring proceedings to an end. Each of them has its specific interests, roles, tasks, and responsibilities, which sometimes coincide but could also be opposed to each other. Directing one's eye toward the court, two different characterizations could be used, corresponding with different approaches: the court as a referee and the court as a manager–

investigator. These approaches will be described by examining the distinction between adversarial and inquisitorial procedures and by exploring the concept of «case management».

Inquisitorial System

A major distinction between types of procedure is between inquisitorial and adversarial systems. In an inquisitorial system, the main roles are for the judge and, in criminal cases, the public prosecution. They have the responsibility to find out whether a crime has been committed and who did it and to get a criminal conviction. It is also their responsibility to avoid punishing innocent persons. The suspect and his counsel play a lesser role in the proceedings.

In civil cases, the judge in an inquisitorial system conducts the fact finding himself, questions witnesses, issues orders to the parties and experts, and could even go beyond the claims of the claimant or beyond the defenses of the defendant if he considers this just.

Adversarial System

In an adversarial system in criminal cases, the public prosecutor and the suspect have (relatively) equal standing. In a sense, each side participates in a contest, with the conviction of the suspect at stake. The judge has to make sure that the contest is fought according to the rules, and the judge or the jury will determine who has won the contest.

In civil cases, the judge is only a referee, leaving the procedure to the parties. The claimant determines what the proceedings will be about, and the scope or contents of each party's defense will not be altered by the court, not even if a strong defense is missed.

It should be emphasized that neither the inquisitorial nor the adversarial system in their pure forms are to be found anywhere. All systems are mixed systems, although the emphasis in the common law tradition used to be more on the adversarial side and in the civil law tradition more on the inquisitorial side. However, this difference in emphasis is gradually becoming less pronounced as civil law countries borrow adversarial procedures (like greater powers for defense counsel and defendant) and the common law countries borrow inquisitorial procedures (cases only decided by judges).

Case Management

Especially in a more or less adversarial civil context, proceedings can last a long time. The court does not take initiatives and just waits until the parties decide to move on. In recent years, this made the call for a form of «case management» by the courts stronger and stronger.

Recognizing that a less reactive and more active judge could save time and money for both the parties and the State, in many jurisdictions, inquisitorial elements have been introduced into proceedings before the courts. The problem is always finding the right balance between the rights and autonomy of the parties and the powers of the judge.

In England, for instance, much attention is paid to the preparatory phase of proceedings, forcing the parties to explore out-of-court solutions and to submit a file to the court that is already complete. In France, a special judge (*juge de la mise en état*) has been created to supervise civil proceedings.

What is meant by «case management» is therefore rather diverse. However, the core of this notion reflects the insight that adversarial elements in proceedings may be sacrificed for the sake of efficiency.

4.8   Legal Remedies

Even in proceedings before the courts, mistakes can easily be made. Those mistakes could concern the law, as well as the facts, and can be made by the court, as well as the parties. The resulting judgment will not reflect the «real» legal situation, and that is generally felt to be highly unjust. Therefore, all jurisdictions provide for extra procedures to have these erroneous judgments overturned, although not in all cases.

The extra procedures are labeled «legal remedies». They come in an incredible variety of forms. The variety concerns the procedure to follow, the court or instance that has to be applied to, the (legal or natural) person the legal remedy is created for, the time limits to be observed, the relief that can be obtained, and the standards to be applied by the court.

Appeals can be dealt with in two different ways, either as a review of the first instance decision or as a new appraisal of everything the parties have submitted (*novum iudicium*, full appeal). If the appeal is a *revisio prioris instantiae* (review), the case will be remitted to the court of first instance if any mistake is found in the appeal. Appeal

This can be time-consuming, with cases going up and down the court system without reaching a final judgment. Therefore, many jurisdictions treat the appeal as «devolving», meaning that the entire case is submitted to the appeal court, which will give a final judgment itself.

A special legal remedy is cassation. Cassation is meant to secure the uniform interpretation of the law. A cassation court will therefore be devoid of investigative powers and has to accept the facts as they have been established by the lower Cassation courts. This court will decide on matters of law only. Since uniformity is the ultimate aim, logically not more than one cassation court can be created within a single jurisdiction.

Especially countries in the French civil law tradition will have a cassation court. Among them are France (*Cour de Cassation*), the Netherlands (*Hoge Raad*), Belgium (*Verbrekingshof*), and Italy (*Corte di Cassazione*). Other highest courts like the Supreme Court of the United States are not cassation courts, although any fact finding by these courts will be extremely exceptional.

5   Conclusion

The brief overview of elements of procedural law showed an enormous variety in the way litigation can be shaped in different jurisdictions. Nevertheless, the margins are set by the principles discussed in the first sections, which have the objective to ensure that cases will be dealt with in a fair way. This is a guarantee for the parties that they will be proved right when their case is just.

Recommended Literature

Chase OG, Herschkoff H, Silberman L, Taniguchi Y, Varano V (2007) Civil litigation in comparative context. Thomson West, St. Paul
Damaska M (1975) The faces of justice and state authority: a comparative approach to the legal process. Yale University Press, Yale
Jolowicz JA (2000) On civil procedure. Cambridge University Press, Cambridge
Van Rhee CH (ed) (2005) European traditions in civil procedure. Intersentia, Antwerp
Zekoll J (2006) Comparative civil procedure. In: Reimann M, Zimmermann R (eds) The Oxford handbook of comparative law. Oxford University Press, Oxford. Chapter 41

14

Philosophy of Law

Jaap Hage

© Springer International Publishing Switzerland 2017
J. Hage et al. (eds.), *Introduction to Law*, DOI 10.1007/978-3-319-57252-9_15

1   What is Philosophy of Law?

Unlike private law, constitutional law, or criminal law, philosophy of law does not deal with a particular subfield of law. Philosophy of law is rather a branch of philosophy that deals with philosophical questions about law. Examples of the types of questions raised within the discipline are:

- How the punishing criminals can be justified
- What the essence of the rule of law is
- Whether human rights would still exist if they were not included in a statute or treaty
- Why contracts are binding
- What the nature of law is

In this chapter, it will not be possible to discuss all legal philosophical questions. We will opt instead for the last question, as it is perhaps the most fundamental one: what is the nature of law? Philosophers of law have discussed this question for centuries, and apparently still disagree. This disagreement is partly caused by the fact that the question itself is ambiguous and can be asked with different purposes in mind.

The Normative Question

The question about the nature of law is often asked in the context of legal decision-making. For instance, a judge may ask herself how a particular case should be decided. She wants to apply the law, and as such, the question of the true nature of law is in fact a step toward the solution for the case at hand.

Riggs v. Palmer, 115 N.Y. 506 (1889)
Francis Palmer made a last will in 1880 in which he left most of his large estate to his grandson Elmer Palmer. After that, Francis Palmer remarried. Elmer knew this and was afraid that his grandfather might change his will. To preclude this possibility, Elmer poisoned his grandfather. For this reason Mrs. Riggs, the daughter of Francis Palmer, sought to invalidate the last will.

New York State law at that time did not contain any written provisions to deal with such cases, and the question that was raised by this case was whether the rule that a convicted murderer cannot inherit from his victim was nevertheless part of the law.

The New York Court of Appeals decided that Elmer could not inherit from his grandfather and invoked the principle that nobody should profit from his own wrongs. Implicitly it also adopted the view that such unwritten principles are part of the law, which is a view about law's nature.

If the question concerning the nature of law is raised in the context of a decision-making procedure, it is a normative question. It addresses the issue of what is to be done, and the underlying assumption is that the law determines what is to be done. For instance, a judge should apply the law, but not morality, and therefore it is important to know which rules count as *legal* rules.

It is also possible to inquire after the nature of law out of a more theoretical interest. Philosophers are sometimes interested in questions without immediate practical interests. They may want to know the nature of law in terms of how legal norms differ from customs and moral norms, purely to have more insight. From this perspective, the question asking about the nature of law is completely disconnected from the question how to act. It is possible to say «This is prohibited by law, but that does not at all affect what I will do».

This conceptual question aims at giving insight into the nature of law but not at answering the question of what is to be done. An important part of the confusion in the discussion about the nature of law can be explained by the fact that people ask the question from one perspective and receive an answer from another.

In the remainder of this chapter, we will discuss the nature of law in some detail. In the ▶ Sects. 1 and 2, we address the conceptual approach, while the normative approach is the central topic of the ▶ Sects. 4 and 5. The chapter is concluded in ▶ Sect. 6.

The Conceptual Question

2 Hart: Law as System

Ask a modern lawyer what law is, and the most likely answer will be along the line that law consists of rules that are made and enforced by the State. This lawyer will likely consider his answer to be a purely factual observation. *As a matter of fact*, law consists of those rules that have been made, or at least are enforced, by the State.

This view on the law has been elaborated by the English philosopher of law Herbert Hart (1907–1993). His seminal work, and our focus in answering the question about the nature of law, is the book *The Concept of Law*. In order to make the exposition easier to follow, we will simplify Hart's views, sometimes at the cost of a little distortion to Hart's sophisticated ideas.

The title of Hart's book is indicative of the question addressed in it. Hart was not interested in the contents of the law of a particular jurisdiction but rather in the characteristics of law in general. That is why he writes about the *concept* and not about the content of law. Moreover, Hart approaches law as a social phenomenon. He considers his work to be a study in descriptive sociology. It may be disputed whether Hart's characterization of his own work is correct. This, however, does not subtract from Hart's intention to study the law as a social phenomenon nor from his intention to identify the general characteristics of this phenomenon.

2.1   Primary and Secondary Rules

One of the findings of Hart is that law does not consist solely of rules that prescribe behavior. In this connection, Hart introduces the distinction between primary and secondary legal rules. Primary rules aim to guide behavior. They include rules that prohibit theft, tell us to drive on the right-hand side of the road, or to compensate the damage that results from contractual default.

Next to primary rules, law also contains secondary rules. These rules do not prescribe behavior but have as their function the organization of the legal system itself. In this connection, one may think of rules that point out the organs of the State and their competences, rules that specify which of two conflicting rules has precedence, and rules that govern legal procedures.

For our present purposes, one particular category of secondary rules is most important; these are the rules that indicate which other rules count as law. Indeed, one of the most important conclusions of Hart's theory is that the law itself determines which rules are legal rules and which rules are not. The law does so mainly by pointing out who has the power to make legal rules.

The underlying idea is that most law has been laid down. There are many bodies that can create law; at the EU level States make treaties, while internally there are national legislators, and in common law countries the judiciary, as well as subnational legislators on the level of provinces and municipalities. Further, private persons can create laws for themselves in the shape of contracts or last wills. All these law creators succeed in making laws because they were empowered to do so. They received this power from other legal rules, and in this way, law itself determines what counts as valid law.

2.2   A Chain of Rules

Two comments must be made about the above characterization of valid law as that which has been made by a law creator (also empowered by law). The first comment is that this characterization is a purely factual statement, which is in principle vulnerable to falsification. Hart did not claim that competently created rules *deserve* to count as legal rules or *deserve* to be obeyed. The only thing he claims is that modern legal systems identify legal rules as rules that were created by somebody who had the legal competence to do so. Whether the law is good or bad is a different issue, an issue that lies beyond the problem field that Hart wants to cover. Hart is—in *The Concept of Law*—concerned not with the question of what we should do or which rules ought to be obeyed, but rather with giving an adequate characterization of law. His presupposition is that such an adequate characterization is given only through focusing on social practices and by avoiding normative issues.

The second comment is that valid legal rules are identified by powers that were themselves conferred by valid legal rules. In other words, the rules that assign the powers required for making valid law must also belong to the law themselves. This means that these power-conferring rules must have been made by persons or bodies who were assigned the competence to do so by power-conferring rules that must have been valid legal rules, meaning that these latter rules … etc.

Let us consider an example to see what this means in practice. Suppose that the Dutch city of Maastricht has parking regulations for the market place. This regulation is valid law because it has been created by the Mayor and Aldermen of Maastricht. This body received the power to make parking regulations for particular streets and squares from a local bylaw on parking. This bylaw was created by the municipality council of Maastricht, which received the power to make such bylaws from a statute created by the Dutch parliament and government.

So we have a chain of validity in which rules and powers alternate: a valid rule was created on the basis of a power to create rules, and this power was assigned by a valid rule that was created on the basis of a power … etc. This last «etc.» signals a complication, however. The chain ends with statutory rules. Why are statutory rules valid law then?

According to Hart, the validity of statutory rules is based on the *recognition* of legislation as a source of law. Since legislation and what follows from it is recognized as valid law, it *is* valid law. The same holds for case law (in common law countries) and for treaties.

One might object to Hart's view by pointing out that most people are not even aware what sources of law are, let alone that they recognize them as sources of valid law. Hart's rebuttal to this objection is that it is not the recognition by «ordinary» people that is of importance, but the recognition by the «officials» of the legal system. Among these «officials,» judges and other legal decision-makers take a prominent place. If these officials recognize legislation and everything that follows from it as valid law, then legislation and what is directly or indirectly created on the basis of it counts as valid law.

Obviously, this raises the question of why these «officials» are officials with such an important role. The only acceptable answer, based on Hart's conception, is that these officials can play this role because they are recognized as having this role in social life.

This last answer demonstrates why Hart could describe his project as a study in descriptive sociology. It is a social practice, with citizens who recognize officials and officials who recognize the validity sources of valid law, that determines what law is.

2.3   A Practical Application: EU Law

What are the practical implications of the view that social practice determines what law is? The answer to this is illustrated by the difference of opinion between the Court of Justice of the European Union and the German Constitutional Court (*Bundesverfassungsgericht*) about why the law of the European Union directly applies to the citizens of the EU Member States. According to the Court of Justice, this question is governed by EU law; however, according to the German Constitutional Court, German law, and in particular the German constitution, governs this issue.

As it happens, EU law as interpreted by the Court of Justice is in agreement with the German constitution as interpreted by the German Constitutional Court, so no actual problems arise. However, this situation would change the moment when the German Constitutional Court declares a European rule invalid because it conflicts with the German constitution. In that case, the European rule would be valid according to the EU and all Member States that assign the highest authority to the European Court of Justice, while the same rule would be invalid in the eyes of the German Constitutional Court and the German judges who will, most likely, follow the Constitutional Court. According to Hart, this issue would be decided by social practice. If the practice is not uniform within the EU, the law will not be uniform within the EU, not even if the law was created by the EU itself.

2.4   Hart as a Legal Positivist

Positive law is law that has been created or «laid down» (*positus*) by the decision of a competent legislator. In the European continent, this will often be the formal legislator, the legislative body at the State level where national parliaments play an important role. It may also be a cooperation of States in the case of treaties, the European Union in the case of European regulations and directives, or a legislator on a decentralized level such as the council of a municipality. In common law countries, the judiciary is also competent to create law. This means that all positive law stems from a official source of law.

Legal positivism is the view that law coincides with positive law: all positive laws are valid law, and there is no valid law outside positive law. It is not hard to see why Hart's views about the nature of law make him a legal positivist. According to Hart, all legal rules stem from an official source. This means that all law is positive law. Moreover, all positive law is law because it stems from an official source. Law and positive law coincide, and this is exactly the point that legal positivists such as Hart want to make.

If all law is positive law and all positive law is law, it only depends on social reality to decide what the law is. Usually, it will be determined by legislation or judicial decisions. Whether a thus created rule is morally just or whether it is prudent to live in accordance with such a rule is, from the perspective of legal positivism, not relevant for the question of whether the rule is a legal rule. This does not mean that morality and reason have no influence on the contents of the law. They have an influence, but it is according to Hart, that morality and reason influence the content at the level of the sources of law, in particular of legislation and case law. Whether a rule is a legal rule is not determined by whether the rule is just or prudent but by whether the rule was created by means of legislation or could be found in a judicial decision.

According to legal positivists, there can be unjust and imprudent laws. In the words of the nineteenth century legal positivist John Austin, «the existence of law is one thing, its merit or demerit another». If law is «merely» a social phenomenon and its validity does not depend on what is just or prudent, it is not obvious that legal rules should be complied with. Paraphrasing Austin, Hart might have said: «the existence of law is one thing, the reason to comply with it another».

Legal Positivism

The Separation of Law and Morality

3   Dworkin's Criticism

It was Hart's intention to characterize law as it really is, not as it should be. Did he succeed in that endeavor? Is law really, as Hart writes, a union of primary rules that guide conduct and secondary rules that regulate the law itself? Is the legal validity of rules really only determined by their pedigree and not by their content? One of Hart's students, Dworkin, dared to doubt this. In one of his first publications, he attempted to show that Hart's theory about the nature of law is wrong, even if this theory is measured against the standard that Hart proposed himself, the standard that the law should be described as it actually is.

3.1   An Example

In ► Sect. 1 we encountered the case of Riggs versus Palmer. The plaintiffs in that case, Mrs. Riggs and Mrs. Preston, sought to invalidate the will of their father Francis Palmer. The defendant in the case was Elmer Palmer, the grandson of the testator. The will gave small legacies to the two daughters, Mrs. Preston and Mrs. Riggs, but the bulk of the estate went to Elmer Palmer.

The reason why Mrs. Riggs and Mrs. Preston wanted to invalidate the will was because Elmer had murdered his grandfather. The grandfather had recently remarried, and Elmer feared that he would change the will, giving Elmer a smaller inheritance. The plaintiffs argued that by allowing the will to be executed, Elmer would be profiting from his crime. While a criminal law existed to punish Elmer for the murder, there was no statute that invalidated his claim to the estate.

Legal Justification

Should Elmer inherit his grandfather's estate given that he murdered his grandfather and also given the fact that there was no statute invalidating his claim to the estate? A yes or no answer to this question would be a legal judgment. Legal judgments need to be justified. In its most basic form, the justification of a legal judgment consists of an argument in which the facts of a case are *subsumed* under a rule formulation and in which the legal judgment is derived from these two premises. An example would be the following argument:

Rule	A person cannot inherit from a person whom he has murdered
Facts	Elmer murdered his grandfather
Legal judgment	Elmer cannot inherit from his grandfather

15

This justification of a legal judgment is nothing more than a logical derivation of the judgment from a rule formulation and a case description.

If the rule formulation can be read off from the available legal sources, the justification of a legal judgment is no harder than producing such a simple argument. However, the rule that «a person cannot inherit from a person whom he has murdered» could not be found in the law of New York when the case appeared before the court. There was a relevant rule that was easy to find, the rule that if someone had been appointed as the beneficiary in a last will of some person, and this last person died, the first-mentioned person inherits the estate. This rule however, which could be found in the available sources, was not the rule that the court applied. The court applied the rule mentioned in the primary justification, a rule that could not be found in any source. How did the court arrive at this «new» rule?

Here another aspect of justification comes into play. The court produced an argument with a conclusion that the rule that «a person cannot inherit from another person whom he has murdered» is a valid rule of New York law. This was not an obvious argument, as we will see later. However, even if the court would have adopted the obvious rule according to which Elmer could inherit, the court should have justified the use of this rule as well.

3.2   Hard Cases, Gaps, and Discretion

According to legal positivists such as Hart, law is a social phenomenon. Law consists of rules, and these rules exist as a matter of fact in social reality for the mere fact that they were created by a person or an institution that was empowered to do so. Moreover, rules attach legal consequences to cases. These legal consequences are as «objective» as the rules themselves. In this way, legal «decision-making» is not really a form of decision-making at all; rather, it is the process of establishing which consequences legal rules already have attached to the case at hand.

For example, if somebody negligently causes a car accident, this person must compensate the damage. This obligation to pay damages does not depend on the judgment of a court. It comes into existence at the moment the accident took place. If the case nevertheless comes before a judge, it is in the positivist picture of law, the duty of the judge to establish that which was already the case, namely, that the tort-feasor has to compensate the damage. The court's judgment is not necessary to create the obligation to pay damages; it is only needed to make enforcement of this obligation possible.

Just like other phenomena in social reality, positive law is finite. There are no more rules of positive law than were explicitly created by means of legislation or judicial decision-making. As a consequence, there may be cases that lack an applicable legal rule. If the law has no solution for these cases, then it contains a *gap*.

If a judge nevertheless has to take a decision on an issue in a gap, she must by necessity create new law. In taking her decision, she may take all kinds of things into account, such as governmental policies, the demands of morality, or even her personal preferences. However, there is one thing on which she cannot base her decision, and that is the law. She cannot do this because for the case at hand there is no law. Such cases, where there is no law or where the law is hard to discover, are called «hard cases». In such a hard case, the legal decision-maker must exercise discretion in the sense of making a decision that is unbound by law.

Arguably, as soon as a court has taken a decision, there is law for hard cases. First there is law for the concrete case at hand, because the court had the power to create legal consequences for this particular case. Second, there is also law for new cases which are similar because the court decision can function as a precedent for future cases. This means that although a type of case used to be hard, it may become easy after a court decision.

3.3   The Donut Theory of Law

The above account of hard cases in which the law is finite and contains a gap and in which courts must exercise discretion because there is no applicable law was offered by Ronald Dworkin. Dworkin called this account the «donut theory of law»; however, he himself considered this account to be wrong; see ◘ Fig. 15.1. The donut stands metaphorically for the law. The opening in its middle symbolizes the space that the law leaves available for a judge to decide on a hard case. Judicial decision-making is confined by law, but the law does not determine the decision. The donut theory was meant to be an account of legal decision-making according to legal positivism, and *it was meant to illustrate why legal positivism is wrong*.

One Right Answer

According to Dworkin, legal positivism is wrong because legal decision-making does not work as it should work accord-

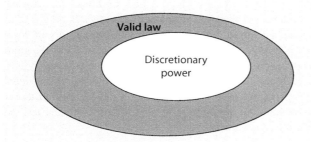

▢ Fig. 15.1   The donut theory of law

ing to legal positivism. Courts that must deal with hard cases do not take a decision that is unbound by law. They do not exercise discretion. Instead they argue as if the case at hand has one unique solution (one right answer) and as if it were their task to find that single right answer to the case. In producing these arguments, courts invoke more «law» than only the positive law, such as legal principles that were not laid down by an official legislator.

This point can be illustrated by the case of Elmer, who murdered his grandfather in order to inherit. The court which decided this case invoked the legal principle that nobody should profit from his own wrongs. Elmer would profit from the murder if he inherited from his grandfather's estate, and therefore he should not inherit. This principle prevails over the rule that last wills should be honored. Therefore, the court decided that Elmer would not inherit.

The decision made by the New York Court of Appeals was no doubt an attractive one. But why is it problematic for legal positivists such as Hart? Dworkin writes that it is problematic because legal principles such as the principle that «nobody should profit from his own wrongs» are not recognized as part of the law by the legal rules that define the law. The principle does not have the relevant source. In fact, it has no «source» at all because it was not made. And still, as a matter of fact, this principle is a part of law. Dworkin uses Hart's approach to determine law's nature, namely, looking at social reality, and more particularly to examine what courts do; however, in Dworkin's view of social reality, there is more law than what can be identified by means of what has been created by an empowered lawmaker. Social reality contains legal principles that are law, not because they were competently created but because they have the «right» content.

Legal Principles

If this argument is correct, it has profound implications for the nature of the law. It implies that there is more law than positive law alone. Therefore, Dworkin's point about legal decision-making has implications that reach farther than legal decision-making alone. It regards the very nature of law. The crucial point in Dworkin's argument is that the legal decision-makers *as a matter of fact* consider these other materials as legal materials too. This means that, in their eyes, *the Hartian picture of law is wrong.*

4   Fact and Norm

Law finds itself on the borderline in between fact and norm. On one hand, law aims to answer the question of what we should do. From this perspective, law is similar to morality, and legal reasoning is essentially the act of determining what the best thing is to do. On the other hand, law aspires to be factual, something that is the same for everybody and that can be established objectively. From this perspective, legal reasoning is establishing the legal facts.

Reasons Arbitrary

There are some who think that these two aspects of law cannot be reconciled. They emphasize the gap between fact and norm. Facts are objective, the same for everybody, but these facts do not tell us what we should do. Admittedly, facts do play a role in deciding what to do. If your house is on fire, this fact is of utmost importance for the decision of whether you will leave the house. Theoretically, however, you might decide to stay in the house. Facts by themselves cannot determine what you should do; they can only do so if they are given meaning as reasons for behavior. Whether they have that meaning is not given with the facts themselves; it is a matter of choice. Reasons are, in this view, arbitrary.

If law were purely a matter of fact, it would be an open question whether it provides us with reasons for acting. Someone might, for instance, ask himself: «According to the law I must pay taxes, but should I really do so»? This person then treats valid law as if it were the law of a foreign country or from the far past.

Reasons Nonarbitrary

There are others who think that facts, including facts concerning law, can by themselves provide us with reasons for acting. According to them, it is not an arbitrary matter whether we assign facts meaning as reasons for behavior. If you are wise, they argue, you *know* what meaning the facts have for you. No sane person remains in a house that is on fire unless he believes that he can extinguish the fire. It is not good for humans to suffocate in smoke or—possibly even worse—to burn alive. It is part of human nature that we want to stay alive, do not want to suffer pain, and in general want to be happy. For this reason, it is good for human beings—objectively good—that they want to live, to avoid pain, and to pursue happiness. Maybe there are circumstances in which this is not the case, but such circumstances are exceptional. There are things that are normally good for humans, and it would be a fallacy to use the existence of exceptions to argue that the main rule that people want to live, to avoid pain, and to pursue happiness does not hold.

This last line of thinking, which assumes that some things are objectively good and others are objectively bad, can be found in the work of, among others, Thomas Aquinas.

5   Thomas Aquinas: Positive Law and Natural Law

Thomas Aquinas was a Dominican priest, who lived from 1225 to 1274. In that time, continental Western Europe still had a feudal system. Members of the higher nobility were the local rulers, and although they were officially the subordinates of the German Emperor or the King of France, they were for most practical purposes independent. Most law in those days was customary law. The role of legislation was limited, and its function was mostly to codify existing customs. In the Middle Ages, Aquinas formulated a theory about the nature of law that has remained influential even in the present day. According to this theory, law is an ordinance of reason for the common good, made and promulgated by he who has care of the community.

5.1   Common Good

A first characteristic of law is that it concerns the common good and not merely the interests of individual persons. There are also guidelines for behavior that only concern the individual good. A modern example is the guidelines for living in a healthy way, for instance, eating healthy food. Since the consequences of unhealthy eating habits mostly affect the eating person alone, this is a matter of individual interest and not a topic for the law.

One can have a different opinion on this and it is very possible nowadays that a State introduces a tax on fattening foods. (As a matter of fact, Denmark briefly had such a tax.) This does not show that Aquinas' distinction does not hold true, but rather that as almost everything touches the interests of others, they thereby become issues concerning the common good.

5.2   Law and Reason

A second characteristic of law is, according to Aquinas, that law is an ordinance of reason. The content of the law is determined by reason (in Latin, *ratio*), and therefore the law can be known by reasoning about the best way to organize human society. We will refer to this kind of law as *rationalist law*. The modern counterpart of this view would be that the content of what the law should be is a matter of science. However, most present lawyers are legal positivists according to whom the law can be known by studying and interpreting authoritative texts, such as legislation and case law.

Natural Law

For many centuries, the view that law can be established by means of reason went in the form of a belief in natural law. Natural law theory assumes that there is a kind of law, *natural law*, for which the contents can be obtained by means of reasoning from human nature. Perhaps the most important representative of this view was Thomas Aquinas. According to Aquinas, human nature determines what the best way to organize society is. Following the Greek philosopher Aristotle (384–322 BCE), Aquinas assumed that there is such a thing as human nature and that this nature determines what the best way is for a human being to live. Since human beings are social by nature, the best way to live is in a society with other human beings. Such a society should allow human beings to flourish; consequently human nature also determines what a good society is. The law that governs such a society should be based on human nature, and given this link with human nature, it is called *natural law*. As we have already seen, Aquinas held the opinion that the content of this natural law can in principle be established by human reason.

Customary Law

This rationalist foundation of law can be contrasted with two alternatives, custom and will. Both alternatives assume that law exists purely as a matter of fact. In the time of Aquinas, most law was still customary law: rules that were generally accepted and often assumed to have existed for time immemorial. Customary law and rationalist law have in common the fact that they both see law as independent of the will of the reigning monarch. An important difference between the two is that customary law is in a sense arbitrary. Its content might just as well have been different from what it actually is, and at different times and in different places customary law is different. Rationalist law, on the contrary, tends to be the same everywhere and always unless different circumstances make different things rational.

This last clause should be taken seriously. Even if human nature is always and everywhere the same, the circumstances under which human beings live vary considerably with time and place. This would imply that even if the most abstract principles of natural law are universal, its concrete elaborations would still exhibit important differences.

The other alternative for rationalist law is law that has been made by the sovereign, the content of which is determined by the sovereign's will. This sovereign would, in the time of Aquinas, have been an emperor, king, or a member of the higher nobility. Nowadays, the people are often taken to be the sovereign. Regardless of who the sovereign may be, the view of the law is the same: the law corresponds to the will of the sovereign, the content of the law in this sense is arbitrary. Aquinas explicitly considers this alternative for his rationalist view of law. He recognizes that the will is one the factors that determine what we should do. Reason tells us how we can reach our goals, while the will determines what our goals will be. But, writes Aquinas, if the will is to have the authority of law, it must be rational. Only then can the will of the sovereign be the law. If the will is not rational, it is not law but evil.

> Sovereign's Will

Suppose you are walking in a forest, and have become thirsty. You would like to drink something and you know that there is a brook in the neighborhood with potable water. It is rational to walk to the brook and to drink some water. This example illustrates that what you should do depends on both what your goal is (to drink) and on reason, which tells you how you can reach your goal (go to the brook). But how can the will be irrational? The following adaptation of the example can show this. Suppose that you know that the brook's water has been polluted and is not potable. But your thirst is so great that you nevertheless want to drink the water. Should you then drink the water from the brook? You should not, because in this version of the example your will is not rational.

In the rationalist view of how to act and on the content of law, like the view of Aquinas, reason is not only a tool to find the means to reach a pre-given goal but also a standard to evaluate

> Reason as Standard

goals with. An unreasonable will should not guide our actions. Already during the Middle Ages, Aquinas' views on this subject were controversial. Particularly, there was a discussion on whether law was the manifestation of God's will. In that age, nobody disputed that the natural law was commanded by God, but the discussion was concerning to what extent God was autonomous in commanding natural law. One view, defended by Aquinas, was rationalist: reason determines what is good law, and God has prescribed this law because it is rational. So, the law depends on the will of God, but this will depends on reason because God is rational.

The other view on the nature of law is voluntaristic (*voluntas* is Latin for will). In this view, the content of natural law depends on the will of God, and it is good *because God willed it*. In this connection, it would not matter whether God's will and the law are rational. It is this voluntaristic view of law that, in a secularized version, has gained prominence in the legal positivist account of law.

5.3   Positive Law and Natural Law

Another characteristic that Aquinas attributed to law is that law is promulgated by he who is charged with the care of the community. This third characteristic has two aspects. The first aspect is that the person who has the power to make laws is the one who has the care for the community as a whole. Aquinas opposes this explicitly to the head of a family, who can only make rules for family life. Such rules are not laws, because they do not concern the common good, but only the good of the family.

The second aspect is that this person who is charged with the care of the community has the power to make laws. According to Aquinas, human beings are social beings. No single person on his own possesses the capabilities that are necessary to lead a full human life. That is why human beings need to live together with other human beings. Given the differences between humans and their interests, a society could easily fall apart if there were not a person who directs the society toward the general interest. So there must be a monarch who furthers the common good. The existence of a society governed by a monarch therefore fits in the natural order in which human beings partake. Such a society is not something that is outside or opposed to natural law but is rather required by natural law. In order to promote the common good, the monarch should make law, positive law.

Positive law must be in service of the common good and therefore should not conflict with natural law. This raises the question of why there should even be positive law. Does natural law not suffice? The answer to this question is that natural law must be supplemented by positive law because natural law is very abstract and needs to be made concrete. One example would be that the natural law in principle prohibits the killing of human beings, but that it does not inform us about the sanctions that should be applied to those who violate this prohibition.

Moreover, there are some issues that need to be regulated, but reason does not tell us what the correct law is, because these are too arbitrary. An example is whether we should drive on the right- or the left-hand side of the road. It is reasonable that there must be a rule for this, but both solutions seem to be equally good. In short, there are a large number of issues that need regulation, but where the content of that regulation cannot be determined by reason alone. There is a need for decision-making and for positive law next to, or—even better—within the framework of, natural law. In fact, it can be determined purely on the basis of reason that there is a need for positive law and therefore natural law prescribes that there must be positive law. The duty to comply with this positive law follows from the facts that human beings need to live together in a society and that such a society can only exist if it has positive law.

In the view of Aquinas, natural law and positive law would ideally supplement each other and would together constitute a coherent set of guidelines for how humans should live in accordance with their nature. It is possible however that positive law and natural law conflict; then the difficult question arises of how such a conflict should be dealt with.

At first sight, the issue seems easy to solve. Law has, in Aquinas' view, the function to let human beings lead their lives in accordance with their nature. If positive law does not fulfill this function, if it is counterproductive, then it would not be law. This simple solution can be summarized by the slogan «Positive law that conflicts with natural law is not law at all».

Taken to its extreme, this slogan is too simple. If people are given the possibility to invoke natural law as a reason to disobey positive law, there is a serious risk that chaos will result. Indeed, anybody who disagrees with a rule might argue that the rule is not binding because it is in conflict with natural law. Moreover, there can be disagreement about the content of natural law because not everybody's «reason»

Why There Must Be Positive Law

When Positive Law and Natural Law Conflict

is to the same extent rational. The chaos that threatens if an (alleged) conflict with natural law is a sufficient ground not to comply with positive law is against the idea of natural law itself because natural law aims at making human society possible.

Law that Is a Little Wrong

Considerations like the ones above brought Aquinas to conclude that positive law that is only «a little» wrong should still be obeyed. The disruption of social order that results from non-compliance with positive law is worse than that which derives from the compliance with law that is unreasonable. However, if the violation by positive law of natural law is sufficiently serious, the duty to comply with positive law ends. Obviously, it is far from simple to draw a clear line where a violation of natural law is serious enough to warrant disobedience of positive law. The German legal philosopher Radbruch stated it as follows:

» The conflict between justice and the reliability of the law should be solved in favor of the positive law, law enacted by proper authority and power, even in cases where it is unjust in terms of content and purpose, except for cases where the discrepancy between the positive law and justice reaches a level so unbearable that the statute has to make way for justice because it has to be considered 'erroneous law'.

5.4   Conclusion on Aquinas

According to Thomas Aquinas, law consists of rules that tell us what kinds of actions serve the common good. In his view, the question of what promotes the common good can be answered by means of reason. Law is therefore a matter of *ratio*, reason.

It may be tempting to oppose natural law theories such as the one proposed by Thomas Aquinas to views according to which law is positive law, the work of human beings. However, we have seen that even from a natural law point of view, it is in general wise to comply with positive law. The practical differences are therefore not as big as they might seem at first sight. Yet the fundamental difference is huge. According to Aquinas, law is ultimately not a matter of rules that exist in social practice, but a matter of knowing which rules lead to the common good. The reason why we should comply with positive law is not that it is by definition the law, but because it is rational to do so.

6   Thomas Hobbes: Normative Legal Positivism

According to Thomas Aquinas, positive law constitutes an important part of law, but in last instance natural law determines how we should act. Thomas Hobbes held a fundamentally different view on this issue. With Aquinas, he shared the normative approach to law: law is an answer to the question of how we should act. Even though he has the same starting point, Hobbes arrives at an answer that is quite different from that of Aquinas.

Thomas Hobbes lived from 1588 to 1679, mostly in   *Leviathan* England, but also for some time in Paris. During this period, England was divided by civil wars. Hobbes' seminal work, the *Leviathan*, was named after a monster that was mentioned in the Bible. The Leviathan about which Hobbes writes is the State, which is more powerful than individuals.

In the *Leviathan*, Hobbes addresses many themes. Here we focus on the way in which Hobbes answers the question pertaining to the nature of law. Law is in the first place an answer to the question of how we should act. According to Hobbes, this question can be answered by means of reason. Much more than Aquinas, Hobbes focuses on the certainty offered by law and on the fact that law can be enforced, even to the extent that he prefers positive law above rational law if an effective State organization exists.

The reason why Hobbes is so strongly attached to the enforceability of law and to legal certainty is that he was rather pessimistic about human nature and the possible consequences if an effective State authority is lacking. This pessimism might very well be the result of the civil wars that Hobbes experienced.

6.1   **The State of Nature**

As starting point for his theory about the nature of law, Hobbes sketches a picture of how the world would look if there were no State. Hobbes calls this situation the *state of nature*. Although according to Hobbes, people differ from each other, these differences are relatively small; even the weakest person is capable to kill the strongest in a rash moment. Therefore, in the state of nature, nobody has a claim to something that cannot also be claimed by somebody else. This equality gives everybody an equal hope to realize his desires. The consequence of this is that two people who want the same thing will become enemies if they cannot both have it. To realize their own desires, they will try to destroy or at least to subject the other. (We are talking about a situation without a State.) Further, everybody knows that everybody else will try to realize their own desires, and as such, they will distrust one another.

War of Everybody Against Everybody

By way of precaution, people will try to safeguard their positions by means of double-crossing one another until there is nobody left who might constitute a danger. According to Hobbes, this is permitted in the state of nature because it is necessary for everybody's survival. The result of this is an all-out war of everybody against everybody. This war may consist not only of actual fights, but in particular of the preparation for possible future fights, like a kind of cold war. While such a war continues, there can be no good opportunities to develop agriculture, industry, or trade. Combined with the continuous fear of actual fights, this makes life disagreeable. In the famous words of Hobbes:

«(…) the life of man [is] solitary, poor, nasty, brutish, and short».

Laws of Nature

The state of nature is disagreeable, but the feelings and reason of human beings make it possible to escape from it. The fear of death, the desire for a pleasant life, and the hope to achieve such a life through diligence provide the inclination to strive for peace. Reason tells man under which conditions peace can be achieved. Hobbes calls these conditions the *laws of nature.*

The first and most fundamental law of nature that Hobbes mentions is that everybody should strive for peace as long as there is hope to achieve it, but that one should fall back on the advantages of the state of nature if peace turns out to be unattainable.

From this first law follows a second. Everybody should be prepared to give up their rights and to be content with as many rights against others as one allows others to have against them. This should be followed to the extent that it is required for peace and self-preservation, on the condition that the others are prepared to do the same.

6.2   The State

Contracts

A renunciation of rights as recommended by the second law of nature is a kind of contract. In the state of nature, contracts are problematic. In many contracts, parties promise to do something in the future. One of the parties must perform, and then wait for the other party to perform. Performance is uncertain however, as in the state of nature there is nobody to enforce the contract. In the state of nature, everybody is entitled to do anything, including nonperformance of agreements. Not only is it risky to perform as the first party, no contract party is obligated to do so. It then makes little sense to engage in contracts at all. Hobbes' conclusion is therefore that in the state of nature all contracts are void.

This becomes different if there is a government with the power to enforce performance. Then the party who performed first can count on the fact that the other party will also perform. On the basis of that certainty, there can be an obligation to perform on the first party, meaning that in civil society (if there is a government) contracts are binding.

This example about contracts illustrates why enforceability is, according to Hobbes, essential for law. Law can only bind people if it is prudent to comply. Because people are approximately equal in strength, it is not prudent to comply with rules in the state of nature because one cannot assume that others will do the same. The most important function of the State is to make it prudent to comply with the rules. If everybody complies, out of fear of government enforcement or for other reasons, then everybody is better off than if nobody complies with the rules. It is in everybody's interest if everybody is forced to obey the law.

According to Hobbes, there can only be law within the context of a State. The reason is because law imposes duties and obligations and that duties and obligations can only exist if it is prudent for people to comply with them. Given the equality of human beings, under which people cannot force each other, a superhuman entity is necessary to force people to obey the law. This entity is the State. | Law and State

Following up on this, Hobbes defines law as what the State has ordered its subjects. The government is the legislator but is itself not bound by law. Indeed, it can revoke laws if it desires to do so.

The laws of nature that hold in the state of nature merely indicate what is required for a safe and pleasant life. They do not obligate. However, as soon as there is a State that enforces the law, the laws of nature become binding too.

6.3 Positive Law and Natural Law

It is remarkable that in Hobbes' view, natural law plays a much more limited role than in Aquinas' view. According to Aquinas, natural law and positive law constitute a coherent whole that must guide man to his natural destination. Both kinds of law have a single purpose in common, and the major difference between the two kinds is the source from which they originate. Natural law is embodied in creation and amenable to being known through reason, while positive law is man-made.

According to Hobbes, natural law in the shape of the laws of nature almost only plays a role in the state of nature. Moreover, it does not indicate how man can achieve his natural destination but only how it is possible to escape from the misery of the state of nature. As soon as the State exists, the State determines the law. More specifically, natural law no longer plays a role in combination with positive law. Natural law is the foundation for positive law because it recommends the formation of a State and to obey positive law when there is a State. However, as soon as an effective State exists, the only law is positive law, which is created and enforced by the State.

This difference between Thomas Aquinas and Thomas Hobbes can be explained by their different views of mankind. Aquinas assumes that something like human nature exists and that it is possible to establish on its basis what is good for mankind. That is the foundation for natural law. According to Hobbes, the only thing that humans have in common is that they pursue their own interests; what these interests constitute is different for everybody. A natural foundation for legal rules is lacking; such a foundation must be created. It is the task of the State to create this foundation—and to enforce it—in the form of positive law.

6.4   Review of Rules Against Legal Principles

Let us have another look at the case Riggs versus Palmer. The New York Court of Appeals decided this case by reviewing the statutory rule about inheritance and last wills against the legal principle that nobody should profit from his own wrongs. The difference between the views of Thomas Aquinas and Thomas Hobbes is well illustrated by this example. The principle against which the judges reviewed the statutory rule was unwritten; it only held because it is reasonable. Although Aquinas would plead for caution when reviewing positive law (legislation) against what is reasonable, reason would in his view be the ultimate standard for what is law. Arguably, therefore, the decision by the New York Court of Appeals to deny Elmer his inheritance would be supported by Aquinas.

Hobbes would probably not have supported that decision. If written rules can be reviewed against what is considered to be reasonable, this opens the way to cast doubt on all law. The result is uncertainty and possibly endless litigation about cases in which parties disagree on what is reasonable. It is the function of positive law to end uncertainty, and therefore reviewing statutory law against unwritten principles is undesirable.

7   Conclusion

In this chapter, we focused on a central question of legal philosophy, the question of the nature of law. We have seen that this question can be asked with different intentions in mind. It may be a normative question, aimed at guidelines for behavior. It may also be a purely conceptual question: what is the nature of this social phenomenon that we call «law»?

Hart answered the conceptual question, and his answer was that law consists completely of positive law, made by rule makers (including judges) who derive their power to create law from positive law. Whether a rule is a legal rule depends only on whether this rule was made by a competent law creator; the content of the rule does not play any role. In this way, Hart emphasized the legal positivist view that there are no moral requirements for the validity of legal rules.

Dworkin also answered the conceptual question, but he pointed out that judges use substantive arguments in taking their decisions. Moreover, they do so to determine the content of the law and not merely when there is a gap in the law and they are in need of creating new laws. Apparently, the content of the rules does play a role in determining what the law is. Dworkin arrived at a non-positivist view of law on the basis of the conceptual question of the nature of law.

Both Thomas Aquinas and Thomas Hobbes answered the normative question of the nature of law. They both assumed that natural law determines what is good for mankind. However, Hobbes did not see much that humans have in common, and the role of natural law was therefore confined to prescribing the need for a State. The «real» law would then be the rules that are created and enforced by the State. Hobbes therefore arrived at a legal positivist conclusion on the basis of the normative question of the nature of law.

Thomas Aquinas assumed that human nature could constitute the foundation for substantive natural law. There is a need for positive law, but positive law should always function within the framework of natural law. As such, Aquinas arrived at a non-positivist view of law on the basis of the normative question of the nature of law.

Recommended Literature

Bix B (2015) Jurisprudence. Theory and context, 7th edn. Sweet & Maxwell, London

Dworkin R (1996) Taking rights seriously. Duckworth, London

Finnis J (2011) Natural law and natural rights, 2nd edn. Oxford University Press, Oxford

Hart HLA (2012) The concept of law, 3rd edn. Oxford University Press, Oxford

Kelsen H (1960) Reine Rechtslehre, 2e Auflage edn. Franz Deuticke, Wien

Supplementary Information

© Springer International Publishing Switzerland 2017
J. Hage et al. (eds.), *Introduction to Law*, DOI 10.1007/978-3-319-57252-9

Index

A

B

C

Printed by Printforce, the Netherlands